Arts of Healing

CRITICAL PERSPECTIVES ON THEORY, CULTURE AND POLITICS

Critical Perspectives on Theory, Culture and Politics is an interdisciplinary series, developed in partnership with the Centre for Critical and Cultural Theory, which is based in the School of English, Communication and Philosophy at Cardiff University, UK. The series focuses on innovative research produced at the interface between critical theory and cultural studies. In recent years much work in cultural studies has increasingly moved away from directly critical-theoretical concerns. One of the aims of this series is to foster a renewed dialogue between cultural studies and critical and cultural theory in its rich, multiple dimensions.

Series Editors:

Glenn Jordan, Visiting Research Fellow, Cardiff School of Journalism, Media and Cultural Studies, Cardiff University. Former Director of Butetown History & Arts Centre.

Laurent Milesi, Tenured Professor of English Literature and Critical Theory, Shanghai Jiao Tong University.

Radhika Mohanram, Professor of English and Critical and Cultural Theory, Cardiff University.

Christopher John Müller, Lecturer, Department of Media, Music, Communication & Cultural Studies, Macquarie University.

Chris Weedon, Professor Emerita and Honorary Chair, Centre for Critical and Cultural Theory, Cardiff University.

Titles in the Series:

Arts of Healing

Cultural Narratives of Trauma

Edited by Arleen Ionescu
and Maria Margaroni

ROWMAN & LITTLEFIELD
INTERNATIONAL
London • New York

Published by Rowman & Littlefield International Ltd.
6 Tinworth Street, London SE11 5AL
www.rowmaninternational.com

Rowman & Littlefield International Ltd. is an affiliate of Rowman & Littlefield
4501 Forbes Boulevard, Suite 200, Lanham, Maryland 20706, USA
With additional offices in Boulder, New York, Toronto (Canada), and Plymouth (UK)
www.rowman.com

British Library Cataloguing in Publication Data

A catalogue record for this book is available from the British Library

ISBN: HB 978-1-78661-097-3

Library of Congress Cataloging-in-Publication Data Is Available

Library of Congress Control Number: 2020934799

ISBN: 978-1-78661-097-3 (cloth)
ISBN: 978-1-5381-4826-6 (pbk)
ISBN: 978-1-78661-098-0 (electronic)

Contents

Acknowledgements

This book was first conceptualized in the context of a conference titled *Arts of Healing*, which we, the editors, Arleen Ionescu and Maria Margaroni, co-organized at the University of Ploieşti, Romania, in 2016. However, it includes the revised versions of only two papers that were presented in the conference. Developing out of our shared concerns and growing dialogue (which became a strong bond of friendship), the scope of the project opened up, permitting us to include contributions by scholars in many disciplines who are specialists in different forms of trauma across the globe.

We are grateful to all our friends and academic colleagues, without whose support, generosity and constructive views on several aspects of trauma and healing, this volume would not have seen the light of day. We would also like to thank the series editors as well as Gurdeep Mattu, Scarlet Furness and Brianna Westervelt from the commissioning editorial team at Rowman & Littlefield International. Our gratitude needs to be extended to the anonymous reviewers for their appreciative response and valuable advice. Finally, we would like to thank our respective academic institutions, Shanghai Jiao Tong University and the University of Cyprus, for creating an auspicious environment within which the research informing this volume was conducted.

Our love and gratitude go to our families, who shared our enthusiasm and remained patient during the long gestation of this project.

Introduction

Arleen Ionescu and Maria Margaroni

According to Jean Laplanche and Jean-Bertrand Pontalis's *The Language of Psychoanalysis*, the concept of 'trauma' (from the Greek τραῦμα meaning 'wound') was associated with 'the idea of a violent shock, the idea of a wound and the idea of consequences affecting the whole organisation.'[1] The term was first employed in medicine and surgery with the meaning of an external injury that was the consequence of violence. When we think of trauma we have in mind both individual and collective traumas, or, to follow Dominick LaCapra's distinction, both historical trauma (whose representation is necessarily linked to the distinction among victims, perpetrators, and bystanders[2]) and structural trauma ('often figured as deeply ambivalent—as both shattering or painful and the occasion for *jouissance*, ecstatic elation, or the sublime'[3]). While individual traumas (extreme life events such as sexual abuse, rapes,[4] criminal assaults, life-threatening illnesses) are impossible to keep evidence of, history gives us indications of events that shattered people's trust in humanity and that provoked deep psychological wounds that require far more in restorative efforts.

A comprehensive list of the traumas of the twentieth and twenty-first centuries seems an impossible task, but it would certainly include the following: the Armenian Genocide (1915–1917); the two World Wars (1914–1918; 1939–1945), especially WW2, which was the first human enterprise to industrialize death and the first time when nuclear bombs were dropped, on Hiroshima and Nagasaki (1945); the post-WW2 division of the world between the East and the West that started from the very heart of the most traumatized city in the world, Berlin; Stalinism with its gulags and prisons;[5] communism in Eastern Europe with its horrendous work camps and prisons, some of which were considered the most atrocious experiments in world history;[6] the system of racial segregation known as apartheid in South Africa; dictatorial regimes in different countries in Asia as well as in South America with a huge number of innocent victims; the Vietnam War (1955–1975), whose survivors were diagnosed with Post-Traumatic Stress Disorder (PTSD);[7] the Rwandan Genocide (1990); and 9/11, the fall of the Twin Towers in New York (2001), preceded and followed by many terrorist attacks in different parts of the world.

Nowadays, the focus of trauma studies moves from Holocaust-centric reflection to the increasingly terror-haunted world where individual and collective traumas have become much of an everyday occurrence, as well as the fate of refugees in search of a better place to live[8] and the victims of natural disasters (environmental catastrophes such as tsunamis, floods, earthquakes and fires).

Since the aim of this book is to address urgent questions within the field of trauma studies and to contribute fruitfully to ongoing debates by focusing on cultural narratives and practices of healing, the next section will delve into delineating the main directions that trauma studies has followed in relation to healing, from the end of the nineteenth century, when Sigmund Freud set up the discipline of psychoanalysis, to the present.

HEALING IN TRAUMA STUDIES: POSING THE PROBLEM

Sigmund Freud developed a method of treatment for mental-health disorders. His patients suffered from both 'accident neurosis' that triggered 'traumatic hysteria,' 'traumatic neurosis,' and *'precipitating trauma'*[9] and 'war neurosis': WW1 combat veterans' nightmares brought them back to the moment they encountered death on the battlefield. Freud discussed these veterans' symptoms in his groundbreaking work 'Beyond the Pleasure Principle.' He regarded melancholia as compulsive repetition (possessed by his past, the patient narcissistically identifies himself with the lost object), and he saw in mourning a possibility to engage with trauma and build a new life. Freud did not live long enough to write on WW2, whose indirect victim he was, being forced to escape Nazi Austria for London and leaving behind in Vienna his elderly sisters, who died in Nazi concentration camps.

With WW2 and the Vietnam War, the world was to be shattered by collective trauma, a type of suffering that led to a shift away from Freud's solution to trauma, mourning, to 'a potential public space for retelling' one's traumatic experience. It might be useful, however, to rewind Freud's main discoveries that have helped many scholars embarking in trauma studies. According to Freud, victims can 'act out' trauma, reliving the past through repetition, or 'work through' it, which means that they manage to put the past behind. Trauma undermines self-respect and trust in other people. It damages the very structure of the self. Either victims of trauma dissociate, blocking out conscious memories of the trauma (which produces numbness), or they experience a series of other feelings, such as guilt, shame and self-loathing. Intrusive memories coming from the subconscious in the form of flashbacks, nightmares, increased arousal, re-enactment of trauma and compulsively repeated behavior prevent them from working through their trauma. The first step towards healing is gaining critical distance from the traumatic event one has experienced, a distance that allows the individual to continue living in the present, although one cannot disengage completely from the traumas of the past.

In 'Landscapes of Memory' Laurence Kirmayer differentiated between a patient suffering from dissociative disorder and a Holocaust victim: the former lives in the 'private space of shame'; the latter shares his experience in the 'public space of solidarity.'[10] It was in this spirit of sharing in order to develop forms of solidarity that in the early 1980s an acute need emerged to gather survivors' testimonies in an effort to honour the dead and to cry out loud 'Never again.' In these years, trauma studies developed as a discipline deriving from Freudian psychoanalysis and a contemplation of the Holocaust. The Holocaust was regarded by Philippe Lacoue-Labarthe as a 'caesura,' which, 'within history, interrupts history and opens up another possibility of history, or else closes off all possibility of history.'[11] Josh Cohen, in his own approach to the Holocaust, employs 'interrupting' as a 'participial adjective,' suggesting 'the effect of the inassimilable trauma of Auschwitz on thinking ("'Auschwitz' interrupts")' and as 'present participle,' meaning 'the imperative of thinking and acting against the recurrence of Auschwitz ("'Auschwitz' must be interrupted").'[12]

The Eichmann trial (1961) had already demonstrated that no healing was possible, that 'there was no escape from Auschwitz.'[13] These words belong to Yehiel Dinur, who gave an emotional opening statement on his two-year imprisonment at Auschwitz. Unable to cope with the attorney general's and the presiding judge's repeated attempts to make him answer questions instead of letting him tell his story, he literally collapsed on the floor in front of the court members and a large audience, and was taken out of the room in an unconscious state on a stretcher.[14] As this incident demonstrated, his mind still tortured his body with the memory of Auschwitz, which he called the 'planet of ashes.' In his later book he revealed that he had fainted because he had subconsciously associated the authoritative Judge Landau with an SS officer. In 1979 the televised interview of the practicing psychoanalyst Dori Laub, a former victim of the Transnistrian concentration camps, marked the onset of a huge testimonial enterprise named the Fortunoff Video Archive for Holocaust Testimonies at Yale, containing fourteen hundred videotaped interviews; many victims testified that healing their wounds was impossible. In his 1982 *To Mend the World*, Emil Fackenheim emphasized the difference between healing and mending and in the second edition of the book (1994), in his response to Susan E. Shapiro's criticism that emphasizing physical and spiritual resistance in the death camps is implicitly a denigration of 'the mute testimony of the *Muselmänner*,' he reiterated that '. . . while a mending of the wound of Spirit is possible, a healing is not.'[15] In 1985, after eleven years of work, Claude Lanzmann's *Shoah*, totalling nine hours of testimonies of survivors but also of perpetrators from four sites across Poland,[16] was released to the public. The series of interviews included in the film showed that the victims' journeys back to the camps via testimony not only reopened their wounds that had no time to heal but also left little hope that they would ever heal.

Starting with the 1990s, trauma theory has become the dominant framework of investigating the transmission of catastrophic experiences. More specifically, the works of Cathy Caruth (*Unclaimed Experience: Trauma, Narrative, and History*), Shoshana Felman and Dori Laub (*Testimony: Crises of Witnessing in Literature, Psychoanalysis, and History*), Dominick LaCapra (*History and Memory after Auschwitz* and *Writing History, Writing Trauma*) and Lawrence Langer (*Versions of Survival* and *Holocaust Testimonies: The Ruins of Memory*) showed, although from slightly different angles, that a traumatic event leaves traces that cannot be completely cured. For Caruth, whose work drew inspiration from Freud, Lacan and Paul de Man, trauma is 'the response to an unexpected or overwhelming violent event or events that are not fully grasped as they occur, but return later in repeated flashbacks, nightmares and other repetitive phenomena.'[17] Comparing the original meaning of 'trauma' as a wound inflicted on one's body with what it has come to represent in trauma studies, psychological grievance, Caruth concluded that 'the wound of the mind—the breach in the mind's experience of time, self and the world—is not, like the wound of the body, a simple and healable event.'[18] Caruth's investigation of the way trauma often disrupts the mechanisms by which memory is represented was highly significant because she stressed the victims' 'absolute inability to know.'[19] This impossibility to relate to what happened to them confers on victims' narratives both an amnesic and 'unspeakable' characteristic. The amnesia and unspeakability that Caruth remarked in survivors' stories, the ones whose 'mind,' not only the body, was wounded,[20] are proofs that suffering is not easy to translate into a logical frame.

In his *Representing the Holocaust: History, Theory, Trauma*, invoking Freud's 'acting out,' 'working through,' 'mourning,' 'melancholy' and 'the sublime,' Dominick LaCapra pleas for a correct understanding of psychoanalysis, which 'is misunderstood as merely a psychology of the individual,' and its concepts, which 'are overtly reduced when they are confined to a clinical context.'[21] The aim of LaCapra's *Writing History, Writing Trauma* was to treat 'trauma and post-traumatic symptoms in a manner that links them to inquiry into other significant problems, including the relations between the individual and society, the political implications of a research orientation, and the limitations and possibilities of an emphasis on melancholia, the sublime, transhistorical, mourning, acting out, and working through, problems that bear on social and political issues.'[22] LaCapra doubts that historiography can heal open wounds. In fact, it can just help victims 'to come to terms with the wounds and scars of the past.'[23] However, even this limited possibility could be but an optimistic assumption in post-apartheid South Africa and post-Nazi Germany, where reflecting on historical losses focused on 'whether attempts to work through problems, including rituals of mourning, can viably come to terms with (without ever fully healing or overcoming) the divided legacies, open wounds, and unspeakable losses of a dire past.'[24] A complete mastery of the past is impossible, and what psychoanalysis can do is just to make the victim aware of the duality between remembering the past, which can still return in the form of flashbacks or nightmares, and living in the present. Hence, the traumatized can neither be blamed for being 'tragically possessed by the past and reliving its suffering to such an extent that present life and the assumption of its responsibilities become impossible' nor presupposed to have achieved complete 'mastery or full dialectical overcoming of the past in a redemptive narrative or a speculative *Aufhebung* and *Versöhnung*—a stereotypically Hegelian overcoming and reconciliation—wherein all wounds are healed without leaving scars and full ego identity is achieved.'[25] Irrespective of their origin, personal or historical, wounds do not 'simply heal,' but rather bring their 'scars or residues in the present.'[26]

In his own turn, Yosef Hayim Yerushalmi contradicted Eugen Rosenstock-Huessy, who had named the historian a 'physician of memory,' honoured 'to heal wounds, genuine wounds.' Yerushalmi preferred the term 'pathologist' for historians and added that the 'Jewish memory cannot be "healed" unless the group itself finds healing, unless its wholeness is restored or rejuvenated.'[27] Lawrence Langer's *Holocaust Testimonies: The Ruins of Memory*, which also cites this famous dispute, has questioned the possibility of healing through narrating survival stories. For example, Zoltan G. 'distinguishes between the self who "does" and the self who is "done to" but cannot reconcile the two roles,' thus suffering 'from a scarred memory, too honest to conceal the original wound, but helpless to heal it.'[28] Leon H.'s story of survival illustrates his anger with all who remained passive while Jewish people were being killed in the gas chambers. This anger, Langer comments, has never

stopped and has remained on his face and transmitted to the next generation. His children had to live with it.[29] Viktor C., who survived but left his
brother behind, confessed that the dilemma whether to stay with his brother
or strengthen his own chance to outlive the others was 'his albatross, the re-
sultant wound,' 'a hurt that he has tried all his life to heal, without success.'[30]
To this example, we may add that of Itzhak Zuckerman, a surviving leader
of the Warsaw Ghetto Uprising, who towards the end of *Shoah* confesses to
Lanzmann: 'If you could lick my heart, it would poison you.'[31]

Such narratives are, as Langer concludes, the very proof that when talking
to Holocaust survivors, one cannot conceive the complete cure of past inju-
ries. Victims are still in a 'blighted convalescence,' with 'festering' wounds
that will never heal.[32] The scars of their memories are 'gaps, amnesia, distor-
tion, revision, or even fugue states or intrusive flashbacks.'[33] As wounded
memory, these are indirectly inherited by the later generations under the
form of what Marianne Hirsch has called 'postmemory,' which is made up
of narratives, images and behaviours that enable them to know, and thus to
'remember.'[34]

While Langer analysed Holocaust victims and their next generations,
Alexander and Margarete Mitscherlich and Eric Santner studied the first
and second generations of the perpetrators. In their *The Inability to Mourn*,
published in 1967, the Mitscherlichs attempted to explain the psychic immo-
bility in post-war Germany by emphasizing that the nation was in depression,
German people seeing themselves as collateral victims. 'The Mitscherlichs'
diagnosis of an impossible collective *Trauerarbeit* and of an unconscious
narcissistic identification of the German people with Hitler and the ideology
of National Socialism chimed with Adorno's appeal to a form of Freudian
working-through to avoid turning the tables on whom the real mourning victims were.'[35] For Eric Santner, '[t]he post-war generations have . . . inherited
not guilt so much as the denial of guilt, not losses so much as lost opportunities to mourn losses.'[36] Two years after the publication of his book in which
he interpreted, among others, several interviews Peter Sichrovsky made with
children and grandchildren of several more or less known Nazi figures,[37]
Santner published a chapter in Friedländer's edited book *Probing the Limits
of Representation*, where he coined the term 'narrative fetishism.' This means
'the construction and deployment of a narrative consciously or unconsciously
designed to expunge the traces of the trauma or loss that called that narrative
into being in the first place.'[38] He contrasted the use of narrative as fetish
to the 'symbolic behaviour that Freud called *Trauerarbeit*, or "the work of
mourning",' and explained that

> [b]oth narrative fetishism and mourning are responses to loss, to a past that
> refuses to go away due to its traumatic impact. The work of mourning is a pro-

cess of elaborating and integrating it in symbolically and dialogically mediated doses; it is a process of translating, troping, and figuring loss and, as Dominick LaCapra has noted in his chapter, may encompass 'a relation between language and silence that is in some sense ritualized.' Narrative fetishism, by contrast, is the way an inability or refusal to mourn emplots traumatic events; it is a strategy of undoing, in fantasy, the need for mourning by simulating a condition of intactness, typically by situating the site and origin of loss elsewhere. Narrative fetishism releases one from the burden of having to reconstitute one's self-identity under 'posttraumatic' conditions; in narrative fetishism, the 'post' is indefinitely postponed.[39]

With the new discoveries about trauma, specialists started to realise something that otherwise Jean-François Lyotard had phrased at the Cerisy-la-Salle colloquium on Derrida ('Les Fins de l'homme,' 1980): '[O]ne must link after Auschwitz but without speculative result.'[40] Lyotard emphasized the need to find idioms for what he called 'differends' and voice them in spite of their seeming unnarratability. In 2010, admitting the unrepresentability of traumatic experiences and the fact that 'traumatic memories entrap us in the prison house of repetition compulsion,'[41] Gabriele Schwab contended that narrative, storytelling and testimonies 'are necessary for healing trauma.'[42] She confessed that 'writing about histories of violence' has countered her own helplessness when she ran away to the States from violent Germany to notice later on that she had stepped into another country of violence.[43] It was then she realised the need for 'a theory of traumatic narratives that deals with the paradox of telling what cannot be told';[44] in other words, traumatic narratives might be conceived as restoring possibilities of healing and mending. This is precisely what Shoshana Felman did after she realised that her course on trauma, especially after her students had watched two of the testimonies from the Fortunoff Archive, put them into the position of witnesses who could no longer cope with the trauma they were exposed to. 'Worried by the critical dimensions of this crisis which the class was obviously going through,'[45] a crisis manifesting itself as 'a sort of *panic* that consisted in both emotional and intellectual disorientation, *loss of direction*,'[46] and helped by Dori Laub, she devised a therapeutic session for her students, asking them to write a paper as *their testimony to the course* they had witnessed.[47] Students' reactions (explained in detail by Felman) seemed to suggest an empathy that extended to their identification with the victims. In response to such unexpected reactions, Hirsch's work encouraged students' empathy, yet introducing an awareness that contributed to their distancing from the event. She preferred 'to think in terms of a form of solidarity that is suspicious of empathy, shuttling instead between proximity and distance, affiliation and disaffiliation, complicity and accountability.'[48]

In recent years, the field of trauma studies has indeed begun questioning some of its foundational narratives. It has paid increasing attention to
collective rather than individual traumas, and to systemic forms of trauma
produced by ongoing, slow forms of violence. It has extended its reach to
areas of the globe that were not under its purview in the past. Caruth's theory
was challenged by Ruth Leys, who disapproved of the ambiguous definitions
of victimhood that blur the difference between victim and perpetrator,[49] and
Wulf Kansteiner and Harald Weilnböck, who questioned her assertion that
the traumatic event is 'unspeakable' and 'unrepresentable,' since that 'contra-
dicts the consensus in psychotherapy studies that narration is an indispensable
tool for healing.'[50]

Many of the ethical issues raised by Holocaust scholars in relation to the
artistic representation of trauma have been contradicted. At the end of the
century, Holocaust trauma transmitted through historical accounts was perceived positively, but its artistic representation was characterized in negative
terms. According to Ernst van Alphen, 'the dubious, even nefarious, features
of fictional, imaginative discourse,' was considered 'not only less effective,
but even objectionable' because of rhetorical ornamentation, the reconstruction of 'an indirect and skewed image of the Holocaust, using flights of fancy
and trivializing imaginative techniques.'[51] Even after Adorno's admission of
having committed an error when asserting that 'to write poetry after Auschwitz is barbaric' (orig. 1949)[52] and the retraction of this famous dictum in
Negative Dialectics (orig. 1966), where he advocated that 'perennial suffering has as much right to expression as a tortured man has to scream; hence
it may have been wrong to say that after Auschwitz you could no longer
write poems,'[53] the debate on Holocaust representation continued for many
decades. Towards the turn of the century, scholars realized that the need to
verbalize pain gives expression to the feelings that the victim or the direct or
indirect witness has repressed;[54] thus the transformation of traumatic memory
into narrative memory was not only necessary but part of the gift of psychoanalysis, known under the name of 'the talking cure.'

Narrating Our Healing: Perspectives on Working Through Trauma by
Chris van der Merwe and Pumla Gobodo-Madikizela offers illuminating
perspectives on the process of 'narrating healing' in the context of the South
African post-apartheid era. Their claim is that when remaining unacknowledged, traumatic events 'continue to disempower victims, and intensify the
feelings of shame and humiliation that are part of the legacy of trauma and
its internalisation,' which they call the 'unfinished business' of trauma.[55]
Healing trauma, with its positive effects of 'the restoration of the self and the
reclaiming of one's sense of control of memory, of the capacity to reflect, understand, and to perceive things as they are or were, requires transformation

of traumatic memory into narrative memory.'[56] Van der Merwe and Gobodo-Madikizela underline the necessity of turning one's life into a narrative, since this has always happened with communities and nations narrating their past in order to grasp the present and to be guided by these stories in the future.[57] However, narratives of trauma are different because they point to the inter-ruption of the coherence and meaning of life ('the traumatized person has "lost the plot"' that was shattered into bits and pieces). According to Paul Ricoeur, the psychiatrist's duty is to help his patient rearrange these bits and pieces into 'a story that is both more intelligible and more bearable.'[58] Susan Brison has defined narrative as a 'remaking' of the self in opposition with the undoing of the self, caused by trauma.[59] Likewise, van der Merwe and Gobodo-Madikizela consider narrating traumatic memory 'a piecing together of a "dismembered self", an attempt at re-mastering traumatic memory,'[60] which is actually the beginning of healing.

Having in mind this edited collection, we have not included in the present volume a chapter on post-apartheid trauma. This is why we would like to linger over what is perhaps the best example of *Narrating Our Healing.* An African woman whose eleven-year-old son was killed greeted Gobodo-Madikizela, a member of the Truth and Reconciliation Commission, aggressively, asking her whether she had come to hurt them. With a mixture of anger and tears she defined TRC as 'a pointless exercise' that would only hurt the wounded more and re-open their scars. However, afterwards she invited Gobodo-Madikizela to her house and started telling her story, an 'exploded silence,' 'a narrative that speaks of the world where helpless parents grieved because they could not protect their children inside or outside the home, but could only cover over the memory of their grief and hope that, someday, grass would grow over it.'[61] This deeply and irreparably wounded woman cried out her pain: 'My anguish was beyond anything I ever thought I could experience. . . . I can feel the wetness of his blood—I felt his last breath leave him. He was my only child.'[62]

As van der Merwe and Gobodo-Madikizela explain, the woman is a typi-cal victim of trauma whose behaviour was detailed by Judith Herman:[63] on the one hand, she wanted to forget 'because remembering reopens the wound of trauma'; on the other hand, she wanted 'to remember because silence is unbearable' and because narrating her trauma meant paying honour to her son's memory.[64] Her loss could not be healed, but the very fact that she was keeping everything in the house in the exact position in which her son had left it when running out for school after getting his peanut butter sandwich ready, was her way of keeping her son's memory alive, as well as freezing that moment as a moment of the present. It was as if her boy just went out to play with his friends, and as if he would return to clean the crumbs he had left after making his sandwich.

Autobiographies were prioritized in the second decade of the millennium as accounts that allow victims to rewrite the histories that were written twice for them: first by the historians who interviewed them and secondly by their readers. Thus, autobiographies became privileged cultural narratives of trauma that could continue the interminable task of working through from the point where classical trauma theory stopped: finding a resolution to the endurance of trauma.[65]

Apart from literary narrative, another way to break the victim's literal silence and overcome the prevailing malaise in verbal representation is to bypass the literary and appeal to a non-literary way of representing trauma. Traumatic memory is not always verbal but can also be re-experienced visually. Traumas can be healed not by eliminating traumatic memories, but by communicating them in any form, including nonverbal, 'iconic' forms of communication like drawing, painting, films, the erection of monuments, the building of museums. From the end of the 1990s onwards, scholars have proposed different healing practices through the use of the arts. Aware of the central role of visual images in an era that is saturated by media coverage, contemporary scholars have suggested that victims and witnesses of trauma make sense of what feels like an illogical experience through visual expression and communication, a fact which makes creative art therapies more effective than the ambiguous healing offered by verbal representation.[66]

Catherine Malabou's *The New Wounded: From Neurosis to Brain Damage*[67] has introduced a radical challenge to psychoanalysis and psychoanalytically inflected trauma theories. Malabou argues that the frontier separating organic from socio-political traumatisms is becoming more and more fluid, given that all forms of trauma transform neuronal organisation, especially those cerebral sites known as 'the affective brain.' She moves on to propose a general theory of trauma that seeks to understand the distinctness of 'the new wounded'—victims of accidental traumatisms, chronic degenerative maladies or different forms of extreme violence devoid of reason. As she insists, these new patients cannot be understood by traditional psychoanalysis because cerebral trauma destroys the core of psychic life, leaving behind only the form of an absence. What is more, cerebral trauma breaks the hermeneutic thread that sustains the talking cure and arrests the transferential process that both psychoanalysis and classical trauma theory consider an inextricable part of the 'art of healing.'

But the most drastic change in the first decade of the twenty-first century was the turn towards critical trauma studies as a discipline of the social sciences. Critical trauma studies include not only those who experienced trauma and narrated it but also those who study it. Critical trauma studies does not see trauma as stemming only from a major catastrophe, but, as Peter Levine has shown, also from accidents, routine invasive medical procedures, loss of loved ones and cataclysms such as earthquakes and hurricanes.[68] If scholars of trauma studies in the past originated primarily from the fields of the humanities, nowadays they are joined by social scientists, medical specialists, rescue workers, police, counsellors and government officers, each playing a different role in helping the victims of trauma. They seek to foster a 'new humanities,' 'keen to meld the scientific with the affective.'[69] However, if classical trauma studies have foregrounded the unrepresentability of the traumatic experience, these new approaches do not engage critically with dominant paradigms in trauma theory and psychoanalysis but remain mostly oriented towards eliminating the stress stemming from a traumatic event.[70] Although no doubt valuable, the various practical solutions they offer in order to deal with and prevent trauma seem to be miraculous recipes of working through trauma, but they do not take into account the fact that we are living in an age of extreme vulnerability where there is no absolute protection or ultimate solution. Acknowledging vulnerability, an important contemporary keyword, promises ways out of the cyclical temporality of trauma by activating possibilities of care, interdependence and empathic intervention. Marianne Hirsch has coined the notion 'unforgiving temporality' to refer to the distinct temporality of trauma, since '[t]rauma offers new conceptions of time, in that it always occurs in the present, as a form of perpetual return.'[71] The 'unforgiving temporality' of a traumatic experience connotes the impossibility to heal, repair or alleviate the pain, which lives on into the future. An alternative may be opening up 'alternative temporalities that are more porous and future-oriented and that galvanize a sense of urgency about the need for change, now.'[72]

Within this context and assimilating the predicaments that Hirsch invokes, our volume proposes a return to the resources of the humanities in an attempt to investigate, reflect on, remember or imagine old and new arts of healing at the intersection of critical and cultural theory, psychoanalysis, philosophy, neurology, literature, the visual arts, film studies and gender and queer studies. We believe that there is an urgent need for the critical humanities to give up an overgeneralized concept of trauma which subsumes 'all forms of violence, dislocation, and psychic pain under its categorical singularity.'[73]

HEAL/LINKS: FROM HOLOCAUST REPRESENTATION TO THE NEW WOUNDED

As Ivan Callus, one of our contributors, suggests in the opening essay of this book, *healing*, the idea of wholeness, putting together the fragments, invokes the enormity of a task that remains unimaginable. Indeed, healing is a big, lumpy, cumbersome word. It makes your mouth full when you try to pronounce it. Hard and round like the pebbles Demosthenes,[74] the Ancient Greek rhetorician, put in his mouth, the word 'healing' (and the thought it conjures) is nevertheless a necessity if, like Demosthenes, our aim is to learn how to speak anew, how not to stay silent, how to avoid stuttering, how to continue speaking *in spite of the stuttering* at the sight of the current faces of trauma.

Although they often interrogate or doubt the possibility of healing, remaining modest in their claims, all contributors in this volume commit themselves to a rigorous reflection on the particular contexts, the conditions, the effects, the tentative temporalities, the inevitable cost of any attempt at healing. Writing from different disciplines, located in different parts of the world, focusing on a variety of traumatogenic cultures, they raise a number of important questions that force us to control a compulsive reiteration of the word and to qualify each one of its uses—without abandoning what we might call the *gift* of its thought. Predictably, at the end of the venture undertaken in the volume, the gift remains intangible, nothing more than the constellation formed by a series of *heal/links* which associate the gift with the creative function of imagination; the plasticity of the human brain; the difficult leap across the temporal and affective gap that prevents forgiveness; the unfamiliar, queer or counter-temporalities produced by the tensions between memory and forgetting; and finally, with a form of empathy cultivated through writing, reading, listening, showing or, simply, through the bio-psychic traces of a maternally connoted being-with that make possible a tactful touching, a careful tending of the still festering wound.

Ultimately, the writers in this volume interrogate any understanding of healing as the restoration of a lost wholeness, the end of subjective or communal crisis, the retrieval of personal or national sovereignty. Callus notes that healing as a process might be helped by 'little moments in a life, little devices to living.' Nicholas Chare, another contributor, suggests that the process of healing involves the commitment to offering an 'enhanced understanding' of our legacies of trauma. Mieke Bal, Ernst van Alphen, Radhika Mohanram and Irene Scicluna retrace this process in a multidirectional politics of place.

The ethical horizon of *life* is central in all the essays, from Lucia Ispas's analysis of Roberto Benigni's *La vita è bella* and Arleen Ionescu's concluding anticipation of a forgiveness-to-come that will inaugurate new life-enhancing possibilities for the descendants of victims and perpetrators alike to Maria Margaroni's interrogation of the biopolitical strategy of a flat, indifferent survival and the testimonies of life offered by Laurent Milesi, Olga Michael and Nicholas Chare against the workings of a homophobic/trans*phobic thanatopolitics and in the face of the vicissitudes of the death drive.

Arts of Healing is structured in three parts, each bringing together essays that share a particular focus or a cluster of concerns. The first part, titled 'Holocaust Trauma and the Ambivalence of Healing: Irreverent Takes,' pays tribute to the centrality of the Holocaust in the emergence and development of trauma studies, while insisting on the need to break away from what Karyn Ball has called 'the disciplinary imaginary' that has determined 'an "appropriate" (rigorous and ethical) approach to the Holocaust.'[75] Hence the irreverent take each of the essays adopts towards particular orthodoxies in the field.

Ivan Callus's self-reflexive essay, titled 'Unfamiliar Healing: Reconsidering the Fragment in Narratives of Holocaust Trauma,' is an apt opening for Part I since it performs the difficulty and tentativeness that characterize contemporary returns to the trauma of the Holocaust, given the bibliography that has already been compiled on it, the extent of psychic devastation it has produced, the time that has elapsed, and the new generations' temporal and emotional distance from the event, its contexts and the actual victims. Callus's point of departure in this chapter is the privileging of the fragment and the fragmentary in accounts of the Holocaust. This is why he chooses to foreground the formal conventions of the *essay* and its connection with the fragmentary, the inconclusive and the elliptical. Since he conceives fragmentation as a redrawing of borders and crossovers into the uncharted, his tour-de-force of an essay involves a strikingly unorthodox performance that suspends accepted stylistic, formatting or referencing practices in order to draw the reader into the vortex of the intellectual *trial* that the word 'essay' connotes. Through close engagement with theoretical reflections on the tradition of the essay as a genre, Callus both restages and exposes (or, in Shklovskyan terms, defamiliarizes) the essay's resistance to the conclusive, its allergy to 'the Great Thought.' Demonstrating how the same kind of resistance dominates narratives of the Holocaust from Maurice Blanchot to Georges Perec, G. W. Sebald, Peter Weiss and Bart van Es (among others), Callus comes to wonder if a different kind of *tone* might, after all, be imaginable in our attempt to produce a form of writing commensurable to traumatic experience. The foil narratives he uses in his critical re-reading of the ethics of the fragment include Victor Shklovsky's autobiographic *A Sentimental Journey* as well as Robert Walser and Robert Musil's own accounts of trauma. One of the key threads that binds together the different fragments (or lexias) that Callus assembles in this creatively orchestrated chapter relates to the function of writing, and especially of the literary, in the process of working towards 'improbable healing.' Does the trauma of the other register only if rendered in the genre of the literary?, he asks. Hasn't literature lost its authority after the crisis of humanity and humanism at the camps? In light of the increasing emphasis on the new media, can we continue to assume that literature will remain an effective art of healing? Important as they are, these questions constitute a challenge and prepare the ground for the theoretical investigation attempted by other contributors in Parts II and III of this volume.

In her own irreverent take on one of the most debated questions in the context of Holocaust studies, 'Forgiving as Self-Healing? The Case of Eva Mozes Kor,' Arleen Ionescu focuses on the philosophical and ethico-political dilemmas of forgiveness, its unconditionality as a pure, ethical gesture, its performative effects, its healing potential as well as its political risks and impasses. Drawing on the thought of Vladimir Jankélévitch, Hannah Arendt, Emmanuel Levinas and Jacques Derrida, Ionescu sets out to elaborate some of the key premises that determine the possibility or impossibility of forgiveness as a form of collective or personal healing. In a spirit similar to that adopted by Callus, she too insists on the *tone* in which forgiveness as a speech act is performed, neither on the subject's intentions nor its effects. She focuses in particular on Eva Mozes Kor, one of the child twins on whom Dr. Mengele had experimented in Auschwitz, and her 1995 declaration of amnesty, which, as Ionescu notes, breaks with a dominant taboo in the Jewish community that rendered any gesture of forgiving the Nazi perpetrators of the Holocaust impossible. Ionescu begins her analysis of Mozes Kor's declaration by comparing it with the Judaic tradition of forgiveness, as this is exemplified in Simon Wiesenthal's *The Sunflower*. With close reference to the film *Forgiving Dr Mengele* and the autobiographical book *Surviving the Angel of Death*, Ionescu examines the validity and operative function of Mozes Kor's speech act, tracing the discourse of empowerment that has informed her controversial gesture. She demonstrates how, on a subjective level, forgiveness has helped Mozes Kor restore her sense of selfhood and her empathy towards others. Despite its obvious beneficial effects, however, Ionescu does not refrain from questioning the selfish motives behind what appears to be a daring, magnanimous stance. Returning to Derrida's analysis of forgiveness, she suggests that Mozes Kor's forgiving gesture is circumscribed by the interest structure of an economy of exchange and ends up becoming an act of sovereignty performed by an individual who presumes to speak in the name of other victims, even in the name of the dead. In her critical approach to Mozes Kor's utilitarian employment of forgiveness as a form of self-healing, Ionescu emphasizes Jankélévitch's refusal to grant forgiveness to a young German who had no involvement in the Nazi crimes. As Ionescu argues in her conclusion, the juxtaposition of these two attitudes allows us to perceive the difference between 'conditional' and pure, 'unconditional' forgiveness, which, following Derrida and in light of the persistence of crimes against humanity, remains 'to-come.'

The last essay included in Part I is titled '(Mis)Representing Trauma through Humour? Roberto Benigni's *La vita è bella*.' In this chapter Lucia Ispas sets out to reflect on one of the central orthodoxies in Holocaust studies, namely the tacit proscription of comedy and humour in Holocaust representation. The focus of her analysis is Roberto Benigni's *La vita è bella*, a controversial 1997 film, which employs a Chaplinesque kind of humour and a fairy-tale structure in what is admittedly an unfamiliar account of life and death in a Nazi concentration camp. Ispas offers an overview of the key debates on Holocaust representability and takes a firm stance in favour of the power of humour to heal trauma and preserve hope in the face of horror. Through a close reading of Benigni's film and its contexts, she points out the connections between the first part and the second, more sober, part, traces the development of Benigni's comic anti-hero and elaborates on the director's employment of fairy-tale conventions, discussing the effects of his decision to mix historical fact and fiction. Engaging with the criticism directed at the film, Ispas meticulously maps out the workings of the gift process mobilized by and propelling Benigni's narrative, a process that renders the spectator the privileged recipient of what, according to the author, constitutes Benigni's ultimate gift: that is, his reclamation of the value of life and his tribute to the survival instinct of human beings. Ispas insists that humour, rather than sugar-coating the dire conditions experienced in a Nazi camp, paradoxically emphasizes them, functioning as both a therapeutic medium and an act of resistance against the absurdity of Nazi ideology. Following her argument, humour in Benigni's hands resembles Perseus's shield, which enables spectators to face the traumatic event while protecting them and future generations from the petrifying effects of its horror.

The second part of the volume, titled 'Mass Trauma, Art and the Healing Politics of Place,' brings together essays that exemplify the transcultural turn in trauma studies, shifting the emphasis onto the global scenes of war, violence, terror, forced migration and human trafficking, and colonial and neo-colonial politics. Focusing on collective experiences of trauma that have endured and infiltrated the textures of life of particular cultures (from India, Colombia and Palestine to the diffused sites of global terrorism), contributors in this part demonstrate their faith in the power of *showing* and communal practices of memorialization when words fall short of the affective weight that renders traumatic events or situations unbearable. The four essays included in Part II turn their attention to the public function of art and its ability to transform the national, transnational and colonial politics of place, changing the ways memory is invested spatially and experienced materially through the sensory body.

The first chapter, by Mieke Bal, 'Improving Public Space: Trauma Art and Retrospective-Futuristic Healing,' opens with the aporia posed by the task of imagining the suffering of others. Imagination is 'all we have,' she insists, but how can imagination be cultivated to turn into an empathetic faculty that can tune into the dissonant noise produced by an experience of trauma? Bal's point of departure is the story of Miguel de Cervantes, author of *Don Quixote*, who, when a young soldier, was captured and spent five years as a slave in Algiers. Reading *Don Quixote*, she emphasizes its traumatic subtext, focusing in particular on the character of Cardenio, a madman, who in vain seeks an attentive listener with whom he might share his traumatic story. The novel, according to Bal, integrates the necessity and limits of witnessing into its literary form, dramatizing a hysterically repetitive process of storytelling which is always interrupted, never allowed to work itself through to some sort of closure. Reflecting on the impasses of narrative witnessing as represented by Cervantes, Bal suggests that perhaps art, the medium of showing, may be capable of teaching us a silent, attentive, non-interruptive way of witnessing. In her view, we need to stop approaching art as an elitist form of cultural expression. Referring to the Baumgartian notion of aesthetics, she argues that art is, instead, a form of community binding in public space through the senses. This is what renders art a powerful vehicle of mediation between the traumatized subject(s) and the interested observers. To demonstrate her argument, she turns to the work of two contemporary female artists, both based in heavily traumatogenic cultures, namely, India and Colombia. As she explains, the challenge that Indian Nalini Malani and Colombian Doris Salcedo face is to produce art capable of resisting the voyeuristic instinct that fetishizes and takes pleasure in violence. In response to this challenge, the two artists create works that 'move and move us,' in an attempt to commemorate the forgotten victims, re-activate memory as a connecting device among sensitized spectators and, by creating empathy, restore the healing potential of traumatized communities. In conclusion, Bal refers to the audio-visual project she has created in collaboration with Mathieu Montanier based on Cervantes's novel. The project exemplifies the need to invent new forms of witnessing trauma and facilitating healing. Like Malani and Salcedo's installations, it constitutes an experiment that reiterates Bal's faith in imagination and its power to break the media and institutional complicity that perpetuates violence. In her analysis of Malani and Salcedo's art, Bal emphasizes the function of cultural memory as a tool of countering orchestrated processes of 'mis-remembering and dis-remembering' our legacies of violence.

In 'Transforming Trauma into Memory,' Ernst van Alphen sets out to demonstrate the role of art in opening up the vicious cycle of trauma into the temporal work of memory. Drawing on Michael Rothberg's seminal *Multidirec-*

tional Memory, he points out the connections between artistic activity and the act of remembering, both aiming at the creation of new worlds out of older resources or material. This is precisely where the healing potential of art lies. Van Alphen is interested in the work of Marjan Teeuwen, a Dutch artist who visualizes and materializes the temporalizing activity of memory, its opening of the frozen traumatic moment to the unpredictability of the future and the movement of collective history. In particular, he concentrates on *Destroyed House Gaza*, an installation created in the destroyed family house of a Hamas member in Gaza. Van Alphen shows how Teeuwen mobilizes the interplay between destruction and creation, order and chaos, in order to produce new connections, to introduce openings where there were only blocked views, to alleviate the sense of loss and restore a feeling of peace that comes out of the loving rearrangement of destroyed and discarded material. Through this patient and tactful work, van Alphen argues, Teeuwen succeeds in making an important intervention in the context of the Israeli-Palestinian conflict, a war in which memories of rootedness and violent uprooting become defensive or aggressive weapons. In situations where traumatic memory is inscribed and survives in the spaces we inhabit, one of the tasks of art appears to be the commemoration, the restoration and renewal of the bond between land and its uprooted people. In this light, Teeuwen's creative practice aims at undoing the effects of war. In tending to the material ruins of Palestinian lives, she contributes to the development of collective resilience and initiates a healing process that, due to the multidirectionality of human memory, can turn both Israeli and Palestinian 'owned' traumas into the learning experience traced in shared pasts.

Like van Alphen and Bal, Radhika Mohanram in 'Textures of Indian Memory' is concerned with the spatial and embodied politics of remembering. Opening her essay, she asks how one might recuperate the memory of a place, especially those layers which may have been forgotten or obliterated. She sets out to examine Chandigarh, the post-independence city, built as the new capital of Punjab after the partition of British India. Mohanram aims at retrieving the traumatic legacy of this event behind the official narratives of independence, which attempt to heal national wounds through promoting an attitude of cultural amnesia. As the author argues, Chandigarh was intended to function precisely as a site of amnesia. Designed by the modernist architect Le Corbusier, it was built as a city of the future, a space where the Indian people could come together beyond the losses of the past. Yet, despite the nationalist agenda, which is literally inscribed in public space and affecting the body politic, the traumatic past, according to Mohanram, cannot be obliterated without a trace. Turning her attention to the Martyrs' Memorial in Chandigarh, she demonstrates how memories of partition are revived through the body's experiential connection to what is silenced, what is not allowed to surface for the sake of national health and unity. Hence Mohanram's insistent question throughout this essay, a question which remains central in the volume: Is amnesia a medium of healing or does it perpetuate trauma, allowing it to fester underneath? In response to this question, Mohanram suggests that the potential for communal healing may, instead, be activated through an agonistic politics of memorialization, what Michel Foucault has called 'counter-memory.' Her essay, however, ends on a more dubitative note, since she considers that the two countries will heal only after the issue of Kashmir is finally resolved.

'How Do We Mourn? A Look at Makeshift Memorials' is the final essay included in Part II. In this essay Irene Scicluna turns to the emergent tradition of the makeshift memorial in an attempt to trace the conditions that helped establish this collective mourning practice, understand its nature and outline its place in our contemporary societies as well as its cultural effects. Opening her essay, Scicluna discusses historical precedents to this twenty-first-century phenomenon, demonstrating how subtle shifts in the ways we approach death and the erosion of the 'great taboo' of mourning have led to this spontaneous expression of communal grief that is becoming more and more common today. Scicluna moves on to analyse the key characteristics of makeshift memorials, concentrating on their immediate, impromptu nature; their combination of individual affect and collective social force; their limited duration and palimpsestic function. She argues that makeshift memorials need to be approached, not as static objects, but as a dynamic system bringing together conflicting feelings, desires, discourses and perspectives. This is why she insists on their socio-political significance as non-hegemonic practices of mourning which have the potential to create the conditions necessary for what Judith Butler in *Frames of War* has called the recognizability of suffering and grief that would otherwise go unnoticed. Finally, Scicluna focuses on the temporary nature of makeshift memorials, their eventual removal from public view, which, as she notes, is 'a fraught issue.' On the one hand, the clearing away of the memorial may feel like a form of disloyalty or betrayal. On the other hand, it is necessary both for reasons of safety but also for the sake of completing the work of mourning. Drawing on Freud, Scicluna suggests that such performative closure that transposes grief from the public to the private domain is important if communal healing is to take place.

Part III, 'Intimate Healing,' marks a shift away from public, collective concerns, concentrating instead on testimonies and theoretical reflections on intimate forms of healing. Bringing together chapters that focus on different media and genres (autofiction, comics, the novel, the film script, installation art), this part looks at more personal responses to collective trauma as well as at traumatic experiences that are the product of family and intergenerational dynamics and gender- or sexuality-related violence. Given the focus of the chapters, psychoanalytic theory is (explicitly or implicitly) a key framework within and against which the authors seek to articulate distinct narratives of healing. Undoubtedly, this reiterates the centrality of psychoanalysis in trauma studies. At the same time, however, the approaches adopted in the essays are proof of the increasing trends towards a more critical employment of classical psychoanalytic discourses and a growing openness to possible interfaces with the field of neurobiology.

In 'Literature between Antidote and Black Magic: The Autofiction of Chloé Delaume,' Laurent Milesi takes up the question raised by Callus in Part I of this volume regarding the effectiveness of writing and, in particular, literature as an art of healing. He focuses on a contemporary French writer, Chloé Delaume, who has been diagnosed with bipolar psychosis and insists on using writing as a weapon of aggression, a poison, and a form of black magic rather than a therapeutic medium. As Milesi points out, Delaume repudiates the healing power of both literature and psychoanalysis. In this spirit, she defines the type of autofiction she is practicing as an 'autopsy,' that is, the post-mortem examination of an ego damaged by familial trauma. In his analysis of Delaume's death-driven writings, Milesi aims at tracing the various negative forms of the ego, as Delaume represents them, associating each form with the collective fictions imposed on her by others. Hence her singular perspective on the genre of autofiction, her employment of it as a kind of antidote, a form of chemotherapy that attempts to kill death by inflicting death. Despite Delaume's repeated pronouncements against the hope or possibility of healing, Milesi concludes by suggesting that what he calls her 'death-write' may have therapeutic effects, after all, in that it offers the subject engaged in writing a space of empowerment where reality can be modified, different roles or scenarios can be tried out and a new, enfranchised 'I' has the chance to emerge.

In 'Queer Trauma, Paternal Loss and Graphic Healing in Alison Bechdel's *Fun Home: A Family Tragicomic*,' Olga Michael's concern remains familial trauma and a subject's attempt at liberating herself from the oppressive hold that the past has on her. More specifically, Michael demonstrates the devastating effects of compulsory heterosexuality on individuals, tracing Bechdel's representation of inter-generationally transmitted queer trauma. Michael makes her own intervention in the debate centred on the healing power of writing, arguing that the comics medium (in its fragmentary nature and its combination of showing with telling) lends itself to an effective working through of intimate trauma. In her analysis of Bechdel's graphic autobiographical novel, Michael pays close attention to the writer's use of Gothic elements as well as her intertextual references to Oscar Wilde and his queer aestheticism. Drawing on queer studies of the Gothic, Michael shows the connections among monstrosity, secrecy, guilt, possession and 'unspeakable desire.' She argues that these connections are thrown into relief in Bechdel's depiction of her family home, which Michael reads as the 'autotopography' of Bechdel's homosexual father and his repressed desire. At the same time, Michael is attentive to Bechdel's subtle undoing of the Gothic narrative, precisely through the relationship she establishes between Wilde and her father. Employing Carolyn Dinshaw's concept of 'queer temporalities,' Michael succeeds in demonstrating the significance of this cross-temporal relation in Bechdel's graphic novel, which allows the author to reconfigure the space of her family home (the intimate site of her trauma) and the character of her closeted homosexual father. As she suggests, through the portrayal of her father as a Wildean aesthete, Bechdel offers her father *post*-death the life of the artist he had declined in favour of passing as a heterosexual family man. In doing so, not only does Bechdel come to possess her traumatic familial past but, more importantly, she is able to project herself as a queer artist onto the possibility of an alternative past in the context of which Wilde becomes her literary (fore)father.

Like Michael, Nicholas Chare is interested in the gendered contexts of intimate trauma caused by the inflexibility of a binary logic that prescribes and proscribes particular life choices. His chapter is titled 'Concrete Loss: Attesting to Trauma in Teresa Margolles's *Karla, Hilario Reyes Gallegos*' and focuses on Margolles's 2016 installation on the life and death of Karla, a sixty-four-year-old trans* woman who was murdered in 2015. In his analysis, Chare is attentive to Margolles's concern with the economic disparities in Mexico and how these affect specific powerless groups, especially trans* people and sex workers. This is why in his approach to *Karla*, Chare pays close attention to the materiality of this artwork, in particular to Margolles's use of a concrete block taken from the scene of the crime. As he informs the reader, concrete is Margolles's signature material that connects her to the tradition of minimalism. Unlike other minimalist artists, however, Margolles seeks to expose not only the dead ends of a capitalist economy but also the ineluctable processes of social abjection that lead to gendered, homophobic and trans*phobic violence. Chare notes the culture-specific connections of concrete as a material with such scenes of violence and argues that Margolles's employment of concrete is both indexical (i.e., pointing to the unequal socio-economic conditions in Mexico and their heavy toll on human life) and therapeutic, since the artist's aim is to offer victims a kind of concrete grave, a resting place. Through her art, which takes the form of a meditation on memory and loss, Margolles performs the mourning ritual that was denied the abjected victims, reclaiming the value of their lives and their power to name themselves. In his reading of *Karla*, Chare turns to the thought of artist and psychoanalyst Bracha Ettinger who, in her critical engagement with Jacques

Lacan, connects processes of social abjection with a form of cultural anxiety in the face of the maternal. As Chare explains, Ettinger's concept of the 'matrixial,' referring to the intra-uterine connection between mother and infant, can help us rethink the maternal beyond fear or anxiety as an experience that fosters encounters, what Ettinger calls 'wit(h)nessing.' According to Chare, it is precisely this experience that Margolles shares with spectators, opening up for them a matrixial dimension of subjectivity that enables compassion and life-enhancing reflection on our legacies of trauma.

The concluding chapter of Part III weaves together a number of threads pursued in earlier essays, namely, the lasting traumas of the Holocaust, the emerging global contexts which introduce new forms of violence and theoretical challenges, the cultivation of the value of life against the diverse faces of contemporary thanatopolitics, as well as the reclamation of the mother/child bond that can function as an important resource for traumatized individuals. In 'The Monstrosity of the New Wounded: Thinking Trauma, Survival and Resistance with Catherine Malabou and Julia Kristeva,' Maria Margaroni directly addresses questions relating to the crisis of classical psychoanalytic theories and their viability in a fast-changing world. Her focus is Catherine Malabou's *The New Wounded* and her materialist rethinking of Freudian psychoanalysis, especially Freud's theorization of trauma. In her analysis of Malabou, Margaroni unpacks the contexts that have informed the philosopher's conceptualization of a new type of traumatized patient, one characterized by cool indifference. Margaroni goes on to demonstrate the close relation between cool indifference as the symptom of our contemporary pathology and a flat mode of existence that Malabou refers to as 'survival.' She proceeds to trace the history of Malabou's concept of survival, from Walter Benjamin and Shoshana Felman to Bruno Bettelheim and Giorgio Agamben. In tracing the layered history of this concept, Margaroni exposes its complicity with the workings of contemporary forms of biopower and emphasizes Malabou's concern with rethinking life as a form of resistance to mere survival. According to Margaroni, despite the insights it offers, Malabou's theory of the new wounded is limited because she privileges the organic over the social causes of trauma and fails to appreciate sufficiently the affective depth that an attitude of cool indifference may, in fact, hide. This is why Margaroni believes it is important to open up the space for a productive dialogue between the philosopher and Julia Kristeva, a literary theorist, writer and practicing psychoanalyst. The writings of Marguerite Duras provide precisely this space of a possible encounter, since they have attracted the attention of both the philosopher and the psychoanalyst. Through a comparative study of Malabou and Kristeva's analyses of Duras, Margaroni points to their distinct aims and perspectives, their dependence on the biological concepts of 'apoptosis' and 'necrosis' as well as their shared faith in the therapeutic value of tenderness.

As Margaroni argues, whereas Malabou has not fully explored this value and its healing potential, Kristeva has recently approached tenderness as the indispensable life-resource cultivated by what she calls 'maternal reliance.' Close to Ettinger's concept of the matrixial, this refers to a bio-psychic economy rooted in each subject's corporeal memories of gestation that, following Kristeva, serves to regulate the processes of death in the interests of life. Reading Duras's film-script of *Hiroshima mon amour* through the lens of Kristeva's essay on 'maternal reliance,' Margaroni concludes her chapter and Part III of this volume with a reaffirmation of the continuing relevance of psychoanalysis and its ability to mobilize the resistances of the subject against the deadening forms of an ambivalent survival.

The present collection aims at contributing to current efforts to pluralize and decolonize our theories of trauma, taking into consideration the varied transcultural contexts that shape both individual and collective experiences of violence, terror, victimization or injustice. Though not aiming to be exhaustive in its selection of different histories and topographies of trauma, it does make an attempt in Part II to move beyond a Euro-American focus towards a better appreciation of the material traumatogenic situations that have changed and continue to change the course of human destinies in South as well as Western Asia. Taking on board the distinctness of contemporary traumatic experiences, the volume intends to offer a fresh consideration of the generic possibilities of cultural narratives developed through the visual arts, literature, film and practices of memorialization or mourning. Contributors' essays adopt a theoretical trajectory that goes beyond traditional approaches to trauma studies, committing themselves to a politically—as much as ethically—invested investigation of the empowering potential and inevitable limits of cultural representation. By foregrounding the commitment to (if not the hope for) repair, healing, resistance and care, the collection opens up the aporetic narratives that have dominated trauma studies to alternative possibilities and conceptions of the future, fostering a broad interrogative and interdisciplinary dialogue in order to develop unfamiliar approaches to the psychic crisis produced by trauma.

NOTES

1. Jean Laplanche and Jean-Bertrand Pontalis, *The Language of Psychoanalysis*, Intro. Daniel Lagache (London: Hogarth Press, 1973; reprinted by Karnac Books, 1988), 656–66.

2. Dominick LaCapra, 'Trauma, Absence, Loss,' *Critical Inquiry* 25.4 (Summer 1999): 723.

3. LaCapra, 'Trauma, Absence, Loss,' 724.

4. See Susan Brownmiller, *Against Our Will: Men, Women, and Rape* (London: Secker and Warburg, 1975). In the United States, in the aftermath of Brownmiller's revealing study, in the 1980s trauma theorists and feminists in the arts and literature wrote and researched massively the issue of childhood physical and sexual abuse, rape, and sexual violence.

5. For a detailed study on Stalinism see Stephen J. Lee, *Stalin and the Soviet Union* (London and New York: Routledge, 1999) and Norman M. Naimark, *Stalin's Genocides* (Princeton, NJ and Oxford: Princeton University Press, 2010). For the effects of Stalinism in the Soviet Union and some of its 'satellite' states, see Vladimir Tismăneanu, *Stalinism for All Seasons: A Political History of Romanian Communism* (Berkeley: University of California Press, 2003). For an excellent account on gulags, see Leona Toker, *Return from the Archipelago: Narratives of Gulag Survivors* (Bloomington and Indianapolis: Indiana University Press, 2000). Leona Toker is also the author of the more recent volume testifying to the similarities between the Gulag and the Holocaust, *Gulag Literature and the Literature of the Nazi Camps* (Bloomington and Indianapolis: Indiana University Press, 2019).

6. See especially the Piteşti prison in communist Romania. For a full description of the Piteşti experiment methods that were supposed to 'heal' the inmates' souls through re-education, but in fact were combining terror and brainwashing techniques, see Arleen Ionescu, 'Witnessing Horrorism: The Piteşti Experiment,' *SLOVO* 32.1 (Spring 2019): 53–74.

7. The diagnostic was included in the *Statistical Manual of Mental Disorders.* See American Psychiatric Association, *Diagnostic and Statistical Manual of Mental Disorders*, 3rd ed. (Washington, DC: American Psychiatric Association, 1980), 236–39. See also Paul Lerner and Mark S. Micale, eds, *Traumatic Pasts: History, Psychiatry, and Trauma in the Modern Age, 1870–1930* (Cambridge: Cambridge University Press, 2001), 2. The psychological legacies of Vietnam were discussed in a five-volume study that 'clearly delineated the syndrome of PTSD and demonstrated its direct relationship to combat exposure.' See Anne Whitehead, *Trauma Fiction* (Edinburgh: Edinburgh University Press, 2004), 4.

8. According to a 2000 survey conducted by the United Nations High Commissioner for Refugees, the number of refugees was approximately twelve million as of January 1998, with an additional one million asylum seekers who had not yet been granted refugee status. See Susan F. Martin, 'New Issues in Refugee Research: Forced Migration and the Evolving Humanitarian Regime,' UN High Commissioner for Refugees (UNHCR), 5 July 2000, https://www.refworld.org/docid/4ff5860e2.html, accessed 14 April 2019.

9. For an elaborate list of symptoms see Breuer, J. and Sigmund Freud, 'On the Psychical Mechanism of Hysterical Phenomena: Preliminary Communication' (1893), in *The Standard Edition of the Complete Psychological Works of Sigmund Freud*, trans. under the General Editorship of James Strachey, in collaboration with Anna Freud, vol. II (1893–1895) (London: Hogarth Press, 1955), 5, original emphasis of terms. See also John Fletcher, *Freud and the Scene of Trauma* (New York: Fordham University Press, 2013).

10. Laurence J. Kirmayer, 'Landscapes of Memory: Trauma, Narrative and Dissociation,' in *Tense Past: Cultural Essays on Memory and Trauma*, eds. Paul Antze and Michael Lambek (London: Routledge, 1996), 188–89.

11. Philippe Lacoue-Labarthe, *Heidegger, Art and Politics: The Fiction of the Political*, trans. Chris Turner (Oxford: Blackwell, 1990), 45.

12. Josh Cohen, *Interrupting Auschwitz: Art, Religion, Philosophy* (London and New York: Continuum, 2005), xviii.

13. Yehiel Dinur (Ka-Tzetnik), *Tzofan E.D.M.A* (Tel Aviv: Hakibutz ha-Meuhad, 1987), 57. English edition: *Shivitti: A Vision* (San Francisco: Harper and Row, 1989), 40. For an analysis of this case see also Michal Shaked, 'The Unknown Eichmann Trial: The Story of the Judge,' *Holocaust and Genocide Studies* 29.1 (Spring 2015): 1–38.

14. See his testimony and collapse at https://www.youtube.com/watch?v=o0T9tZiKYl4, accessed 5 April 2019.

15. Emil Fackenheim, *To Mend the World: Foundations of Post-Holocaust Jewish Thought*, 2nd ed. (Bloomington: Indiana University Press, 1994), 336. To understand the false premises of Shapiro's critique and the distinction between Hegelian and post-Hegelian thought, see Josh Cohen's explanations in note 27, in *Interrupting Auschwitz*, 148.

16. The sites are the Chełmno extermination camp, where gas vans were used to exterminate Jews, the death camps of Treblinka and Auschwitz-Birkenau, as well as the Warsaw Ghetto.

17. Cathy Caruth, *Unclaimed Experience: Trauma, Narrative, and History* (Baltimore: John Hopkins University Press, 1996), 91.

18. Caruth, *Unclaimed Experience*, 4.

19. Caruth, *Unclaimed Experience*, 92.

20. Caruth, *Unclaimed Experience*, 4.

21. Dominick LaCapra, *Representing the Holocaust: History, Theory, Trauma* (Ithaca, NY: Cornell University Press, 1994), 8.

22. Dominick LaCapra, *Writing History, Writing Trauma* (Baltimore: Johns Hopkins University Press, 2014), ix.

23. LaCapra, *Writing History, Writing Trauma*, 42.

24. LaCapra, *Writing History, Writing Trauma*, 44–45.

25. LaCapra, *Writing History, Writing Trauma*, 90.

26. LaCapra, *Writing History, Writing Trauma*, 144.

27. Yosef Hayim Yerushalmi, *Zakhor: Jewish History and Jewish Memory* (Seattle and London: University of Washington Press, 1982), 94.

28. Lawrence L. Langer, *Holocaust Testimonies: The Ruins of Memory* (New Haven, CT: Yale University Press, 1991), 46–47.

29. Langer, *Holocaust Testimonies*, 92.

30. Langer, *Holocaust Testimonies*, 98.

31. Itzhak Zuckerman, in *Shoah*, dir. Claude Lanzmann (The Criterion Collection, Blu-Ray, 1985 [DVD, 2013]). The entire interview of Simha Rotem and Itzhak Zuckerman, who talk about their involvement in the Jewish combat organization in the Warsaw Ghetto and the Warsaw Ghetto Uprising, can be seen at the United States

Holocaust Memorial Museum, Film Accession Number 1996, 166, https://collections.ushmm.org/search/catalog/irn1004790, accessed 5 April 2019.

32. Langer, *Holocaust Testimonies*, 92.

33. Gabriele Schwab, *Haunting Legacies: Violent Histories and Transgenerational Trauma* (New York: Columbia University Press, 2010), 14.

34. Marianne Hirsch, *The Generation of Postmemory: Writing and Visual Culture After the Holocaust* (New York: Columbia University Press, 2012).

35. Arleen Ionescu, *The Memorial Ethics of Libeskind's Berlin Jewish Museum* (London: Palgrave Macmillan, 2017), 36.

36. Eric L. Santner, *Stranded Objects: Mourning, Memory and Film in Postwar Germany* (Ithaca, NY and London: Cornell University Press, 1990), 34.

37. Peter Sichrovsky, *Born Guilty: The Children of the Nazis*, trans. Jean Steinberg (London: I. B. Taurus, 1988). For an analysis of both Santner's and Sichrovsky's books, see also Ionescu, *The Memorial Ethics of Libeskind's Berlin Jewish Museum*, 36–37.

38. Eric L. Santner, 'History Beyond the Pleasure Principle: Some Thoughts on the Representation of Trauma,' in *Probing the Limits of Representation: Nazism and the 'Final Solution,'* ed. Saul Friedlander (Cambridge, MA and London: Harvard University Press, 1992), 144.

39. Santner, 'History Beyond the Pleasure Principle,' 144.

40. This sentence, part of his paper 'Discussions, ou: phraser 'Après Auschwitz,' was then left out from the text Lyotard published later, *The Differend: Phrases in Dispute*, trans. Georges Van Den Abbeele (Manchester: Manchester University Press, 1988). It was 'saved' by Avital Ronell who recorded it in *Finitude's Score: Essays for the End of the Millennium* (Lincoln: University of Nebraska Press, 1994), 256.

41. Schwab, *Haunting Legacies*, 2.

42. Schwab, *Haunting Legacies*, 48.

43. Schwab, *Haunting Legacies*, 6.

44. Schwab, *Haunting Legacies*, 48.

45. Shoshana Felman, 'Education and Crisis, or the Vicissitudes of Teaching,' in *Testimony: Crises of Witnessing in Literature, Psychoanalysis, and History*, Shoshana Felman and Dori Laub (New York and London: Routledge, 1992), 48.

46. Felman, 'Education and Crisis,' 49.

47. See Felman, 'Education and Crisis,' 52, text paraphrased, with the original emphasis kept.

48. Marianne Hirsch, 'Connective Histories in Vulnerable Times,' *PMLA* 129.3 (2014): 339.

49. Ruth Leys, *Trauma: A Genealogy* (Chicago and London: The University of Chicago Press, 2000), 266–97.

50. Wulf Kansteiner and Harald Weilnböck, 'Against the Concept of Cultural Trauma or How I Learned to Love the Suffering of Others without the Help of Psychotherapy,' in *Cultural Memory Studies: An International and Interdisciplinary Handbook*, eds. Astrid Erll and Ansgar Nünning (Berlin: De Gruyter, 2008), 7.

51. Ernst van Alphen, *Holocaust Effects in Contemporary Arts, Literature and Theory* (Stanford, CA: Stanford University Press, 1997), 17.

52. Theodor W. Adorno, 'Cultural Criticism and Society,' in *Prisms*, trans. Samuel Weber and Shierry Weber (Cambridge, MA: MIT Press, 1983 [1955]), 34; also 70, 73.

53. Theodor W. Adorno, *Negative Dialectics*, trans. E. B. Ashton (London and New York: Routledge, 2004 [1973]), 362.

54. Although it is impossible to draw up a comprehensive list of important Holocaust testimonials, apart from Primo Levi's, Elie Wiesel's, Charlotte Delbo's, Tadeusz Borowski's and Simon Wiesenthal's, among others, mention should be made of several works analysing how cultural narratives of trauma are constructed: Avril Alba, *The Holocaust Memorial Museum: Sacred Secular Space* (Houndmills, Basingstoke: Palgrave Macmillan, 2015); Sara R. Horowitz, *Voicing the Void: Muteness and Memory in Holocaust Fiction* (Albany: State University of New York Press, 1997); Jakob Lothe, Susan Rubin Suleiman and James Phelan, eds., *After Testimony: The Ethics and Aesthetics of Holocaust Narrative for the Future* (Columbus: Ohio State University Press, 2012); Jakob Lothe, ed., *Time's Witnesses: Women's Voices from the Holocaust*, trans. Anne Marie Hagen (Edinburgh: Fledgling Press Ltd., 2017); Annette Wieviorka, *Era of the Witness*, trans. Jared Stark (Ithaca, NY: Cornell University Press, 2006); James Young, *The Texture of Memory: Holocaust Memorials and Meaning* (New Haven, CT: Yale University Press, 1993); and Barbie Zelizer, *Remembering to Forget: Holocaust Memory through the Camera's Eye* (Chicago: University of Chicago Press, 1998).

55. Chris N. van der Merwe and Pumla Gobodo-Madikizela, *Narrating our Healing: Perspectives on Working through Trauma* (Newcastle: Cambridge Scholars Publishing, 2007), vii.

56. van der Merwe and Gobodo-Madikizela, *Narrating Our Healing*, vii.

57. van der Merwe and Gobodo-Madikizela, *Narrating Our Healing*, 2 and 4.

58. Paul Ricoeur, 'Life: A Story in Search of a Narrator,' in *A Ricoeur Reader: Reflection and Imagination*, ed. Mario Valdés (Toronto: University of Toronto Press, 1991), 435.

59. Susan Brison, *Aftermath: Violence and the Remaking of the Self* (Princeton, NJ: Princeton University Press, 2002), 71.

60. van der Merwe and Gobodo-Madikizela, *Narrating Our Healing*, 28.

61. van der Merwe and Gobodo-Madikizela, *Narrating Our Healing*, 31.

62. van der Merwe and Gobodo-Madikizela, *Narrating Our Healing*, 30–31.

63. See Judith Herman, *Trauma and Recovery: The Aftermath of Violence—From Domestic Abuse to Political Terror* (New York: Basic Books, 1992).

64. van der Merwe and Gobodo-Madikizela, *Narrating Our Healing*, 32.

65. John Masterson, David Watson and Merle Williams, 'Mending Wounds? Healing, Working through, or Staying in Trauma: An Introduction,' *Journal of Literary Studies* 29.2 (2013): 2.

66. See Linda Bushell Spencer's *Heal Abuse and Trauma Through Art: Increasing Self-worth, Healing of Initial Wounds, and Creating a Sense of Connectivity* (1997), Stephen K. Levine's *Trauma, Therapy: The Arts and Human Suffering*, Kathy Luethje's *Healing with Art and Soul: Engaging One's Self through Art Modalities* (2008) and Esther Dreifuss-Kattan's *Art and Mourning: The Role of Creativity in Healing Trauma and Loss* (2016).

67. Catherine Malabou, *The New Wounded: From Neurosis to Brain Damage*, trans. Steven Miller (New York: Fordham University Press, 2012).

68. See Peter A. Levine, *Healing Trauma: A Pioneering Program for Restoring the Wisdom of Your Body* (Boulder, CO: Sounds True, 2005), 14.

69. Monica J. Casper and Eric Wertheimer, eds., *Critical Trauma Studies: Understanding Violence, Conflict and Memory in Everyday Life* (New York: New York University Press, 2016), 2.

70. See Jasmin Lee Cori's *Healing from Trauma: A Survivor's Guide to Understanding Your Symptoms and Reclaiming Your Life* (2009), Ann Goelitz and Abigail Stewart-Kahn's *From Trauma to Healing: A Social Worker's Guide to Working with Survivors* (2013), Michael Orlans and Terry M. Levy's *Attachment, Trauma, and Healing: Understanding and Treating Attachment Disorder in Children, Families and Adults* (2014), Carolyn Yoder's *The Little Book of Trauma Healing: When Violence Strikes and Community Security Is Threatened* (2005), and Gerald Kiesman's *Trauma Healing Guide: Understanding Trauma with Healing Exercises* (2017).

71. Hirsch, 'Connective Histories in Vulnerable Times,' 335.

72. Hirsch, 'Connective Histories in Vulnerable Times,' 335–37.

73. Michael Rothberg, 'Preface: Beyond Tancred and Clorinda—Trauma Studies for Implicated Subjects,' in *The Future of Trauma Theory: Contemporary Literary and Cultural Criticism*, eds. Geert Buelens, Sam Durrant and Robert Eaglestone (New York: Routledge, 2014), xiii.

74. According to Plutarch, Demosthenes got rid of his stuttering through a rigorous practice of speaking with pebbles in his mouth. See Plutarch, 'Demosthenes,' trans. John Dryden, *The Internet Classics Archive*, http://classics.mit.edu/Plutarch/demosthe.html, accessed 19 April 2019.

75. Karyn Ball, *Disciplining the Holocaust: Traumatic History as an Object of Inquiry and Desire* (Albany: State University of New York Press, 2008), 8.

BIBLIOGRAPHY

ALBA, Avril. *The Holocaust Memorial Museum: Sacred Secular Space*. Houndmills, Basingstoke: Palgrave Macmillan, 2015.

ADORNO, Theodor W. 'Cultural Criticism and Society.' In *Prisms*. Translated by Samuel Weber and Shierry Weber. 17–34. Cambridge, MA: MIT Press, 1983 [1955].

ADORNO, Theodor W. *Negative Dialectics*. Translated by E. B. Ashton. London and New York: Routledge, 2004 [1973].

American Psychiatric Association, *Diagnostic and Statistical Manual of Mental Disorders*. Third Edition. Washington, DC: American Psychiatric Association, 1980.

BALL, Karyn. *Disciplining the Holocaust: Traumatic History as an Object of Inquiry and Desire.* Albany: State University of New York Press, 2008.

BREUER, J. and Sigmund Freud. 'On the Psychical Mechanism of Hysterical Phenomena: Preliminary Communication' (1893). In *The Standard Edition of the Complete Psychological Works of Sigmund Freud.* Translated under the general editorship of James Strachey, in collaboration with Anna Freud. Volume II (1893-1895), 3–17. London: Hogarth Press, 1955.

BRISON, Susan. *Aftermath: Violence and the Remaking of the Self.* Princeton, NJ: Princeton University Press, 2002.

BROWNMILLER, Susan. *Against Our Will: Men, Women, and Rape.* London: Secker and Warburg, 1975.

CARUTH, Cathy. *Unclaimed Experience: Trauma, Narrative, and History.* Baltimore: John Hopkins University Press, 1996.

CASPER, Monica J. and Eric Wertheimer, editors. *Critical Trauma Studies: Understanding Violence, Conflict and Memory in Everyday Life.* New York: New York University Press, 2016.

COHEN, Josh. *Interrupting Auschwitz: Art, Religion, Philosophy.* London and New York: Continuum, 2005.

DINUR, Yehiel (Ka-Tzetnik). *Tzofan E.D.M.A.* Tel Aviv: Hakibutz ha-Meuhad, 1987.

DINUR, Yehiel (Ka-Tzetnik). *Shivitti: A Vision.* San Francisco: Harper and Row, 1989.

FACKENHEIM, Emil. *To Mend the World: Foundations of Post-Holocaust Jewish Thought.* Second Edition. Bloomington: Indiana University Press, 1994.

FELMAN, Shoshana. 'Education and Crisis, or the Vicissitudes of Teaching.' In *Testimony: Crises of Witnessing in Literature, Psychoanalysis, and History.* Shoshana Felman and Dori Laub. 1–56. New York and London: Routledge, 1992.

FLETCHER, John. *Freud and the Scene of Trauma.* New York: Fordham University Press, 2013.

HERMAN, Judith. *Trauma and Recovery: The Aftermath of Violence—From Domestic Abuse to Political Terror.* New York: Basic Books, 1992.

HIRSCH, Marianne. 'Connective Histories in Vulnerable Times.' *PMLA* 129.3 (2014): 330–47.

HIRSCH, Marianne. *The Generation of Postmemory: Writing and Visual Culture After the Holocaust.* New York: Columbia University Press, 2012.

HOROWITZ, Sara R. *Voicing the Void: Muteness and Memory in Holocaust Fiction.* Albany: State University of New York Press, 1997.

IONESCU, Arleen. *The Memorial Ethics of Libeskind's Berlin Jewish Museum.* London: Palgrave Macmillan, 2017.

IONESCU, Arleen. 'Witnessing Horrorism: The Piteşti Experiment.' *SLOVO* 32.1 (Spring 2019): 53–74.

KANSTEINE, Wulf and Harald Weilnböck. 'Against the Concept of Cultural Trauma or How I Learned to Love the Suffering of Others without the Help of Psychotherapy.' In *Cultural Memory Studies: An International and Interdisciplinary Handbook.* Edited by Astrid Erll and Ansgar Nünning. 229–40. Berlin: De Gruyter, 2008.

KIRMAYER, Laurence J. 'Landscapes of Memory: Trauma, Narrative and Dissociation.' In *Tense Past: Cultural Essays on Memory and Trauma.* Edited by Paul Antze and Michael Lambek. 173–98. London: Routledge, 1996.

LACAPRA, Dominick. *Representing the Holocaust: History, Theory, Trauma.* Ithaca, NY: Cornell University Press, 1994.

LACAPRA, Dominick. *History and Memory after Auschwitz*. Ithaca, NY: Cornell University Press, 1998.

LACAPRA, Dominick. 'Trauma, Absence, Loss.' *Critical Inquiry* 25.4 (Summer 1999): 696–727.

LACAPRA, Dominick. *Writing History, Writing Trauma*. Baltimore: Johns Hopkins University Press, 2014.

LACOUE-LABARTHE, Philippe. *Heidegger, Art and Politics: The Fiction of the Political*. Translated by Chris Turner. Oxford: Blackwell, 1990.

LANGER, Lawrence L. *Holocaust Testimonies: The Ruins of Memory*. New Haven, CT: Yale University Press, 1991.

LANGER, Lawrence L. *Versions of Survival*. Albany: State University of New York Press, 1982.

LANZMANN, Claude, director. *Shoah*. The Criterion Collection, Blu-Ray, 1985 [DVD, 2013].

LAPLANCHE, Jean and Jean-Bertrand Pontalis. *The Language of Psychoanalysis*. Introduction by Daniel Lagache. London: Hogarth Press, 1973; Reprinted by Karnac Books, 1988.

LEE, Stephen J. *Stalin and the Soviet Union*. London and New York: Routledge, 1999.

LERNER, Paul and Mark S. Micale, editors. *Traumatic Pasts: History, Psychiatry, and Trauma in the Modern Age, 1870-1930*. Cambridge: Cambridge University Press, 2001.

LEVINE, Peter A. *Healing Trauma: A Pioneering Program for Restoring the Wisdom of Your Body*. Boulder, CO: Sounds True, 2005.

LEYS, Ruth. *Trauma: A Genealogy*. Chicago and London: The University of Chicago Press, 2000.

LOTHE, Jakob, Susan Rubin Suleiman and James Phelan, editors. *After Testimony: The Ethics and Aesthetics of Holocaust Narrative for the Future*. Columbus: Ohio State University Press, 2012.

LOTHE, Jakob, editor. *Time's Witnesses: Women's Voices from the Holocaust*. Translated by Anne Marie Hagen. Edinburgh: Fledgling Press Ltd, 2017.

LYOTARD, François. *The Differend: Phrases in Dispute*. Translated by Georges Van Den Abbeele. Manchester: Manchester University Press, 1988.

MALABOU, Catherine. *The New Wounded: From Neurosis to Brain Damage*. Translated by Steven Miller. New York: Fordham University Press, 2012.

MARTIN, Susan F. 'New Issues in Refugee Research: Forced Migration and the Evolving Humanitarian Regime.' UN High Commissioner for Refugees (UNHCR). Working Paper No. 20. 5 July 2000. https://www.refworld.org/docid/4ff5860e2.html. Accessed 14 April 2019.

MASTERSON, John, David Watson and Merle Williams. 'Mending Wounds? Healing, Working through, or Staying in Trauma: An Introduction.' *Journal of Literary Studies* 29.2 (2013): 1–5.

MITSCHERLICH, Alexander and Margarete. *The Inability to Mourn: Principles of Collective Behaviour*. Translated by Beverley R. Placzek. New York: Grove Press, 1975.

NAIMARK, Norman M. *Stalin's Genocides.* Princeton, NJ and Oxford: Princeton University Press, 2010.

PLUTARCH. 'Demosthenes.' Translated by John Dryden. *The Internet Classics Archive.* http://classics.mit.edu/Plutarch/demosthe.html. Accessed 19 April 2019.

RICOEUR, Paul. 'Life: A Story in Search of a Narrator.' In *A Ricoeur Reader: Reflection and Imagination.* Edited by Mario Valdés. 425–37. Toronto: University of Toronto Press, 1991.

RONELL, Avital. *Finitude's Score: Essays for the End of the Millennium.* Lincoln: University of Nebraska Press, 1994.

ROTHBERG, Michael. 'Preface: Beyond Tancred and Clorinda—Trauma Studies for Implicated Subjects.' In *The Future of Trauma Theory: Contemporary Literary and Cultural Criticism.* Edited by Geert Buelens, Sam Durrant and Robert Eaglestone. xi–ix. New York: Routledge, 2014.

SANTNER, Eric L. 'History Beyond the Pleasure Principle: Some Thoughts on the Representation of Trauma.' In *Probing the Limits of Representation: Nazism and the 'Final Solution.'* Edited by Saul Friedlander. 143–54. Cambridge, MA and London: Harvard University Press, 1992.

SANTNER, Eric L. *Stranded Objects: Mourning, Memory and Film in Postwar Germany.* Ithaca, NY and London: Cornell University Press, 1990.

SCHWAB, Gabriele. *Haunting Legacies: Violent Histories and Transgenerational Trauma.* New York: Columbia University Press, 2010.

SHAKED, Michal. 'The Unknown Eichmann Trial: The Story of the Judge.' *Holocaust and Genocide Studies* 29.1 (Spring 2015): 1–38.

SICHROVSKY, Peter. *Born Guilty: The Children of the Nazis.* Translated by Jean Steinberg. London: I. B. Taurus, 1988.

TISMĂNEANU, Vladimir. *Stalinism for All Seasons: A Political History of Romanian Communism.* Berkeley: University of California Press, 2003.

TOKER, Leona. *Gulag Literature and the Literature of the Nazi Camps.* Bloomington and Indianapolis: Indiana University Press, 2019.

TOKER, Leona. *Return from the Archipelago: Narratives of Gulag Survivors.* Bloomington and Indianapolis: Indiana University Press, 2000.

VAN ALPHEN, Ernst. *Holocaust Effects in Contemporary Arts, Literature and Theory.* Stanford, CA: Stanford University Press, 1997.

VAN DER MERWE, Chris N. and Pumla Gobodo-Madikizela. *Narrating Our Healing: Perspectives on Working through Trauma.* Newcastle: Cambridge Scholars Publishing, 2007.

WHITEHEAD, Anne. *Trauma Fiction.* Edinburgh: Edinburgh University Press, 2004.

WIEVIORKA, Annette. *Era of the Witness.* Translated by Jared Stark. Ithaca, NY: Cornell University Press, 2006.

YERUSHALMI, Yosef Hayim. *Zakhor: Jewish History and Jewish Memory.* Seattle and London: University of Washington Press, 1982.

YOUNG, James. *The Texture of Memory: Holocaust Memorials and Meaning.* New Haven, CT: Yale University Press, 1993.

ZELIZER, Barbie. *Remembering to Forget: Holocaust Memory through the Camera's Eye.* Chicago: University of Chicago Press, 1998.

Part I

HOLOCAUST TRAUMA AND THE AMBIVALENCE OF HEALING: IRREVERENT TAKES

Chapter One

Unfamiliar Healing

Reconsidering the Fragment in Narratives of Holocaust Trauma

Ivan Callus

Fragmentary writing is risk, it would seem: risk itself.

> —Maurice Blanchot, *The Writing of the Disaster* (1980)

Normally, one goes on.

> —Georges Perec, 'I was born' (1970)

She feels whole.

> —Bart van Es, *The Cut-Out Girl* (2018)

To ask what there remains to say about the Holocaust, or how to say it, is to confront the question of whether there is anything to which it is possible to not grow inured.

Familiarity, unfamiliarity, defamiliarization: they set the challenge to writing about the Holocaust, to discover a relating that is not rehearsed, that maintains urgency, that dispels the recognizable to reveal something of the undiscerned. It is no defence to pass up the challenge by saying that the issues converging there are of an order that absolves the missed response, the one that justifies that it isn't happening by disclaiming possession of the background or of familiarity with the intertext, possibly anticipating its inevitable meagreness before the scale of what was perpetrated and the consequences. The inadequacy, it is true, is systemic to any conceivable response before the unpresentable. True too, however, that the magnitude of what is in view suffices to solicit reflection, ever and again.

The risks for the response lie in triteness or anomaly, into which the (un)familiar can quite easily fall. The disbelief, so different to denial, that it happened. To inconceivable system and scale. But it did. Separation, death, survival, the indescribable trauma defeating empathy's effort, the disaster that is not so absolute that it can keep at bay subsidiary or subsequent traumas.

The entirety of Maurice Blanchot's *The Writing of the Disaster* could as well be given in epigraph, if that were possible. Fragmentary, elliptical, it nevertheless contrives to seem an inexhaustible statement on the Holocaust. It could seem like there is little or nothing to say after it. However, Blanchot himself warns against that thought, as will be seen.

Can healing's attestation, its ministry, its process, its effects, be rendered by academic genres' regularities and conventions? Doubtless they can. Yet the form of the book chapter can feel sclerotic and inapt in relation to the Holocaust, trauma and the rigours of recovery. Unfamiliarity, not familiarity, might alternatively prevail: of reference, approach, expectation, response, form. And of such healing, such reparative and readapted wholeness, as might be witnessed.

What might be required is a different essaying. Even, simply, the essay again, in some play of form that deviates from the frame, range or propriety of the academic. Hence also, after Blanchot, the risk of fragmentary writing.

The essay: consequently Montaigne.

In an essay of his own called 'The Habitus of the Text,' included in *Grimspound and Inhabiting Art* (2018), Rod Mengham considers Montaigne's foundational *essais* on the essayistic. He characterizes the 'movement of thought' at work there as 'hesitant, impulsive' and 'snared by the memory of other texts.'[1] He adds that it involves 'above all else . . . an "attempt" (an "essai") to compose something out of scattered materials, out of the books that chance to be at hand, the ideas that happen to rise to the surface of the mind.' The emerging aesthetic, the evolving *discipline*, is one of fragmentary composition. Shape, cohesion, appropriateness, logic are not thereby betrayed. There is a different responsibility at work, even when argument is brought back to its 'point of origin' seemingly 'more by homing instinct than by design,' in 'a recoiling movement' that keeps 'the reader's attentiveness . . . afloat [by] seeming to lead it astray.'

Mengham's grounding quotations recall Montaigne recording a pointed faith in the force of the fragmented, but also in the fanciful:

> . . . I leaf through now one book, now another, without order and without plan, by disconnected fragments. One moment I muse, another moment I set down or dictate, walking back and forth, these fancies of mine.

Montaigne is surely being disingenuous here. There is method in the meandering, in the ideas that happen to rise to the surface of the mind and in what the transcription sets down.

And there is, too, a decorum that is quite distinct. The method, the decorum, will guide this piece and its own disconnected fragments from 'now one book, now another,' 'without order and without plan,' in an associative moment that must discover its own rigour.

Mengham also notes 'an allergic resistance' in Montaigne 'to the conclusive, the legislative, the incontrovertible,' the avoidance of 'the shape, texture, weight and odour of the Great Thought,' the fascination, rather, with 'the brittleness and elusiveness of the process of thinking.'

Such resistance is more suited still when the theme is the Holocaust and traumatic memory, when the converging concerns and the challenges of form are what they are, when healing offers itself to consideration shadowed by the irresolvable. Then . . .

. . . the ellipsis. Because there is nothing else to say or write that could be more charged.

In lieu of great thought or searing conclusion, the pathos within scatter, the pregnancy of the unuttered.

Alternatively, as here, the truth lying in contiguities. Or rather, *truth* being too large a word, the fit of contiguities.

It's a hopeful word, *healing*. The act, the process, can be helped by little moments in a life, little devices to living. Quite like the ones Montaigne describes, which helped him recover a little every day, off fragments read in fragments of time.

'Disconnected fragments,' was Montaigne's phrase.

Fragment, the fragment.

A big word, a big idea too, despite the implicit sense of rupture, of wholeness rent.

The fragment has form. It is 'the romantic genre par excellence,' write Philippe Lacoue-Labarthe and Jean-Luc Nancy soon into their chapter on 'The Fragmentary Exigency' in *The Literary Absolute* (1978). They then refine this statement. 'If the fragment is indeed a fraction, it emphasizes neither first nor foremost the fracture that produces it,' they note of the conception they have in view, which evidently does not lean towards repair of what was broken, or healing. They acknowledge *ruin*, in 'the tradition of Diderot' and 'the philological fragment,' but the greater pertinence here lies with their acknowledgement of Montaigne, when they note, 'Fragment is also a literary term: "Fragments," or what, in terms of form, amounts to *essays* in the style of Montaigne.' In this mode,

> the fragment designates a presentation that does not pretend to be exhaustive and that corresponds to the no doubt properly modern idea that the incomplete can, and even must, be published (or the idea that what is published is never complete). In this manner the fragment is delimited by a two-fold difference: if it is not simply a pure piece, neither is it any of the genres-terms employed by the moralists: *pensée*, sentence, *maxim*, opinion, anecdote, remark. . . . The fragment, on the contrary, involves an essential incompletion.

The idea of fragment 'contrary' to Montaigne's conception is discernible in Fragment 22 of the *Athenaeum*. There the fragment is identical to the *project*, a 'fragment of the future' borne from 'the ability to idealize objects immediately and simultaneously.' It could seem that this suggests a history and a writing more innocent, less traumatized than the present, less shadowed by the disaster.

Looking at arrays of the fragment across literary history, it is critical to know which to pick up.

Following upon the sentence in *The Writing of the Disaster* that provides the first epigraph is this thought: 'It is not based on any theory. . . .' And following soon upon that, in turn, is the thought that the fragment attests to 'the absence of time, absence in a nonnegative sense, time anterior to all past-present, as well as posterior to every possibility of a present yet to come.' This radicalizes what was discerned in Fragment 22 of the *Athenaeum*.

It ought also to be observed that Blanchot notes, '*When all is said, what remains to be said is the disaster. Ruin of words, demise of writing, faintness merely murmuring: what remains without remains* (the fragmentary)' (italics in the original). This, the answer to the question that opens this piece, affirms the risk of the fragmentary. Blanchot writes of the disaster seemingly in snatches of prose, in fragments, in the keenest awareness of the distinct trajectory of that tradition in the history and forms of literature and theory.

That history of the fragment and its forms overwhelms the method, itself 'not based on any theory,' of *this* writing, which though it keeps the aesthetics of the fragment in view, together with the pertinence of that aesthetics to the forms by which it is possible to recover (from) the Holocaust, is to be more modestly thought of as an organization of *lexias* in the sense envisaged by Barthes early in *S/Z* (1970): 'blocks of signification,' 'units of reading.'

Units of reading come in different dispensings. Mengham's attention to that aspect of Montaigne's essayistic-cum-fragmentary method shaped by 'the books that chance to be at hand' is worth recalling, when the books that chanced to be to hand in the midst of this essay's composition included Mengham's own but also Brian Dillon's *Essayism* (2017), Sarah Manguso's *300 Arguments* (2017) and Don Paterson's *The Fall at Home* (2018), all in readier reach than the standard works in trauma studies, or the necessary points of reference when considering the aesthetics of the fragment. There is disinclination in this piece to route the argument in a manner oriented to the canonical intertext in regard to trauma and memory. A re-crafting of familiarity, unfamiliarity, is what is at stake.

There is the reception of a different time and a different temper at work.

But there remains lodged the memory of familiar Holocaust accounts, of the various reflections on what happened and its import, across different genres and forms and media and in all kinds of association and relation: Anne Frank, Hannah Arendt, Hermann Langbein, Martin Niemöller, Miklós Radnóti, Primo Levi, Giorgio Bassani, Paul Celan, Edmond Jabès, Elie Wiesel, George Steiner, Art Spiegelman, Steven Spielberg, Roberto Benigni and many others. Including, with varying levels of broader familiarity, Blanchot and Georges Perec and, not dissociatively, Viktor Shklovsky, Robert Musil, Robert Walser and W. G. Sebald. And more recently, Bart van Es.

It is off, or with, texts by these last six authors that this essay mostly works, off lexias that serve for structure and draw other lines of association in.

Dillon, whose *Essayism* chanced to be at hand, quotes Theodor Adorno's *Minima Moralia* (1951), itself a work in fragments, on the essay being fragmentary and random. That is in a section 'On Essayism,' while in another, 'On the Fragment,' he notes that 'the fragment stands alone but speaks, or must be made to speak by a reader, to the fragment that surrounds it.' And elsewhere, he brings up

> the problem of pattern. By what principle should these fragments abut one another, rub up against each other, speak to or seduce their fellow fragments across the page or in the memory of a reader? . . . The deliberate writer of fragments behaves differently, in fact fusses constantly about the correct composition or constellation. . . . There are several sorts of relation from which to choose.

The relevance of Dillon's question is evident, once the issue of structure and lines of association is raised. Pattern forms and relation proffers itself, without the need for over-driven seeking.

And what would be the relevance of Manguso and Paterson, and of their books as *objets trouvés*, as it were?

Manguso . . . who has moved from memoir and short stories to *300 Arguments* (2017), each cast to pithy succinctness. When she published *The Two Kinds of Decay* in 2008, the form was there even then. It is an account, a memoir, in fragments, the theme her long and distressing recovery from autoimmune disease. Healing and the fragmentary are in affinity there.

Paterson . . . who has moved from poetry to aphorisms, most recently in *The Fall at Home* (2018), but without leaving the former behind. Among the aphorisms, this one: 'To heal without a scar is a waste of a good wound.' And elsewhere: 'Time heals so well it erases us. We *are* its wounds.'

There are contexts in which the truth in the fragments or aphorisms that are happened upon is searing, but where the fit to the context and text in hand can be excellent or variable.

Genres change; their rationales and what they carry evolve.

The book chapter, itself a genre, can bear some rearrangement too. Coming in that place, an essay on the themes in view cannot quite be an essay, however, not straightforwardly so.

The smoothness of the essay, its suave ease, the fluency of its form must itself suffer some disturbance. Especially if it is to bear apter lines.

Blanchot's *The Writing of the Disaster*, which speaks of 'interruption' and 'intermittence,' understands disturbance. A meditation on the apocalyptic that is itself composed in fragments, to a form that is short of the *essai* and in excess of the essayistic, it contains a disjunctive reflection that places in question its entire method and rationale. 'Let us heed this warning,' Blanchot writes at one point, before going on to this statement:

> There is reason to fear that, like ellipsis, the fragment—the 'I say practically nothing and take it back right away'—makes mastery over all that goes unsaid possible, arranging in advance for all the continuities and supplements to come.

Blanchot adds, in attribution and parentheses, '(Jacques Derrida.).' He leaves this fragment on the fragment like this, uncommented. This is in keeping with that dynamic of fragmentary writing, whatever its intent and pitch, that invites comparison with the compilation of a commonplace book. Blanchot must have been composing almost like Montaigne: to a principle of scatter, to an ethic of associativeness, though the greater deliberation in the method can be sensed. Not that this deliberation goes so far as for him to place the quotation precisely. It remains unreferenced, the exact source in Derrida unspecified. It could be looked up, of course. But as it is a fragment on the fragment, that somehow seems incongruous with the spirit of the method or the piece.

Nancy and Lacoue-Labarthe recall Fragment 206, the idea that '[a] *fragment, like a small work of art, has to be entirely isolated from the surrounding world and be complete in itself like a hedgehog*' (italics in the original). It is what Blanchot, invoking Derrida in the quotation given above, was warning about when considering the ellipsis.

'Not every narrative is an arc,' notes Manguso. This surely applies to critique's narratives, as well. This essay, for instance, seeks to dispense with any very obvious one. Yet there is line, even in the absence of arc. Line: in the sequence of what has been read, in the order of the presentation, in the stringing of fragments that could take on the tone of the aphoristic and the portentousness of the elliptical, this last being '"the deficient displacement, doubtless,"' as Michael Naas cautions while quoting Derrida in his essay on 'Blanchot . . . Writing . . . Ellipsis,' 'of the dot, dot, dot.'

In *Essayism*, Dillon speaks of a 'tension . . . between the fragment and the aphorism.' In his five rules for aphorisms, Don Paterson's first is that an aphorism must 'be short, but not fragmentary.' Elsewhere, he notes that poetic truth provides, contrastingly, a definition of the aphorism, which is 'its talentless, tone-deaf brother.'

The fragment, possibilized by the aleatory, can always seem close to the accident of the aphoristic. The deeper reach, the gnomic knowingness, tends to find the higher pitch with the aphoristic, which is not necessarily more truthful.

It is difficult to ignore Derrida on the aphoristic. 'The bad aphorism, the *bad* of aphorism is sententious, but every aphorism cuts and delimits by virtue of its sententious character: it says the truth in the form of the last judgement, and this truth carries [*porte*] death.'

The truth is that *The Writing of the Disaster*, where the fragmentary can acquire aphoristic tonalities and which if it does not carry death certainly speaks of it, is not sententious. There is another truth nonetheless, which is that its idiom and style and tone are a previous generation's.

Trauma, healing, representation devise different rhetorics across time.

This is a different time.

Blanchot prefigures Paterson. 'An isolated sentence—aphoristic, not fragmentary—tends to reverberate like an oracular utterance having the self-sufficiency of a commentary to which nothing need be added,' he writes. This is another example of his own alternative wording for the Derridean reflection, seen above, that he quotes. The intent, the insistence, is on the conceit that invests the fragmentary with the wisdom of the ages, even, possibly, 'a life of the Spirit,' as *Athenaeum* fragment 451 has it, or the 'Spirit in Becoming,' as *Critical Fragment* 86, which he also quotes, has it. To quote a wry remark on another topic from a different Derridean source, *Demeure*: 'Nothing is less certain.' Friedrich Schlegel's thought, recalled by Lacoue-Labarthe and Nancy, that 'aphorisms are coherent fragments' seems blithe in the midst of such jaded experience. Yet the effect glimpsed beguiles, reliably. Isolated utterance, independently of whether it is quoted or placed elliptically or clipped or entered in a commonplace book or positioned otherwise, takes on the heft afforded by the cut, the break, the compression, the insular immensity. An almost-Aleph of meaning.

The wiles of the aphoristic can be very distracting while in thrall to what the fragment and its textualizations have cast over representation of trauma, of recovery as and where it is even possible.

Blanchot understands this in *The Writing of the Disaster*: 'The isolated aphoristic sentence is attractive because it affirms definitively, as if nothing beside this sentence spoke anymore in its vicinity.'

The distraction is such that it predetermines trajectory. To write about the fragment's co-implications with that thematic, their history and their dynamic, their aesthetic and their ethic, imposes an established intertext.

There would be the legacies of attention, as has been acknowledged, to the *Athenaeum*, the Schlegels, the emerging idea of Romanticism and the literary absolute, modernist experimentation, post-structuralist commentary, the canons of trauma studies. All of that at least, across all of which the fragment is both device and trope.

The predeterminism that binds critical route must occasionally be resisted. Even while remaining cognizant of the exorbitant opportunity cost, which is clear when reading Blanchot. As, for instance, in *The Writing of the Disaster*'s characterization of the Holocaust as 'the absolute event of history—which is a date in history—the utter-burn where all history took fire, where the movement of Meaning was swallowed up.' Or in this characterization in these two separate statements of why, implicitly, healing, the very idea of it, is illusory, even unthinkable:

Time has radically changed its meaning and its flow. Time without present, I without I.

'I' too disappeared in the disaster which never appears. The fact of disappearance is, precisely, not a fact, not an event; it does not happen, not only because there is no 'I' to undergo the experience, but because since the disaster always takes place after having taken place, there cannot possibly be any experience of it.

But there *can* be a different intertext here. Even if the italics set the tone for the nervousness over the procedure.

There *can* be a different intertext because the very familiarity of reference that suggests itself most readily leaves too little space for familiarization with that which is only now coming to view, or that which is being written now around this thematic, or that which was written some time ago and is now ripe for recovery and recall.

There *can* be a different intertext. For instance, that which brings back Shklovsky and his theory that ironically is too familiar in terms of 'defamiliarization,' translated alternatively and pointedly in terms of 'estrangement' and more recently by Alexandra Berlina in terms of e*n*strangement.

The missing letter, the superadded letter. This is where referencing Perec, master of the lipogrammatic, will become relevant.

Fragments, episode, syncopation. Not untypically the writing of trauma, of Holocaust, proceeds to the protocols they set.

For instance, in counter-example, Perec, who eliminates and excises letters in *La Disparition* (1969), a defamiliarizing, e*n*stranging novel that is lipogrammatically entire-integral in its lack of a single instance of the letter *e*, the most common in French and in English, as Edgar Allan Poe's 'The Gold-Bug' did not fail to instrumentalize.

La Disparition refracts Holocaust experience and loss. David Bellos, Perec's biographer, reveals:

> In the case of *La Disparition*, the double cover hid something that none of the author's closest friends could have guessed at, unless they, too, were orphans of the *shoah*. The novel's title is a slightly arch euphemism for death, but it is also something much more special: it is the term used in administrative French for persons missing and presumed dead. In his drawer at Rue de Bac, Perec still had the certificate issued in 1947 by the Ministry of War Veterans in re Perec Cyrla née Szulewicz, last seen alive at Drancy on 11 February 1943, a document headed ACTE DE DISPARITION.

Bellos also notes that after *La Disparition* Perec felt he could attempt '*something more ambitious*,' which would be '*a vesperal autobiography*' (all italics are in the original and indicate Perec's own words). The work he had in mind would be published as *W* (1975). *W* provides the letter-title to his memoir as a child of the Holocaust; the subtitle is *Or, the Memory of Childhood*. Bellos refers to an interview in which Perec asserted, 'All of this autobiographical work was organised around a single memory which, for me, was profoundly obscured, deeply buried and, in a sense, denied.' This would be a writing for a different sense of recovery, then. Perec wrote to Jacques

Lederer, Bellos also recalls, to say that 'his need to write derived from his absent relationship to his first family. Writing would not alleviate the pain, *for there are wounds too deep ever to heal over entirely.*'

Family: what the Holocaust prevented from growing familiar. As will be seen, this will be an important motif in van Es's *The Cut-Out Girl*.

But for the sake of chronology, a return to Shklovsky first.

Chronology has a bearing in any case. The first work on this essay co-incided with the commemorations, leading up to the eleventh hour of the eleventh month, that marked the hundredth year since the end of WW1. That other holocaust. Of which the survivors, those who remember with minds clearly still traumatized, as the many archives of transcribed and filmed in-terviews reveal, are now gone.

Not, though, many of their accounts, including Shklovsky's. Shklovsky saw action in the war and wrote about his experiences in a bid to come to terms with the effects and the trauma. And there was Robert Walser too, who withdrew to a mental hospital in the years after the war. He was still there in the second conflict.

Healing, if that is the word, worked a little better for Shklovsky than it did for Walser.

Shklovsky's memoir, *A Sentimental Journey*, echoes a title of Laurence Sterne's. This is not surprising. It's Shklovsky, with *his* intertexts. He ex-presses dissatisfaction with Henri Barbusse's novel *Under Fire* (1916), which influenced Remarque's *All Quiet on the Western Front* (1928). 'I don't like Barbusse's *Under Fire*,' Shklovsky asserts. He adds:

> It's glossy and contrived. Writing about war is very difficult. . . . To describe the mood of a front without resorting to false and artificial passages is hard. . . . Un-til I'm shown the statistics, I will never believe there was so much fighting with bayonets or that it was possible to destroy a German foxhole with your hands and cave in the hole with your feet. I will never believe in this book, with its jumble of corpses, its end washed away by a flood and various conclusions. So I will speak. I will try to relate everything that happened.

And so Shklovsky, who suffered a serious stomach wound in 1917 during the fighting, relates in unforgiving detail. His theme becomes 'war in all its na-kedness,' 'the inner lining of war, its predatory essence.' His intent is to urge the undoing of what the novelist and journalist Ben Ehrenreich has referred to as 'pre-existing patterns of thought,' not unlike his urging of defamiliariza-tion. 'Man has been given the tool of art,' Shklovsky notes. 'It revitalizes the world.' But for this revitalization of pre-existing thought, art must 'extricate' itself from 'the cluster of associations in which it is bound.' Only like this can it find the 'dissimilarity of the similar,' as he calls it in a late book of essays, *Bowstring* (1975). *On the Dissimilarity of the Similar* is, in fact, the subtitle.

Mainly about poetics though it is, *Bowstring* carries ample references to the war, none more pointed than when he quotes a line from Vladimir Mayakovsky's 1916 poem, 'War and the World.' The line reads, 'In the rotting boxcar, four legs for forty men.' Humanity, in fragments.

It all connects with Shklovsky's ongoing interrogation of literary forms and their relation to content, not least in relation to an emerging aesthetics of fragmentation.

Literary forms, Shklovsky is convinced, need to be reinvented for post-war literary aesthetics to attain integrity of representation. He uses a military metaphor: 'In art, humanity . . . searches for truth, like artillerists at war get close to hitting their target—they shoot, missing the target, then they try again.' His inquiry is whether the target for art about the war and its traumatic fallouts could best be struck, or missed, using naturalistic realism or, alternatively, techniques of fragmentation: 'contradiction, anachronism, disharmony,' as Ehrenreich has it.

Later, the emerging intertext. *The Cut-Out Girl* (2018), the recipient of the Costa Prize for 'Book of the Year,' is written by a Dutch-born academic teaching Shakespeare in Oxford. Its topic is not Early Modern drama or poetry. The book centres on the traumas surrounding the fostering by van Es's grandparents of a Jewish girl, Hesseline (Lien for short), one of the 'hidden children' whose parents perished in the camps and who was taken into fraught and dangerous safekeeping by family and friends, by that other resistance which defied National Socialism not by tactical sabotage or clandestine operations but by helping the hunted survive. Lien had been sent away by her parents before their inevitable deportation to the camps. Her experience of the war years was of serial concealment in various properties across the Netherlands by that wider network.

The Cut-Out Girl is an account of 'anachronism, contradiction and disharmony' of another kind, traumatic enough. It emerges from the disorientation, across time, occasioned by friction in and after survival, but also improbable help with some level of healing. For in writing the story of Lien's trauma and survival, of her fragmented and disorienting memories, van Es knows early on that he must also narrate the story of friction between her and his family after the war, and the bid to overcome that aspect of the past while working through the larger trauma.

The Cut-Out Girl discovers that Holocaustic trauma does not protect against succeeding or different trauma. It potentiates it further.

There forms a tension in Shklovsky between how he writes about the war and trauma, and the forms and styles he starts to expect of literary art. About the war he himself will write something like this (the italics are in the original):

> *After the explosion our soldiers . . . busied themselves by picking and putting*
> *together the shattered pieces of their comrades' bodies.*
> *They picked up pieces for a very long time.*
> *Naturally, some of the pieces got mixed up.*
> *One officer went up to a long row of corpses. The last body had been put*
> *together out of the leftover pieces. It had the torso of a large man. Someone had*
> *added a small head; on the chest were small arms of different sizes, both left.*
> *The officer looked for a rather long time; then he sat on the ground and burst*
> *out laughing . . . laughing . . . laughing . . .*

This is forensic realism on human sensibilities denaturing themselves before the horror of war. The trauma is commented as it sets.

Shklovsky defamiliarizes through hyper-realism when the relation is his own. In *Bowstring*, as its translator Shushan Avagyan notes in the 'Preface,' the defamiliarization also works through 'a technique of textual montage' comprising 'autobiography, biography, memoir, history, and literary criticism.' Shklovsky suggests that '[a]rt moves, transforming,' something he sees it doing by 'reinterpreting old structures . . . not for the sake of changing, but to impart the sensation of things in their difference through rearrangement.'

Montage, rearrangement: they serve criticism too.

The Cut-Out Girl, its form and style perspicuous enough, is overshadowed throughout by the *punctum*, the ache of the sense of absence occasioned by looking at the photographs, the writings, of those who are no more.

In Ted Hughes's 'Six Young Men,' a poem on a photograph taken at Hebden Bridge of the six young men in the title who would go on to die in WW1, there is a line that reads, 'To regard this photograph might well dement.' The poem ends as follows: 'Such contradictory permanent horrors here / Smile from the single exposure and shoulder out / One's own body from its instant and heat.' It captures what is felt when reading *The Cut-Out Girl*.

The punctum in photographs like Hughes or van Es write about is immediately apprehensible. But sometimes the trauma takes much longer to register, as it does with Robert Walser's work.

Walser, suddenly, is everywhere. Perhaps this is because, in the words of the novelist and critic Benjamin Kunkel, 'he fulfils the modern criterion: he sounds like no one else.' Unfamiliar, then, as well as dissimilar. Certainly, Walser attracts commentaries now by figures like J. M. Coetzee or Ben

Lerner, and literary criticism has been recovering reflection on his work by Franz Kafka, Stefan Zweig, Herman Hesse, Walter Benjamin and W. G. Sebald.

Walser was born in 1878, in Biel, Switzerland. His wartime involvement appears to have been limited to the obligatory military service in the National Guard. Switzerland was neutral. But there is some evidence to suggest that he carried some patrolling and orderly duties sufficiently close to action near the border. As Ben Lerner notes, it is surely 'impossible to separate the interplay of independence and conformity in Walser's work from the surpassing catastrophes of the twentieth century.' It does appear that Walser's withdrawal upon himself, his increasing reclusiveness that grew pathological and meant that he lived most of the post-war years in a mental hospital, coincided with acute depression suffered during the war years.

Trauma and life in an institution made for Walser's writing. A sentence of stayed healing.

Robert Musil writes 'On the Essay' but not so much in fragments, rather in unfinished pursuit of something more whole in *The Man without Qualities*, which even though it is incomplete runs to over a thousand pages in its English translation. He and Walser both write about war and soldiering. Musil, in his 1928 novella *Die Amsel*, depicts the experience of bombardment. Walser, in an essay called 'In the Military,' speaks about the contrary attractions, as Ben Lerner reports, of refusal and obedience, whereas in his 1917 novella *The Walk*, references to the war are rife, as has been discussed by Melissa Kagen in a fine article. But the Walser texts deserving of closer view now are rather shorter, practically illegible in manuscript form because they were inconceivably *smaller*: *Microscripts*, as the English translation classes them. Walser wrote them in an extraordinarily minute script just two millimetres long, in pencil. Pens gave him cramp, he noted. He fitted them into discarded or stray paper, cards, tickets. For a long time they were indecipherable, before the remarkable deciphering labours of Jochen Greven, the editor of Walser's work in German, made them accessible.

Musil goes large-scale, as unfragmentary as anything, in *The Man without Qualities* (1930–1943). The result, in a fine irony, remains a fragment of the undelivered whole. Mega-fragment, but fragment still.

Unresolved: Musil's oblique, one might say allegorical, narrative of the history of Europe, the holocaust of WW1 as background, written in the midst of the Holocaust.

It is not a small detail that he and his Jewish wife lived in Switzerland from 1938.

'Without families, you don't have stories.'

This is the first sentence of the 'Prologue' to *The Cut-Out Girl*, whose subtitle is *A Story of War and Family, Lost and Found*. The subtitle may instigate suspicion of feel-good sentiment within the chronicling of individuated experience of the disaster. Reception of Benigni's *La vita é bella* (1997), with its insinuation of comedic uplift, of the ruses of paternal ingenuity devised to keep the *bambino* at the centre of the narrative distracted from what was really taking place in the camp, was affected by some critical ambivalence on that score.

The sentence is spoken by the woman who Lien grows up to be, Hesseline de Jong-Spiero. For her too, the familial was what the fragmentation of wartime experience took away, the experience of family life othered and defamiliarized across long years, dissimilar to what would have been expected. There is precision in the book's subtitle.

'The Cut-Out Girl' would surely refer to Lien herself, an idea reinforced by the choice for the translated title in Italian, *La ragazza cancellata*. Certainly, the sense in Hesseline of cancellation of a life, of suspension and deviation, is strong.

The German translation of the title is *Das Mädchen mit dem Poesiealbum*. A *poesiealbum* is, essentially, a child's commonplace book, a scrapbook of well-wishing sentiments, typically expressed in simple and sometimes familiar verse by friends and relatives. In his 'Prologue' van Es describes a *poesiealbum* as 'a kind of poetry scrapbook that nearly all girls in the Netherlands used to keep.' In other words, it is a compilation of fragments, looking forward to a life of completeness. The earliest entry in Lien's is marked 'The Hague, 15 September 1940.' It is signed, 'your father,' and reads (italics in the original):

This is a little book where friends can write
Who wish for you a future bright
To keep you safe throughout the years
With many smiles and never tears.

It is rare for the unpretentious verse in a *poesiealbum* to carry such heavy dramatic irony. Or to transcend quite as poignantly the 'bad sententiousness' of the quasi-aphoristic, of the fragmentariness in evidence here.

To regard this punctum might well dement.

There *is* another cut-out girl in the *poesiealbum*. 'Opposite, on the left' of the inscription, van Es observes, there are 'three paper cut-outs in pastel colours: at the top, a wicker basket of flowers; and below, two girls in straw hats. The one on the right smiles and looks happy, like Lien's mother in the photo, but the cut-out girl on the left purses her lips as she clutches her posy. She glances sideways, as if unable to meet the viewer's eyes.'

Van Es will spend a lot of time seeking to engage the story of the woman who was the girl symbolized in the cut-out figure in Lien's *poesiealbum*. The missed gaze will be invited to turn and tell the story of missing and missed family, until, improbably, the last line in the chronicle can be an affirmation of wholeness. It is the one reproduced in the epigraphs heading this piece.

Scepticism on wholeness and its possibility is not the right tone to strike in reception of this book. It would be entirely the wrong response, a crass misreading, to find the epigraph trite.

Perec, in *W*, is himself eloquent enough on the effects of how a young mind apprehends disaster. The letter-title, *W*, is a pun turning on the sense of the double *v*, or double *vie* in French, the double life, except that in this case there is nothing akin to the literary tropes of doubling of the kind seen in Nabokov's *The Real Life of Sebastian Knight* (1941), where the narrator is known as *V*. Rather, the memoir is shaped by a double narrative. One appears to be an account of family, of aunts and uncles but above all absent parents, recalled with evident unreliability and the sense of necessary re-creation since, to echo Lien, there are no stories without families. The other, which initially seems fanciful, even surreal, is of a remote island whose inhabitants are engaged in hyper-organized, hyper-competitive sporting contests whose governance contrives to double up as the island's polity, all of which seems increasingly surreal until it starts to become clear that its brutalities stand in allegory for the camps' perpetrations of atrocity.

As always, such healing as there is does not arrive, if it does at all, equitably. Some recover, if that is the word, a little better than others. Others not at all.

Writing finds different rearrangements, to use Shklovsky's word, to represent recovery, if recovery it is. Perec's ingenuity with rearrangement conveys the trauma, though whether it configures healing is another question altogether.

The writing that might bear witness to the trauma and such healing as there could be does not necessarily arrive in proportions easy to take in, either—as is shown by Walser, who unlike Musil, goes miniscule. He turns himself, as Sebald put it, into 'a clairvoyant of the small.' But both Musil and he write from, on, in traumatized space, whether it be a continent's or one person's psyche.

What both Musil and Walser come up against, in their very different ways with scale, is the intractability of proportioning literary art in any way that is commensurable with the wartime upheaval they lived. This becomes a formal problem for Modernism, for High Modernism. How to defamiliarize, in art, authentically and with apt measure, war and worse? Adorno's famous statement reverberates. In line with that reflection on barbarity, another one from Blanchot to say, 'There is a limit at which the practice of any art becomes an affront to affliction.'

What readership reactions can be expected of, primed by, the art that affronts? More pressingly, how does art move to a practice without affront when it positions itself before affliction, which may be one's own or another's or a people's or a continent's or the world's? Musil responded by inflating nineteenth-century classic realism at the same time as he was pioneering the anti-hero narrative, with a protagonist, Ulrich, seemingly intent on self-unmaking. Walser, in contrast, becomes, before Maurice Blanchot, J. D. Salinger or Thomas Pynchon, the very figure of the author withdrawn from the world. He is self-impoverished and self-abjected. He does not even own his pencils or any paper. The texts he writes are illegible and erasable. Here is defamiliarization indeed.

Of course there can grow familiarity of readerly response even there. Every next literary experiment that confounds perspicuity in reaction to and representation of imponderable atrocity, but that then finds readerships, demonstrates the inevitability of accommodation.

Even of the work of Walser, he who sounds like no one else.

Against the idea that readers and critics are inured to everything, there remains the possibility of a sentence that would start like this: 'As far as I know there is nothing else in literature like . . .'

The sentence is Sebald's. It occurs toward the end of *A Natural History of Destruction* (1999). He is referring to *Die Ästhetik des Widerstands* (1975–1981), 'that thousand-page work of fiction which [Peter Weiss] began when he was well over fifty . . . in the company of *pavor nocturnus*, the terror of the night . . . a magnum opus which sees itself, almost programmatically, not only as the expression of an ephemeral wish for redemption, but as an expression of the *will* to be on the side of the victims at the end of time.'

The potential literary repertoire occasioned by the disaster, it turns out, is inexhaustible.

Literature, history, are supple enough to take in anything and everything. *Even the disaster.*

And here is Musil, in 'Helpless Europe,' on such accommodation, on what happens when carrying on regardless amid and after the disaster, on chronic invalidity and unachieved healing.

> Life goes on just as before, only a little more feebly, with a touch of the invalid's condition. . . . So we have seen many things, but we haven't changed; we have seen a lot and perceived nothing.

I think there is only one explanation for this: we were lacking the concepts with which to absorb what we experienced; or perhaps lacking the feelings whose magnetism sets the concepts in motion. All that remains of the experience is an astonished restlessness . . .

The astonished restlessness can be felt as history and in history. Before it writes itself in literature.

'Normally, one goes on,' writes Perec, echoing Musil on life and the invalid's condition.

Healing . . . 'keeping on keeping on,' in the wry words of Alan Bennett.

'The words of . . .': argument by quotation, one of the methods of this piece, is, like the fragmentary, a risk. The risk is not necessarily allayed by the hope that a different discipline, a different rigour, might prove itself.

Looking at Shklovsky again, through the recent translation of 'Art, as device' by Alexandra Berlina, reveals how many extravagantly long but pointedly apt quotations he indulges in. Sometimes fragments, or lexias, from others already bear everything. They are enough.

They may be enough, but not unconditionally so. *The Writing of the Disaster* observes that '[i]f quotations, in their fragmenting force, destroy in advance the texts from which they are not only severed but which they exalt till those texts become nothing but severence [*sic*], then the fragment without a text, or any context, is radically unquotable.' Quotation is only justifiable if it prompts the return to the texts it derives from and recalls the context of which they are a part. When that context involves the disaster, the task is unsustainable yet governed by the obligation to the unwritable and the irrecoverable.

In *The Cut-Out Girl* van Es reflects on his own justification for his project and what it seeks to recover after Hesseline asks him, 'What is your motivation?' This is his answer on the obligation involved:

> I think hers could be a complex and interesting story. Recording these things is important, especially now, given the state of the world, with extremism again on the rise.

And he adds, 'There's an untold story here that I don't want to lose.'

There are untold stories that can still be retrieved. They can still be made to matter, in ongoing response to what is etched in Birkenau and what is quoted by Blanchot in *The Writing of the Disaster* and by Ann Smock, in the foreword to her translation: 'Know what has happened, do not forget, and at the same time never will you know.'

Another kind of record reveals itself gradually. In his 'Foreword' to *On the Natural History of Destruction*, Sebald recalls that the idea for his book, a collection of essays based on his lectures on the Allied bombing of Germany, came from Carl Seelig. Seelig, a German-Swiss poet and writer, was a friend and guardian to Walser. Sebald records that

> [t]he idea behind the first lecture came from Carl Seelig's account of an excursion he made in the summer of 1943 with Robert Walser, then a patient in a mental hospital on the very day before the night when the city of Hamburg went up in flames. Seelig's reminiscences, which make no mention at all of the coincidence, gave me a clearer view of the perspective from which I myself looked back on the trauma of those terrible years. Born in a village in the Allgäu Alps in May 1944, I am one of those who remain untouched by the catastrophe then unfolding in the German Reich. In my first Zürich lecture I tried to show, through passages of some length taken from my own literary works, that this catastrophe had nonetheless left its mark on my mind.

There is a lot to take in here. Walser, still unhealed from his own trauma, on the eve of devastation around him; Seelig overlooking the outing with him in his own chronicles; Sebald, on the contrary, intrigued by the tableau, so that he decides he must write himself; and Sebald again, admitting to his writing having in fact already been the oblique testimony to the trauma around and within and even from infancy, yet one in cultural memory that, as he notes, for understandable reasons 'never became an experience capable of public decipherment' in Germany. Sebald's method works not dissimilarly to Montaigne, as it happens: he notes, in a 'postscript,' that what he presented in Zürich was 'merely a rough-and-ready collection of various observations, materials, and theses,' which would need to be 'complemented and corrected.' So he does that, and *On the Natural History of Destruction* is the result. It has many notable attributes, and careful documentation is one of them.

As is the realization, toward the end, that it is all part of 'the *historia calamitatum* of mankind.' It is what drives writing of disaster, even if not singularly of *the* disaster. Toward the end, Sebald studies 'the justification for the sadomasochistic preoccupation, the repeated and virtuoso representation of suffering manifest in the literary work of two poets more than half a millennium apart in time, yet very much alike in spirit.'

The two poets are Dante and Peter Weiss.

Trauma diffuses across space and time. The challenge to memory and any healing is unconfined by the situatedness of atrocity.

Nevertheless, the specificity of the atrocity demands chronicling. For Sebald, the challenge and the failed ethics are in the 'abstract memory of the dead.'

This is 'of little avail against the lure of waning memory if it does not also express sympathy—sympathy going beyond mere pity—in the study and reconstruction of an actual time of torment.'

The diffusion of memory touches literature. The trauma denatures it.

In 'Robert Antelme, or the Truth of Literature' (1962), Perec writes, 'We don't quite know whether it is literature that we look down on, in the name of the concentration camps, or the concentration camps, in the name of literature.' The result is that

> Literature has lost its authority. It searches in the world for the signs of its defeat: angst oozes out from bare walls, from moorlands, from corridors, from petrified palaces, from impossible memories, from vacant stares. The world is congealed, placed between parentheses.

This is grimmer than Adorno on barbarity, or Blanchot on art's affront. It is ultimately why, as Perec observes at the start of the same essay, 'The literature of the concentration camps does not get attacked.'

Healing, wholeness: the very idea. Not after the 'utter-burn of the disaster,' as Blanchot has it, not before the utter alterity to any normality in which one, or literature, goes on.

Writing on Weiss's *Die Ermittlung* (*The Investigation*), Sebald notes in his last chapter that '[c]ompensation for the subjective sense of personal involvement in genocide, in which the writer's guilt neurosis assumes almost unmanageable proportions, could be made only if he placed the objective social conditions and preconditions of the tragedy at the center of his discourse.' Weiss could only contain the 'almost metaphysical dimension to this negative balance sheet' by referencing the Dantesque. And then, Sebald notes, 'The mere fact that, in the thirty-three cantos of *Die Ermittlung*, he could describe only the circles of the Inferno is the verdict on a period that has left any hope of salvation far behind.'

Of healing likewise.

So much reflection on what the aptest form might be for writing incalculable trauma, improbable healing.

'To call a piece of writing a fragment, or to say it's composed of fragments, is to say that it or its components were once whole but are no longer,' writes Manguso.

'Fragments, indeed. As if there were anything to break.' That's Don Paterson in *The Fall at Home*.

When and where might it be out of place, poor form, this otherwise under-standable scepticism about the whole?

There is a distinct change of temper at work in Manguso's and Paterson's observations on the fragment and the assumed relation to the whole and its possibility. The tone is different to the numerous lines on that relation in *The Literary Absolute* and *The Writing of the Disaster*. They are too many to quote. But the orthodoxy of critical and writerly assumption is evolving, as is intuited in *After Testimony: The Ethics and Aesthetics of Holocaust Narra-tive for the Future*, edited by Jakob Lothe, Susan Rubin Suleiman and James Phelan (2012).

To stand by the intuition is to invite the different intertext that's doing preliminary work here.

They are not alien to thought on the unpresentable, but the tone and the dis-position in a comment by Manguso appear nevertheless contrasting:

> Nothing is more boring to me than the re-restatement that language isn't suffi-ciently nuanced to describe the world. Of course language isn't enough. Accept-ing that is the starting point of using it to capacity. Of increasing its capacity.

'The world,' pragmatically. Not the disaster.

Derrida, Blanchot, so many others of that generation which had the 'bread of apocalypse in [their] mouths,' to use a phrase from *Specters of Marx*, increased language's capacity and reinvented it through their self-recasting philosophy, their *essais* and *récits*. The viabilities they introduced remain, alongside the opportune other idioms, capacities, intertexts and canons that proffer themselves in the present.

Before the Holocaust, the hush of history, which will not be quiet, as el-lipsis.

The witness of writing, the tribute of reading. The commitment at least to the latter, to the letter that is late by definition but for which the destination lies across and in time.

From the *Los Angeles Times*, this headline comes up online on the day that this essay is being finalized: '25 years after genocide, can Rwanda heal?'

The article speaks of 'artificial apology.' One scholar of the genocide is reported saying, 'Many survivors forgive because they are poor and need shelters or school fees.' A Tutsi widow says, 'I found I could not live with anger forever.'

The healing, its trauma, and sometimes healing as trauma: recognized, observed, offered to notice.

Why is it that to a certain kind of mind and for all the evidence in newsreels and in the copy of foreign and war correspondents, the trauma of the other caught in the disaster registers only if rendered in, as, the (para-)literary?

How are trauma and healing eased, or not, disturbed, or not, by the presence, the absence, of such (post-)literary texts? Why does the traumatized imaginary still discern a primacy of urgency, perhaps even of authenticity, in what Blanchot referred to as *l'éspace littéraire*?

It would be thought that the resources and affordances of twenty-first-century intermediatic space, across the filmic, the virtual, and more, decentre assumptions on the centrality of literary space.

And why is there the concern, still, with authentic representation, when as Blanchot notes in *The Writing of the Disaster*, 'If there is, among all words, one that is inauthentic, then surely it is the word "authentic."'

An earlier lexia observed the flight from the conclusive in Montaigne's essayistic method.

The protocols of conclusion tend to be averse to critical writing ending on a quotation. The technique seems lazy, devolving the responsibility onto another's better words. But here, where the ethic has been to bring others' heterological chronicling into contiguity, in order to bear witness after sixty years and more to the disaster, to incalculable trauma, to (im)possible healing, one quotation carries a sense, against the odds, of an unexpected, improbable resolution that stands in counterposition to all the accumulated doubt over the possibility of recovery and wholeness. It can be given here in the form of a hypograph. It comes from the last chapter of *The Cut-Out Girl*, just a few pages before the last sentence of that book which served, above, as the third epigraph, and which counters the cultural suspicion of wholeness exemplified in the reflections encountered in Manguso and Paterson. It is apt because of what converges at the end of van Es's book, which itself has a fragmentary ethic to its structure: the thinkability, the writability against the odds and against familiar assumptions, of a different stance on thoughts of healing and of its impossibility.

It is given below and brings this essay to a close. Balancing it out, for less hopeful dispositions, is this reflection on Weiss's art by Sebald, which turns on the impossibility of remedy, through art or otherwise.

> The purpose of representing cruelty . . . , as we now know, has never been fulfilled and probably never can be, since our species is unable to learn from its mistakes. Consequently, such arduous cultural efforts can no more come to a conclusion than the pain and torment they seek to remedy. The torture of those never-ending efforts is the true wheel of Ixion on which the creative imagination is always binding itself again, so that it can at least be absolved in doing penance.

Realizing that the writing of the disaster is penitential, self-repeating, in step with humanity's propensity to perpetrate disaster again in an irresolvable cycle, is what makes it all the more important for such healing as can occur to be affirmed. Hence:

> The way Lien introduced me . . . as a 'nephew' in January 2015 confirmed something special, the healing of a breach. . . . Lien has done the healing herself.

NOTES

1. The essay as a genre—as remarked on by, say, John D'Agata or Brian Dillon in recent books on its tradition and praxis—does not typically provide page references when it quotes. They are not provided here either, as to do so would have felt counter to the shape and spirit of what is being essayed. However, bibliographic references for works mentioned in this text are provided at the end, as that practice does not depart from the conventions of the essay.

If this explanation seems unacceptable nonetheless, it is worth pointing out that the quotations used are from short texts or specified sections from books, and that they are in fact easily locatable. The exceptions might be the quotations from *The Writing of the Disaster*. But then the point, precisely, is the exceptional quality of that book and its aptness in its entirety for the epigraphic, hence for that which must be read ahead and self-sufficiently of everything else.

BIBLIOGRAPHY

Associated Press. '25 Years after Genocide, Can Rwanda Heal? Six Villages Try.' *Los Angeles Times* 6 April 2019. https://www.latimes.com/world/la-fg-rwanda -genocide-anniversary-20190406-story.html. Accessed 24 April 2019.

BARTHES, Roland. *S/Z: An Essay*. Translated by Richard Miller. New York: Hill and Wang, 1975.

BELLOS, David. *Georges Perec: A Life in Words.* London: Harvill, 1999.

BENNETT, Alan. *Keeping On Keeping On*. London: Faber and Faber, 2016.

BLANCHOT, Maurice. *The Writing of the Disaster*. Translated by Ann Smock. Lincoln and London: University of Nebraska Press, 1995.

BLANCHOT, Maurice and Jacques Derrida. *The Instant of My Death / Demeure*. Translated by Elizabeth Rottenberg. Stanford, CA: Stanford University Press, 2000.

BUDICK, Sanford and Wolfgang Iser, editors. *Languages of the Unsayable: The Play of Negativity in Literature and Literary Theory*. Stanford, CA: Stanford University Press, 1987.

COETZEE, J. M. 'The Genius of Robert Walser.' *The New Yorker*, 2 November 2000. https://www.nybooks.com/articles/2000/11/02/the-genius-of-robert-walser/. Accessed 24 April 2019.

D'AGATA, John, editor. *The Lost Origins of the Essay*. St Paul, MN: Graywolf Press, 2009.

DERRIDA, Jacques. 'Aphorism Countertime.' Translated by Nicholas Royle. In *Acts of Literature*. Edited by Derek Attridge. 414–33. New York and London: Routledge, 1992.

DERRIDA, Jacques. *Specters of Marx: The State of the Debt, the Work of Mourning, and The New International*. Translated by Peggy Kamuf. New York and London: Routledge, 1994.

DILLON, Brian. *Essayism*. London: Fitzcarraldo Press, 2017.

EHRENREICH, Ben. 'Making Strange: On Victor Shklovsky.' *The Nation*, 5 February 2013.

HUGHES, Ted. 'Six Young Men.' In *Collected Poems of Ted Hughes*. Edited by Paul Keegan. London: Faber and Faber, 2005.

KAGEN, Melissa B. 'The Wanderer as Soldier: Robert Walser's *der Spaziergang*, Switzerland in World War I, and Digression as Occupation.' *German Quarterly* 89.1 (2016): 36–50.

KUNKEL, Benjamin. 'Still Small Voice: The Fiction of Robert Walser.' *The New Yorker*, 30 July 2007. https://www.newyorker.com/magazine/2007/08/06/still-small-voice. Accessed 24 April 2019.

LACOUE-LABARTHE, Philippe and Jean-Luc Nancy. *The Literary Absolute: The Theory of Literature in German Romanticism*. Translated by Philip Barnard and Cheryl Lester. New York: State University of New York Press, 1988.

LERNER, Ben. 'Robert Walser's Disappearing Acts.' *The New Yorker*, 3 September 2013. https://www.newyorker.com/books/page-turner/robert-walsers-disappearing-acts. Accessed 24 April 2019.

LOTHE, Jakob, Susan Rubin Suleiman and James Phelan, editors. *After Testimony: The Ethics and Aesthetics of Holocaust Narrative for the Future*. Columbus: The Ohio State University Press, 2012.

MANGUSO, Sarah. *300 Arguments*. St Paul, MN: Graywolf Press, 2017.

MANGUSO, Sarah. *The Two Kinds of Decay: A Memoir*. New York: Farrar, Straus and Giroux, 2008.

MENGHAM, Rod. *Grimspound and Inhabiting Art*. Manchester: Carcanet, 2018.

MUSIL, Robert. 'Helpless Europe.' Translated by Philip H. Beard. In *Precision and Soul: Essays and Addresses*. 116–33. Edited and translated by Buton Pike and David S. Luft. Chicago: University of Chicago Press, 1990.

MUSIL, Robert. 'On the Essay.' In *Precision and Soul: Essays and Addresses*. 48-51. Edited and translated by Buton Pike and David S. Luft. Chicago: University of Chicago Press, 1990.

MUSIL, Robert. *The Man without Qualities*. Translated by Sophie Wilkins and Burton Pike. New York: Picador, 1997.

PATERSON, Don. *The Fall at Home: New and Collected Aphorisms*. London: Faber and Faber, 2018.

PEREC, Georges. 'I Was Born.' In *Species of Spaces and Other Pieces*. 95–99. Edited and translated by John Sturrock. London: Penguin, 1997.

PEREC, Georges. *La Disparition*. Paris: Gallimard, 1990.

PEREC, Georges. 'Robert Antelme, or the Truth of Literature.' In *Species of Spaces and Other Pieces*. Edited and translated by John Sturrock. 249–262. London: Penguin, 1997.

PEREC, Georges. *W, or Memory of Childhood*. Translated by David Bellos. London: Vintage, 2001.

SEBALD, W. G. 'Le Promeneur Solitaire: W. G. Sebald on Robert Walser.' *The New Yorker*, 6 February 2014. https://www.newyorker.com/books/page-turner/le-promeneur-solitaire-w-g-sebald-on-robert-walser. Accessed 24 April 2019.

SEBALD, W. G. *On the Natural History of Destruction*. Translated by Anthea Bell. New York: Modern Library, 2004.

SHKLOVSKY, Viktor. 'Art, as Device.' Translated by Alexandra Berlina. *Poetics Today* 36.3 (2015): 151–74.

SHKLOVSKY, Viktor. *Bowstring: On the Dissimilarity of the Similar*. Translated by Shushan Agavyan. McLean, IL and London: Dalkey Archive Press, 2011.

WALSER, Robert. *Microscripts*. Translated and Introduction by Susan Bernofsky, with 'Some Thoughts on Robert Walser' by Maira Kalman and 'Afterword' by Walter Benjamin. New York: New Directions, 2012.

WALSER, Robert. *The Walk*. Translated by Christopher Middleton and others. New York: Serpent's Tail, 1992.

VAN ES, Bart. *The Cut-Out Girl: A Story of War and Family, Lost and Found*. London: Penguin, 2018.

Chapter Two

Forgiving as Self-Healing?

The Case of Eva Mozes Kor

Arleen Ionescu

WHAT IS FORGIVENESS?

Forgiving the crimes against humanity perpetrated by the Nazis has remained one of the most ethically contentious issues resulting from the barbarity of the Shoah that put to test the moral validity of this philosophical notion and demanded its complete rethinking. After dealing with the ontology of evil and ethics in *Le Mal* and *Traité des Vertus*, in his main philosophical text, titled *Le Pardon* (*Forgiveness*), Vladimir Jankélévitch enlarged upon all moral and social-political compulsions on forgiving. He placed 'pure' forgiveness in the realm of a possible impossibility, no matter how 'mad' it may seem.[1] Jankélévitch defined the notion of forgiveness by what it is not rather than by what it is,[2] differentiating between its concrete and abstract gestures. Judeo-Christian traditions record concrete acts of what can be called *transactional forgiveness*:[3] *excusing*, which rationalizes the wrongdoing and the wrong-doer, and *renouncing*, which denies justice. When one forgives, one works through one's past, that roundabout process required in traumatic situations that helps the victim gain critical distance from the traumatic event s/he has experienced in order to be able to continue living in the present. Jankélévitch called 'similiforgiveness' or 'apocryphal forgiveness' those traditions meant to end a critical situation (such as in a post-conflict society) and bring acceptance or reconciliation. 'Pure forgiveness' is something that 'has perhaps never been granted in the concrete acts of forgiveness.'[4] In contrast with the excuse, which can be always rationalized and motivated by understanding the nature of the perpetrator's wrong deed, it is unmotivated and neither conditional on the perpetrator's subsequent actions nor a way to achieve certain goals, since it 'renounces justice,'[5] thus remaining 'foreign to the criterion of any "according to".'[6] Spontaneous and gratuitous, 'pure forgiveness' is akin to a divine act, a 'gracious gift' that goes beyond moral or juridical contexts.[7] It becomes 'the impossibility par excellence' paradoxically when 'absolute wickedness'[8] is forgiven. The 'madness' of forgiveness was inscribed by Jankélévitch into what he called a 'hyperbolical' ethics, whereby evil is always forgiven because forgiveness must be stronger than evil. Otherwise, for Jankélévitch, evil represented both the prerequisite of and the main *obstacle* to forgiveness.

By the 1960s, in Jankélévitch's France, there were public debates around a moratorium that would set a period of twenty years, after which crimes could no longer be prosecuted. In *L'Imprescriptible*,[9] a section of which, 'Pardonner?,' was translated as 'Should We Pardon Them?,' appeared as part of the debates around the irrevocability or the inexpiability of the Nazi war crimes. The French Parliament eventually passed a law on the imprescriptibility of crimes against humanity in 1964, upholding the notion of crime against humanity adopted in the Nuremberg tribunal in 1945.

Engaging with 'Should We Pardon Them?' one should first note that it does not entirely contradict *Forgiveness*, where Jankélévitch had stated that crimes against values, especially the ones against humanity, 'stand morally outside the confines of time'[10] and that '[t]he prescription of a colossal crime is a monstrous caricature of ordinary prescription.'[11] It is also important to emphasize that Jankélévitch had insisted on the condition that forgiveness should be requested in order to be granted, an issue that was emphasized by many scholars. For instance, according to Charles Griswold in his genealogy of forgiveness, forgiveness is a two-person process involving a moderation of anger and a cessation of projects of revenge, in response to the fulfilment of several conditions on the part of the perpetrator: acknowledging the guilt, repudiating the deeds, expressing regret, understanding the injury they committed, promising not to inflict injury again, and finally proving to be worthy of approbation.[12]

For twenty years after the Nazi crimes, Jankélévitch had waited for a plea for forgiveness (a plea that actually came later, and which will be dealt with in the last section of this chapter). In the lack of 'a single word of understanding and sympathy'[13] and 'the absence of gestures of repentance, offers of reparations, or requests for forgiveness on the side of the perpetrators,'[14] his resentment grew, as one can easily observe from the bitterness of his language that 'portends a certain mythologization of the crimes and the criminals, tending to demonize the perpetrators.'[15] According to Jankélévitch, Auschwitz was a metonym for the unforgivable and the Shoah was 'a truly infinite crime whose horror deepens the more it is analyzed,'[16] a 'metaphysical abomination' that transformed the six million Jews who perished into 'the top of the list of martyrs for all time.'[17] The comparison of the perpetrators with dogs was thus 'unfair to dogs,' as '[d]ogs would not have invented the crematoria, nor thought to inject phenol into the hearts of children.'[18] Therefore, the best term to use about the Nazi perpetrators was 'monsters' who constructed a 'monstrous machine for crushing children, for destroying Jews, Slavs, and Resistance fighters by the hundreds of thousands,' and who were tacitly supported by all Germans, whom Jankélévitch found guilty for their 'innumerable complicities' and their 'complacent silence.'[19] It was precisely this monstrosity that made their crimes unforgivable, since forgiveness is human, and the crimes committed demonstrated that the Nazis were inhuman. Under such circumstances, Jankélévitch simply proclaimed that 'forgiveness died in the death camps,'[20] consonant with Elie Wiesel's certainty that his God and his soul were murdered the night he stepped into the camp,[21] and Levinas's contention that 'Nietzsche's God, the God who is dead is the one who committed suicide at Auschwitz.'[22] Jankélévitch did not seem to mind denying the power of the spirit to forgive that he had dealt with in his earlier book. He even went further, asserting that even the alternative of forgiveness, punishing the perpetrators, was suspended by the proportion of the crime:

> One cannot give life back to that immense mountain of miserable ashes. One cannot punish the criminal with a punishment proportional to his crime: for in relation to the infinite all finite magnitudes tend to equal one another; hence the penalty hardly seems to matter strictly speaking, what happened is inexpiable.[23]

In what follows, I will attempt to put Jankélévitch in dialogue with other philosophers who have offered similar as well as different readings of forgiveness.

Hannah Arendt, who had written a thesis on 'The Concept of Love in St. Augustine,' pointed out that forgiveness can create new future relationships that eliminate revenge. In *Responsibility and Judgement*, she doubted the possibility to either punish or forgive 'the horror itself in its naked monstrosity,'[24] a position which brings her very close to Jankélévitch's in 'Should We Pardon Them?'. Before *The Origins of Totalitarianism* appeared in bookstores, Arendt sent a copy as a birthday present to Karl Jaspers, her former PhD supervisor, with whom she shared a lasting friendship. In her correspondence with Jaspers on the book, Arendt defined radical evil as making 'human beings superfluous,'[25] through the elimination of 'unpredictability,' or 'spontaneity.'[26] Since total domination killed both the juridical and moral person in man,[27] both juridical punishment and forgiveness cease to be valid options. This consideration was maintained in *Eichmann in Jerusalem: A Report on the Banality of Evil*, where she showed that Eichmann was beyond any forgiveness or punishment, since even if he had been sentenced to death, this form of punishment would be rather a symbol for the community of humanity.[28] Arendt's convictions were highly criticized by several Jewish authorities (including Gershom Scholem, the well-known scholar of Jewish mysticism), who refused to translate her work into Hebrew. *The Human Condition* put forward a clear-cut discussion on forgiveness where she included it alongside promise as the two framing 'actions' of political life; forgiveness was regarded here as an open possibility for 'redemption from the predicament of irreversibility.'[29]

Emmanuel Levinas's belief in ethics as 'first philosophy' is close to Jankélévitch's. For both philosophers, ethics came before ontology and metaphysics, epistemology and even self-consciousness,[30] and the question 'What should I do?' was more important than the question 'Who am I?.'[31] According to John Llewelyn, Levinas placed the 'I' in 'an ethical universe' where it is 'elected not to be saved, but to serve.'[32] In *Totality and Infinity*, Levinas referred to the '*infinity of responsibility*,' a responsibility that increases 'in the *measure that it is assumed. . . .* The better I accomplish my duty the fewer rights I have; the more I am just the more guilty I am.'[33] The culpability, justice and duty are to be seen in relation to 'the judgement of God,' which for Levinas meant the truth. Thus, the communication of 'I' with the Other[34] in apologetic discourse can be addressed to him only under 'what might be called the judgement of God,' and, therefore, maintained as truthful.[35] In a subsection of *Totality and Infinity* titled 'The Infinity of Time,' Levinas showed that the gift of forgiveness could undo the past and give another chance.[36] In this way, forgiveness interrupts 'what would otherwise be a continuous accumulative duration,' since the reality of a past misdeed is renewed by forgiveness.[37] This is the situation when one is forgiven beyond their death: '[t]he fissure (*faute*) of infinite temporality going towards the good is the ethical infinition of goodness expressed in the forgiveness of fault (*faute*) beyond the face, across dead time, across the death of the person forgiven, therefore beyond the reciprocity of response.'[38]

Levinas asserted that the ethics of love and of forgiveness can be neglectful of what he called *le tiers* (the third party).[39] When one forgives the one who has done them harm and when one repents for the wrong they did to the other, the third party may be injured. If we extend this notion to the Shoah, 'the third party' are the dead; forgiving the perpetrators who murdered them would be equivalent to killing them twice. Thus, consonant with Jankélévitch's thinking and, as we will see in the next section, with Simon Wiesenthal's argument, forgiving involves also the dead who did not authorize the forgiver to forgive.

As I showed in *The Memorial Ethics of Libeskind's Berlin Jewish Museum* in a discussion on the impossibility of forgiving the Nazi crimes,[40] Levinas's *Talmudic Lesson* (1963) was a response to Jankélévitch's passionate analysis of German guilt.[41] Emphasizing that he did not speak on behalf of the Jewish people but in his own name, Levinas agreed with Jankélévitch on the impossibility of forgiveness in the case of aggression, and confessed his own 'difficulty' to forgive 'some Germans,' namely those who consciously supported National Socialism, including Martin Heidegger.[42]

In a seminar on forgiveness, Jacques Derrida questioned the validity of Jankélévitch's 'Should We Pardon Them?,' responding to its two main axioms: the necessity of asking for forgiveness and the imprescriptibility of the Shoah. Unlike Aaron T. Looney, who unconvincingly attempted to reconcile the contradiction between Jankélévitch's opinions as a Western philosopher and as a Jew,[43] Derrida criticized the general tone and 'violence' of the texts of *L'Imprescriptible*, which he found 'unjust and unworthy of what Jankélévitch had elsewhere written on forgiveness.'[44] Jankélévitch had insisted on the Abrahamic tradition according to which the one who was forgiven needs to go through the precondition of repentance so that forgiveness is not made a 'simple buffoonery.'[45] Derrida dismissed this precondition, maintaining that forgiveness takes place without or before repentance.[46] Jankélévitch excluded 'the infinity of human forgiveness and thus the very hyperbolicity of the ethics' that was the guiding thread of his eponymous book.[47] Owing to such an exclusion, Jankélévitch refused to see that the very fact that the Nazi crime was unforgivable precisely remained 'the only thing to forgive.'[48] Derrida, the philosopher who believed in the impossibility of an absolute gift without return and in unconditional hospitality,[49] believed also in a 'pure and unconditional forgiveness' that 'escapes the rules of normality' and 'is a madness of the impossible.'[50] Like any 'mad' thing, '[i]t must plunge, but lucidly, into the night of the unintelligible.'[51]

Unlike Jankélévitch and Arendt, Derrida regarded forgiveness and punishment not as alternatives, but as simultaneously possible through the shift in perspective between the person who offers forgiveness and the institution whose responsibility is to establish justice and punish wrongdoers. Only such a separation of responsible agents can bring justice and love together, even if the institutional right to punish does not mean that 'the person is relieved of the decision between justice and forgiveness.'[52]

Derrida believed that pure forgiveness should overcome any limits, including those of Auschwitz: '[I]f pure forgiveness, with regard to Auschwitz or anything whatever, is to take place, it is for each person to come to it, to take responsibility for it in a unique way without entering into any economy of judgement, of penalty, of punishment, etc.'[53] In order to be worthy of its 'purity,' forgiveness has to give up any power, it has to be *unconditional but without sovereignty,* because while to forgive 'gives the most splendor to greatness, to the highness of the sovereign, to sovereignty,' it can also run 'the risk of being unjust, of acting unjustly . . . in the highest degree.'[54] As soon as this 'most difficult task, at once necessary and apparently impossible' has been assumed, we can believe in a forgiveness-to-come.[55]

In accordance with Jankélévitch, Derrida claimed that forgiveness as communication is essential. Jankélévitch saw forgiveness as a face-to-face between torturer and victim, and mentioned that forgiveness can take place only if the victim is still alive. Derrida agreed that the scene of forgiveness involves a language that the forgiven and the forgiver should share, 'an agreement on the meanings of words, their connotations, rhetoric, the aim of a reference.'[56] Without it, forgiveness remains 'deprived of meaning.'[57] Forgiveness cannot occur unless the two sides agree 'on the nature of the fault,' and are conscious of 'who is guilty of which evil toward whom.'[58]

One last aporia called 'the most artful perhaps'[59] was offered to us in Derrida's 'Hostipitality.' Derrida showed that telling someone 'I forgive you' both obliges and wounds the one who is forgiven. In addition, it implies 'I give,' and such a gift is already destroyed by being acknowledged, thus inscribing forgiveness within an economic exchange, a 'transaction of gratitude, a commerce of thanking.' However, he agreed that forgiveness must be voiced, since 'silent forgiveness' of which 'the forgiven one would know nothing' would be 'as disastrous [*néfaste*] as what silence would have wanted to avoid.'[60]

To conclude, from all these philosophers' slightly different views on forgiveness, we retain those that will be primarily investigated in relation to the analysis of Eva Mozes Kor's case: that in order to grant forgiveness, one needs to be asked for it, that one cannot forgive on behalf of the dead, and that, in order to be unconditional, forgiveness cannot be equated to any form of economic exchange.

FROM AUSCHWITZ TO FORGIVENESS: THE CASE OF EVA MOZES KOR

Eva Mozes Kor, the protagonist of the film *Forgiving Dr Mengele* (2005) and author of the book *Surviving the Angel of Death: The True Story of a Mengele Twin in Auschwitz* (2011),[61] is the only Holocaust survivor who claimed to have silently forgiven her aggressor, Dr. Mengele, and all the Nazi perpetrators 'across dead time,' to echo Levinas on the fissure of temporality discussed in the first section. This section discusses how her position broke with 'a powerful taboo—both among survivors of the Holocaust and within the Jewish community more generally,'[62] and asks whether her gesture can be actually called forgiveness. Following closely the gradation in the implementation of her decision to forgive, the first part of this section attempts to compare her views with the Judaic conception of forgiveness as exemplified in Simon Wiesenthal's book *The Sunflower: On the Possibilities and Limits of Forgiveness*. The last part of this section enquires whether Mozes Kor's forgiveness can be regarded as an operative speech act.

When the two ten-year-old twin sisters, Eva and Miriam, arrived on the platform at Auschwitz, they were brutally ripped apart from their family and selected to become Josef Mengele's twins. Despite the atrocious conditions and terrifying experiments, they stepped out of the camp as survivors on 27 January 1945. For forty years, the two sisters did not bring up the subject of their detention at Auschwitz between themselves (*FDM*, 25.08–25.15). However, Nazi atrocity had an unrelenting impact on Mozes Kor's life, who, beyond her chronic silence about this tragedy, remained embittered, tormented, enslaved by the past that she refused to remember. She experienced the shame of the survivor that many scholars talked about.[63] Her negative feelings made her act out constantly. Flashes of memory and constant fears repetitively came back: she was unable to cope with Halloween children's plays, which reminded her of the way in which her family was harassed in Portz (*SAD*, 128); in adolescence she had a recurring nightmare in which soap bars would speak in the voice of her parents and sisters and ask why she was washing with them (*SAD*, 118); hearing flight attendants' instructions in German on a Lufthansa flight, she was paralysed by fear and felt 'physically sick' (*FDM*, 24.19–25.07).

In 1984 the two sisters founded the CANDLES (Children of Auschwitz Nazi Deadly Lab Experiments Survivors) support group, managing to locate 122 survivors living in different parts of the world (*SAD*, 130).[64] Miriam discovered that the unknown chemicals injected in her body prevented her kidneys from growing more than the size of a ten-year-old's; she died in 1993 in spite of Eva donating one kidney to her a few years before. Her twin's more fragile disposition had given Eva additional strength in keeping herself alive in Auschwitz in spite of Dr. Mengele's estimation that she would have only two weeks to live. Once her sister passed away, unable to participate in the funeral since the Judaic law imposes that the dead must be buried within twenty-four hours, Eva started to exorcise the ghosts of her past. In 1995, she transformed CANDLES into the Holocaust Museum and Education Center in Terre Haute, Indiana. She anxiously started looking for perpetrators who worked or knew about Mengele's experiments, and she met Dr. Hans Münch, a former SS officer who had been acquitted at Krakow because several Auschwitz survivors gave evidence that he had saved their lives. Since it was important for her 'to prove to the deniers and the revisionists that there were gas chambers at Auschwitz' (*FDM* 35.50–58), she asked him to go with her on the fiftieth anniversary of the camp's liberation[65] and sign a declaration testifying to the functioning of gas chambers. He agreed to do so, confessing that he still had nightmares about Auschwitz. The process of editing her letter of thanks to Dr Münch revealed to her that she still felt as Dr. Mengele's victim. On 27 January 1995, once Dr. Münch signed his declaration, she made a puzzling declaration of amnesty in front of television cameras:

> Fifty years after liberation, I, Eva Mozes Kor, in my name only hereby give amnesty to all Nazis who participated directly or indirectly in the murder of my family and millions of others, because it is time to forgive, but not to forget. It is time to heal our souls. (*FDM*, 38.02–38.26)

In order to understand Mozes Kor's gesture and to see whether it works for her as a Jewish woman, we need to return to Jankélévitch's insistence on the Abrahamic traditions, which are different from the Christian view on forgiveness. Christianity, among other religions, states that one has to forgive in order to abide by God's teachings. 'Forgive us our trespasses as we forgive those who trespass against us' (Mathew 6:12) is part of the Lord's Prayer. David Watson, who recalls Kenneth McCall's words, glosses the word 'forgiveness' (made up by 'fore' [before, situated or placed in front] and 'to give') as follows: 'Fore-give-ness is love given before another has either given it, earned it, accepted it, or even understood it. That is the nature of God's love who sent his Son to bear this long before we ever thought of loving him. Love takes the initiative.'[66] For Christians, the subject of forgiveness is an 'I' that is not related to egocentrism but to love. Forgiveness is an imitation of God's love, thus unknown, since God's ways are unfathomable. Christians should forgive those who wrong them even when the latter do not make any gesture of contrition, since Christian forgiveness does not depend on the repentance of the wrongdoers, as epitomized by Christ on the cross, who utters: 'Father forgive them, they know not what they do' (Luke 23:34).

Conversely, in the ten days of repentance that culminate in Yom Kippur, the Day of Atonement, Jewish people look back over the past year, confess their sins and ask for forgiveness of anyone they have wronged. Moreover, the Mishnah says: 'For sins against God, the Day of Atonement brings forgiveness. For sins against one's neighbor, the Day of Atonement brings no forgiveness until one has become reconciled with one's neighbor.'[67] The very first stage of atonement consists in asking for forgiveness from both God and the victim. This process involves the repentance and the return of the perpetrator (*teshuvah*) to the right path, after the victim's forgiveness is asked for on three occasions, a moment when the victim is obliged to forgive.[68]

That one cannot forgive on behalf of the dead according to Judaic laws is something that has been agreed on. Jankélévitch makes it clear in his texts

and so does Derrida in 'On Forgiveness': 'The survivor is not ready to sub-
stitute herself, abusively, for the dead. The immense and painful experience
of the survivor: who would have the right to forgive in the name of the disappeared victims?'[69] Jankélévitch's position that a common 'we' (including the
dead whom survivors represent) should not forgive is congruent with that of
many Holocaust survivors, among whom the former Holocaust victim Simon
Wiesenthal, who became the most famous Nazi hunter after WW2, and who
cites the Mishnah Yoma in his book *The Sunflower: On the Possibilities
and Limits of Forgiveness*.[70] His book recounts that while being worked to
death, starved and humiliated outside his concentration camp, Wiesenthal
was approached by a nurse to see the deadly wounded SS soldier, Karl. Karl
repented for having become part of Hitler's killing machine, asking Wiesenthal for forgiveness. The latter listened to the soldier's story yet left without a
word. Back in the camp, he shared his concerns with his closest fellow prisoners, who assured him that he had respected the Judaic laws.[71] At the end of
the book, Wiesenthal mused not only on the duty not to forget but also on the
'many kinds of silence' that limited the possibility of forgiveness:

> Well, I kept silent when a young Nazi, on his deathbed, begged me to be his
> confessor. . . .
> And how many bystanders kept silent as they watched Jewish men, women,
> and children being led to the slaughterhouses of Europe?[72]

Mozes Kor's book testifies to a similar silence which is synonymous
with cowardice and passivity; neighbours, classmates, even her best friend
watched silently as her family was marched out from Portz, the village where
she grew up (*SAD*, 18). Their silence meant indifference to the fate of human
beings with whom they shared a past. Mozes Kor claimed to be prepared to
cross the uncrossable gap from the silence in which her family left their birth-
place, being deported to their destruction, to forgiveness. This shift is marked
by a change of her lexicon from that of disruption and irreversible loss to one
of empowerment.

In her declaration of amnesty which she mistook for forgiveness, Mozes
Kor insisted that she spoke in her name 'only,' which is indicative of her
awareness of the need not to hurt what Levinas called 'the third party,' as I
have shown in the previous section.[73] However, as Peter Banki rightly suggests, her declaration still had a 'public, political character.'[74] My contention
is that although she took great care to act only in her own name, she ended
up acting synecdochically as a representative of the victims. She forgave the
Nazis not only for what they had done to her, but also for having killed 'millions of others,' including her family. Therefore, she implicitly gave voice
to the voiceless. In her discourse she unconsciously shifted from first-person

singular to first-person plural. The imperative 'It is time to heal *our* souls' refers to all the victims who survived, a gesture that the other victims found improper. Her hasty deliberation that her fellow survivors' emotional and physical baggage from the past would continue haunting them to the end of their lives is illustrative of her lack of empathy: 'Most of my fellow survivors are so hurting that they do not have the ability to even understand what I am talking about—and so many of them will die without ever feeling free from that pain' (*FDM*, 39.34–39.53). From the superior position (hence of 'power') she assumed, she failed to understand that the solution that worked for her may not work for others. Claiming that she respected their decision, in her turn she invoked the right to differ from them when in 2001 Dr. Hubert Markl, the president of the Max Planck Society, publicly asked for the victims' forgiveness (*FDM* 47.09–47.30).

Through the lens of John Austin's theories on 'performative utterance,' Mozes Kor's 'speech acts'—'I forgive Dr. Mengele / I forgive everybody'— are highly problematic. Speech acts that were included by Austin in the category of 'behabitives,' 'those reactions to other people's behavior and fortunes and of attitudes and expressions of attitudes to someone else's past conduct or imminent conduct,'[75] should performatively effectuate forgiveness. Any 'illocutionary act of performance is in the performed locutionary act, as is the perlocutionary act of communicating to the listener that he is forgiven.'[76] In this light, Mozes Kor could not seek forgiveness or atone for Dr. Mengele's and the Nazi crimes in general; her bestowal of forgiveness could not have any perlocutionary effect on them since Dr. Mengele was dead and the Nazi perpetrators were impossible to identify. Making a speech act means performing 'an action, perhaps, which one could scarcely perform, at least with so much precision, in any other way.'[77] The locution 'I forgive' can be included in those performative utterances that presuppose six general conditions, out of which the first four are compulsory for the act to be successful: (1) the acceptance of a conventional procedure and an effect, (2) the appropriateness of the invoked procedure, (3, 4) the correct and complete execution of the procedure, and (5, 6) the sincerity and the consistency of the participant, which strengthen the speech act in order for it not to be 'hollow' or 'abused' and thus ineffective.[78]

In the speech act performed by Mozes Kor, the forgiven is not present (the first addressee, Dr. Mengele, is dead and the second addressee, the Nazis, is a general referent that cannot be precisely determined). In addition, since there is no acceptance of a certain procedure, we cannot speak of the appropriateness of the procedure. It is clear that Mozes Kor's forgiveness falls short of the first four points and is incorrect, incomplete, and, thus, inoperative. Points 5 and 6 are strengthened by her conviction that forgiveness gives her nothing but liberation. In the film, her gestures, including her facial expression and the tone of her voice, are indicators of her sincerity and her belief in her message. What is also crucial is that she signed her declaration. Signatures, as well as authenticating acts, are endowed with a performative force that makes them accomplish what they ratify. In Austin's mapping of how to do things with words, a signature acts as a tether because, unlike in the case of an utterance, the written document is linked to its source.[79] By signing the document, Mozes Kor endorsed it, and framed it as a moment of political transformation.

One possible way to read her gesture is in terms of ego psychology:[80] not unlike 'emotional forgiveness,'[81] her notion of forgiveness converges towards the removal of the emotional pain resulting from traumatic life events, and has healing effects on the forgiver. The ego state therapy that explores covert ego states resulting in behaviour change derives from ego psychology. In ego state therapy, forgiveness is not for the benefit of the perpetrator but for that of the victim, since it enables the latter to move on with his/her life, let go of grievances and regain control.

The object-relations theory approach to trauma theory has identified in the Holocaust victims a blockage in the communication between the victim's self and its good internal objects. This blockage is known as a 'breakdown of the empathic process': '[t]he internal good object becomes silent as an empathic mediator between self and environment, and the trust in the continual presence of good objects and the expectation of human empathy is destroyed.'[82] Mozes Kor grew up as an orphan who experienced all the symptoms of someone whose human empathy was destroyed: 'a catastrophic isolation, an inner abandonment that not only paralyzes the self and its possibilities of action, but also annihilates it, which is at the same time accompanied by mortal fear, hatred, shame, and despair.'[83] She confessed in the book that after forgiving the Nazis she also forgave herself for hating her parents due to their inability to protect their children (*SAD*, 133).

Both the film and the book insist on representing Mozes Kor as stretching beyond physical and psychological limits. One of the most used words in *FDM* and *SAD* is 'power' (with all its derivatives and synonyms). The book mentions that she was 'strong and brave and more outspoken' than all her siblings (*SAD*, 3). At Auschwitz, she felt 'helpless': 'things are done to us, we have no power over it' (*FDM*, 40.52–41.03). When she was injected with an unknown germ and taken to the infirmary to die, she no longer had the ability to decide what happened to her. Without food or liquid in the block where she was sent to die, she was 'overpowered' by 'the need to get water' (*SAD*, 66). Yet she empowered herself with the little physical strength she still had in order to prevent dehydration: she crawled on the floor every day to get to the tap at the end of the barracks. She took her 'power' back, 'refusing to die': 'I made a silent pray that I would do anything within my power to prove him wrong, to survive, to be reunited with Miriam' (*FDM*, 14.58). She alludes that feeling like a mother rather than a sister to Miriam (*FDM*, 25.34) helped her 'become sturdier and more forceful, too' (*SAD*, 75). She was the one in charge of 'organizing'[84] potatoes and flour to assuage their hunger or a scarf which could help her sister stay warm.

Empowering becomes the leitmotif of the film once the viewer sees her declaration of amnesty. Her children, Alex and Rina Kor, allude constantly to their mother's strong personality. Her friend Mary Wright invokes Eva's 'power as an individual' (*FDM*, 40.08). Mozes Kor admits that she had 'a very strong need' to thank Dr. Münch (*FDM*, 36.35–36.41), also pointing out that she 'had no idea' that she 'had the power to forgive a Nazi,' a power that no one could have given or taken away from her (*FDM*, 41.04–41.15). On the fiftieth anniversary of the liberation of Auschwitz, she dominated the whole event. She seemed to be in control of everything: it was she who read both Dr. Münch's declaration and her own amnesty document. The other Mengele twins witnessed the whole process in silence. Her forgiveness was a self-centred, cathartic act of self-healing through which she reached self-empowerment that can be equated to a regained sovereignty of the self, a release from persistent fears as a former Nazi victim. Her gesture, then, cannot be pure, unconditional forgiveness, as Derrida theorizes it. It is the product of a calculation, an economy, a transaction, a deal: by forgiving, she got back her power to live her life as a normal person, leaving her status as a victim behind.

She asserted that she had not foreseen the overwhelming power of forgiving:

> So I thought about it [about forgiving Dr Mengele],[85] and the feeling that I had the power to forgive that god of Auschwitz, me, the little nothing, the little guinea pig, made me feel very good inside. And so, if I forgive Doctor Mengele, I might as well forgive everybody (*FDM*, 37.40–38.01).

Mozes Kor admitted the madness of her gesture: 'If anyone would have told me ten years ago today that I was going to forgive the Nazis, I would have told them, please go and find the best psychiatrist and have your head examined, because you are crazy' (*FDM*, 42.57). It is not a coincidence that the scene in which she speaks about her newly acquired empowerment takes place in a fitness centre where she trained herself to have stronger muscles and improve her posture. In this setting, she forced her 'power' onto her viewers in order to rid herself of the burden of her past, speaking to the reporter while she was exercising: 'Once I read it and signed it [the declaration of amnesty] the feeling of complete freedom from all the burden the pain has inflicted upon me . . . it's a life changing experience' (*FDM*, 40.22–40.38, my insertion).

Banki's reading of '[t]he feeling of self-empowerment to which Mozes Kor testifies after having made her declaration of amnesty-forgiveness' foregrounds 'the restoration of a feeling of narcissistic self-sufficiency, which results from the dismissal of those who for the longest time have been most hated and feared.'[86] There is indeed a lot of self-sufficiency in her gesture, which Mozes Kor did not deny. In the film, she informed us that, for her, forgiveness was neither a moral nor a religious experience: it 'has nothing to do with the perpetrator, has nothing to do with any religion, it has only everything to do with the way the victim is empowering himself or herself and taking back their life' (*FDM*, 48.44–49.03). In her book she wrote: '[W]hat I discovered once I made the decision was that forgiveness is not so much for the perpetrator, but for the victim. I had the power to forgive. . . . That made me feel powerful. It made me feel good to have any power over my life as a survivor' (*SAD*, 132). In her view, this would mean making sure that the offenders would never offend again, yet without forgetting or condoning what happened. That the offenders will never offend again, that anti-Semitism will cease to exist, are clearly mere illusions, even looking only at the fact that a still unidentified neo-Nazi arsonist burnt down her museum in 2003. The museum was beyond repair, but she found the strength to rebuild it from scratch and reopen it fifteen months later.

'Restorative justice'[87] emphasizes repairing the harm of criminal behaviour through a tripartite representation of victim, offender and community; therefore, we cannot interpret Mozes Kor's forgiveness in this vein since she did not participate in a cooperative process including all stakeholders. Nevertheless, a definition of forgiveness which can aptly illustrate Mozes Kor's aims was given by the pioneer of restorative justice, Howard Zehr:

> letting go of the power the offense and the offender have over a person. It means no longer letting that offense and offender dominate. Without this experience of forgiveness, without this closure, the wound festers, the violation takes over our consciousness, our lives. It, and the offender, are in control. Real forgiveness, then, is an act of empowerment and healing. It allows one to move from victim to survivor.[88]

On the one hand, Mozes Kor's empowerment (the fact that she found the power over herself) led to her judging her fellows who were also Dr. Mengele's victims. Uttering 'it is time to heal *our* souls,' she identified herself as the representative of a group that had not appointed her to speak on its behalf. Thus, empowerment became sovereignty, since she invested herself with power over the others. According to Derrida, sovereignty annuls forgiveness because 'what makes the "I" forgive you' sometimes unbearable or odious, even obscene, is the affirmation of sovereignty.'[89] On the other hand, the victim cannot be 'stripped of the minimal, elementary *possibility* of *virtually* considering forgiving the unforgivable' because they would be deprived 'of life, or the right to speak, or that freedom, that force and that power which *authorises*, which permits the accession to the position of "I forgive."'[90] Mozes Kor's story shows that she was deprived of all her rights when in Auschwitz, including that of forgiving. Forgiving her enemy was one of the rights she acquired after she was ready to confront her past.

One last feature of forgiveness as 'the ultimate act of self-healing' is its association with peace: 'Anger and hate are seeds that germinate war. Forgiveness is a seed for peace' (*SAD*, 133). The invocation of peace, when forgiveness is possible, versus war, when it becomes too hard to grant, also appears in the film when, after forgiving the Nazis, she was challenged by Dan Bar-On to take part in a reconciliation meeting with Palestinians. This challenge proved to be not only above her 'power' of forgiveness but also beyond her understanding. The Palestinians objected to her overbearing sense of self-importance and her certainty that she was special. She admitted having been dominated by the fear of becoming a hostage on Palestinian ground and feeling threatened by the Palestinians' reproaches about what 'her' people did to 'their' people. The meeting ended on her inability to cope and her justification that in times of war it is not possible to reconcile (*FDM*, 01.07.32).

HEALING AND FORGIVENESS

Derrida believed that with the passing of time and the change of generations, forgiveness and reconciliation would be possible.[91] I would like to return, by way of a short conclusion, to Jankélévitch's waiting for a plea for forgiveness, which I mentioned in the first section of this chapter. Thirty-five years after Jankélévitch asserted that no gestures of remorse from the perpetrators came, a young man named Wiard Raveling asked Jankélévitch for forgiveness. Their correspondence was published in the *Magazine Littéraire*, a little while before the French philosopher was visited at his home by his interlocutor. Raveling was a young man who by chance was born German, who was 'completely innocent of Nazi crimes,' yet felt 'a mixture of shame, pity, resignation, sadness, incredulity, revolt' when thinking about them, who thought of 'Anne Frank, and of Auschwitz and of *Todesfuge* and of *Nuit et Brouillard: "Der Tod ist ein Meister aus Deutschland."'[92] Raveling invited Jankélévitch to visit him, promising he would welcome him in a neutral space free of any reference to German philosophy or culture that might have upset the French philosopher (they would neither speak of Hegel, Nietzsche, Jaspers or Heidegger, nor listen to Schubert or Schumann, but rather talk about Descartes and Sartre and listen to Chopin, Fauré or Debussy).[93] Though Jankélévitch thanked him profusely for the letter, he did not go to Germany, his justification being that he was 'too old to inaugurate' such 'a new era.'[94] When they finally met in France, he still could not utter 'I forgive.'

Perhaps the best explanation for Jankélévitch's reaction was given by Derrida. He thought Jankélévitch hesitated to respond to this invitation which would have eased the way towards an 'illusory and false' forgiveness; such a gesture would have been 'a therapy of forgetting,' a 'healing away' that has nothing to do with pure forgiveness but rather is 'a sort of narcissism, reparation and self-reparation, a healing that re-narcissizes,'[95] terms in which I actually analysed Mozes Kor's gesture throughout this chapter.

Raveling's gesture can be put in parallel with Hubert Markl's request for forgiveness mentioned previously. At the time Dr. Mengele was conducting experiments at Auschwitz, Markl was a child. In spite of being innocent of the Nazi crimes, he did ask for forgiveness from Mengele's victims. Similarly to Jankélévitch, the twins did not grant him that forgiveness. It was only Mozes Kor who asserted that she had already forgiven all the perpetrators.

While Jankélévitch feels too old to inaugurate a new era, Mozes Kor's forgiveness seems a venture in this direction. Despite her motives and self-centred approach, Kor's forgiveness gives us hope in a new age: that of an *arrivant* that 'surprises, like a revolution, the ordinary course of history, politics, and law.'[96] In her *Hatred and Forgiveness*, Julia Kristeva has invoked tragedies of the twentieth and twenty-first centuries—God's martyrdom in Auschwitz, the Gulag, the planes that crashed into the Twin Towers in New York—and asserted that there are only two solutions to counteract the hatred and violence surrounding us in our days: love or forgiveness.[97] From the two, Mozes Kor preferred the latter, which for Kristeva is 'the only possible alternative to hatred that can still heal our world.' Through forgiveness, she argues, 'time for vengeance is suspended, allowing a rebirth for men, always already petrified by hate.'[98] Unlike Jankélévitch, Mozes Kor did not wait for the change of generations but came up with her solution on the fiftieth anniversary of the liberation of Auschwitz. Dr. Münch's daughter, son and granddaughter as well as Mozes Kor's children, thus second and third generations of victims and perpetrators, attended the event.

Mozes Kor remained committed to testimony as a medium of forgiving and healing until the end of her life on 4 July 2019.[99] She died at the venerable age of eighty-five in Krakow while literally testifying: she was accompanying a CANDLES delegation on the annual educational trip to Auschwitz.[100]

In his own turn, in *Forgiving Dr Mengele*, Alex Kor, her son, refrains from commenting on whether he himself has forgiven Dr. Mengele and the Nazis for having killed his grandparents and aunts. He simply mentions the duty of the new generations to let the world know what happened. This may mean that after Mozes Kor's death the time for pure, unconditional forgiveness with its supreme healing effects has not yet come.

NOTES

1. See Vladimir Jankélévitch, *Forgiveness*, trans. Andrew Kelley (Chicago and London: University of Chicago Press, 2005), 141–42.
2. Jankélévitch used the apophatic method to describe 'pure' forgiveness. 'Apophatic' (coming from the Greek ἀποφατικός, 'negative') is generally employed in theology to refer to 'knowledge of God obtained by way of negation.' (*Oxford English Dictionary*, 2nd ed. on CD-ROM (v. 4.0.0.2), Oxford: Oxford University Press, 2009).
3. Martha C. Nussbaum, *Anger and Forgiveness: Resentment, Generosity, Justice* (Oxford: Oxford University Press, 2016), 60.
4. Aaron T. Looney, *Vladimir Jankélévitch: The Time of Forgiveness* (New York: Fordham University Press, 2015), 10.
5. Jankélévitch, *Forgiveness*, 119.
6. Looney, *Vladimir Jankélévitch*, 68.
7. See Jankélévitch, *Forgiveness*, 3–4.
8. Vladimir Jankélévitch and Béatrice Berlowitz, *Quelque part dans l'inachevé* (Paris: Gallimard, 1978), 129, translated by Looney in *Vladimir Jankélévitch*, 162.
9. 1971, originally published in *Le Monde* (January 3, 1965).
10. Looney, *Vladimir Jankélévitch*, 90.
11. Jankélévitch, *Forgiveness*, 48–49.
12. Griswold, Charles L., *Forgiveness: A Philosophical Exploration* (Cambridge: Cambridge University Press, 2007), 149–50.
13. Vladimir Jankélévitch, 'Should We Pardon Them?,' trans. Ann Hobart, *Critical Inquiry* 22.3 (Spring 1996): 567. Cf. Jankélévitch, *Forgiveness*, 157.
14. Looney, *Vladimir Jankélévitch*, 9.
15. Looney, *Vladimir Jankélévitch*, 51.
16. Jankélévitch, 'Should We Pardon Them?,' 558.
17. Jankélévitch, 'Should We Pardon Them?,' 563.
18. Jankélévitch, 'Should We Pardon Them?,' 565.
19. Jankélévitch, 'Should We Pardon Them?,' 556 and 565.
20. Jankélévitch, 'Should We Pardon Them?,' 567, translation modified. The term the translator used is 'pardoning.'
21. 'Never shall I forget those moments which murdered my God and my soul and turned my dreams to ashes.' See Elie Wiesel, *Night*, trans. Marion Wiesel (London: Penguin, 2006), 34.
22. Levinas, quoted in Stéphane Mosès, 'Emmanuel Levinas: Ethics as Primary Meaning,' trans. Gabriel Motzkin, in *Emmanuel Levinas: Critical Assessments of Leading Philosophers*, eds. Claire Katz and Lara Trout, vol. 1: *Levinas, Phenomenology and His Critics* (London and New York: Routledge, 2005), 335.
23. Jankelevitch, 'Should We Pardon Them?,' 558.

24. Hannah Arendt, *Responsibility and Judgement*, ed. and Intro. Jerome Kohn (New York: Schoken Books, 2003), 23.

25. Hannah Arendt and Karl Jaspers, *Correspondence, 1926–1969*, ed. Lotte Kohler and Hans Saner, trans. Robert and Rita Kimber (New York: Harcourt Brace & Co., 1992), 166.

26. Hannah Arendt, *The Origins of Totalitarianism*, new ed. (San Diego: Harcourt Brace and Company, 1979), 447.

27. Arendt, *The Origins of Totalitarianism*, 451.

28. See Hannah Arendt, *Eichmann in Jerusalem: A Report on the Banality of Evil* (New York: Penguin, 1994).

29. Hannah Arendt, *The Human Condition* (Chicago: University of Chicago Press, 1958), 212–13.

30. See Levinas's counterarguments against considering ontology as 'first philosophy,' since ontology is 'a philosophy of power' that does not call into question the same,' hence 'a philosophy of injustice.' *Totality and Infinity: An Essay on Exteriority*, trans. Alphonso Lingis (Pittsburgh, PA: Duquesne University Press, 1969), 46.

31. See Jankélévitch, *Cours de philosophie morale. Université libre de Bruxelles 1962–1963* (Paris: Éditions du Seuil, 2006), 43 and Levinas's definitions of ethics from *Totality and Infinity*, 304.

32. John Llewelyn, *Emmanuel Levinas: The Genealogy of Ethics* (London and New York: Routledge, 2005), 99.

33. Levinas, *Totality and Infinity*, 244, italics in the original.

34. The Other means in phenomenology the other human being, the counterpart entity that can define the self.

35. See Levinas, *Totality and Infinity*, 246.

36. Levinas, *Totality and Infinity*, 281–85.

37. See Llewelyn, *Emmanuel Levinas*, 122.

38. Llewelyn, *Emmanuel Levinas*, 122.

39. Emmanuel Levinas, 'The Ego and the Totality,' trans. A. Lingis, in *Collected Philosophical Papers* (Dordrecht: Martinus Nijhoff, 1987), 33. For a definition of *le tiers*, see Robert Bernasconi, 'The Third Party: Levinas on the Intersection of the Ethical and the Political,' in *Emmanuel Levinas: Critical Assessments of Leading Philosophers*, ed. Claire Katz with Lara Trout, vol. 1: *Levinas, Phenomenology and His Critics* (London and New York: Routledge, 2005), 45.

40. See Arleen Ionescu, *The Memorial Ethics of Libeskind's Jewish Museum* (London: Palgrave Macmillan, 2017), 15–16.

41. Michael L. Morgan, *Discovering Levinas* (Cambridge: Cambridge University Press, 2007), 36.

42. Levinas, *Nine Talmudic Readings*, trans. Annette Aronowicz (Bloomington: Indiana University Press, 1990), 25. See also my analysis of this fragment in *Memorial Ethics*, 16.

43. See Looney, *Vladimir Jankélévitch*, 9.

44. Jacques Derrida, 'To Forgive: The Unforgivable and the Imprescriptible,' in *Questioning God*, eds. John D. Caputo, Mark Dooley and Michael J. Scanlon (Bloomington and Indianapolis: Indiana University Press, 2001), 28, tenses modified.

45. Jankélévitch, *Forgiveness*, 157.

46. Derrida, 'To Forgive,' 27.

47. Derrida, 'To Forgive,' 34.

48. Jacques Derrida, 'On Forgiveness,' in *On Cosmopolitanism and Forgiveness*, trans. Mark Dooley and Michael Hughes, preface by Simon Critchley and Richard Kearney (London and New York: Routledge, 2005), 32.

49. See Jacques Derrida, *Given Time: I. Counterfeit Money*, trans. by Peggy Kamuf (Chicago and London: University of Chicago Press, 1992); Jacques Derrida, 'Hostipitality,' trans. Barry Stocker and Forbes Morlock, *Angelaki: Journal of the Theoretical Humanities* 5.3 (2000): 1–18 and *Of Hospitality, Anne Dufourmantelle Invites Jacques Derrida to Respond*, trans. Rachel Bowlby (Stanford, CA: Stanford University Press, 2000).

50. Derrida, 'On Forgiveness,' 45.

51. Derrida, 'On Forgiveness,' 49.

52. Looney, *Vladimir Jankélévitch*, 175.

53. Michal Ben-Naftali, *An Interview with Professor Jacques Derrida*, trans. Moshe Ron, Shoah Resource Center, The International School for Holocaust Studies, The Multimedia CD 'Eclipse of Humanity,' Jerusalem: Yad Vashem, 2000, 17.

54. Derrida, 'To Forgive,' 33.

55. Derrida, 'On Forgiveness,' 59.

56. Derrida, 'On Forgiveness,' 48. This echoes Jean-François Lyotard's sense of what would remain as a 'differend' otherwise, in *The Differend: Phrases in Dispute*, trans. Georges Van Den Abbeele (Manchester: Manchester University Press, 1988).

57. Derrida, 'On Forgiveness,' 48.

58. Derrida, 'On Forgiveness,' 49.

59. Jacques Derrida, 'Hostipitality,' in *Acts of Religion*, ed. and Intro. Gil Anidjar (New York: Routledge, 2002), 398.

60. Derrida, 'Hostipitality,' 398.

61. *Forgiving Doctor Mengele*. A film by Cheri Pugh and Bob Hercules, First Run Features, 2005. The quotations that follow within the text under the abbreviation *FDM* have been transcribed from the documentary. Eva Mozes Kor and Lisa Rojani Buccieri, *Surviving the Angel of Death: The True Story of a Mengele Twin in Auschwitz* (Terre Haute, IN: Tanglewood, 2011). Hereafter abbreviated as *SAD*, with page numbers in the text. For reasons of space, this chapter does not cover other more recent films featuring Eva Mozes Kor: the CNN documentaries *Voices of Auschwitz* (2015) and *Incredible Survivors* (2016); the documentary *The Girl Who Forgave the Nazis* (2016), which explores her meeting with Oskar Gröning; and *Eva*, a documentary by Ted Green Films and WFYI Indianapolis (2018).

62. Peter Banki, *The Forgiveness to Come: The Holocaust and the Hyper-Ethical* (New York: Fordham University Press, 2018), 10.

63. See Giorgio Agamben, *Remnants of Auschwitz: The Witness and the Archive* (New York: Zone Books, 1999), 87–136; and Ruth Leys, *From Guilt to Shame: Auschwitz and After* (Princeton, NJ: Princeton University Press, 2007).

64. The survivors and 'others with firsthand knowledge of Mengele's activities' gathered at Yad Vashem in 1995 where they were questioned 'in a trial-like manner'

by a panel on what happened. Some of the testimonies were translated into English and published in Michael A. Grodin, Eva Mozes Kor and Susan Benedict, 'The Trial that Never Happened: Josef Mengele and the Twins of Auschwitz,' *War Crimes, Genocide and Crimes against Humanity* 5 (2011): 3–89.

65. We should also recall that 1995 was the year when the Truth and Reconciliation Commission in South Africa was set up with the purpose of addressing the issue of human rights violations that had been perpetrated during the years of apartheid rule. Victims gave statements about the ordeals they experienced, and perpetrators requested amnesty from both civil and criminal prosecution. Such practices raised two different approaches to forgiveness: political amnesty, handled by the state, and interpersonal forgiveness in interpersonal contexts. The setting up of TRC came at a time when it became 'useful to consider the intrapsychic processes that may operate when individuals confront the question of whether to forgive on behalf of a family member who was killed, disabled or disappeared. See Fathima Moosa, Gill Straker and Gill Eagle, 'In the Aftermath of Political Trauma: What Price Forgiveness?,' in *Forgiveness and the Healing Process: A Central Therapeutic Concern*, eds. Cynthia Ransley and Terri Spy (Hove and New York: Brunner-Routledge, 2004), 135.

66. Kenneth McCall quoted in David Watson, *Fear No Evil* (London: Hodder and Stoughton, 1984), 149.

67. *Yoma 8:9, Mishnah*, quoted in Harriet Kaufman, *Judaism and Social Justice* (Cincinnati, OH: Kaufman House Publishers, 1986), 30.

68. This summary of the ritual of forgiveness is based on Cynthia Ransley, 'Forgiveness: Themes and Issues,' in *Forgiveness and the Healing Process: A Central Therapeutic Concern*, eds. Cynthia Ransley and Terri Spy, 13.

69. Derrida, 'On Forgiveness,' 44.

70. I would like to thank Peter Banki for this suggestion in an earlier draft of this chapter. In his volume *The Forgiveness to Come*, Banki includes a detailed analysis of Wiesenthal's *Sunflower* from this perspective (20–48).

71. For instance, his friend Josek explained: 'You would have had no right to do this in the name of people who had not authorized you to do so. What people have done to you yourself, you can, if you like, forgive and forget. That is your own affair. But it would have been a terrible sin to burden your conscience with other people's sufferings'; 'I believe in Haolam Emes—in life after death, in another, better world, where we will all meet again after we are dead. How would it seem then if you had forgiven him? Would not the dead people from Dnepropetrovsk come to you and ask: 'Who gave you the right to forgive our murderer?.' Simon Wiesenthal, *The Sunflower: On the Possibilities and Limits of Forgiveness*, with a symposium edited by Harry James and Bonny V. Fetterman (New York: Schocken Books, 2008), 60, 62.

72. Wiesenthal, *The Sunflower*, 86.

73. Levinas, 'The Ego and the Totality,' 33.

74. Banki, *The Forgiveness to Come*, 12.

75. J. L. Austin, 'Performative—Constative,' in *The Philosophy of Language*, ed. J. R. Searle (Oxford: Oxford University Press, 1971), 13.

76. Looney, *Vladimir Jankélévitch*, 189.

77. Austin, 'Performative—Constative,' 13.

78. J. L. Austin, *How to Do Things with Words* (Cambridge, MA: Harvard University Press, 1962), 16.

79. See Austin, *How to Do Things with Words*, 60–62.

80. Ego psychology was a school of psychoanalysis rooted in Freud's structural model of id-ego-superego that was chiefly concerned with personality. With Anna Freud's discovery that the ego supervises and opposes the id through defensive functions (see *Ego and the Mechanisms of Defense*), Henz Hartmann, David Rapaport, René Spitz, Margaret Mahler, Edith Jacobson and Erik Erikson attempted to explain human behaviour through a psychoanalysis that was based in general psychology.

81. For an exploration of emotional forgiveness see Richard Fitzgibbons, 'Anger and the Healing Power of Forgiveness: A Psychiatrist's View,' in *Exploring Forgiveness*, eds. Robert D. Enright and Joanna North (Madison: University of Wisconsin Press, 1988), 67.

82. Werner Bohleber, 'Treatment, Trauma and Catastrophic Reality,' in *Psychoanalysis and Holocaust Testimony: Unwanted Memories of Social Trauma*, eds. Dori Laub and Andreas Hamburger (London and New York: Routledge, 2017), 23.

83. Bohleber, 'Treatment, Trauma and Catastrophic Reality,' 23.

84. 'Organizing' in camp language meant 'stealing from the Nazis' (*SAD*, 48).

85. Her son testifies that during the ceremony she was also challenged by a reporter to forgive Dr. Mengele, which according to him brought about the whole process of forgiveness (*FDM* 37.14–23). It is unclear how she changed her letter of forgiveness to Dr. Hans Münch into a declaration of amnesty to all the Nazis. She claimed that she had thought about forgiving Dr. Mengele, but the film seems to indicate she changed the declaration on the spot. The speed with which she turned a letter of forgiveness into a public declaration of amnesty suggests further that there was no 'working through' as defined psychoanalytically, but rather a deep sense of coming to terms with it all.

86. Banki, *The Forgiveness to Come*, 12.

87. Restorative justice is meant to bring about the reconciliation of victims and the community at large with offenders.

88. Howard Zehr, *Changing Lenses: A New Focus for Crime and Justice* (Ontario: Herald Press, 1990), 47. For an analysis on the dyadic forgiveness, see Marilyn Armour and Mark S. Umbreit, *Violence, Restorative Justice and Forgiveness: Dyadic Forgiveness and Energy Shifts in Restorative Justice Dialogue* (London and Philadelphia: Jessica Kingsley Publishers, 2018).

89. Derrida, 'On Forgiveness,' 58.

90. Derrida, 'On Forgiveness,' 58.

91. Derrida, 'To Forgive,' 41.

92. Wiard Raveling, 'Lettre de Wiard Raveling' (June 1980), in *Magazine Littéraire* 333 (June 1995), 53. Fragments from the letter are reproduced here with the English translation provided in Derrida, 'To Forgive.'

93. Raveling, 'Lettre de Wiard Raveling,' 53.

94. Jankélévitch, quoted in Derrida, 'To Forgive,' 40.

95. Derrida, 'To Forgive,' 41. I would add that the gesture would have also meant a way of appropriating liberal humanism, a commitment to man, the subject that has become free in his pursuit of happiness, which Derrida criticized in *Specters of Marx*.

See Jacques Derrida, *Specters of Marx: The State of the Debt, the Work of Mourning and the New International*, trans. Peggy Kamuf, Intro. Bernd Magnus and Stephen Cullenberg (New York and London: Routledge, 1994), especially 70–71.

96. Derrida, 'On Forgiveness,' 39.

97. Julia Kristeva, *Hatred and Forgiveness*, trans. Jeanine Herman (New York: Columbia University Press, 2005), 222.

98. Kristeva, *Hatred and Forgiveness*, 192.

99. While the writing of this chapter was in process, Mozes Kor was still lecturing and travelling round the globe to share her Auschwitz experience. Her death came before the final revision stage of the present chapter.

100. BBC Radio 4 featured the obituary programme *Last Word* dedicated to Mozes Kor on 12 July 2019.

BIBLIOGRAPHY

AGAMBEN, Giorgio. *Remnants of Auschwitz: The Witness and the Archive*. New York: Zone Books, 1999.

ARENDT, Hannah. *Eichmann in Jerusalem: A Report on the Banality of Evil*. New York: Penguin, 1994.

ARENDT, Hannah. *The Human Condition.* Chicago: University of Chicago Press, 1958.

ARENDT, Hannah. *The Origins of Totalitarianism*. New Edition. San Diego: Harcourt Brace & Company, 1979.

ARENDT, Hannah. *Responsibility and Judgement*. Edited and Introduction by Jerome Kohn. New York: Schoken Books, 2003.

ARENDT, Hannah and Karl Jaspers. *Correspondence, 1926–1969*. Edited by Lotte Kohler and Hans Saner. Translated by Robert and Rita Kimber. New York: Harcourt Brace & Co., 1992.

ARMOUR, Marilyn and Mark S. Umbreit. *Violence, Restorative Justice and Forgiveness: Dyadic Forgiveness and Energy Shifts in Restorative Justice Dialogue*. London and Philadelphia: Jessica Kingsley Publishers, 2018.

AUSTIN, J. L. *How to Do Things with Words.* Cambridge, MA: Harvard University Press, 1962.

AUSTIN, J. L. 'Performative—Constative.' In *The Philosophy of Language*. Edited by J. R. Searle. 13–22. Oxford: Oxford University Press, 1971.

BANKI, Peter. *The Forgiveness to Come: The Holocaust and the Hyper-Ethical*. New York: Fordham University Press, 2018.

BEN-NAFTALI, Michal. *An Interview with Professor Jacques Derrida*. Translated by Moshe Ron. 1–29. Shoah Resource Center. The International School for Holocaust Studies, The Multimedia CD 'Eclipse of Humanity.' Jerusalem: Yad Vashem, 2000.

BERNASCONI, Robert. 'The Third Party: Levinas on the Intersection of the Ethical and the Political.' In *Emmanuel Levinas: Critical Assessments of Leading Philosophers.* Edited by Claire Katz with Lara Trout. Volume 1: *Levinas, Phenomenology and His Critics*. 45–57. London and New York: Routledge, 2005.

BOHLEBER, Werner. 'Treatment, Trauma and Catastrophic Reality.' In *Psycho-analysis and Holocaust Testimony: Unwanted Memories of Social Trauma*. Edited by Dori Laub and Andreas Hamburger. 19–31. London and New York: Routledge, 2017.

DERRIDA, Jacques. *Given Time: I. Counterfeit Money*. Translated by Peggy Kamuf. Chicago and London: University of Chicago Press, 1992.

DERRIDA, Jacques. 'Hostipitality.' In *Acts of Religion*. Edited and Introduction by Gil Anidjar. New York: Routledge, 2002.

DERRIDA, Jacques. 'Hostipitality.' Translated by Barry Stocker and Forbes Mor-lock. *Angelaki: Journal of the Theoretical Humanities* 5.3 (2000): 1–18.

DERRIDA, Jacques. *Of Hospitality, Anne Dufourmantelle Invites Jacques Derrida to Respond*. Translated by Rachel Bowlby. Stanford, CA: Stanford University Press, 2000.

DERRIDA, Jacques. 'On Forgiveness.' In *On Cosmopolitanism and Forgiveness*. Translated by Mark Dooley and Michael Hughes. Preface by Simon Critchley and Richard Kearney. 27–60. London and New York: Routledge, 2005.

DERRIDA, Jacques. *Specters of Marx: The State of the Debt, the Work of Mourning and the New International*. Translated by Peggy Kamuf. Introduction by Bernd Magnus and Stephen Cullenberg. New York and London: Routledge, 1994.

DERRIDA, Jacques. 'To Forgive: The Unforgivable and the Imprescriptible.' In *Questioning God*. Edited by John D. Caputo, Mark Dooley and Michael J. Scanlon. Bloomington and Indianapolis: Indiana University Press, 2001.

FITZGIBBONS, Richard. 'Anger and the Healing Power of Forgiveness: A Psychia-trist's View.' In *Exploring Forgiveness*. Edited by Robert D. Enright and Joanna North. 63–74. Madison: University of Wisconsin Press, 1988.

Forgiving Dr Mengele. A Film by Cheri Pugh and Bob Hercules, First Run Features, 2005.

GRISWOLD, Charles L. *Forgiveness: A Philosophical Exploration*. Cambridge: Cambridge University Press, 2007.

GRODIN, Michael A., Eva Mozes Kor and Susan Benedict. 'The Trial that Never Happened: Josef Mengele and the Twins of Auschwitz.' *War Crimes, Genocide and Crimes against Humanity* 5 (2011): 3–89.

IONESCU, Arleen. *The Memorial Ethics of Libeskind's Jewish Museum*. London: Palgrave Macmillan, 2017.

JANKÉLÉVITCH, Vladimir. *Cours de philosophie morale. Université libre de Brux-elles 1962–1963*. Paris: Éditions du Seuil, 2006.

JANKÉLÉVITCH, Vladimir. *Forgiveness*. Translated by Andrew Kelley. Chicago and London: University of Chicago Press, 2005.

JANKÉLÉVITCH, Vladimir. 'Should We Pardon Them?.' Translated by Ann Ho-bart. *Critical Inquiry* 22.3 (Spring 1996): 552–72.

JANKÉLÉVITCH, Vladimir and Béatrice Berlowitz. *Quelque part dans l'inachevé*. Paris: Gallimard, 1978.

KAUFMAN, Harriet. *Judaism and Social Justice*. Cincinnati: Kaufman House Pub-lishers, 1986.

KRISTEVA, Julia. *Hatred and Forgiveness*. Translated by Jeanine Herman. New York: Columbia University Press, 2005.

LEVINAS, Emmanuel. 'The Ego and the Totality.' Translated by A. Lingis. In *Collected Philosophical Papers*. 25–45. Dordrecht: Martinus Nijhoff, 1987.

LEVINAS, Emmanuel. *Nine Talmudic Readings*. Translated by Annette Aronowicz. Bloomington: Indiana University Press, 1990.

LEVINAS, Emmanuel. *Totality and Infinity: An Essay on Exteriority*. Translated by Alphonso Lingis. Pittsburgh, PA: Duquesne University Press, 1969.

LEYS, Ruth. *From Guilt to Shame: Auschwitz and After*. Princeton, NJ: Princeton University Press, 2007.

LLEWELYN, John. *Emmanuel Levinas: The Genealogy of Ethics*. London and New York: Routledge, 2005.

LOONEY, Aaron T. *Vladimir Jankélévitch: The Time of Forgiveness*. New York: Fordham University Press, 2015.

LYOTARD, Jean-François. *The Differend: Phrases in Dispute*. Translated by Georges Van Den Abbeele. Manchester: Manchester University Press, 1988.

MOOSA, Fathima, Gill Straker and Gill Eagle. 'In the Aftermath of Political Trauma: What Price Forgiveness?.' In *Forgiveness and the Healing Process: A Central Therapeutic Concern*. Edited by Cynthia Ransley and Terri Spy. 128–50. Hove and New York: Brunner-Routledge, 2004.

MORGAN, Michael L. *Discovering Levinas*. Cambridge: Cambridge University Press, 2007.

MOSÈS, Stéphane. 'Emmanuel Levinas: Ethics as Primary Meaning.' Translated by Gabriel Motzkin. In *Emmanuel Levinas: Critical Assessments of Leading Philosophers*. Edited by Claire Katz and Lara Trout. Volume 1: *Levinas, Phenomenology and His Critics*. 326–36. London and New York: Routledge, 2005.

MOZES KOR, Eva and Lisa Rojani Buccieri. *Surviving the Angel of Death: The True Story of a Mengele Twin in Auschwitz*. Terre Haute, IN: Tanglewood, 2011.

NUSSBAUM, Martha C. *Anger and Forgiveness: Resentment, Generosity, Justice*. Oxford: Oxford University Press, 2016.

RANSLEY, Cynthia. 'Forgiveness: Themes and Issues.' In *Forgiveness and the Healing Process: A Central Therapeutic Concern*. Edited by Cynthia Ransley and Terri Spy. 10–32. Hove and New York: Brunner-Routledge, 2004.

RAVELING, Wiard. 'Lettre de Wiard Raveling' (June 1980). *Magazine Littéraire* 333 (June 1995): 51–8.

WATSON, David. *Fear No Evil*. London: Hodder and Stoughton, 1984.

WIESEL, Elie. *Night*. Translated by Marion Wiesel. London: Penguin, 2006.

WIESENTHAL, Simon. *The Sunflower: On the Possibilities and Limits of Forgiveness*. With a symposium edited by Harry James and Bonny V. Fetterman. New York: Schocken Books, 2008.

ZEHR, Howard. *Changing Lenses: A New Focus for Crime and Justice*. Ontario: Herald Press, 1990.

Chapter Three

(Mis)Representing Trauma through Humour?

Roberto Benigni's La vita è bella

Lucia Ispas

SHUSHING THE SHOAH

The Holocaust represents not only one of the most tragic events of the twentieth century but also of the history of mankind, an unfathomable catastrophic episode that produced trauma. In the years since, the world has endeavoured to find a way to contemplate its profound implications and to explain the unexplainable. The long debate on whether it might be appropriate or not to represent the Shoah in narratives or films originated, on the one hand, from the assumption that representing the horrors survivors were exposed to would be equivalent to re-enacting the tragedy over and over again and, on the other hand, from the belief that words cannot describe events as they actually happened. Primo Levi, for example, believed that one cannot adequately portray authentic horror and made it clear on numerous occasions that the witnesses need to describe the 'tragic world of Auschwitz' assuming 'the calm, sober language of the witness, neither the lamenting tones of the victim nor the irate voice of someone who seeks revenge,'[1] while Elie Wiesel doubted the possibility of translating the implications of the catastrophe he went through, precisely because of the impossibility of rehabilitating and transforming words that were 'betrayed and perverted by the enemy.'[2] However, both Levi and Wiesel left us testimonies of their ordeals in the concentration camps, since for survivors, telling the story of what happened becomes a duty originating from the imperative, 'Do not forget!'

If the reservations against approaching the Shoah in art or literature have been abandoned, consensus seems not to have been reached on how to represent it. Since 'the Holocaust transgresses our categories and therefore no description can do justice to it,'[3] writers, visual artists and film producers alike need to find the most appropriate and meaningful way to bear witness (to

communicate a traumatic experience, to process it, to obtain empathy and ca-
tharsis). The traumatic experience of the Holocaust must be communicated,[4]
because, as Giorgio Agamben has shown, '[r]emembrance is impossible but
imperative.'[5]

Since this chapter focuses on a film, I will start with Judith E. Doneson,
a world authority on Holocaust motion pictures, who has proclaimed the
supremacy of the film over other forms of art, since it is a means of visually
expressing the unimaginable, acknowledging its potential to educate, 'albeit
often in an attenuated manner.'[6] An image is more powerful than words; thus
the film becomes a privileged medium of representation. Drawing on the
recurrent comparison of the Holocaust with Medusa, the monstrous creature
who turned to stone anyone risking to gaze at her, Siegfried Kracauer argues
that 'the film screen is Athena's polished shield,'[7] the mirrored shield that
allowed Perseus to look at (and kill) Medusa without directly meeting her
gaze. This view, based on the metaphor of the indirect power that the arts
have, is shared by Ilan Avisar, who considers film to have primacy over
literature in its quest for realism. He sees the photographic image as being 'a better means of objective representation' with 'a stronger immediate
and sensuous impact on the viewer.'[8] In her own turn, the reputed memory
studies scholar Alison Landsberg argues that films play the most important
part in forming 'prosthetic memory,' a form of memory that 'teaches ethical
thinking by fostering empathy.'[9] Unlike history, memories are based on a
subjective relationship with the past. They are not a natural product derived
from a direct experience but from a mediated one, similar to watching a
movie. Images appropriately mediate the transfer of events into history;
moreover, motion pictures are an accurate instrument that faithfully provides
a much-needed insight.

In more than seventy years after WW2, there have been thousands of films
about the Shoah, some dealing with purely historical facts,[10] others being
dramatic representations with an ironic twist.[11] This chapter will focus on a
more unusual representation of the Shoah, Roberto Benigni's production *La
vita è bella* (*Life Is Beautiful*), which has caused a real maëlstrom since 1997
when it was released, because the audience was shaken, overwhelmed by the
humorous way in which the director chose to tell his story. There is an apparent fracture between the two parts of the film. Part I is dominated by laughter,
Part II is centred around a tragicomedy of games and impossible riddles. Both
facets of the protagonist, Guido, seem far from the common idea of a hero:
on the one hand, the peculiar picaresque Prince Charming fighting against
villains (especially against Dora's fiancé) in order to rescue Dora, his chosen
one, from a lifetime of marital imprisonment; on the other hand, Giosuè's
father, desperate to protect his only child by concealing the true genocidal

nature of the camp. The ebullient waiter in the first part turns into the loving husband and father in the second one, in which he protects his son in the
concentration camp where they were sent by playing a role, putting on a mask
of a funny face for Giosuè even when his physical pain is excruciating. Such
features are admittedly representative of the *hoi polloi*, the quintessence of
an anti-hero, a Kafkaesque/Chaplinesque figure. Yet, he acquires, through his
actions, the status of an authentic heroic character, at a time when 'the heroes
become less and less fabulous.'[12]

THE DUCKLING OR THE PLATYPUS

The title of this section is the answer to a riddle that one of the characters,
Dr. Lessing, is preoccupied with. Dr. Lessing, who in the first part is a guest
in Guido's hotel and in the second part a cruel Nazi who is in charge of the
selections, is seen quite obsessed with solving a hard riddle that reads: 'Fat
fat, ugly ugly, all yellow in reality. If you ask me what I am I answer "cheep
cheep cheep." Walking along I go "poopoo," who am I, tell me true?' The
two possible answers he comes up with, 'the duckling or the platypus,' are
actually both incorrect. As Benigni himself pointed out, the riddle simply has
no answer. 'The duckling or the platypus' means nothing. This section, which
covers the reception of the film, takes this emblematic title with the aim of
demonstrating the irrationality of several of the arguments put forward by
Benigni's detractors.

Life Is Beautiful has garnered many awards and prizes. It was nominated
for seven Academy Awards, winning three Oscars, including one for Best
Actor. At the Cannes Film Festival in 1998, it won the Grand Prize of the
Jury. It vexed and fascinated at the same time, thus separating the world
of critics and viewers into two irreconcilable parties: on the one hand, the
'highbrow' who have objected to its mystifying the truth, its irreverence, callousness, sentimentalism and humour; on the other, the 'lowbrow' who have
lionized Benigni.

His critics attacked his audacious attempt to re-write the bl(e)ackest page
in recent history, an attempt seen by many as a form of Holocaust denial, a
blasphemy or a way 'to wash Europe's hands, the hands of Christian civiliza-
tion, clean of the Jewish blood it spilled during World War II.'[13] Appalled by
Benigni's production, Art Spiegelman, who created an infamous caricature
depicting a prisoner holding an Oscar in a death camp, described the film in
virulent terms: '[I]f you can keep your sense of humour you can even survive
a bummer. And the Holocaust is just a metaphor for a bummer.'[14] After winning the Oscar, *Life Is Beautiful* was regarded as 'soothing and anodyne—a

hopeful fable of redemption' that proved that 'the audience is exhausted by the Holocaust, that it is sick to death of the subject's unending ability to disturb,' a mood that was understandable for the audience, but not for an artist who, in spite of knowing that a young child entering Auschwitz would have been immediately gassed, ignored that and protected his audience 'as much as Guido protects his son.'[15] My contention is that Benigni does not sugar-coat a painful episode in history; moreover, he does not trivialize the Holocaust but merely dresses his dramatic story in a clownish outfit that does not disguise horror but, paradoxically, emphasizes it.

Kobi Niv believed that Benigni showed 'the audience just a small part, a very particular doctored, cute little *frame* out of the whole picture, and he thus creates in them the impression that his fake reality is in fact what took place in the death camps and, by implication, what happened to the Jews in the Holocaust.'[16] However, no piece of art could dare capture and present the whole magnitude of such a catastrophe. Ilan Avisar has argued that any treatment of the Holocaust must commemorate the sufferings of the victims with dignity and compassion and understand the monumental injustice inflicted on the Jewish people.[17] On my reading, *Life Is Beautiful* pays homage to the victims by producing an emotional response to their situation and suffering.

The most controversial and highly criticized element of the film was Benigni's humorous approach to such a difficult topic as the Holocaust. 'Benigni's irreverent combination of slapstick gags and filial melodrama elicited more vituperative condemnations because he eschewed any pretext of realism and found humour in the dire circumstances of a concentration camp.'[18] Benigni's untainted humour was at the same time praised by others, since Guido was associated with a Charlie Chaplin whose humour has been recognized as equally subversive and critical of the dehumanization brought about by technology and capitalism. Similarly to Chaplin's sketches, Guido's humorous approach does not pacify or tame the camp conditions but exposes them in all their ruthlessness and absurdity. Guido's humour can be seen as a way of resistance against an absurd yet strong enemy.[19]

Abandoning any reservations about the film, some scholars were won by the way in which, almost invisibly, the comedy mingled with the sweetness of a modern fairy tale, creating a delicate framework for the buffoonish actions of a Don Quixotesque Prince Charming caught between the love for his wife and child and the unseen, yet extremely present, horror of mass murders in a lager. Gilbert Adair, for instance, commented that he dreaded the very idea of 'a comedy about the Holocaust' but admitted:

> so powerful is humour as an agent of transgressive subversion, so uncontrollably instinctive is a belly laugh, that in spite of all my misgivings I capitulated to the film. As Spielberg demonstrated, to make audiences cry at a Holocaust

movie is child's play. But to make them laugh! That takes both talent . . . and some sort of foolhardy genius. . . . That it has absolutely no pretension to re-creating the realities of the camps is precisely the grandeur, not the weakness, of Benigni's film.[20]

Gefen Bar-on in her own turn argued: '[T]o condemn *La Vita è Bella* on the basis of its alteration of the facts is to assume that art's role in relation to history is to document, to give a human face to events in order to inform the public about them.'[21]

Although this section cannot fully cover the debates around Benigni's par-adoxical approach to the Holocaust, the views presented above are sufficient to demonstrate the centrality of humour in these debates. If for Benigni's fierce critics bringing laughter into the context of such a tragedy meant a presumptuous, offending and unforgivable gesture, for the ones who were readier to go along with Benigni's invention of tricksters, riddles and fun, humour was perceived as acquiring a therapeutic function. In what follows, this is precisely what this chapter aims to point out.

LAUGHING WITH THE LIZARDS

In an account on the use of humour in Holocaust films, Justin Geldzahler discusses Benigni's film and quotes Henry Eilbert's words from *What Is a Jewish Joke?*. Eilbert had classified Jewish humour as 'bitter' and 'ironic,' a sort of combination between laughing and crying which can be traced back to a common Yiddish phrase identified as *lachen mit yashtsherkes*, 'which means literally "laughing with the lizards" but is best translated as "laugh-ing through the tears."'[22] Perhaps 'laughing with the lizards' is the best way to describe Benigni's film, which in the second part presents a tragedy, but whose title would pass for that of a comedy.

In their *Historical Dictionary of the Holocaust Cinema*, Robert Reimer and Carol Reimer argued that Benigni's title may have been inspired by Leon Trotsky's final words before his execution: 'Life is beautiful. Let the future generations cleanse it of all evil, oppression and violence and enjoy it to the full.'[23] According to Maurizio Viano, at first glance 'the title has no apparent narrative justification, puzzles viewers, and forces them to ask questions. Be-nigni was certainly aware that, while nobody would recognize the reference to Trotsky, the title *Life Is Beautiful* would expose the film to further critical venom.'[24] This testifies to the fact that Benigni was conscious of the critique his choice of title would expose him to.

In *My Mother's Voice*: *Children, Literature, and the Holocaust*, Adrienne Kertzer thought the reference to Trotsky should be ignored, since Benigni repeatedly asserted that his film is based 'on his childhood memory of his father magically transforming war experience into reassuring and comic narrative for his children.'[25] Her own interpretation is that Benigni's title is reminiscent of a paradoxical assertion in Primo Levi's *Survival in Auschwitz* (the American title of the English *If This Is a Man*, which was initially published in Italian as *Se questo è un uomo*) that Benigni was familiar with: 'I was thinking that life was beautiful and would be beautiful again, and that it would really be a pity to let ourselves be overcome now.'[26] Benigni seems confident that, by the end of the film, the viewers' final thoughts will come to echo Guido's words, which give his son the chance to live: *dai, la vita è bella!*

Roberto Benigni was fully aware of the risks involved in producing and directing this controversial film, but had the courage to follow his own principles epitomized in the idea that 'fear can be mastered.'[27] As he declared, his main concern was not to offend the sensitivity of the survivors, as 'the Holocaust is still an open wound'; his intentions were 'not to *scandalize* it [the sensitivity of survivors], or *sensationalize* it':

> The feeling for the movie came to me. I didn't go fetch it. Like Rossini said, he was visited by ideas and creativity from heaven. The idea came to me. I hesitated, then threw myself into the idea. I am a megalomaniac in using beauty. You need courage in love. There was love there. The Holocaust occurred in a place in the imagination. It became an image of basic images.
>
> Now about comedy used in an extreme situation. In the first part and second part of the movie, the character is basically the same. But in the second part, the situation is extreme. There were risks involved.[28]

Benigni defined the film as a 'modern fairy-tale,'[29] which made Jeremy Maron think that 'the performance/reality dyad lends the film's fabulist historiography a logical explanation' and becomes a sort of 'historiographical method that transcends the filmic text.'[30] Benigni used thorough documentation, based on detailed readings of Holocaust texts (including Primo Levi's works),[31] and his father's accounts of his imprisonment in a work camp, as well as on talks with Holocaust survivors whose testimonies he indirectly employed methodically. He consulted historian Marcello Pezzetti and Shlomo Venezia, an Auschwitz survivor and a former member of the *Sonderkommando*.[32] He patterned the main character, Guido, after his own father, Luigi Benigni, who spent time in the Bergen-Belsen work camp between 1943 and 1945.[33] 'The hardships of a work camp cannot be compared to the devastation of a concentration camp,' Benigni said.[34] However, his father's almost obsessive need to talk about his traumatic experience was not very different from that of a concentration camp survivor.

The renowned psychoanalyst Cathy Caruth sees psychic trauma as a valuable model of history, because although the traumatic experience gets implanted directly in the psyche, it is never fully available to consciousness; therefore, to speak trauma out is to re-live an 'unclaimed experience,' an event one never truly experienced the first time around.[35] Analysing Freud's work, where he shows that the traumatic accident takes place too soon, too suddenly, too unexpectedly to be fully grasped by one's consciousness, and Lacan's work, where this peculiar accidentality, lying at the heart of Freud's notion of trauma, is linked to the larger philosophical significance of traumatic repetition, Caruth poses an intriguing question: 'Is it not remarkable that, at the origin of the analytic experience, the real should have presented itself in the form of that which is *unassimilable* in it—in the form of the trauma, determining all that follows, and imposing on it an apparently accidental origin?'[36] In the light of Caruth's theory, re-telling the story means re-living it. Benigni's father felt the urge to tell his story. Yet, if for him his firsthand experience was what Caruth has named 'unclaimed experience,' for his son, it became what Landsberg has called 'prosthetic memory.'[37] Benigni chose to represent his father's trauma in his film in an attempt that, to quote Dominick LaCapra's words on art in general, assesses the responsibility of art itself with respect to 'traumatic events that remain themselves invested with value and emotion.'[38] Unlike history, the memories presented in the film, based on the subjective account of Luigi Benigni's past, inherited and mediated by his son, carried in themselves 'a distorted, but bearable view of a horrific history. Life is only beautiful if memory allows for it to be constructed as such.'[39]

In Ruth Ben-Ghiat's opinion, the film forces its viewers to revisit their own anti-Semitism; it is also the indirect product of configurations of contemporary memory that function to obscure Italy's position as Germany's ally and an anti-Semitic state during WW2.[40] Echoing Ben-Ghiat's and Maurizio Viano's views, Tama Leaver remarked that the first half of the film attempted not to victimize Italians but rather to point out their complicity, which consisted of two attitudes: not opposing, and actively supporting Hitler's policies converging towards the Final Solution.[41] I agree with Leaver, since the viewer can see, for instance, how the town officials, prepared to hail and to applaud, welcomed whom they thought to be Nazi officers with a grotesque display of enthusiasm, even if, eventually, the car brought down the road two common people. The film shows how parents chose dictators' names to baptize their children (Adolpho or Benito), or how a third-grade math problem on the amount of money necessary to support epileptics and physically or mentally challenged people finds a shocking solution: the state would significantly save if these individuals were eliminated. It was precisely this way of thinking that germinated the Nazi ideology, centred around the utopian idea of the perfect man belonging to the Aryan race. The Nazis began to put their ideology into practice with the support of German scientists who believed that the human race could be improved by limiting the reproduction of people considered 'inferior,' mainly those belonging to what they considered 'the poisonous race' of the Jews. When Guido, impersonating a school inspector, is asked to demonstrate the superiority of the Aryan race, he insists on showing his navel to the children in class, pointing hereby to the irrationality of attributing to one specific ethnic group a superior position, as the phrase *l'ombelico del mondo* may suggest.[42]

THE COMEDIAN AS GIFT-BEARER

In one of his interviews, Benigni confessed: 'I had a strong desire to make the film. I had to make the film. This is a message to be heard to future generations. It tells a story, although I am just a comedian. It tells the story directly and precisely, but it is a gift from heaven. An act of love. A gift.'[43] Indeed, *Life Is Beautiful* can be centred on the theory of the gift, a gift that comes through the employment of humour that has a healing effect. If we focus on the possible gift-bearers the film brings into the foreground, we may identify a donor, a gift and a donée. The donor is Luigi Benigni, who represents the filmmaker's source of inspiration. Roberto Benigni's role in this triad is that of both a donée and a donor of the gift. In its own turn, the audience, the donée, is also given a Pandora's box, a fragile hope that life is beautiful. Finally, Guido is endowed with the attributes of a donor, offering his son the chance to live and to appreciate the beauty of life.

According to Ruth Ben-Ghiat, the film was based on the tension between family memory and public history, with Benigni practising a discourse of victimhood mixed with the culture of shame. Ex-prisoners, like Luigi Benigni, shut themselves off from the rest of the world and opened up only in a familiar environment, where confession was possible. In order to protect the innocent loved ones from trauma, he felt compelled to distort his story by re-telling it, employing humour and irony, becoming thus the initiator of the donation act. Sharing his experience, he offered himself and his family the *Tikkun olam* (in ancient Hebraic meaning 'repair of the world soul, good for the psyche'):

> The spiritual sight that has enough of a glowing heart behind it to see beneath the surface of things; to care for others beyond oneself; to translate suffering into meaning; to find the edges of hope, and to bring it forward with a plan; a willingness to find insight through struggle; an ability to stand and withstand what one sees that is painful; and, in some way, to gentle the flurry; to take

up broken threads as well and tie them off; to reweave and mend what is torn, to patch what is missing; to try for perception far beyond the ego's too-often miniscule understanding.[44]

On such a reading, *Life Is Beautiful* may be seen as performing an authentic gesture of bearing witness. Apolitical and ahistorical in nature, it is able to depict the full horror of the Shoah through a skilfully mastered mixture of document and tale, historical fact and imagination, depicting actually the power of the survival instinct of the individual.

Another riddle that Lessing, the Nazi doctor, poses in the first part of the film is 'If you say my name, I am no longer there. Who am I?.' Its answer is 'silence,' which becomes one of the film's leitmotifs. In the second part of the film, when Lessing is in charge of the selection of prisoners, Guido tells him the riddle again hoping to refresh his memory, but he receives no answer. Lessing's silence stands for his paralysis and myopia; it translates into the Nazi regime's blindness to human suffering. In another scene, a female guard urges Guido to keep quiet ('always quiet!,' she tells him), reinforcing her dominating position over the disposable prisoners. Benigni's obstinate refusal to let himself be silenced echoes his character's. Hence, when Benigni speaks through his characters, he gives a gift to the contemporary spectator. Through giving voice to those who can no longer speak, he proves, in his own manner, that humanity resists all evil.

The film places its producer in the middle of the donor-donée dyad: Benigni simultaneously honours his father's memory, after having benefited from his story, and pays homage to the victims of the Shoah. Benigni initiates the gift-exchange process with his viewers, offering them a gift that will help them work through the trauma of the Holocaust. In the end, Benigni receives back from his spectators the gift of understanding that what he called *just a simple story* carries *in nuce*, 'the tragedy of mankind.'[45]

In contrast, having the potential of becoming a genuine gift-bearer, giving Guido and his family the chance to escape, Lessing fails to complete his task. A complex character, Lessing initially seems to have a human face, yet, at a moment of maximum tension, he proves nevertheless to be the ultimate representative of an oppressive system. His actions develop mechanically, as he chooses the ones to be sent to their imminent death in complete detachment. Placing himself at a distance from the events in the camp, withdrawing into his own obsessions, Lessing shows more passion when it comes to his riddles. Portrayed as an intriguing, benevolent person in the first part of the film, he eventually gets dissolved in the crushing gears of an irrational apparatus, thus losing any contact with the appalling reality. Moreover, oblivious to Guido's life and death situation, Lessing is tormented to maniacal proportions by his ridiculous riddle. Frustrated, muttering, he leaves Guido in total stupefaction:

the good doctor could have been his family's ticket to freedom and life, but instead, Lessing isolates himself in his own petty needs and worries. In comparison to Guido's extremely volatile position, his conundrum appears to be a simulacrum of a personal tragedy. At the time when he had the absolute power to decide whether an individual is kept alive or sent to the gas chamber, when he possessed the ultimate gift of saving a human's life, in his self-centred universe, Lessing proves to be unable to rise to the occasion— not because he is afraid to offer it, but rather, because he is unaware of his gift-bearer position. Although Leaver concedes that 'in some way (albeit on a completely different level to the prisoners) Lessing, too, is a victim of the "grey zone" of the concentration camps,'[46] the character is, nonetheless, the embodiment of callousness and short-sightedness, pointing to the Nazis' lack of any logic and empathy.

Further exploring the paradigm of the gift in *Life Is Beautiful*, we need to mention the position of Guido's son, Giosuè, who, in the closing scene of the film, referring to his father's final gesture, confesses: 'This is my story. This is the sacrifice my father made. This was his gift to me.' Guido sacrifices his own life so that his son can live. His gift is an individual's response to the *mysterium* of life, waiting for no reward or assurance.[47] It is only much later that Giosuè understands the value of the gift of life he received, its true significance. Benigni hides Guido's death by placing it off-screen, away from the child's sight, in a final attempt to preserve his innocence. Guido is seen walking towards his own execution while dancing, pretending to be still the master of his destiny. Aware of the film critics who disapproved of this choice, such as, for instance, Gilbert Adair, who thought that '[i]f he had dared to shoot such a scene, then the film would have been a masterpiece,'[48] I concede that this is the most appropriate way to drop the final curtain over this representation of the Holocaust without undermining its message. In fact, Benigni chose to hide extreme images of the Holocaust horror. Their absence from the screen suggests that they are actually beyond representation. There is one exception though: a shocking scene of the horrific pile of corpses only lingers on the foggy screen, but stays enough seconds to convince the audience that the terror was always present and undeniable.

A VOYAGE FROM GALLOWS HUMOUR TO A HUMOROUS FAIRY TALE

After noting the architectural construction of the film and its 'weird symmetry,' Viano insists on the schizophrenic aspect of *Life Is Beautiful*, its staging of a comedy (first part) versus a developing tragedy (second part), a dualism that is actually an artistic device: 'Spatially, the two opposites are kept separate and yet overdetermine one another, a bit like the Yin-Yang symbol, where the black and the white are well defined and symmetrically juxtaposed but each contains a speck of the other as a memento of their interdependence.'[49] The two aspects negate each other, creating a symbolic message that can be deciphered only after interpreting the sub-textual insertions in the film: the riddles, the numerous symbols, the metaphors, all those elements constituting what Laura Leonardo calls 'mythopoeia.'[50]

My own claim is that there is no real fracture between the two parts of this film, which forces the boundaries of tragedy towards those of comedy, since neither is the first a pure comedy nor is the second a pure tragedy. The first part, a conventional romantic comedy, allows us to become familiar with the main characters: we see them falling in love in spite of all odds, joking, playing at, mocking the absurdity of Fascism. We witness the humorous moment when the prince saves his princess on a horse that was initially white but had been painted green by anti-Semites who had marked it as a Jewish horse. Due to the intimate view of characters we get in the first part, the story of the couple in the camp becomes more personalized. Given this framework, Benigni offers his audience a number of details pointing to the drama depicted in the second part. He gives clues, hints that create the tragic canvas he depicts his funny love story on—note, for instance, Guido's gesture in the brakeless car, a gesture meaning 'Out of the way!' which gets mistaken for the Fascist salute. Another hint to what will follow can be found at the beginning of the film when Guido meets a little girl at a farm. He introduces himself to the little girl as a prince who owns a lot of land. The place he owns he calls Addis Ababa. The reference to Ethiopia's capital is part of the game, as he informs the little girl that he is going to completely change the farm, get rid of the animals one usually sees at a farm (like cows) and repopulate the place with camels and hippopotami. In fact, Guido caricatures Mussolini's Fascist imperialist doctrine, mimicking the Fascists' attempt to reconstruct Rome and referring to several major building programmes initiated by Mussolini, such as the via dei Fori Imperiali project. Later on, the former effervescent waiter, impersonating an obtuse inspector, caricaturizes the Fascist discourse about race, as discussed in the section 'Laughing with the Lizards.'

Although dramatic and gloomy, the second part hides a multitude of comic elements, placed by Benigni not for irreverent purposes but with respectful restraint in order to make the unrepresentable reality of the death camp at least bearable. For instance, Guido picks up Giosuè's remark about them being participants in a game and invents its rules in his desperate attempt at creating hospitality in a completely hostile environment. When the guard yells the camp regulations to the prisoners, the father takes this opportunity to present the living conditions to his son, as an interpreter, but his 'translation' transforms the brutal commands into elaborate threads to follow in order to accumulate points that could make them the winners of a real tank. He explains, for example, that every day, the person with the least points has to wear a sign that says 'Jackass' on it and that if anyone is afraid or asks for their mummy, they will have points deducted. Furthermore, one can lose points by being hungry and asking for lollipops or bread with strawberry jam. In this fictionalized context, the Nazi guards themselves become part of the game and play the parts of 'mean guys who yell a lot,' and the reason they are not around all the time is because they are in a never-ending game of hide and seek. Imre Kertész poses an intriguing question as to what extent this device of the 'game' might correspond to the reality of Auschwitz, arguing that even if everyone could smell the stench of burning human flesh, they still did not want to believe that all of this could be true: 'One would rather find some notion that might tempt one to survive, and *a real tank* is, for a child, precisely this kind of seductive promise.'[51]

On another occasion, almost caught by the Nazis as he was placing his son at the table alongside the German children in the camp, Guido pretends to teach them the Italian word for 'thank you.' The humorous effect is a fragile one, undermined by the tragedy that could have happened. He finds the strength to make jokes all the time (even about the atrocity of making soap out of the victims) and even to risk his life only to play *The Barcarolla* on the speakers so that his wife could hear it and know that he is alive.

The film displays two main categories of tricksters/jokers, juxtaposed in order to make more visible the difference between more or less effective ways of using humour to improve our perception of life, making it *beautiful*, and thus partly healing trauma. These tricksters are the embodiment of the principles of Good and Evil, situated on antithetic poles: innocence/ignorance as opposed to knowledge/participation in the Holocaust. We can place Guido and Giosué in the first category and Lessing in the second category. Interestingly, once Lessing becomes part of the Holocaust machine, unable to comprehend the chance he was given to prove that he is a human being, he loses his sense of humour. By contrast, Guido's humour in the second part of the film acquires both a therapeutic and a cathartic value. As Costică Brădătan signalled in an excellent article, 'To Die Laughing,' one sentence from Primo Levi's *If This Is a Man* describing his arrival at the camp, 'My impression is that all this is a huge machine [whose purpose is] to laugh at us' (*la mia idea e che tutto questo e una grande macchina per ridere di noi*),'[52] is particularly striking. That is because, Brădătan thinks, 'paradoxical as it may sound, if somebody or something is laughing at your suffering, this suffering is, in a sense, not redeemed, of course, but somehow graspable, *made* graspable. If you can say that your ordeals, terrible as they are, have been *meant* by an entity—if an evil one—as a way of laughing at you, that's already a *promise of meaning.*'[53] The example that Brădătan uses to support his views is precisely Benigni's *La vita è bella*, where the suffering Benigni describes 'becomes part of a game (*gioco*), the cruelest of games, no doubt, but still a game, something you can play, engage in, or just follow.'[54] For Brădătan, Guido decides to play along with the cathartic laughter: 'The "machine" laughs at him, but at the same time this is precisely what "saves" him in a way. He joins in the laughter and, in so doing, shows that he still has some autonomy left: that he can decide to do or *not* do certain things, which still means a lot when you are in a limit-situation. The machine kills him in the end, but it cannot crush him. He is "saved" by his laughter, and ours. There is thus a sense in which Benigni's film comes very close to Levi's insight, if it is not born right out of it.'[55]

Omer Bartov argues that although humour, however crazy and infectious, is not known to have actually saved anyone in the Holocaust, love and humour 'are among the most human of all qualities, and devotion to saving the soul of a child is the most notable of all sacrifices.'[56] As scholars Marie Friederichs and Chaya Ostrower have shown, humour was actually used by the prisoners in the death camp as a defence mechanism. Friederichs argues that 'the use of humour when addressing traumatic events is not an inexplicable peripheral phenomenon that functions as an arbitrary and provocative leitmotiv, but that it originates from a profound psychological reasoning.'[57] She believes that humour in *Life Is Beautiful* 'functions more as a kind of anointment, to cope with the self [that is] surrounded by the impending world. It is also directed towards the absurdities of the real world, but with a witty and less aggressive inclination.'[58] Benigni uses humour in order 'to beautify the world' and to give 'a rosy picture of reality.'[59]

Ostrower's monograph, dedicated to gallows humour, aimed to investigate and understand the types of humour used and their role during the Holocaust. Ostrower conducted a number of interviews with fifty-five participants, Jewish Holocaust survivors who were adolescents during the Shoah. One of the interviewees, Felicia, confessed that 'they wanted to turn us into robots, and it was the integral part of our inner mental struggle for our human image, that we were still capable of laughing at this or that. Humor was one of the integral components of our spiritual coping.'[60] Another interviewee, Helina, admitted that 'the jokes helped us keep our mind alert, gave us a soberer look at things, scorn in the face of constant terror and danger, and that way lessening the terror and fear. The jokes let us feel that we're still human, despite the huge, diabolical power of the conquerors.'[61]

Since gallows humour played the part of a defence mechanism, becoming a way of surviving in the camps, laughter seems to have had a therapeutic value, reshaping reality and offering new perspectives. The Jews employed it in extreme conditions, and Benigni respectfully followed in their steps. With his filial, yet irreverent and acid melodrama, he skilfully walked on the edge of the blade, but managed to convince the audience that humour can be, at the same time, both a tool and a weapon, thus pointing to the irrationality of the Holocaust and, paradoxically, to the (in)ability to (mis)represent it.

Ultimately, *Life Is Beautiful* is a controversial film that has no intention to document the Shoah, as history does. The Italian director has paved the way to the audacious use of humour in Holocaust fiction that attempts to refract the absolute horror by broadening the limits of what is bearable. Therefore, it comes as no surprise to anyone that a documentary about the Holocaust and humour was released (at the Tribeca Film Festival in Manhattan in 2016), titled *The Last Laugh*. This documentary includes interviews with mostly Jewish comedians and a cinema verité portrait of an elderly Los Angeles–area inhabitant, Renée Firestone, who survived the Holocaust with her sense of humour largely intact. Here, the comedian Judy Gold tells this joke: 'If the Nazis forced her to stand naked on a line with other women, would she hold her stomach in?' The joke is by far not as acid as the ones quoted by Ostrower in her monograph: 'Two Jews meet and one of them is eating perfumed soap. The other Jew asks: Moish, how come you're eating this smelling soap? and Moish answers: If they're going to turn me into soap, the least I can do is smell good' (Felicia).[62] The director of this documentary, Ferne Pearlstein, wanted to explore not only the limits of humour and free speech today, but also how Shoah victims and survivors 'used humor as a salve, defence mechanism and weapon despite their powerlessness.'[63]

In a similar way, Roberto Benigni tries to make the unpalatable bearable. As this chapter has endeavoured to demonstrate, Benigni's film is both a gift of hope that is offered to its viewers and an invitation, through laughter mixed with tears, to reflection as part of a healing process. Viewers are indirectly summoned to contribute to the meaning, thus continuing the work of the creator, receiving the gift offered to them and handing it over to future generations.

NOTES

1. See, for instance, Primo Levi, *Voice of Memory: Interviews 1961–87*, eds. Marco Belpoliti and Robert S. C. Gordon (Cambridge: Polity, 2001), 186.

2. Elie Wiesel, *Night*, trans. Marion Wiesel (New York: Hill and Wang, 2006), viii.

3. Thomas Trezise, 'Unspeakable,' *Yale Journal of Criticism* 14.1 (2001): 39.

4. Let us remember Lyotard's famous dictum: 'something which must be able to be put into phrases cannot yet be.' Jean-François Lyotard, *The Differend: Phrases in Dispute*, trans. Georges Van Den Abbeele (Manchester: Manchester University Press, 1988), 13.

5. Giorgio Agamben, *Remnants of Auschwitz: The Witness and the Archive* (New York: Zone Books, 1999), 12–13.

6. Judith E. Doneson, *The Holocaust in American Film*, 2nd ed. (Syracuse, NY: Syracuse University Press, 2001), 6.

7. Siegfried Kracauer, *Theory of Film: The Redemption of Physical Reality* (New York: Oxford University Press, 1960), 305.

8. Ilan Avisar, *Screening the Holocaust: Cinema's Images of the Unimaginable* (Bloomington and Indianapolis: Indiana University Press, 1988), 4.

9. Alison Landsberg, *Prosthetic Memories: The Transformation of American Remembrance in the Age of Mass Culture* (New York: Columbia University Press, 2004), 149.

10. See *The Diary of Anne Frank*, *Judgment at Nuremberg*, *The Boys from Brazil*, *Victory*, *Voyage of the Damned*, *Au nom de tous les miens*, *The Assault*, *La Storia*, *Hanna's War*, *Playing for Time*, *The Wall*, *Escape from Sobibor*, *War and Remembrance*, *The Garden of the Finzi-Continis*, *Les Violons du Bal*, *Lacombe, Lucien*, *Lili Marleen* and *Schindler's List*.

11. According to Annette Insdorf, we can include in this category *The Nasty Girl*, *My Mother's Courage*, *A Self-Made Hero*, *Dr. Petiot*, *Conversation with the Beast*, *Genghis Cohn*, *Train of Life* or *Jakob the Liar*. See *Indelible Shadows: Film and the Holocaust*, 3rd ed. (Cambridge: Cambridge University Press, 2003), 276.

12. Joseph Campbell, *The Hero with a Thousand Faces* (Princeton, NJ and Oxford: Princeton University Press, 2004), 186.

13. Kobi Niv, *Life Is Beautiful, But Not for Jews* (Lanham, MD: Scarecrow Press, 2003), 88.

14. See Spiegelman's caricature at http://www.thirteen.org/nyvoices/transcripts/spiegelman.html, accessed 23 August 2018.

15. David Denby, 'In the Eye of the Beholder,' *The New Yorker*, 15 March 1999, 96–97.

16. Niv, *Life Is Beautiful, But Not for Jews*, xxii.

17. Avisar, *Screening the Holocaust*, 182.

18. Lawrence Baron, *Projecting the Holocaust into the Present: The Changing Focus of the Contemporary Holocaust Cinema* (New York: Rowman & Littlefield, 2005), 3.

19. See, for instance, Francine Stock, 'Tears for a Clown!,' *New Statesman*, 12 February 1999, 43, https://www.newstatesman.com/tears-clown, accessed 10 September 2018.

20. Gilbert Adair, 'The Critics: Fairy-Tales after Auschwitz,' *Independent*, 14 February 1999, http://www.independent.co.uk/arts-entertainment/the-critics-fairy-tales-after-auschwitz-1070749.html, accessed 10 September 2018.

21. Gefen Bar-on, 'Benigni's Life-affirming Lie: "Life is Beautiful" as an Aesthetic and Moral Response to the Holocaust,' in *Beyond Life is Beautiful: Comedy and Tragedy in the Cinema of Roberto Benigni*, ed. Grace Russo Bullaro (Leicester: Troubador Publishing, 2005), 182.

22. Henry Eilbert, *What Is a Jewish Joke?* quoted in Justin Geldzahler, 'We Laugh So We Don't Cry: The Humor in Holocaust Films,' *Vulture*, 31 May 2012, https://www.vulture.com/2012/05/we-laugh-so-we-dont-cry-the-humor-in-holocaust-films.html, accessed 10 September 2018.

23. C. Robert and Carol J. Reimer, *Historical Dictionary of the Holocaust Cinema* (Toronto and Plymouth: Scarecrow Press, 2012), 111.

24. Maurizio Viano, '*Life Is Beautiful:* Reception, Allegory and Holocaust Laughter,' *Jewish Social Studies* 3 (1999): 52. A version of the same, similarly titled article appears in *Film Quarterly* 53.1 (1999): 26–34.

25. Adrienne Kertzer, *My Mother's Voice: Children, Literature, and the Holocaust* (Toronto and Ontario: Broadview Press, 2002), 204.

26. Primo Levi, *Survival in Auschwitz: The Nazi Assault on Humanity*, New Afterword by Primo Levi and Philip Roth, trans. Stuart Woolf (New York and London: Simon & Schuster, 1996), 164.

27. Roberto Benigni and Henri Béhar, '*La Vita è bella' (Life Is Beautiful), Press Conference at the 1998 Cannes Film Festival*, http://www.filmscouts.com/scripts/interview.cfm?File=vit-bel, accessed 10 September 2018.

28. Benigni and Béhar, '*La Vita è bella,*' http://www.filmscouts.com/scripts/interview.cfm?File=vit-bel, accessed 10 September 2018.

29. In an interview published in *Corriere della sera* on 19 December 1997, Benigni asserted that *Life Is Beautiful* was 'a fantastical film, almost science fiction, a fairy-tale with no reality, no neo-realism, no realism in it' (quoted in Niv, *Life Is Beautiful, But Not for Jews*, 24).

30. Jeremy Maron, 'Theatrical Games and the Gift of a Fable,' in *Stages of Reality: Theatricality in Cinema*, eds. André Loiselle and Jeremy Maron (Toronto and London: University of Toronto Press, 2012), 175.

31. Benigni referred to Levi's *The Truce* in the press conference at Cannes in 1998 (Benigni and Béhar, '*La Vita è* bella,*' http://www.filmscouts.com/scripts/interview.cfm?File=vit-bel, accessed 10 September 2018).

32. Sonderkommando was a special unit of prisoners who were forced by the Nazis to help in extracting the dead bodies from the gas chambers and cremating them.

33. 'When my father told me and my three sisters about his experiences, it came out exactly like the character of Guido.' (See Roberto Benigni, in Jessica Lazar and Ann LoLordo, 'A Comic Film's Acid Test: Benigni's "Life Is Beautiful," A Humorous Love Story Set Amid the Holocaust Draws Laughter, then a Telling Silence,' *Baltimore Sun*, 26 July 1998, http://articles.baltimoresun.com/1998-07-26/features/1998207191_1_benigni-jerusalem-film-festival-silence, accessed 10 September 2018).

34. Benigni and Béhar, '*La Vita è bella,*' http://www.filmscouts.com/scripts/interview.cfm?File=vit-bel, accessed 10 September 2018.

35. Cathy Caruth, *Unclaimed Experience*: *Trauma, Narrative, and History* (Baltimore: Johns Hopkins University Press, 1996), 11.

36. Caruth, *Unclaimed Experience*, 79.

37. See Landsberg, *Prosthetic Memories*, 149.

38. Dominick LaCapra, *History and Memory after Auschwitz* (Ithaca, NY: Cornell University Press, 1998), 1.

39. Maron, 'Theatrical Games and the Gift of a Fable,' 179.

40. Ruth Ben-Ghiat, 'The Secret Histories of Roberto Benigni's *Life Is Beautiful*,' in *Jews in Italy under Fascist and Nazi Rule, 1922–1945*, ed. Joshua D. Zimmerman (Cambridge and New York: Cambridge University Press, 2005), 332.

41. See Tama Leaver, 'Rationality, Representation and the Holocaust in Life is Beautiful,' *Limina* 10 (2004): 75.

42. This phrase has the same significance in French and in Romanian, two other Romance languages.

43. Benigni and Béhar, *'La Vita è bella,'* http://www.filmscouts.com/scripts/interview.cfm?File=vit-bel, accessed 10 September 2018.

44. Campbell, *The Hero with a Thousand Faces*, 23.

45. Benigni and Béhar, *'La Vita è bella,'* http://www.filmscouts.com/scripts/interview.cfm?File=vit-bel, accessed 10 September 2018.

46. Leaver, 'Rationality, Representation and the Holocaust in Life is Beautiful,' 76.

47. For the debates around the second level or mode of giving, see Jacques Derrida, *The Gift of Death*, trans. David Wills (Chicago: University of Chicago Press, 1995), 91.

48. Adair, 'The Critics: Fairy-Tales after Auschwitz.'

49. Viano, *'Life Is Beautiful,'* 56.

50. Laura Leonardo, 'La torta etiope e il cavallo ebreo: Metaphor, Mythopoeia and Symbolism in *Life Is Beautiful*,' in *Beyond Life is Beautiful: Comedy and Tragedy in the Cinema of Roberto Benigni*, ed. Grace Russo Bullaro (Leicester: Troubador Publishing, 2005), 203.

51. Imre Kertész, 'Who Owns Auschwitz?,' *Yale Journal of Criticism* 14.1 (2001): 271.

52. Primo Levi, *Se questo e un uomo* (Torino: Einaudi, 1986), 33, Brădătan's translation.

53. Costică Brădătan, 'To Die Laughing,' *East European Politics and Societies* 25.4 (2011): 739.

54. Brădătan, 'To Die Laughing,' 739.

55. Brădătan, 'To Die Laughing,' 739.

56. Omer Bartov, *The 'Jew' in Cinema*: *From the Golem to Don't Touch My Holocaust* (Bloomington and Indianapolis: Indiana University Press, 2005), 123.

57. Marie Friederichs, 'Humour as a Way of Dealing with the Trauma of the Holocaust: Discussion of the Use of Humour to Approach the Holocaust by Two Members of the Second Generation; Melvin Jules Bukiet and Roberto Benigni' (MA dissertation), University of Ghent, 2014–2015, 8, https://lib.ugent.be/fulltxt/

Lucia Ispas

RUG01/002/212/982/RUG01-002212982_2015_0001_AC.pdf, accessed 22 September 2018.
    58. Friederichs, 'Humour as a Way of Dealing with the Trauma of the Holocaust Discussion,' 59, my addition.
    59. Friederichs, 'Humour as a Way of Dealing with the Trauma of the Holocaust Discussion,' 63.
    60. Chaya Ostrower, *It Kept Us Alive: Humor in the Holocaust* (Jerusalem Yad-Vashem, 2014).
    61. For all these examples and more, see Ostrower, *It Kept Us Alive.*
    62. See Ostrower, *It Kept Us Alive.*
    63. Andrew Sillow-Caroll, 'New Documentary Asks If We're Ready to Laugh at the Holocaust,' *Jewish Telegraphic Agency*, 26 April 2016, http://www.jta.org/2016/04/26/arts-entertainment/new-documentary-asks-if-were-ready-to-laugh-at-the-holocaust, accessed 10 September 2018.

BIBLIOGRAPHY

ADAIR, Gilbert. 'The Critics: Fairy-Tales after Auschwitz.' *Independent* 14 February 1999. http://www.independent.co.uk/arts-entertainment/the-critics-fairy-tales-after-auschwitz-1070749.html. Accessed 10 September 2018.
AGAMBEN, Giorgio. *Remnants of Auschwitz: The Witness and the Archive.* New York: Zone Books, 1999.
AVISAR, Ilan. *Screening the Holocaust: Cinema's Images of the Unimaginable.* Bloomington and Indianapolis: Indiana University Press, 1988.
BAR-ON, Gefen. 'Benigni's Life-affirming Lie: "Life is Beautiful" as an Aesthetic and Moral Response to the Holocaust.' In *Beyond Life is Beautiful: Comedy and Tragedy in the Cinema of Roberto Benigni.* Edited by Grace Russo Bullaro. 179–200. Leicester: Troubador Publishing, 2005.
BARON, Lawrence. *Projecting the Holocaust into the Present: The Changing Focus of the Contemporary Holocaust Cinema.* New York: Rowman & Littlefield, 2005.
BARTOV, Omer. *The 'Jew' in Cinema: From the Golem to Don't Touch My Holocaust.* Bloomington and Indianapolis: Indiana University Press, 2005.
BEN-GHIAT, Ruth. 'The Secret Histories of Roberto Benigni's *Life Is Beautiful.*' In *Jews in Italy under Fascist and Nazi Rule, 1922–1945.* Edited by Joshua D. Zimmerman. 330–49. New York: Cambridge University Press, 2005.
BENIGNI, Roberto and Henri Béhar, *'La Vita è bella' (Life Is Beautiful), Press Conference at the 1998 Cannes Film Festival.* http://www.filmscouts.com/scripts/interview.cfm?File=vit-bel. Accessed 10 September 2018.
BRĂDĂTAN, Costică. 'To Die Laughing.' *East European Politics and Societies* 25.4 (2011): 737–58.
CAMPBELL, Joseph. *The Hero with a Thousand Faces.* Princeton, NJ and Oxford: Princeton University Press, 2004.
CARUTH, Cathy. *Unclaimed Experience: Trauma, Narrative, and History.* Baltimore: Johns Hopkins University Press, 1996.

DENBY, David. 'In the Eye of the Beholder.' *The New Yorker* 15 March 1999: 96-97.

DERRIDA, Jacques. *The Gift of Death*. Translated by David Wills. Chicago: University of Chicago Press, 1995.

DONESON, Judith E. *The Holocaust in American Film*. Second Edition. Syracuse, NY: Syracuse University Press, 2001.

FRIEDERICHS, Marie. 'Humour as a Way of Dealing with the Trauma of the Holocaust: Discussion of the Use of Humour to Approach the Holocaust by Two Members of the Second Generation; Melvin Jules Bukiet and Roberto Benigni' (MA dissertation). University of Ghent. 2014–2015. 8. https://lib.ugent.be/fulltxt/RUG01/002/212/982/RUG01-002212982_2015_0001_AC.pdf. Accessed 22 September 2018.

GELDZAHLER, Justin. 'We Laugh So We Don't Cry: The Humor in Holocaust Films.' *Vulture*, 31 May 2012. https://www.vulture.com/2012/05/we-laugh-so-we-dont-cry-the-humor-in-holocaust-films.html. Accessed 10 September 2018.

INSDORF, Annette. *Indelible Shadows: Film and the Holocaust*. Third Edition. Cambridge: Cambridge University Press, 2003.

KERTÉSZ, Imre. 'Who Owns Auschwitz?.' *Yale Journal of Criticism* 14.1 (2001): 267-72.

KERTZER, Adrienne. *My Mother's Voice: Children, Literature, and the Holocaust.* Toronto and Ontario: Broadview Press, 2002.

KRACAUER, Siegfried. *Theory of Film: The Redemption of Physical Reality.* New York: Oxford University Press, 1960.

LACAPRA, Dominick. *History and Memory after Auschwitz*. Ithaca, NY: Cornell University Press, 1998.

LANDSBERG, Alison. *Prosthetic Memories: The Transformation of American Remembrance in the Age of Mass Culture*. New York: Columbia University Press, 2004.

LAZAR, Jessica and Ann LoLordo. 'A Comic Film's Acid Test: Benigni's "Life Is Beautiful," A Humorous Love Story Set Amid the Holocaust Draws Laughter, then a Telling Silence.' *Baltimore Sun* 26 July 1998. http://articles.baltimoresun.com/1998-07-26/features/1998207191_1_benigni-jerusalem-film-festival-silence. Accessed 10 September 2018.

LEAVER, Tama. 'Rationality, Representation and the Holocaust in Life is Beautiful.' *Limina* 10 (2004): 70–80.

LEONARDO, Laura. 'La torta etiope e il cavallo ebreo: Metaphor Mythopoeia and Symbolism in Life Is Beautiful.' In *Beyond Life Is Beautiful: Comedy and Tragedy in the Cinema of Roberto Benigni.* Edited by Grace Russo Bullaro. 201–24. Leicester: Troubador Publishing, 2005.

LEONE, Massimo. 'Shoah and Humour: A Semiotic Approach.' *Jewish Studies Quarterly* 9.2 (2002): 173–92.

LEVI, Primo. *Se questo e un uomo.* Torino: Einaudi, 1986.

LEVI, Primo. *Survival in Auschwitz: The Nazi Assault on Humanity.* New Afterword by Primo Levi and Philip Roth. Translated by Stuart Woolf. New York and London: Simon and Schuster, 1996.

LEVI, Primo. *Voice of Memory: Interviews 1961–87*. Edited by Marco Belpoliti and Robert S. C. Gordon. Cambridge: Polity, 2001.

LYOTARD, Jean-François. *The Differend: Phrases in Dispute*. Translated by Georges Van Den Abbeele. Manchester: Manchester University Press, 1988.

MARON, Jeremy, 'Theatrical Games and the Gift of a Fable.' In *Stages of Reality: Theatricality in Cinema*. Edited by André Loiselle and Jeremy Maron. 160–82. Toronto and London: University of Toronto Press, 2012.

NIV, Kobi, *Life Is Beautiful, But Not for Jews*. Lanham, MD: Scarecrow Press, 2003.

OSTROWER, Chaya. *It Kept Us Alive: Humor in the Holocaust*. Jerusalem: Yad-Vashem, 2014.

REIMER, Robert C. and Reimer, Carol J., *Historical Dictionary of the Holocaust Cinema*. Toronto and Plymouth: Scarecrow Press, 2012.

SILLOW-CAROLL, Andrew. 'New Documentary Asks If We're Ready to Laugh at the Holocaust.' *Jewish Telegraphic Agency*, 26 April 2016. http://www.jta.org/2016/04/26/arts-entertainment/new-documentary-asks-if-were-ready-to-laugh-at-the-holocaust. Accessed 10 September 2018.

SPIEGELMAN, Art. *Healing Images*. http://www.thirteen.org/nyvoices/transcripts/spiegelman.html. Accessed 10 September 2018.

STOCK, Francine. 'Tears for a Clown!.' *New Statesman*, 12 February 1999. https://www.newstatesman.com/tears-clown. Accessed 10 September 2018.

TREZISE, Thomas. 'Unspeakable.' *Yale Journal of Criticism* 14.1(2001): 38–63.

VIANO, Maurizio. '*Life Is Beautiful*: Reception, Allegory and Holocaust Laughter.' *Jewish Social Studies* 3 (1999): 47–66.

WIESEL, Elie. *Night*. Translated by Marion Wiesel. New York: Hill and Wang, 2006.

Part II

MASS TRAUMA, ART AND THE HEALING POLITICS OF PLACE

Chapter Four

Improving Public Space

*Trauma Art and
Retrospective-Futuristic Healing*

Mieke Bal

I died in Auschwitz, but no one knows it.

—Charlotte Delbo[1]

Formerly is today.

—Françoise Davoine[2]

In the late sixteenth century, a young Spanish soldier was captured by Corsairs and sold into slavery in Algiers. This was, so to speak, common practice in the Mediterranean area, primarily a commercial endeavour. From 1575 to 1580, the young man had no idea if and when he would ever get out. Imagine the feeling—or rather, the incapacity to have any. His parents did not have the money to redeem him. A few texts have been written by eyewitnesses or fellow slaves describing the everyday life in the *baño*, the confrontations with cruelty and benevolence, in what has been called an 'early modern dialogue with Islam.' But not much transpires about how the detained experienced their situation. We can only imagine. Yes, we need the imagination in the face of such un-representable events and situations that we call 'traumatic.' Internment is a horrific experience, but the worst of it, I would think, is not knowing if there will ever be an end to it. Time loses its meaning. And it stretches endlessly. More about this captive fellow in Act 3 below.[3]

What can art do? In a domain where expertise is medical, psychiatric and psychoanalytical, what is the point of using art, a privileged and even, according to many, elitist form of cultural expression? How can art effectively address the brutalities of cultures where violence generates trauma on an everyday basis, and even pretend to contribute to healing trauma? The works described below insert themselves into a large body of contemporary art that is aimed at attending to traumatic situations and states. In a convoluted way and with modest, indirect results, I believe art can do, at least, something. I am not interested in artworks that *represent* the event of traumatizing, nor in a vague overuse of the term 'trauma.' Instead, addressing one work each by two artists coming from and living in a severely traumatogenic culture (India and Colombia), I will make a case for the importance of art as a medium and mediation between the people hurt—in the past and present—and the art viewers who live in a relatively protected environment. It is not because any real connection can be established. What can be done is improve the social fabric of the culture that keeps trauma unspeakable.[4]

It is only possible for art to do something because the imaginative appeal of art can sensitize visitors in order to slowly modify the culture of condoning that makes trauma—that wound that silences—invisible and inaudible, systematically ignored and overlooked. Art acts between what we know but feel free to overlook and what we sense, feel and unreflectively condone but can also actively vomit out: violence, injustice and lethal poverty. The artists I will discuss deploy aesthetics—as in the Baumgartian view of aesthetics as binding through the senses in public space—to contribute to that sensitization, each in her own way. They both literally attempt to modify space.[5]

ACT 1: CREATING COMMUNITY WITH WORDS, HEALING WITH PIGMENT

Indian artist Nalini Malani makes work that *moves*, in all possible ways. Movement, in her work, is not limited to the technical movement of the video shadow plays and video installations that have made this artist famous all over the world; the reflections of her reverse-painted works on glass or Mylar; the erasure of wall drawings in 'erasure performances,' and the cinematic aspect of multi-panel paintings—and more. But also, her work produces a movement that underlies all these technical ones, the emotional movement that the mode of painting and the allusions to real-life situations solicit, as in 'I am moved.'[6]

This movement can move us to *political* movement: a change of opinion, of priorities, and a more active and empathic attitude. Such changes can improve the texture of public space, in order for traumatized people to be able to 'tie up the broken thread.' This is a phrase Spanish baroque writer Miguel de Cervantes wrote several times, lastly in the prologue to his final novel, *The Travails of Persiles y Sigismunda*, which he finished three days before his death and was posthumously published in 1617: 'A time may come, perhaps, when I shall tie up this broken thread and say what I failed to say here and what would have been fitting.' Tying, repairing the broken social bond is also the summary of the goal of the work of Françoise Davoine, psychoanalyst of trauma.[7]

Collectively enabling that reparation of the broken social bond is the multiple and enduring movement that is part of *why* and *how* Malani is a profoundly political artist, and this, *thanks to* her strongly artistic, indeed aesthetic art. She opposes the *representation* of the political situations—most directly, the proliferating violence—that she seeks to indict and resist. But how can art shape such resistance, if it isn't through showing its opponent? The dilemma of representation is the risk of repeating, and exposing to voyeurism, thus giving presence and force to the violence one abhors and wishes to eradicate. But censoring it out of view would be falling in the opposite trap, of making art only for art's sake. This is the dilemma both Malani and Colombian artist Doris Salcedo, in artistically very different ways, both masterfully address.

Malani's most famous shadow play, *In Search of Vanished Blood*, from 2012, addresses traumatogenic oblivion explicitly. Its soundtrack begins with abstract sound. The sound is neither calming nor threatening. It is no illustrative music; it is not music at all. It is difficult to say what it means; that appears to be its point. Sound we cannot give meaning to becomes meaningful when after a while we hear the words, 'This is Cassandra speaking.' Malani's voice speaks these words after more than a minute. The meaning comes from the name: Cassandra invokes the woman from Greek mythology whose prediction of imminent catastrophe could not be heard. And in the well-worn spirit of blaming the victim and killing the messenger, she was killed when she refused to shut up. 'In the heart of darkness,' replies or continues a distorted voice, pluralized by means of asynchronicity.[8]

The shadow play *In Search of Vanished Blood* consists of four elements. The first one consists of five cylinders with images on them in reverse painting. These images are carefully balanced in view of the cylinders' turning. The balance concerns the shadows that the figures will cast, and the need for emptiness between them, for variations in scale, and the effects of colour in semi-darkness, moving from bright pastels to the dark lines of shadows. The second element consists of six video projections that cut through the turning cylinders and add their projections on the walls, sometimes appearing as the primary layer of images, sometimes almost hidden by the shadows. A third element is a soundtrack that includes abstract sounds, voices and silences. And fourth, there are the visitors, adding rumour and voices, whispers and sighs to the soundtrack, and when the cylinders hang lower, on the same level as the projections, the visitors cast their own shadows. The effect of the visitors' presence is so crucial for the shadow plays that I must put them here in the list of the work's material elements.

In addition to an ensemble of moving images that are as such still paintings, this is also a shadow play on the sonic level, as the voice is accompanied
by its own shadow. The pluralization of the voice is meaningful not only because of its eerie mechanical sound but also because it speaks a plural identity
in the linguistic first-person singular. The phrase 'in the heart of darkness'
quotes the title of Joseph Conrad's 1899 novel. This adds the spatial positioning 'in' that might be seen as saying 'Africa, including Conrad's-Kurtz's
"the horror! the horror" is here.' Here is double as well: in India, and here in
this exhibition space in Germany, New York, Torino, or other places where
the work has been exhibited and experienced. The quotation by Christa Wolf
of Aeschylus is indirect, passing through Heiner Müller's *Hamletmachine*
where Ophelia speaks these words, but there, saying, 'This is Electra speaking.' Three mythical women (Cassandra, Ophelia, Electra) speak in one
personal pronoun 'I' and claim their voice. All three were victimized; all
remained strong, refusing to give up their subjectivity. What the voice says,
a bit difficult to understand, becomes grimmer.[9]

The Cassandra story haunts much of Malani's work. She made a thirty-
panel painting in 2009, one of those cinematic paintings that require active
movement on the part of the viewers, who shift from panel to panel while
being confronted with their own reflection due to the shiny surface. From
Aeschylus to Wolf and back again, Malani intensively engages literature
that addresses trauma in complex ways—in this case, as multi-sensorial, or
synesthetic. We can understand Malani's choice of Cassandra-Wolf's words
in the soundtrack of *In Search of Vanished Blood* as a sonic *thought-image*
that comprehends a statement about the field of vision in its relation to time.
To sum this up extremely briefly: according to Malani's varied forms of
movement, vision is dialogic. This dialogic nature of vision is a simultaneous exercising of the subject and object status of the viewer and what is being seen. Within this dialogue, temporally, Malani brings history in, not as
something 'out there' in the past but in its density and inextricable mixture of
the different fields constituting 'culture'—intricately folded, twisted, coiled,
a tangle of movements, alluded to by the tangle of cables; in other words,
convoluted, and entangling the viewer. The enveloping effect of sound is part
of that entanglement.[10]

After Malani's voice, the abstract sound takes over again. But now the visitor has the memory of those words to help her imagination make sense of the
sounds. These continue to reject their function as illustrations. After having
heard the name Cassandra, however, we know that both the difficulty of hearing and the need to understand are crucial. And thus, we make an effort. The
words 'Under the sun of torture / To the capitals of the world / In the name of
the victims' don't tell a story. In this, they are different from, yet reactivate

the myth of Cassandra, galvanized through Christa Wolf's rewriting of it that put it back into the present. And they differ from Conrad's book title; a book the ambivalence of which towards race issues is well-known.[11]

This reactivation of the myth of Cassandra is a good example of the ability of literature to do something, and visual art can make that something function more intensively and collectively. These words only set a story up, recall it, and together they add up. They set the stage, define the addressee and specify the speaker. That speaker is layered, for it is triple. It is up to the visitors to take a place and choose their relationship to what is to come. The visitors must do this for the story to be able to *take place*, and to give the searcher, who is the subject of this work as the title stages it, some respite. They are provided with the clues, the links, to connect what they see to the invisible invoked, with the help of their imagination. They are given all the tools to become part of the searching subject, to join the search and thus increase the chance that a result may be found, to wrench the blood from its erased invisibility.

Art is a product of the imagination, and addresses the imagination of its audiences—and this in the most literal sense. This entails the status of art as fiction. But fiction is not the opposite of reality. It is a special inflection of reality, the latter enriched by the imagination. In this way, art is able to provide visions, including knowledge, that other forms of knowledge production have difficulty achieving. The central motive of *In Search* is something as concrete, real, material, human, ordinary and extraordinary and sticky as *blood*. Related to life and death, to health and violence, blood is starkly sensuous: smelly, adhesive and visible. It is both symbolic, semiotically 'speaking,' and real; and yet, as the work's title suggests, it can vanish. To search for it in an artwork, then, is the task of the imagination.

Malani's work is imaginative to the extreme; at the same time, it always invokes, summons a reality of horror. Addressing a contemporary audience and compelling them to imagine, hence *see*, what history has done to people, Malani seeks to enable Cassandra to be finally heard, so that the future, too, can be seen, or imagined. She cannily uses the device of quotation, literary and visual, to enhance recognizability and thus make visitors part of the game. Through quotation, she also inserts her work in the kind of ephemeral community that art can forge. These works make such imagining almost irresistible. Among the many 'tools'—devices, issues, media, thoughts—brought in to achieve this imagining is *time*. Time is inscribed in the works' stamina to insist, reiterate and yet constantly transform the materiality of the symbolic blood. This prolongs the duration of the experience of the art. Time is also made specific in the temporal itinerary from present to past and back. And time is at work in reading, looking, experiencing and imagining. These are the four activities triggered, each with a temporality of its own. This is one reason for the use of poetry as the primary quotation in this work. Time is brought in through quotation, recognizing the past; and through imagining the future, by Cassandra-the-artist, to whom we must listen this time. The poetics of quotation implies an acknowledgement of the collective nature of art—the works, the experience and what the imagination does with these. It is a form of collaboration, opposing the narcissistic individualism often attached to the idea of the artist. This is an important aspect of Malani's practice. In this respect, as in all choices she makes, there is a politically motivated commitment.

In addition to, or rather, overshadowing or absorbing time and quotation, the primary issue in this work is the search for materiality, for which blood is both a metaphor and the real thing. It is both *comparant* and compared, thus undermining the divide that rules theories of metaphor. Real, material traces are needed in order to believe, acknowledge and feel historic violence. The work of the shadows that define the poetics of *In Search of Vanished Blood*, in particular, is geared to designing such traces, even in a minimal(ist) materiality. In its own uniqueness the work thus stipulates a first conditional feature of the entire body of the shadow plays.

Like the quotations and the tripled voice, the images turn; they pass by, casting their shadows at a pace of four turns a minute. Thanks to the relentless turning, violence emerges, on many different levels at once, although never directly represented. Each body part that flies by on the cylinders or the videos seems cut off in acts of aggression. Innocent butterflies are so out of scale that they seem the product of nuclear disaster. Just one of many images, or rather, one moment in the moving work: on one cylinder we see at some point a man with an Afghan headdress, mouth open, who is holding, perhaps caressing with clumsy oversized hands, a gigantic bird (figure 4.1). A cat sleeping beside him seems indifferent to the bird. On the bottom are some sea creatures, out of place in what could otherwise be considered a scene. A smaller young woman or girl shines through the transparency. At certain moments of the turn, she seems to be inside the man's body. A dog standing on hind legs walks beside her like a circus animal. Is this animal walking on a cloud, or a brain?

So far, I seem to have presented this image as a drawing, interpreting its outlines. But it is a painting. Mute colours make the painting on the cylinder look like watercolours rather than oil painting, with a predominant burnt sienna and phthalocyanine blue only interrupted by the blue feathers of the bird and a touch of scarlet on the dog. On the bottom of the cylinder small creatures move, animals of indistinct identity: birds, salamanders, butterflies. The blue is repeated in the image on the next cylinder, of which we can only see a narrow portion. There, two women, only outlined, are sitting. Under

Figure 4.1. Detail from Nalini Malani, *In Search of Vanished Blood*. Six-channel video/ shadow play with five reverse-painted rotating Mylar cylinders, 4 rpm, sound, 11 minutes. dOCUMENTA (13), Kassel, 2012.

their feet, however, is an isolated spine, made of bones. This spine is blue, the same blue we just encountered on the bird's feathers.

Painting and drawing meet in the details, especially the eyes. The man's eye is strikingly expressive. He seems astounded or horrified by the bird, perhaps by its size, or the tactile substance of its feathers. On the bird's tail the feathers look prickly; perhaps the man feels the pain of thorns. The girl's eyes are striking too. They face us directly, from the other side of the transparent cylinder. And the woman on the left of two women on the next cylinder looks resigned, dejected, with her large eyes.

Meanwhile, sound and language remain hauntingly present. The voice of Cassandra speaks the future, in vain. Blood: vanished, forgotten; yet present not in scarlet splatters but in the innumerable narratives of violence the work holds up, then retracts. Signs of blood, the paintings, the Mylar, the drawings, the sounds all press forward the materiality of the work, which nevertheless remains elusive. They are able to muster the meaning of blood, precisely because they *are* not it but tie themselves to it. And then, the poem from which the title is a quotation slowly passes over the bandaged face of a woman—gagged, her mouth wrapped with semi-transparent gauze (figure 4.2).

This is the emblematic image of the work, reproduced in all publications. It is where poetry meets visuality; where the image asserts its own poetic nature, and a face is both completely obliterated and yet 'live' in the present. Overwritten by the poem, yet dimly visible, the image speaks in its dual medium to state the aliveness of the woman and the way the poem covers her face, as one face of violence.

Like the voices and the sounds, the poem is avoiding narrative, and it is entirely set in negativity. Like Cassandra's words, there is only 'no sign of blood,' and no motivation for shedding it. Normally, according to everyday logic, the negative is vague; it lacks specification. In this it is comparable to

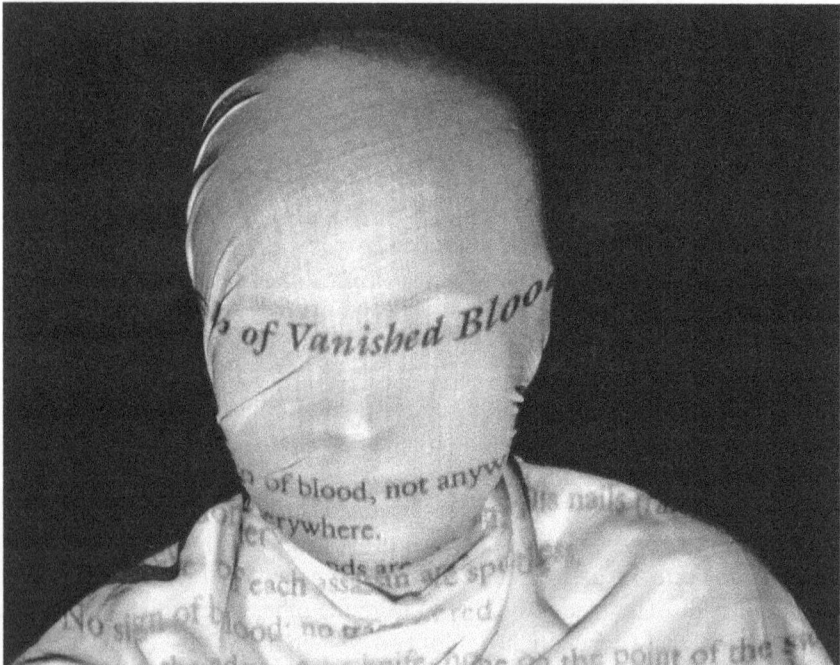

Figure 4.2.   Detail from Nalini Malani, *In Search of Vanished Blood.* Six-channel video/shadow play with five reverse-painted rotating Mylar cylinders, 4 rpm, sound, 11 minutes. dOCUMENTA (13), Kassel, 2012.

abstraction in the traditional sense, where it means figural negativity: without figuration. Here, however, the relentless negativity cries out the demand to find the blood. It hollers the obligation to make historic violence concrete, to bring it to visibility. The repetition of 'no' and 'not' becomes itself a figure; it brings abstraction to potential figuration. A figuration that Malani's work— imaginative, addressing the imagination of its viewers—provides. And as I am using verbs like crying, shouting and hollering, the negativity also affects the poem. It is not spoken aloud.[12]

This work is very full, iconographically; it seems to address all times and all places. At some point during the turns, we see a woman's face, later her body; and many images of hands, some projected 'real' hands, some drawings of American Sign Language spelling out the word 'democracy.' Then there are running dogs taken from Aedwaerd Muybridge's early modernist attempt to turn photography into moving images (1830–1904). A huge fingerprint covers a woman's face. There are pixelated images of a woman's body lying as if dead. Flashes of light move fast, sometimes with heads on the sides. We notice skyscrapers and baroque folds. The projections include animations looking like historical drawings as well as popular styles, at some point overruled by hands. On the cylinders are many images from the archive of Indian and Western mythology, with devouring monsters alternating with men in business suits, gun in hand—the juxtaposition suggests they are equally devouring monsters. And much more. Slowly the title poem scrolls over the bandaged face. Silent, it silences. The poem is present but only so indirectly, projected on the side, literally obliquely. And, although presented as an image, it is primarily written in language, not images. This seemingly secondary element makes the case for the paradoxical materiality of the work through that literary work, and its eponymous search for matter.[13]

It is significant for the transformations necessary to achieve materiality that the poem is not quoted on the soundtrack. We can only *see* it, and subsequently read it. The text moves, and although the movement is slow, it is rather unusual to read when the letters move upwards, away from us. We are bound to someone else's pace—which is a humbling experience, even if the pace is patient. Furthermore, the words compete with the face and its relief, barely visible behind the bandages, and even more difficult to see due to the moving words. Words and face compete. The face opposes to the words the relief of mouth, nose and eyes. The words oppose to the face their attention-grabbing difficulty-to-read due to movement, the face's relief and the enigmatic poetic content, including its negative discourse.[14]

Yet, when due visual attention is paid, we can see, or read, more and more of that face as we read the poem. We can see that it is female, Indian looking and unreadable in its expression. Most importantly, we are feeling the close connection between face and poem, the close adherence of the poem to the face—another bandage. Like the two sides of a coin or a sheet of paper, the face and the poem become a face-poem in movement; the moving image of a face that is a poem, a poem that is a face. In order to read the poem, we must pay visual attention, including to the doubly hidden face itself. Imagine that poignantly semi-invisible face with the text of the poem projected on it as one of six projections on the sides of five cylinders with images and their shadows. And thus, realize that invisibility is not only its theme, but also its material modality.[15]

Wandering among the cylinders, what comes across is not only a turbulent mass, visually and acoustically, but also the mode of existing as part of a mass. This includes a mixture of close-ups and long shots, when you see images wherever your eyes take you, hitting moments when the images are very close and, due to their position close to the ground, low. Eye-to-eye with details, brushstrokes, lines, dripping colours, body parts and animals, while all those other things also keep happening. It is an embodied experience of the constant flipping of scale the images already show by themselves. There is not a single level, in this work, on which linearity remains possible. The utter convolutedness may leave us perplexed, and that is fortunate. For that state of puzzlement will have prepared us for a viewing attitude that makes us permeable to the multiple effects of encounters with people who have been hurt. This is how the artist offers a pathway to the healing of trauma. That pathway is a tightly textured community of sensitive people—sensitized by an art of painting that moves. Such a community can also be summoned without recourse to figurative images, as we can see in the work of Doris Salcedo.

ACT 2: STOP LOOKING AWAY

Movement, of the smallest, subtlest kind, trembles through an immense plaza consisting of large slabs, each 4.5 meters long, 1.28 centimeters wide, in sand colour, with a grainy surface of extremely fine pebbles, engineered to resist the absorption of water. Nearly effaced names are written on them, in a dark hue. These are written in sand. Overwriting these are other names, in the same size and font, engraved in shallow relief in the slabs. Suddenly, a shiny drop of water appears, rolling towards the relief; then more, until the letters of the name are filled and the water becomes a convex shiny surface, surmounting the flatness of the slabs. After a few minutes, the water letters start to tremble, then they disappear. Appearance and disappearance: the names keep moving. Moving, as physical instability, and as emotional effect, producing turmoil. The flat ground on which the visitor must walk, the humble material and

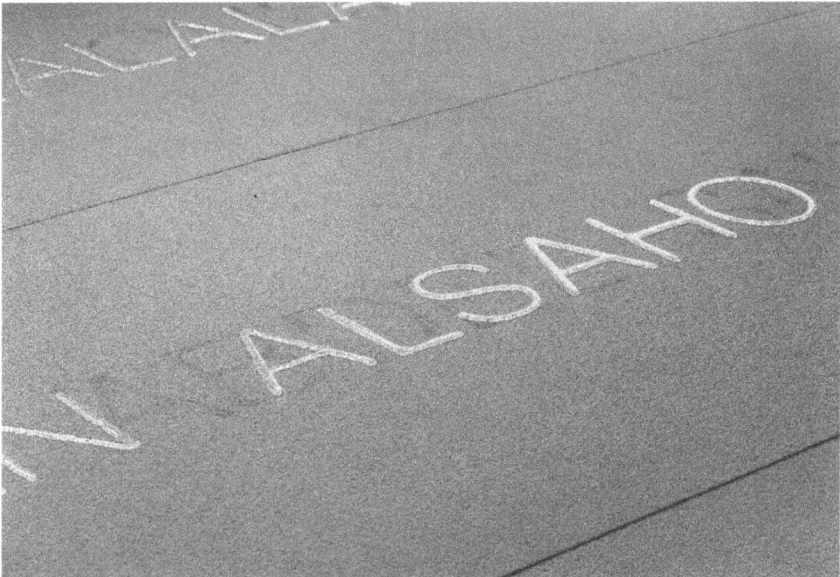

Figure 4.3. Doris Salcedo, *Palimpsesto*, 2013–2017. Water, sand, crushed marble, resin, metal. Dimensions variable. Collection of the artist. Photographer: Juan Fernando Castro.

the constant unsteadiness, these are the basic tenets of a recent artwork by Colombian artist Doris Salcedo titled *Palimpsest*. The water names overwrite the sand names, which remain as a palimpsest, a trace of forgotten people. The naming as the only literary element evokes the importance of naming in the Hebrew Bible. It is stipulating the uniqueness of a human being.[16]

This work opened at the Palacio de Cristal in the Parque del Retiro in Madrid in September 2017. In this work, movement, on the many levels just described, is again key to the work's effectiveness as an attempt at healing. When returning from experiencing it, hours long, and, still under its impact, I wondered how beauty can be at the same time a fierce indictment. Installed on commission by the Museo Reina Sofía, it stayed there for six months. Like Malani, Salcedo, whose art has been devoted from the beginning in the 1980s to counter the oblivion of violence and the violence of oblivion, has made one of the most brilliant political art installations I have ever seen. The term 'counter-monument' (Andreas Huyssen), although in certain ways appropriate, doesn't begin to cover it. It is also a performative work that keeps moving and changing. And by inviting the visitor to walk on it—there is no other space for us—it includes the public in the performance. Every step, one has to decide whether to avoid stepping on the names or, in what seems to me a callous indifference, walk on top of them (figure 4.4). The possibility

Figure 4.4. Doris Salcedo, *Palimpsesto*, 2013–2017. Water, sand, crushed marble, resin, metal. Dimensions variable. Collection of the artist. Photographer: Juan Fernando Castro.

of indifference also hits a nerve, since the names form a recollection of and homage to the innumerable victims of European indifference who drowned in the Mediterranean Sea.[17]

This is not a 'theme'; the work is not 'about' this acutely political issue. Doris Salcedo does not represent the violence she invokes, nor the oblivion she counters. Although her work is never abstract in the traditional sense, it never proclaims political opinions in the loud voice of so much art that calls itself political. Her work 'deconstructs,' in line with Derrida, the binary opposition between abstraction and figuration, which is also in line with Deleuze. The objects in her earlier work are concrete 'things'—stacked shirts, modified pieces of furniture—but they signify on a very different level, deploying affect and subtle light to touch their viewers. Without ever stating a 'theme,' the work concerns, and is committed to, a political cause. In *Palimpsest*, the issue at stake is the most tragic, over-visible due to the media yet too well-known to avoid becoming invisible, of the world in our time. Too much sand and too little water push people to embark on the precarious boats of human traffickers, only to perish on too much water. Sand and water: they are part of the basic conditions that preclude survival, so that people cannot stay where they were born and would like to have stayed if only they had the merest chance to survive the negative dialectic of too much (sand), too little (drink-able water), too much (sea water).[18]

An artwork can hardly be more *contemporary*—happening in our time, today. And it is devoted to that tragedy of ongoing violence we all, in Europe, continue to condone. The names tell us that the drowned are not an anony-mous mass but an enormous group of individuals, whose lives matter—each of them as human as we all are, or pretend to be. After five years of strenuous work and creativity, at great personal expense of time, artistic thought and economic resources, and importantly, in collaboration with a crew of twenty, *Palimpsest* shows the cultural necessity yet difficulty to mourn, to grieve for unknown dead. Salcedo's is a protest against the violence of indifference and of the acceptance, and even a certain stimulation of the murderous violence by governments—not only the Colombian one but by all governments, and in the case of *Palimpsest*, especially the European ones—that accepts the loss (with the tiniest majority) of the referendum for peace with the FARC. Salcedo immediately responded to this disastrous outcome with another enor-mous artwork, *Sumando Ausencias*, covering the entire surface of the central Plaza of Bogotá. This protest is at the same time an homage to each of those persons, now named by their names. That double effect, of soliciting indigna-tion and grief, of beauty and pain, is unspeakable. As Ludwig Wittgenstein stated at the end of the *Tractatus*, of what one cannot speak, one must keep silent. But later, he retracted, or modified that statement, when he said that of what one cannot speak, one must show. I titled my 2010 book on Salcedo's art after Wittgenstein's dictum.[19]

The surface of this work, adapted to the irregular shape of and the many columns in the building, covers the entirety of the Art Nouveau glass build-ing of the Palacio de Cristal, of 1.065 square meters. Each of the 220 slabs is 4.53 by 1.29 meters and weights 980 kilos. One can only imagine the lo-gistics of transporting it. The appearance and disappearance of the water has a strong impact, comparable to the pace of four turns per minute of Malani's cylinders, which makes it impossible to see it all in one turn, so that we want to stay for the next. In *Palimpsest*, it makes the visitor want to stay to see the vanishing water reappear, and thus witness the act of witnessing that this work constitutes and performs. One cannot write on water, and sand will not stay in place. But the artist demonstrates that one can write *with* water, and *with* sand. The names written in sand belong to victims of European indiffer-ence who died before the year 2010; the names written with water, to those who died after 2010. Only a fraction of the individuals who died could find a place in this enormous work. But that each of them counts is clear, as clear as the brilliant drops of water. The name is what distinguishes one human being from another; it is the label of her uniqueness. Against the abjection

Figure 4.5. Doris Salcedo, *Palimpsesto*, 2013–2017. Water, sand, crushed marble, resin, metal. Dimensions variable. Collection of the artist. Photographer: Juan Fernando Castro.

of anonymous death, the brilliance of the water dignifies the persons named. The transparency and the evaporation of the water with which the names are written constitute a subtle metaphor of the fragility of human existence and, in these cases, of the lives cut off too early.

A complex mechanism underneath the slabs pushes the water up, drop by drop, to the surface (figure 4.5). Each drop 'walks' towards the sculpted letters, through the tiniest hole in the stone, between the minuscule pebbles. When the drops merge and take leave from their brilliant appearance where the sun makes them look like precious stones, we realize we must resist that comparison because nothing stays stable and the material is humble. Instead, we see tears; the earth is crying. This weeping of the stone stands in for the absent tears of all of us, who shake off the everyday spectacle of deaths shown, in half a minute, on television. Instead, in Salcedo's installation, one is captivated enough to spend a long time *with* the dead. While waiting for the vanished water to return, we can and must take the time to reflect on the political issue so powerfully made tangible due to the absence of representation. Thus, as in all of Salcedo's art, grief is brought together with at least a minimal effort to suggest that we can, indeed must, break the cycle of silenced violence. The tool: memory.

Memory is usually understood as a *cultural* phenomenon as well as an *individual* and *social* one. Although the term 'cultural memory' has been quite popular for a few decades now, my assumption is that these three 'kinds' of memory cannot be separated. The distinction is only a matter of emphasis, of perspective and interest on the part of the memorizing subject. All memories have an individual, a social and a cultural aspect. This is only logical, since the subjects that remember are also participants in all three of these domains. Moreover, memories have a three-partite temporality. Memory is a connection between the three times of human temporal awareness: the past, in which things happened that the memory engages—or not; the present, in which the act of memorizing takes place and into which the remembered content is retrieved; and the future, which will be influenced by what the subjects in the present, together and embedded in their cultural environment, remember and do with those memories. I focus on 'cultural memory'—as I said, this is a focus only—one that brings forward political aspects, and the plurality of the subjects involved. In the installation, no visitor is alone. The fact of being together in a (social) space is an important aspect of the experience; while developing the thoughts that the work solicits, one is aware of being *with* those others as well as with the dead.[20]

Salcedo's work addresses cultural memory in its negativity, its failure, and seeks to find hints of solutions. Failure of memory is not so much *forgetting*, a very useful concept we should not 'forget' when considering memory; and one which Aleida Assmann, in her book *Formen des Vergessens*, usefully sums up as 'a filter, as a weapon and as a prerequisite for the creation of new things.' Instead, Salcedo's focus is an *actively*, albeit not necessarily purposely, *repressing* or, in a different view, *disassociating.* In other words, *dis-remembering*—as the title of a 2015 work of hers calls it. At the same time, she is referring to wilfully denying and erasing, in what can even go as far as bad faith, *distorting* potentially helpful memories. This is a form of *mis-remembering*. Both dis-remembering and mis-remembering are devastating, wasteful missed opportunities for the present and future. Without moralizing, Salcedo counters these failures. If she eschews representation, I imagine various reasons for this.[21]

These two failures of memory take shape in the cultural imagination in, and with which, humans exist. The *human figure* constitutes the primary subject matter of figurative literature and art, although by no means exclusively. In literature, especially narrative, the human figure takes on the propulsion of narrative thrust. As agent or patient, it carries the action that is the motor of the plot. Here this figure is named *character*. Both figure and character can be seen as figurations: *figurative* in that they embody ideas shaped in forms, and *figures* of anthropomorphic appearance that are, do and appear. It is the convergence of figure and character in their guise of figurations that projects the terms in which we tend to analyse art. A most emblematic manifestation is the recurrence of the self-portrait, and the memoir, autobiography or self-reflexive moments in fiction. I see in the convergence between art and its analysis the work of 'the anthropomorphic imagination.' With this newly coined term I mean a tendency to approach cultural artefacts through the lens or frame of frequently unacknowledged anthropomorphic concepts. The tools of analysis are thus made congruent to the objects.

This telescoping of object and analysis produces a number of tendencies, of which I will point out a few of the problematic ones. One such tendency is the conflation of artwork and the maker's *intention*. Another is the *unification* of the artwork, to resemble a unified human being anxious to hold himself together. A third tendency is the '*spiritualization*,' the de-materialization or dis-embodiment of art, art-making and viewing or reading. These three tendencies produce instances of failures of memory. It is in countering these tendencies that Salcedo's work yields to the victims in need of remembrance—a remembrance that their traumatized survivors badly need but cannot access. While recognizable for their subtlety and that intricate combination of formal beauty with affective bleakness, her works are impossible to 'sign.' They also pluralize the human beings they bring back to memory, thus precluding the anxious unification. And they are profoundly material. The material (above called 'humble') of sand and water make any spiritualizing tendency to disembody them futile. And while the work is so large as to cover an entire museal space, every name, every letter, every drop and every pebble counts as recollection of every human being destroyed by violence. To realize, feel and thus remember this is the *work* of art, which thus becomes a more serious, effective and stronger utterance than any news item or political debate—these days reduced to tweets anyway—can effectuate.

In this work with and for memory, Salcedo joins artists who deploy the shadow as the spectre of the dead returning. This is the profound link with Nalini Malani's shadow plays. The shadow as the trace, such as the names written in sand in *Palimpsest*, becomes a spectre when we take time itself into account. And time is the motor of memory, as well as of forgetting, dis-remembering, mis-remembering. When we think of time, we cannot ignore history, but I am under the impact of the contemporaneity of this artwork, hence, of the history of the present. There, the plurality of experiences of time lead to what I have called 'heterochrony.' One of the durational differences in the various experiences of time is the duration of the look—the Deleuzian 'crystal image,' that tangled unit of an actual image and its virtual image where we see the sprouting of moments of time through the various facets of the crystal, as if doubled. All these temporal forms are activated in the contemporary crystal of this multi-tentacled artwork.[22]

ACT 3: FROM CLASSICAL
LITERATURE TO CONTEMPORARY ART

Let me return to that Spanish soldier and his traumatic situation, the story of whom I began this chapter. In the end, the young man miraculously made it. He was redeemed after five years. But what happened in his mind, personality and body during those five years? How to continue living? He found art as a remedy. Returning to Spain, he proceeded to write the world's all-time bestselling novel, *El Ingenioso Hidalgo Don Quijote de la Mancha*, first published in 1605, the second part in 1615. It is a mad book about a mad man, who runs from adventure to adventure, mostly with unhappy endings. At first sight it reads like a parody of medieval epics and romances, and as a precursor of later novels that mock adventure stories, such as eighteenth-century *Jacques the Fatalist and His Master* (Denis Diderot, 1765–1770) and *The Life and Opinions of Tristram Shandy, Gentleman* (Laurence Sterne, 1759). It also resonates with postmodern novels of the late twentieth century. It is a book that, many say, is hilariously funny. Yet only recently has it been considered for its traumatic texture. It stands out in its intensity and creative expression of prolonged hopelessness. If such a literary work has achieved and retained the worldwide status as a masterpiece that it has, it is first of all because it has not lost any of its actuality. Every epoch knows of such situations that push human beings out of humanity. Formerly, in deep history, things happened that still happen, or happen again, today. Hence the epigraph, 'formerly is today.'[23]

The wandering knight is not the only one driven mad by trauma. In Part 1, chapter 23, a mad young man named Cardenio seeks to heal by telling the story of how he has been driven to madness. He has become attached to his madness, as a protective shield that saves him from worse. A few bystanders try to help, but they fail because they cannot listen well enough. The therapeutic attempt fails. Every time the mad man asks his interlocutors to listen in silence, but when they interrupt the patient's story, the latter falls into a rage and becomes violent. The tale is taken up several times with different addressees who all try to help as well: first a shepherd, who cautions Don Quijote before they meet young Cardenio; then Don Quijote himself, who gets distracted when his own obsession is alluded to; then, at the end, the priest. It begins to look as if Cardenio is searching for a good analyst: one with sympathy, who lets him speak and takes him seriously. He is looking for solidarity. Silence is his condition.

The scene begins with a distant view of the young man jumping around in the mountains. Then a shepherd tries to help Don Quijote, who walks painstakingly after having been beaten up, accompanied and supported by his

squire Sancho Panza, by telling him the story of the young man and his own
failure to help him:

> But he suddenly fell silent in the middle of his speech and fixed his eyes on the
> ground for quite a while. We waited quietly and expectantly, though in some
> alarm to see how this fit would end. . . . From all this we could easily tell that
> some fit of madness had come upon him. . . . in a great fury he got up from
> the ground . . . and attacked the man nearest to him with such reckless rage . . .
> [190][24]

When Don Quijote and Sancho Panza find Cardenio, the good knight tries to
comfort him, showing his understanding of trauma, almost guaranteeing his
help:

> Should your misfortune be such as to close all doors to every kind of consola-
> tion, it is my intention to join you in your grief and lamentations; for it is still
> some consolation in sorrows to find someone to grieve for them . . . I entreat
> you, sir . . . to tell me who you are, and the cause which has brought you to live
> and die in these wastelands like a brute beast, for your dress and your person
> show this . . . I swear that I will serve you with all the loyalty to which who I
> am obliges me, either by relieving your misfortune, if any relief is possible, or
> by joining you in bewailing it, as I have promised. [192; trans. adapted]

Here, he offers solidarity. Again, Cardenio is willing to tell his traumatizing
story on the condition that he not be interrupted. He is explicit enough: 'If you
wish me to explain to you, gentlemen, the immensity of my misfortunes in a
few words, you must promise not to interrupt the thread of my sad tale with
any question or remark; for the moment you do so, my narrative will end.'
[193] And he adds, as if rediscovering who he is: '[M]y name is Cardenio.'
But alas, Don Quijote is incapable of unconditional listening; when Cardenio
mentions Don Quijote's favourite literary genre, his own mad obsession wins,
and he interrupts. The young man bursts into a rage.

The scene reads like a mise-en-abyme of the novel, of trauma theory,
and in addition, of the problem of voyeurism and inter-male rivalry, which
in Cardenio's case is the traumatogenic element. In the course of his story,
Cardenio says:

> I praised Luscinda's beauty, her grace and wit, so much that my praise roused
> a desire in him to see a maiden endowed with such virtues. To my own misfor-
> tune I yielded to him, and let him see her one night by the light of a candle at a
> window through which it was our habit to talk. She was dressed in a loose wrap,
> looking so beautiful that he forgot all the beauties he had ever seen. . . . Now
> Luscinda happened to ask me for a book of chivalry to read, one she was very
> fond of. It was *Amadis of Gaul* . . . [196]

This is the trigger for Don Quijote's failure as a good analyst. He shouts out:

'If you had told me, sir, at the beginning of your story that lady Luscinda was fond of books of chivalry. . . . Pardon me, sir, for having broken our promise not to interrupt your story; but when I hear of matters of chivalry and of knights errant, I cannot prevent myself from talking of them.' [197]

In other words, he cannot listen to the 'you' who speaks to him, but appropriates the latter's story to feed his own. Selfishness wins over the well-meant generosity.

The novel carries not only the traces of the absurdity and madness that suggest, without ever mentioning it, the inevitably traumatic state in which its creator must have been locked, upon his return to Spain, as transpires in the stories told, but also foregrounds this consequence of war and captivity in the madness of its literary form. Often, such literary masterpieces are adapted into films. The sheer endless stream of 'adventures' makes all film adaptations of this novel more or less hopeless endeavours, however. One can barely read, let alone watch all those pointless attempts to help others, the aftermath of which involves cruelty and pain. If we—actor Mathieu Montanier and myself—nevertheless sought to make an audio-visual work based on the novel, it is because the repercussions of violence, of hopeless stagnation in situations of which the end is not in sight, need and deserve exploration, so that viewers can learn from it for dealing with their own experiences as well as those hinted at by others in their surroundings. This is what I call in my title, 'improving public space.'[25]

The challenge to make a video project based on *Don Quijote* appeals to two ambitions. First, the current situation of the world makes a deeper, creative reflection on trauma and its assault on human subjectivity an urgent task for art. The insights the novel harbours uniquely connect to other experiences of war, violence and captivity. Second, the project is also an attempt at facilitating healing. As a mostly narrative medium, film seems the least apt to do justice to the turbulent incoherence, repetitiveness and incongruous episodes told in the novel; yet due to its capacity for audio-visualization, a well-thought-through video project can explore and transgress the limits of what can be seen, shown, narrated and witnessed. Heeding once more Wittgenstein's ending of his *Tractatus* (1921), 'Of what one cannot speak, one should keep silent' in its later modified version into 'Of what one cannot speak, one can still show,' we hoped to explore the importance of showing as a 'silent,' non-interruptive way of enabling *witnessing*. Witnessing, as an engaged activity against the indifference of the world.

In order to do justice to the peculiar, cyclic, perhaps even 'hysterical' form of the novel while pursuing these two goals, only an equally 'incoherent,' episodic artwork can be effective. But this artwork must exceed a plain similarity. In view of the need for witnessing, such a form enables viewers to construct their own story and connect it to what they have seen around them. Thus, we aimed to turn the hysteria of endless storytelling into a reflection on communication beyond the boundaries that madness draws around its captive subjects, and instead, open up their subjectivity; briefly, we aimed to bring Cervantes closer to Proust.

To achieve this, we expected that the creation and production of singular installation pieces would facilitate experimenting with the episodic nature of the literary masterpiece. These pieces, which we called 'scenes,' would be presentations of situations. To give insight into the stagnation that character-izes the adventures, the pieces are predominantly *descriptive*. Any attempt at narrative is 'stuttering,' recurring, without any sense of development, and often, the images do not match the dialogues.

What French theorist of trauma-induced madness Françoise Davoine calls, citing Fernand Braudel, 'poussières d'événements'[26] was the guideline of this work's form: sprinkling situations, moments, over the stage or throughout the gallery space. That space serves as a public space, the texture of which the work aims to improve. Thus, the tenuous line of a single narrative yields to an installation that puts the visitor in the position of making her own narra-tive out of what is there, while witnessing the events. This is adequate to the state of trauma presented in the pieces, and to the need to stretch out a hand to, instead of turning away from, people hurt so deeply.

The traumatic state looms over the entire project, and determines its form. Therefore, we wanted to try something I had never done: completely merge the author's biography, the main character's ostensive and much-commented-upon madness, and the main character of the one narrative unit we had se-lected for a narrative element, 'The Captive's Story,' as three incarnations of the desperate attempt to recover from the world's most horrid crime: to destroy the subjectivity of others by violence—from war to rape to captivity. The name Don Quijote, thus, identifies that hybrid figure.[27]

The form of these pieces is experimental in many different ways, so that a contemporary aesthetic can reach out to, and touch, a situation of long ago, if only because such situations continue to occur. Long, enduring shots predomi-nate, five to eight minutes per shot. Sound-wise, some are quiet, some loud. As far as possible, they consist of single-shot pieces and remain, as far as possible, uncut. Another experimental form concerns the dynamic relationship between visibility and invisibility, image and writing. A frequent deployment of voice-off without synchronicity with the images—also a novelty in our work—fore-grounds this tension. The actor Mathieu Montanier is visible (figure 4.6), but so are the letters of inscriptions, in association with other texts, to foreground

Figure 4.6. Mathieu Montanier as 'The Captive' in the video project by Mieke Bal: *Don Quijote: Tristes Figures*. Photograph: Ebba Sund (2019). With the support of the Linnaeus University Centre for Concurrences in Colonial and Postcolonial Studies and the Linnaeus University Centre for Intermedial and Multimodal Studies.

the nature of video-*graphy* as a form of writing. We also experimented with different combinations of sequences, including mounting multiple images on a screen. Hence, through experimenting with possible forms of the art of video, we sought to invent new forms for the formlessness of trauma.

At the end of this essay, then, I must reiterate my beginning question: What can art do to help the healing of trauma? Not much, but nevertheless, as I hope to have shown, it can do something no other cultural form is capable of. It can create a community, not through coercion, propaganda or manipulation, but through motivating the deployment of the imagination in freedom. Community, and each individual that is, becomes and feels to be part of it do not as such heal trauma, but fulfil a first indispensable condition *sine qua non* for a beginning of healing.

NOTES

1. Charlotte Delbo, *Auschwitz and After*, trans. Rosette C. Lamont, with a foreword by Lawrence L. Langer (New Haven, CT and London: Yale University Press, 1995), 267.

2. This is one of many catchphrases I borrow from Françoise Davoine, *Don Quichotte, pour combattre la mélancolie* (Paris: Stock, L'autre pensée, 2008), and Françoise Davoine and Jean-Max Gaudillière, *A bon entendeur, salut! Face à la perversion, le retour de Don Quichotte* (Paris: Stock, L'autre pensée, 2013). For biographical information, I rely mostly on María Antonia Garcés, *Cervantes in Algiers: A Captive's Tale* (Nashville, TN: Vanderbilt University Press, 2002). Without these authors, I would really not know where to begin reading *Don Quijote*—as a witness, rather than a tourist.

3. The most accessible of these witness statements is María Antonia Garcés, ed., Antonio de Sosa 2011 [second half sixteenth century], *An Early Modern Dialogue with Islam: Antonio de Sosa's* Topography of Algiers *(1612)*, trans. Diana de Armas Wilson (South Bend, IN: University of Notre Dame Press).

4. Examples of the graphic representation of trauma are discussed in Miriam Haughton, *Staging Trauma: Bodies in Shadow* (London: Palgrave Macmillan, 2018). The almost abusive diffusing of the term is devastatingly demonstrated in Margaret Iversen, *Photography, Trace and Trauma* (Chicago: University of Chicago Press, 2017). There the term is equated with shock, even change (18), and in the end, with modernity and photography. This diffusion is an erasure; it is what makes trauma and responsibility unspeakable.

5. My use of 'public space' alludes to the aesthetic theory of Alexander Gottlieb Baumgarten, from 1750.

6. The most comprehensive and most recent account of Malani's work is *Nalini Malani, The Rebellion of the Dead, Retrospective 1969–2018 Part II*, ed. Marcella Beccaria (Ostfildern, Germany: Hatje Cantz, 2018). On her unique erasure performances, see my book *In Medias Res: Inside Nalini Malani's Shadow Plays* (Ostfildern, Germany: Hatje Cantz, 2016), 'Prologue: Entering,' 19–23. For each exhibition she makes a large drawing in charcoal which is then erased during or at the end of the show, leaving traces.

7. She says this several times in a book on which we (Michelle Williams Gamaker and I) have based a video project. See Françoise Davoine, *Mother Folly: A Tale*, trans. Judith G. Miller (Stanford, CA: Stanford University Press, 2014). For the video project—feature film and installations—see http://www.miekebal.org/artworks/films/a-long-history-of-madness/.

8. What follows is partly derived, but revised, from my extended analysis of *In Search* in my book on Malani's shadow plays (see note 6). Fragments from this work can be seen in a trailer on YouTube; see https://www.youtube.com/watch?v=6uK9iRoPds8 (4").

9. The Cassandra myth, best known in the tragedy *Agamemnon* from Aeschylus's trilogy *Oresteia*, has been brought to bear on the present in Christa Wolf's 1983 novel *Cassandra*, published in English in 1988 by Strauss and Farrar, New York, translated by Jan von Heurck.

10. On thought-images, especially literary ones related to trauma, see Gerhard Richter, *Thought-Images: Frankfurt School Writers' Reflections on Damaged Life* (Stanford, CA: Stanford University Press, 2007).

11. Among many critical essays on Conrad's novel, see Edward Said, 'Two Visions in *Heart of Darkness*,' in *Culture and Imperialism* (New York: Random House, 1993), 22–31, to get a sense of the novel in context.

12. That the logic of negativity entailing vagueness has the potential to fill itself up with meaning has been forcefully argued by historiographer Hayden White in a seminal essay, 'The Forms of Wildness: Archaeology of an Idea,' in *The Wild Man Within: An Image in Western Thought from the Renaissance to Romanticism*, eds. Edward Dudley and Maximillian E. Novak (Pittsburgh, PA: University of Pittsburgh Press, 1972), 1–38. For the tradition of negativity in relation to politics, see Diana Coole, *Negativity and Politics: Dionysus and Dialectics from Kant to Poststructuralism* (London and New York: Routledge, 2000). Deleuze and Guattari have amended the traditional meanings of abstraction and the aesthetics derived from it, turning abstraction into the potential for new figuration. See *A Thousand Plateaus: Capitalism and Schizophrenia*, trans. Brian Massumi (London: Athlone Press, 1987). For an explanation and background, see my book on the political force of abstraction, *Endless Andness: The Politics of Abstraction According to Ann Veronica Janssens* (London: Bloomsbury, 2013).

13. Originally written in Urdu, the poem by Pakistani poet Faiz Ahmad Faiz (1911–1984), translated by Agha Shahid Ali, was published in English as part of Faiz's posthumous bilingual collection *The Rebel's Silhouette: Selected Poems* (Delhi: Oxford University Press, 1991).

14. Significantly in another way, the poem is read by Malani in the film *Cassandra's Gift* (2012) by Payal Kapadia, which accompanies the artist book made for the presentation of *In Search of Vanished Blood* at Documenta 13. That title was also used for an exhibition that included this work at the Vadehra Art Gallery in New Delhi.

15. The sign as two sides of a sheet of paper was Ferdinand de Saussure's metaphor for the inseparability of signifier and signified. The work of the Swiss linguist (1857–1913) was posthumously published on the basis of his students' notes. See Jonathan Culler, *Ferdinand de Saussure* (Ithaca, NY: Cornell University Press, 1986), for a brilliant and very accessible introduction to Saussure's thought, including the metaphor of a sign as the inseparable two sides of a sheet of paper.

16. On Salcedo's work up to the 2010s, see my book *Of What One Cannot Speak: Doris Salcedo's Political Art* (Chicago: University of Chicago Press, 2010); an extended version was translated by Marcelo Cohen with Miguel Á. Hernández Navarro as *De lo que no se puede hablar: el arte política de Doris Salcedo* (Bogotá, Colombia: Universidad Nacional de Colombia, sede Medellín / Panamericana, 2014).

17. Among many publications on memory and counter-memory, such as *Present Pasts: Urban Palimpsests and the Politics of Memory* (Stanford, CA: Stanford University Press, 2003), Huyssen also published an online interview that states his position very lucidly. See https://www.politika.io/en/notice/state-of-the-art-in-memory-studies-an-interview-with-andreas-huyssen. Huyssen also wrote about both Malani and Salcedo.

18. Deleuze's view of abstraction is best explained in a clear and lucid article by John Rajchman, 'Another View of Abstraction,' *Journal of Philosophy and the Visual Arts* 5.16 (1995): 16–24.

19. See the final sentence of Ludwig Wittgenstein, *Tractatus Logico-Philosophicus*, trans. David Francis Pears and Brian McGuinness (New York and London: Routledge, 2001). On his change of opinion see *Philosophical Investigations* #41, commented on by Davoine and Gaudillière, 17, 51–52, who quote Maurice O'Drury, *Conversations avec Ludwig Wittgenstein*, trans. J.-P. Cometti (Paris: PUF, 2002), 159, 170, 173.

20. On memory, with special focus on cultural memory and traumatic (non-) memory, see *Acts of Memory: Cultural Recall in the Present*, eds. Mieke Bal, Jonathan Crewe and Leo Spitzer (Hanover, NH: University Press of New England, 1999). In this volume, the contribution by Ernst van Alphen is especially crucial for an understanding of trauma, and that of Marianne Hirsch for photographic expressions of trauma.

21. See Aleida Assmann's important work on memory and community, especially her *Formen des Vergessens* (Göttingen: Wallstein, 2016).

22. On heterochrony, see Mieke Bal and Miguel Á. Hernández Navarro *2MOVE: Video, Art, Migration* (Murcia, Spain: Cendeac, 2008). On the crystal image, Deleuze wrote: 'What constitutes the crystal-image is the most fundamental operation of time: since the past is constituted not after the present that it was but at the same time, time has split itself in two at each moment as present and past, which differ from each other in nature, or . . . it has to split the present in two heterogeneous directions, one of which is launched towards the future while the other falls into the past. Time has to split at the same time as it sets itself out or unrolls itself: it splits in two dissymmetrical jets, one of which makes all the present pass on, while the other preserves all the past. Time consists of this split, and it is this, it is time, that we *see in the crystal*.' (Gilles Deleuze, *Cinema 2: The Time-Image*, trans. Hugh Tomlinson and Robert Galeta (Minneapolis: University of Minnesota Press 1989), 82; emphasis in text.

23. On the humour in Cervantes's novel, see many of the essays in Roberto González Echevarría, ed., *Cervantes' Don Quixote: A Casebook* (Oxford: Oxford University Press 2005). The traumatic background and texture of the novel has been analysed by Garcés (see note 2). This presentation introduces a video project I developed with French actor Mathieu Montanier. See http://www.miekebal.org/artworks/exhibitions/don-quijote-tristes-figuras/, accessed 23 January 2020.

24. For easy access I am quoting from the Penguin edition, in the translation by J. M. Cohen, first published in 1950.

25. Adaptation is an increasingly practised academic discipline. I find the term slightly problematic, as has also been argued by its prime scholar, Thomas Leitch, in his decisive critique of the normative tendencies in the field. See Thomas Leitch, 'Twelve Fallacies in Contemporary Adaptation Theory,' *Criticism* 45.2 (2003): 149–71. I have published an article on this issue, 'Intership: Anachronism between Loyalty and the Case,' *The Oxford Handbook of Adaptation Studies*, ed. Thomas Leitch (New York and Oxford: Oxford University Press, 2017), 179–96.

26. Braudel, in Davoine, *Don Quichotte, pour combattre la mélancolie*, 43–44.

27. The trauma incurred by Cervantes after losing the use of his left hand, almost drowning, then being held in captivity as a slave without any sense of an ending to his disempowered state and his suffering, has been beautifully traced, narrated and ex-

plained by Colombian literary-historical scholar María Antonia Garcés in *Cervantes in Algiers*. The recurrence of traumatogenic situations is demonstrated by the fact that this contemporary author has herself been wounded by captivity at the hands of the FARC, as she states in her book.

BIBLIOGRAPHY

ASSMANN, Aleida. *Formen des Vergessens.* Göttingen: Wallstein, 2016.

BAL, Mieke. *Endless Andness: The Politics of Abstraction according to Ann Veronica Janssens*. London: Bloomsbury, 2013.

BAL, Mieke. *In Medias Res: Inside Nalini Malani's Shadow Plays.* Ostfildern, Germany: Hatje Cantz, 2016.

BAL, Mieke. *Of What One Cannot Speak: Doris Salcedo's Political Art*. Chicago: University of Chicago Press, 2010. Extended version in Spanish translated by Marcelo Cohen with Miguel Á. Hernández Navarro. *De lo que no se puede hablar: el arte política de Doris Salcedo*. Bogotá, Colombia: Universidad Nacional de Colombia, sede Medellín / Panamericana, 2014.

BAL, Mieke, Jonathan Crewe and Leo Spitzer, editors. *Acts of Memory: Cultural Recall in the Present*. Hanover, NH: University Press of New England, 1999.

BAL, Mieke and Miguel Á. Hernández Navarro. *2MOVE: Video, Art, Migration*. Murcia, Spain: Cendeac, 2008.

COOLE, Diana. *Negativity and Politics: Dionysus and Dialectics from Kant to Poststructuralism*. London and New York: Routledge, 2000.

CULLER, Jonathan. *Ferdinand de Saussure.* Ithaca, NY: Cornell University Press, 1986.

DAVOINE, Françoise. *Don Quichotte, pour combattre la mélancolie.* Paris: Stock, L'autre pensée, 2008.

DAVOINE, Françoise. *Mother Folly: A Tale.* Translated by Judith G. Miller. Stanford, CA: Stanford University Press, 2014.

DAVOINE, Françoise and Jean-Max Gaudillière. *A bon entendeur, salut! Face à la perversion, le retour de Don Quichotte*. Paris: Stock, L'autre pensée, 2013.

DELBO, Charlotte, *Auschwitz and After*. Translated by Rosette C. Lamont, with an Introduction by Lawrence L. Langer. New Haven, CT and London: Yale University Press, 1995.

DELEUZE, Gilles. *Cinema 2: The Time-Image*. Translated by Hugh Tomlinson and Robert Galeta. Minneapolis: University of Minnesota Press, 1989.

DELEUZE, Gilles and Félix Guattari. *A Thousand Plateaus: Capitalism and Schizophrenia.* Translated by Brian Massumi. London: Athlone Press, 1987.

FAIZ, Faiz Ahmat. *The Rebel's Silhouette: Selected Poems.* Delhi: Oxford University Press, 1991.

GARCÉS, María Antonia. *Cervantes in Algiers: A Captive's Tale.* Nashville, TN: Vanderbilt University Press, 2002.

GARCÉS, María Antonia, editor. Antonio de Sosa [second half sixteenth century]. *An Early Modern Dialogue with Islam: Antonio de Sosa's* Topography of Algiers

(1612). Translated by Diana de Armas Wilson. South Bend, IN: University of Notre Dame Press, 2011.

GONZÁLEZ ECHEVARRÍA, Roberto, editor. *Cervantes' Don Quixote: A Casebook.* Oxford: Oxford University Press, 2005.

HAUGHTON, Miriam. *Staging Trauma: Bodies in Shadow.* London: Palgrave Macmillan, 2018.

HUYSSEN, Andreas. *Present Pasts: Urban Palimpsests and the Politics of Memory.* Stanford, CA: Stanford University Press, 2003.

IVERSEN, Margaret. *Photography, Trace and Trauma.* Chicago: University of Chicago Press, 2017.

LEITCH, Thomas. 'Twelve Fallacies in Contemporary Adaptation Theory.' *Criticism* 45.2 (2003): 149–71.

MALANI, Nalini. *The Rebellion of the Dead, Retrospective 1969-2018 Part II.* Edited by Marcella Beccaria. Ostfildern, Germany: Hatje Cantz, 2018.

O'DRURY, Maurice. *Conversations avec Ludwig Wittgenstein.* Translated by J. P. Cometti, Paris: PUF, 2002.

RAJCHMAN, John. 'Another View of Abstraction.' *Journal of Philosophy and the Visual Arts* 5.16 (1995): 16–24.

RICHTER, Gerhard. *Thought-Images: Frankfurt School Writers' Reflections on Damaged Life.* Stanford, CA: Stanford University Press, 2007.

SAID, Edward. 'Two Visions in *Heart of Darkness*.' In *Culture and Imperialism.* New York: Random House, 1993. 22–31.

WHITE, Hayden. 'The Forms of Wildness: Archaeology of an Idea.' In *The Wild Man Within: An Image in Western Thought from the Renaissance to Romanticism.* Edited by Edward Dudley and Maximillian E. Novak.1–38. Pittsburgh, PA: University of Pittsburgh Press, 1972.

WITTGENSTEIN, Ludwig. *Philosophical Investigations.* Translated by G. E. M. Anscombe. Oxford: Blackwell, 1958.

WITTGENSTEIN, Ludwig. *Tractatus Logico-Philosophicus.* Translated by David Francis Pears and Brian McGuinness. New York and London: Routledge, 2001.

WOLF, Christa. *Cassandra.* Translated by Jan von Heurck. New York: Farrar, Straus and Giroux, 1988 [1983].

Chapter Five

Transforming Trauma into Memory

Ernst van Alphen

In his book *Multidirectional Memory*, Michael Rothberg quotes Israeli and Palestinian spokespeople in order to illustrate the spiralling logic of memory production: 'After an Israeli defence official warned Palestinians that they would be subject to a "Shoah" (disaster or Holocaust) if they continued firing rockets from the Gaza Strip into Israel, a Hamas official answered that Palestinians were faced with "new Nazis."'[1] In this confrontation of different histories, memories are borrowed and cross-referenced. The confrontation demonstrates well that memory is an act performed in the present and establishing a relationship with the past. In the words of Rothberg: 'memory is the past made present.'[2] This quotation implies that memory is not a past but a contemporary phenomenon, and that memory is 'a form of work, working through, labor, or action.'[3] Acts of memory are performed in order to deal with the present situation and at the same time to work through multiple traumatic pasts.[4]

Multidirectional memory suggests that memories are not owned by groups, nor are groups 'owned' by memories:

> Rather, the borders of memory and identity are jagged; what looks at first like my own property often turns out to be a borrowing or adaptation from a history that initially might seem foreign or distant. Memory's anachronistic quality—its bringing together of now and then, here and there—is actually the source of its powerful creativity, its ability to build new worlds out of the materials of older ones.[5]

The commonsense notion of memory as recall of the past and as privately owned is complicated by the idea that memory builds new worlds out of the material of older ones. The 'powerful creativity' of memory should, however, not be understood in terms of false memory, or silencing 'real' memories, but as displacement according to the logic of a 'screen memory.' As Freud describes it in his essay 'Screen Memories' (1899) and in his book *The Psychopathology of Everyday Life* (1909), a screen memory covers up a traumatic event that cannot be approached directly. 'Screen memory stands in or substitutes for a more disturbing or painful memory that it displaces from consciousness.'[6] The creativity of acts of memory can now be understood in two ways. It is either a displacement or substitution of a traumatic event, or an effort to work through a traumatic event.[7] The first function is a matter of survival, whereas the second function is a matter of healing.

In this chapter I will focus on a striking example of multidirectional memory, namely, the traumatic pasts of two nations: the past of the Holocaust and the past of Al Nakba, the expulsion of more than 700,000 Palestinians from Mandatory Palestine. The common ground of these two disasters, legitimizing the birth of the state of Israel and legitimizing the not-yet-established state of Palestine, is that both disasters have resulted in memories of rootedness. Rootedness in the same land, that is. These multidirectional memories of rootedness will be assessed through the art practice of Dutch artist Marjan Teeuwen.[8] In 2016–2017 she made an installation in the destroyed house of a Hamas member in Gaza. The house had been bombed by the Israeli army, and one son of the owner was killed in the destruction of the family home. I will argue that Teeuwen's installation in the destroyed house in Gaza is an effort to transform symbolically this traumatic event into memory, to work through the traumatic past into the temporality of memory.

ROOTEDNESS IN THE LAND

The conflict between Israel and Palestine originates in historical ruptures of their respective bonds between the land and the people.[9] The ancient Jewish people were exiled by the hands of the Romans from the land they felt connected to and identified with. It was only after two thousand years, in 1948, that they were able to return to the land they originally came from by establishing the State of Israel. This led to a relay of exilic existence: Palestinians have experienced exile in more recent times, since the foundation of the State of Israel in 1948, which has resulted in the expulsion of hundreds of thousands of Palestinians from the land in which they have been rooted for thousands of years.

The Israeli/Palestinian conflict is not just an armed conflict fought by means of conventional weapons. Ultimately it is a war on memory, in which houses and trees are employed as powerful instruments of warfare. Both states claim to be rooted in the same land, and those claims are based on memory. Houses and trees have become the most important cultural symbols that are central in the two peoples' respective articulations of rootedness. Houses and trees remind Israelis as well as Palestinians symbolically of their rootedness in the same contested area. As Laura van Gelder put it, these cultural symbols claiming rootedness and ownership over the land have become major stakes in this war of memory, 'of which some of the most salient examples are Israel's massive uprooting of Palestinian olive trees, the punitive demolition of Palestinian homes, and the Israeli overplanting of bulldozed Palestinian orchards and villages with non-native pine forests,' as well as the construction of settlements in East Jerusalem and at the West Bank.[10] Israeli legal scholar Irus Braverman suggests that the seeming unimportance of houses and trees to the Israeli/Palestinian conflict harbours a denial of their true significance. He argues that acts of planting/uprooting and building/unbuilding are in fact 'acts of war,' regulated by a range of legal strategies.[11]

But what does one destroy when one destroys a house? First of all, the building that the word 'house' refers to. Although today more and more people live in tents or other temporary constructions, and a house can also refer to a boat, as in a houseboat, we first of all think of an architectural construction, a building, in which people live and which they have made their home. But the word 'house' signifies more than just the building that offers a home; it also stands for 'family.' When we talk about the House of Orange, for instance, we do not refer to one of their royal palaces. The term covers the complete lineage and ancestry of the family, not only the family members that are still alive. In other words, the word 'house' also refers to a family and its roots, to genealogical memory.

In languages such as English and Dutch, this use of the word house is metaphorical. Only in special contexts and cases does the word house have the meaning of 'family' as intertwined with the architectural meaning. The best-known example is Edgar Allen Poe's story 'The Fall of the House of Usher.' The House of Usher is not diagnosed by its destruction but by its downfall, which indicates that it concerns primarily a family and not a building, although the collapse of the building materializes the downfall, indeed the extinction, of the family. In Arab and Hebrew, however, there is one term that has these two different meanings systematically. The Arab word 'bait' and the Hebrew word 'bet' have the same double meaning and are pronounced in the same way. In those languages the destruction of a house is completely ambiguous: it refers to the destruction of a building that serves as a home to people and to the destruction of the genealogical memory of a family. It also invokes the one through reference to the other, because the material construction is the equivalent of the roots of the family it harbours.

In the recent art projects of Marjan Teeuwen, the term 'destroyed house' contains yet another ambiguity. The titles of these projects are specified by the location of the house: *Destroyed House* (2007–2008), *Destroyed House Krasnoyarsk* (2009), *Destroyed House Piet Mondriaanstraat* (2010–2011), *Destroyed House Bloemhof* (2012), *Destroyed House Op Noord* (2014), *Destroyed House Leiden* (2015) and, most recently, *Destroyed House Gaza* (2017) (figures 5.1 and 5.2). All these projects were interventions in houses that were discarded and destined to be destroyed. They were old or ruined and there was no reason to renovate them anymore. It was their fate to be destroyed. Teeuwen's interventions in these old, ruined houses look at first sight as a further destruction of houses that are already in the process of being destroyed. She breaks away floors or walls, which gives the impression of performing the finishing stroke or fatal blow. The project of the artist is, then, not an act of creation, but an act of destruction; or better, in her projects, creation is a form of destruction. But there is more to it.

Teeuwen re-uses the remainders of the ruined houses. They are piled up; windows or other kinds of openings are closed off by leftover materials. She also creates sculptures out of debris, rubbish and used materials. These added interventions to the ruined house sometimes consist of an arbitrary collection of materials. Sometimes, however, all the re-used materials are selected and categorized on the basis of materials and colours. Teeuwen did this, for example, in her Archive series and in the architectural sculptures created in several of her Destroyed Houses. Most of the time the re-used materials are selected on the basis of colours, mostly the colour white or black. For instance, she produces harmonious white piles and architectural sculptures consisting of plaster plate, plasterboard, wood, plastics and so on. Other times the piles are intersected by horizontal black stripes of the space in between the layers of plasterboard. Or the use of painted planks, which formerly covered the floors, results in structured piles that counter the desolate disharmony of the discarded houses. Although the structured piles are highly complex, aesthetically they look minimalistic because of the seriality of the structures and the reduced colour scheme: black, the brown colour of wood, but especially white are the dominant colours. Earlier works, like the *Huiskamer* (Living Room) series are extremely colourful. They look as if all the belongings present in a living room have been re-ordered into piles, without making a selection on the basis of colour or kind of object. Although these works do not make a minimalistic impression because of the abundance of colours and the great variety of objects, these works, too, demonstrate an obsessive practice of ordering and structuring.

Whereas a house that is designated to be destroyed tends to look chaotic, Teeuwen's interventions create order and structure. Her ordered piles of

Figure 5.1. Verwoest Huis Gaza 1, 2017, 155 x 225 cm, inkjet print on dibond/framed (courtesy of the artist).

whatever kind of materials adds beauty to the desolate spaces of the deserted building, no longer a house, for no longer the haven of a family. This creation of beauty and harmony out of chaos and destruction is, however, not an end in itself. The beauty of the practice of ordering and structuring is highly significant; it embodies the ordering activity of memory. The activity of memory is explicitly evoked by the titles of a series of works she made between 2007 and 2010 in the Archive series: *Archive 1–4, Archive Sheddak SM's, Archive Johannesburg* and a recent commission, *Archive Temporarily Hall of Justice Amsterdam 1–5*. Although not situated in discarded houses, and not dealing with architectural interventions like destroying walls, floors and ceilings, these works all share characteristics with the Destroyed Houses. Archives are physical storages of memory, and in archival processes we can recognize the activity of memory. Archives and memory collect objects and events. But they do not do this arbitrarily. Archives and memory are selective in how they collect. If they did not select, they would end up as arbitrary storages. But the ordering activity of archives and memory implies that many objects and events are discarded, refused, repressed, forgotten. What is selected to be kept and relished is not just stored. Archives and memory categorize; they put together objects or events with the same or similar qualities. They create links between objects and events that are different in some respects but have qualities in common in other respects.[12]

This view of the archive and, or as, memory suggests that Teeuwen's interventions in discarded houses should be understood as archival practices embodying the work of memory. Her creation of order in chaos concerns both a rebuilding/transformation of the house and a return of memory to the house. She visualizes and materializes the house-as-memory, the work of memory and the rooting of the people who lived there, which are embodied by the house. Not the roots, but the rooting. From this perspective, it is important to notice that her interventions in the discarded houses do not only consist of pilings of selected leftover materials. She also opens up floors or removes walls, creating views in spaces that were so far closed off. Connections and associations established by the activity of memory are enabled by opening up and connecting all spaces in these houses. The house as embodiment of memory depends on the intensification and materialization of links, relations and connections, performed by the opening up of all surfaces that so far blocked views. In this, Teeuwen's projects resonate with the famous view of memory presented by Frances A. Yates, who traced the theories of memory from antiquity on, before the invention of print came along to assist us in memorizing. She focused especially on the art of memorizing by means of a walk through a house. Each room becomes the storage space for particular memories, and space becomes the host of time. Many artists have taken up Yates's vision, among whom the Italian writer Italo Calvino.[13]

Teeuwen's Destroyed Houses are often compared to the works of American artist Gordon Matta-Clark, who died at the age of thirty-five in 1978. These comparisons make sense only at first sight, but become much less meaningful when we look more closely at their projects. Like Teeuwen, Matta-Clark intervened in houses that were going to be demolished. He opened up views in and through the building by removing geometrical forms from walls or floors. Often this gave the impression that the house was hit by a meteorite. In contrast with Teeuwen, he never selected, re-used and re-ordered the materials that came out of the house. He called his artistic practice 'anarchitecture,' conflating the word 'anarchy' with 'architecture.' This condensation added the political twist of anarchy to the domain of architecture and the space of one's home. The personal domain of the home was opened up by the public domain, inside and outside were connected, and the place of the home was converted into a state of mind that refused the political distinction between personal and public.[14]

Both Teeuwen and Matta-Clark transform buildings into artistic statements. But Teeuwen's interventions in discarded houses take a very different direction. Although she also opens up views in and through the houses in which she intervenes, her selecting and re-ordering of the materials of the house resonate with the surrounding social reality in a different way from Matta-Clark's interventions. The devices by means of which Teeuwen embodies the inner activity and process of memory in the ruined houses cannot be recognized in the works of the American artist. Nor are the meanings these interventions generate comparable to Matta-Clark's effects.

The different projects of the Destroyed House series Teeuwen realized have in common that they create order out of chaos, and beauty out of ugliness. Moreover, they deconstruct the notion of destruction itself, proposing creation not as the opposite of destruction, but as intimately entangled with it, namely, as its precondition. By performing creation as an activity that establishes a new architectural sculpture with a new order, structure, links and relations, she evokes the ordering, archival activity of memory. In fact, memory is already suggested by the location of her performances of creation: namely, the house, not only referring to an architectural construction but also to the rooting of human beings and genealogical memory, whether or not the dominant language in the community where the houses are situated uses the word in its double meaning. As a result, memory is evoked in these projects in several ways.

When she realized her Destroyed Houses in several locations in the Netherlands, and even in Russia with *Destroyed House Krasnoyarsk*, this evocation of memory remained abstract or general. The embodiment of memory in these projects remained implicit because no specific memories were involved, no specific pasts imposed themselves. Most critics and visitors of the Destroyed House series were impressed by the beauty of her creations/ destructions and by the obsessiveness of the performance that resulted in this stirring, unconventional beauty, but they did not make the association with the 'work of memory.'[15] In the case of *Destroyed House Gaza*, the recognition of the destroyed house as an embodiment of the work of memory is unavoidable. It is the context of Gaza that transforms the abstract idea of memory into a concrete one.

In the context of this memory war in which houses and trees are powerful cultural symbols as well as instruments of warfare, *Destroyed House Gaza* does not evoke memory abstractly, but utterly concretely and politically, albeit implicitly—as it becomes art. In contrast to political journalism and propaganda, political art achieves its convincing effect by an appeal to viewers to reconsider their routine convictions because they are touched on an affective as well as an intellectual level. Teeuwen's interventions in *Destroyed House Gaza* are at the same time interventions in the Israeli/Palestinian memory war, making visible that the Arab homonym 'bait' and the Hebrew homonym 'bet' refer to a building that serves as a home to people as well as to the

**Figure 5.2.   Verwoest Huis Gaza 3, 2017, 155 x 254 cm, inkjet print on dibond/framed
(courtesy of the artist).**

genealogical memory of a family, hence that both are being destroyed. For
the rooting of human beings is embodied in the cultural symbol of the house;
their uprooting in its destruction.

The house in which Teeuwen performed her intervention in 2016–2017 is
located in the town of Khan Younis, near Rafah, in the south of Gaza near
the Egyptian border. Since 1948 the town consists, for a major part, of a
refugee camp. The centre of the town has been demolished in order to create
a buffer zone between Gaza and Egypt. The concrete wall, which Israel built
to close Gaza off from Israel, also continues here between Gaza and Egypt.
The house put at Teeuwen's disposal was owned by a member of Hamas and
was bombed by Israel in the 2014 Gaza War. The bomb created a big hole in
the roof and in the floor underneath. One son of the owner was killed by the
attack. After the bomb attack the house was uninhabitable and waiting to be
demolished and rebuilt.

The first thing Teeuwen did was dig out the soil under the first floor; she
removed one and a half meters of sand. Next, she opened up the floors of the
second story by cutting open three sides of the floor; the fourth side remained
intact, and as a result, the floors folded downwards due to their weight. Subsequently most of the floors were hanging vertically, some of them supported
by props preventing a completely vertical hanging. Thus, they replaced the
walls that were blown away by the bomb. By means of opening up the floors

and digging out the soil beneath the ground floor, all the spaces in the house became visually connected and new perspectives were created. This intervention created depth, height, distance, and as a result, vistas/views in an architectural space formerly consisting of two closed-off floors connected by a staircase. Whereas in the original building one could see only the room in which one dwelled, after these interventions one had visual access to all the house's spaces at the same time. The illusion of an endless space, with new spaces behind those nearest, was created reminiscent of the images of the eighteenth-century Italian artist Giovanni Battista Piranesi.

Debris and used materials from the house were re-used for the construction of five new walls and two enormous piles, a black one and a white one, reaching from the ground to almost the roof of the building. Windows and other openings in the outer walls were closed with rubbish. These constructions are not creations *ex nihilo* but re-orderings of what was already there. This re-ordering evoked archival organizations, of which memory is one of the prime examples. By closing off all openings to the space outside the house, Teeuwen transformed the house into an inner space. The suggestion of being inside an inner space was also evoked by the two enormous piles reaching from bottom to roof, because they looked like the spines of a body. Not realistically, but rather functionally; they were like the nerve centres of this inner space. The black nerve centre referred to the black spots and traces on walls and floors left by the bomb that had hit the house. The white nerve centre referred to the original white colour of the walls. The five walls created out of debris covering the open architectural structure filtered light into a very fine grid of white dots. This grid of light did not illuminate the inner space; it did not produce lightened areas, but became part of the re-ordered structuring that Teeuwen's interventions brought about. Light was not used to enable vision but was dealt with as one of the materials that constituted the inner space. The grid of light and stone closing off the openings in the walls were like a new skin to the house.

On top of a low pile of ordered stones, Teeuwen showed the fragmented remains of the bomb that had destroyed the house and killed one of its inhabitants. All other material used by Teeuwen was insignificant as such; the re-use of it evoked the ordering process and activity of memory, but not specific memories. The remains of the bomb, however, distinguished themselves from the other materials by signifying a specific memory: the moment in the forty-five-year history of the building when the house was destroyed by being hit by bombs and grenades. This briefest moment in time definitively modified the spatial structure. The small display of remains of bombs and grenade shards could easily be overlooked because it was much less overwhelming than the obsessively structured space in which it was placed. Nevertheless, one could also claim that this modest exhibition is the centre of Teeuwen's Destroyed House, because it is here that memory is not evoked as an ordering, archival process, but in the form of a specific object of memory. It is here, in these traces of that intensely loaded moment, that the location of the Destroyed House, Gaza, is inescapably significant.

By means of her interventions Teeuwen has transformed the bombed, ruined house into an architectural sculpture, as well as into a site of memory. The term 'site of memory' was introduced by French historian Pierre Nora.[16] These sites are places, objects or other phenomena which have become of symbolic significance to a particular group of people when the continuity between past and present is broken. Monuments, memorials, but also specific days of the year during which a specific loss or event is commemorated, can function as sites of memory. Although houses, olive trees and pine trees already have symbolic significance in Palestine and Israel, this significance is general and not tied to specific houses or trees. Teeuwen's interventions in *Destroyed House Gaza* have intensified the symbolical significance of the house and turned it into a site of memory.

After it was finished in December 2016, people from Gaza visited the house, not just to admire the artistic project and the beauty bestowed onto the ruined house, but also to reflect on and to commemorate the broken bond between their land and their people. The space that a house is, and demarcates, commemorates the time that the bond between land and people was not yet broken; it commemorates the house and the family that was rooted in that house. A destroyed house restores the continuity of time by embodying the force of memory. But how is it possible that the spatial dimension of a ruined house can effectuate the re-establishment of memory of the past, of a dimension that is temporal? This is possible because the bombed house is more than a ruined, artistic architectural construction. The materiality of the spatial ruin already embodies time; the holes and wounds caused by the bomb attack embody the temporality of trauma.[17] The chaos and damage caused by the bomb attack is not only material damage, but also a temporal havoc. It was an event, a historical moment, which could not be experienced when it happened. The event, literally a bomb attack, was unimaginable, too enormous in its devastating and killing effects to experience and work through. The traces of that event could be recognized all over the space of the house.[18] They are the symptoms of a failed experience, in other words, of trauma. This failed experience makes it impossible to remember the events voluntarily. In order to do so, the conditions for the possibility of memory first had to be developed. This is precisely what Teeuwen's *Destroyed House Gaza* has done.

This implies that Teeuwen's interventions in *Destroyed House Gaza* did not just transform a discarded space into an artistic statement and an embodiment of memory. Rather, she transformed the temporality of trauma into the temporality of memory. An event that because of its 'explosive' nature could not be worked through was transformed into memory by setting up the conditions for commemoration. By transforming chaos into order and transforming a ruin into an architectural sculpture, Teeuwen transformed trauma into memory. That was Teeuwen's contribution to the restoration of the cultural, social health of a people confined in reiterated traumatogenic situations.

But because of the fact that the memory of rootedness in Palestine and Israel is multidirectional, Teeuwen's work did not only transform the traumatic past of Palestinians into a memory of that past, but also the traumatic past of the Jewish people of Israel. Because her work performed the transformation symbolically, both parties in this war on memory would have been able to identify with the healing transformation of trauma into memory. But of course, this is speculative, because Israelis are not allowed to visit Gaza, and Palestinians are not allowed to leave Gaza. This implies that the healing potential of this artwork remained exclusively accessible to the Palestinians imprisoned in Gaza.

NOTES

1. Michael Rothberg, *Multidirectional Memory: Remembering the Holocaust in the Age of Decolonization* (Stanford, CA: Stanford University Press, 2009), 311.

2. Rothberg, *Multidirectional Memory*, 3.

3. Rothberg, *Multidirectional Memory*, 4.

4. See Mieke Bal, 'Introduction,' in *Acts of Memory: Cultural Recall in the Present*, eds. Mieke Bal, Jonathan Crewe and Leo Spitzer (Hanover, NH: University Press of New England, 1999), vii–xvii.

5. Rothberg, *Multidirectional Memory*, 5.

6. Rothberg, *Multidirectional Memory*, 13.

7. For an explanation of the difference between acting out and working through trauma, see Dominique LaCapra, *Representing the Holocaust: History, Theory, Trauma* (Ithaca, NY: Cornell University Press, 1994).

8. Born in 1953, Marjan Teeuwen lives in Amsterdam. She creates large-scale architectural installations in buildings that are demolished after her interventions. She tears and strips, disrupts construction and structure, and with the remaining material she builds a new artistic image. Based on these installations she also realizes photographic works.

9. See Carol Bardenstein, 'Trees, Forests, and the Shaping of Palestinian and Israeli Collective Memory,' in *Acts of Memory: Cultural Recall in the Present*, eds.

Mieke Bal, Jonathan Crewe and Leo Spitzer (Hanover, NH: University Press of New England, 1999), 148–68.

10. Laura van Gelder, MA thesis, Leiden University (unpublished), 2016.

11. Irus Braverman, *Planted Flags: Trees, Land and Law in Israeli/Palestine* (Cambridge: Cambridge University Press, 2009); 'Powers of Illegality: House Demolitions and Resistance in East Jeruzalem,' *Law and Social Inquiry* 32.2 (2007): 333–72.

12. For an analysis of the principles that determine archival organizations, see my book *Staging the Archive: Art and Photography in Times of New Media* (London: Reaktion Books, 2015).

13. Frances A. Yates, *The Art of Memory* (Chicago: The University of Chicago Press, 1966).

14. See Judith Russi Kirshner, 'The Idea of Community in the Work of Gordon Matta-Clark,' in *Gordon Matta-Clark*, ed. C. Diserens (New York: Phaidon, 2003), 147–60.

15. Several Dutch newspapers mention that.

16. Pierre Nora, 'Between Memory and History: *Les Lieux de Mémoire*,' *Representations* 26 (1989): 7–24; *Realms of Memory: Rethinking the French Past*, vols. 1–4 (New York: Columbia University Press, 1996).

17. The word trauma comes from Greek and it means 'wound.'

18. For an analysis of trauma, and its relation to memory, sees Ernst van Alphen, 'Symptoms of Discursivity: Experience, Memory, and Trauma,' in *Acts of Memory: Cultural Recall in the Present*, eds Mieke Bal, Jonathan Crewe and Leo Spitzer (Hanover, NH: University of New England Press, 1999), 24–38; 'Caught by Images,' in *Art in Mind: How Contemporary Images Shape Thought* (Chicago: University of Chicago Press, 2005), 163–79; *Caught by History: Holocaust Effects in Art, Literature, and Theory* (Stanford, CA: Stanford University Press, 1998).

BIBLIOGRAPHY

BAL, Mieke. 'Introduction.' In *Acts of Memory: Cultural Recall in the Present*. Edited by Mieke Bal, Jonathan Crewe and Leo Spitzer. vii-xvii. Hanover, NH: University Press of New England, 1999.

BARDENSTEIN, Carol. 'Trees, Forests, and the Shaping of Palestinian and Israeli Collective Memory.' In *Acts of Memory: Cultural Recall in the Present*. Edited by Mieke Bal, Jonathan Crewe and Leo Spitzer. 148–68. Hanover, NH: University Press of New England, 1999.

BRAVERMAN, Irus. *Planted Flags: Trees, Land and Law in Israeli/Palestine*. Cambridge: Cambridge University Press, 2009.

BRAVERMAN, Irus. 'Powers of Illegality: House Demolitions and Resistance in East Jerusalem.' *Law and Social Inquiry* 32.2 (2007): 333–72.

KIRSHNER, Judith Russi. 'The Idea of Community in the Work of Gordon Matta-Clark.' In *Gordon Matta-Clark*. Edited by C. Diserens. 147–60. New York: Phaidon, 2003.

LACAPRA, Dominique. *Representing the Holocaust: History, Theory, Trauma.* Ithaca, NY: Cornell University Press, 1994.

NORA, Pierre. 'Between Memory and History: *Les Lieux de Mémoire.*' *Representations* 26 (1989): 7–24.

NORA, Pierre. *Realms of Memory: Rethinking the French Past.* Volumes 1–4. New York: Columbia University Press, 1996.

ROTHBERG, Michael. *Multidirectional Memory: Remembering the Holocaust in the Age of Decolonization.* Stanford, CA: Stanford University Press, 2009.

VAN ALPHEN, Ernst. *Caught by History: Holocaust Effects in Art, Literature, and Theory.* Stanford, CA: Stanford University Press, 1998.

VAN ALPHEN, Ernst. 'Caught by Images.' In *Art in Mind: How Contemporary Images Shape Thought.* 163–79. Chicago: University of Chicago Press, 2005.

VAN ALPHEN, Ernst. *Staging the Archive: Art and Photography in Times of New Media.* London: Reaktion Books, 2015.

VAN ALPHEN, Ernst. 'Symptoms of Discursivity: Experience, Memory, and Trauma.' In *Acts of Memory: Cultural Recall in the Present.* Edited by Mieke Bal, Jonathan Crewe and Leo Spitzer. 24–38. Hanover, NH: University of New England Press, 1999.

VAN GELDER, Laura. MA thesis, Leiden University (unpublished), 2016.

YATES, Frances A. *The Art of Memory.* Chicago: University of Chicago Press, 1966.

Chapter Six

Textures of Indian Memory[1]

Radhika Mohanram

On a trip to Delhi to research this chapter on the sites of partition memory, I resolved to visit Purana Qila, or Old Fort, which is the site of much Indian political history. Purana Qila was built on the remnants of Indraprastha, the capital city of the Pandava rulers from the Indian epic, the *Mahabharata*; later Humayun, the second Mughal Emperor, the son of Babar and the father of Akbar the Great, located his capital Din Panah here. Other rulers followed, using this location as their site of rule until the British developed New Delhi as the capital of British India. Even then, Purana Qila played a role as Edwin Lutyens, the architect of New Delhi, used it to align the central vista, Kingsway, now called Rajpath. Notwithstanding the development of Lutyens's Delhi, this city has been aesthetically and architecturally also a Muslim city for a long time, as it had been the capital for the Mughal rulers, as well as five other previous Muslim dynasties—the Mamluks, the Khiljis, the Tughlaqs, the Sayyids and the Lodis—between 1206 and 1526. Now it is the capital of Hindu India even though, constitutionally, we are secular. Street names have been changed, by and large, in an attempt to erase memories of our Islamic past and to reflect the current Hindu reality. And how has this new incarnation of Delhi affected Purana Qila? In 1947, with the Indian partition, this fort, along with Humayun's Tomb, became one of two refugee camps for Delhi Muslims fleeing to Pakistan. Between 150,000 and 200,000 Delhi Muslims, including 12,000 who belonged to the civil service, took refuge in Purana Qila. In 1948, the camp was eventually closed with their transportation to Pakistan. Purana Qila is not politically charged in the same way anymore, as now there is only the occasional theatre production that takes place here. In April 2016, when I visited it, there were no vestiges of the refugee camp; now the grounds are being used by young lovers trying to get privacy away from their families, holding hands under the trees and walking around.

There is a museum within the fort which highlights Indraprastha or Hindu mythology but not the Islamic past, drawing attention to how each regime of power attempts to forget the memories of its predecessors. But how do the layers of history sedimented within a place reveal themselves? Are some bits of it forgotten or irrecoverable? How is the memory of place recuperated?

Setting out to examine the relationship between place and memories, this chapter aims to address the following questions: 1) Do places contain their inhabitants' memories? 2) How does bodily affect manifest itself in sites of memory? And, finally, 3) how do these affective memories re-manifest themselves in the present? Indeed, it is commonplace to suggest that there is a close imbrication of these terms—place, body and memory—in that bodies shape, and are shaped by, memories as much as these two terms—bodies and memories—are affected by place. In his theorizing of memory, Paul Connerton points to the link among these terms and suggests a two-step process in the excavation of this relationship. He posits that our awareness of the binary opposites up/down, front/back, right/left, and inside/outside, which are all central to our orientation in space, emerges from our body.[2] Here he follows Kant, who in 'On the First Ground of the Distinction of Regions in Space' points out that reading a map requires us to locate directions in relation to our body, and it is only through this orientation that we are able to distinguish between the directions. For Kant, our comprehension of directionality—left from right, up from down, for instance—which gives us a sense of the world surrounding us as well as the knowledge within which we perceive it, require the mediation of our bodies.[3] Thus bodies, spatial orientations, place, one's history and memory, and knowledge are all connected in this pedestrianization of identity. Our bodies give us a sense of direction, and as we walk around places, we memorize the details of what needs to be remembered, and what they mean, to gain a sense of who and where we are through this process.

If individual bodily identity is shaped in affirmative or disruptive ways by places and the past, does the national body politic also get affected in similar ways? How does the affective memory of a nation's people get recorded beyond the writing of history and the collection of archival material, and how is place tied to these memories? Though both are shaped by a negotiation between remembering and forgetting, the difference between history and affective memory is that the former consciously shapes and trains a nation's citizens in how to recollect the past, whereas the latter repeats the past in 'the everyday present.'[4] Memory is often bodily in that we follow certain routines and harbour certain memories. Because memories tend to engage all the senses, often their recall elicits strong physical responses. For instance, certain smells or songs recall instantly a sense of the past, feelings of well-being or of trauma.

Dylan Trigg's suggestive notion—that the term being 'touched by the past' refers to place in that the recollection of the past is both *kinaesthetic and sensual*—is useful to explore the sites of partition memory in India.[5] Questions dealt with here will be: How is partition remembered or deliberately relegated to a national amnesia in India? How is the loss of ancestral memories which are firmly located in specific places forgotten or remembered? How is the filtering, withholding and construction of memory shaped by the various sites that refer to partition? I will examine one sensory site of memory in India, Chandigarh, the post-independence city which was built as the new capital of Punjab because Lahore, the previous capital, had been allocated to Pakistan during independence and partition. By focusing on Chandigarh, I want to underscore the affects of partition, not as it was in 1947, but, rather, as they have continued to haunt the nation right into the present. For this, I am particularly influenced by Pierre Nora's work, whose term *lieux de mémoire* (sites or places of memory) represented the use of places and the different ways people identified with their nation. For him, people remembered their past through monuments, names of streets, flags and institutions, among other material sites.[6] Thus, Nora's work makes explicit the relationship between memory and material remnants of the national past. Nora's work on memory is very useful for my reading of the affects of partition that linger on throughout India even in the present. If the dominant story of independence had placed partition loss under erasure, as I have consistently argued,[7] these sites of memory seem to question the notion of repression in that the nationalist celebration of independence also triggers the melancholic memories of the past in specific places.

PLACING MEMORY

There are two commonplace assumptions about place which originate from different intellectual trajectories: first, in subjects like geology or physical geography, place is perceived to be equivalent to the environment, a sum total of its parts; secondly, especially in the humanities and social sciences, it is understood to be a product of human experience with no intrinsic meaning unto itself.[8] In this the value and nostalgic attachments that the notion of place holds for us and its role in the construction of identity, take it beyond an empirical idea.[9] It is this latter view of place that has been central to memory studies, especially those that have been developed in the wake of Maurice Halbwachs's work. Halbwachs rebelled against the notion of both the investigation of internal memory processes as developed by Freud and the concept of cultural memory. For Halbwachs, memory is social, and it is only in social contexts that we can remember. He argues that 'it is to the degree that our individual thought places itself in [memory and social] frameworks and participates in this memory that it is capable of the act of recollection.'[10] In fact, it is context that not only recuperates memory but also gives meaning to it. Memories of the past are directly related to a system of ideas and events of which we are members in the present.

Halbwachs's work also influenced that of Pierre Nora who, in his three-volume *Lieux de Mémoire* project undertaken between 1984 and 1992, posited that certain sites had the ability to evoke emotional affect which was directly connected to the recuperation of certain forms of memory as well as views of the nation. Nora suggested that these sites of memory were central to remembering because, with the onset of modernity, globalization, massification and democratization, the collective memory of people had withered away and modern media had taken its place. For him, this new form of memory or *lieux de mémoire* had evolved because of the disappearance of the *milieux de mémoire*, which were the 'real environments of memory.'[11] *Lieux de mémoire* required the creation of archives, the maintenance of anniversaries, the organization of celebrations and the like for memory to prevail, as without them history would sweep away the specificity of memories. Thus, *lieux de mémoire* expands our understandings of what sites are: places and things that allow for the resurfacing of affective memories. Nora states that they are the 'moments of history torn away from the movements of history, then returned; no longer quite life, not yet death, like shells on the shore when the sea of living memory has receded.'[12]

The importance of place as an *aide-mémoire* has a long and venerable history. In the classical story told by Cicero in *De Oratore*, the poet Simonides had been invited to a banquet in a rich man's house in Thessaly to recite his poems. Having done so, he had stepped out of the house briefly when the roof of the banqueting hall suddenly came crashing down. The family members of the guests could not identify the bodies, as they were all mangled beyond recognition. Simonides, however, was able to remember each of the guests according to the position he was seated at the table. For Cicero the mnemonics of place and image were key to the art of memory.[13] The 'Art of Memory' emerged in classical culture and was used in the medieval period and through the Renaissance. Here, a set of places functions as 'a grid on which the images of the items to be remembered [were] placed in a certain order; and the items [were] then remembered by mentally revisiting the grid of places and traversing them step by step.'[14]

Nora's focus on sites which function as the repositories of memory intersected with a phenomenological frame proves fascinating, as this intersection not only unites memory with place but also factors in the experiential nature of these in bodily identity. Thus, all three—memory, place and identity—are tightly imbricated such that the body and its identity is also a composite of place and memory. Merleau-Ponty's analysis of Paris suggests such an imbrication in that, for him, Paris is not a sum of its parts but, rather, '[i]ts modalities are always an expression of the total life of the subject, the energy with which he tends towards a future through his body and his world.'[15] Dylan Trigg initiates this phenomenological frame to point out that 'places are defined by their relationship with the particular subject who experiences them.'[16] Trigg suggests that affect is a spark that ignites between the place and the subject. For instance, an agoraphobic's anxiety of public spaces is caused only through a spark between the city and the agoraphobic subject, as anxiety is intrinsic neither to the said subject nor to the city, but only through this constitutive spark is the city experienced as such.[17]

From a phenomenological perspective, then, place is more than the environment or the meanings projected onto it by people or history or memory. It is also to be understood experientially as well as affectively and with particularity.[18] It is affective in the sense that our body's perception of a place becomes the way we apprehend it. Consider what happens to a 1947 refugee fleeing India for Pakistan, or the refugee fleeing Pakistan for India. What was once dear and familiar as home with family memories and a sense of belonging, as the space of one's ancestors, is now fraught with danger for one's life and has become unfamiliar, resulting in the skewing of the notion of home. Place is also particular in that our relationship with it is unique. In the case of the Hindu or Sikh refugees fleeing Lahore, now in Pakistan, their relationship to it involves both a sense of belonging and un-belonging, unique to that city. Moving to India also produces this strange sense of forcible belonging and an emotional un-belonging, as it is not the land of their ancestral memories.

While such a phenomenological reading of place seems to focus on the individual's relationship to it, how do places generate a group affect? How does individual memory become public memory? While individual memory is specific and anchored within lived experience, public memory belongs to the realm of history. Here, memory is located and interpreted as being external to any individual subject, and public memory belongs to a public past, which though external to the subject yet gives a social, historical and cultural meaning to the subject. This public history is commemorated not only in the collective memories of people but also in archives, libraries and monuments, and it is to this last that we will focus our attention in the next section of this paper. However, a caveat. As Trigg points out, monuments that represent a spatialization of the past carry with them 'a sentiment broader than the idiosyncracies of the object representing that remembered event,'[19] or, to put it another way, they are subject to the vagaries of time, taste and interpretations.

In sum, first, the very nature of memories also suggests the restless multiplicity of co-existing versions, the influence of the past in the present and the present in the past, imaginings, replications and interpretations. Second, even collective memories are carried corporeally in repetition, voice, affect and engagements among individuals, nations, sites, objects and images. Third, the concepts of both monuments and memories suggest a survival and a living on, especially through change. To quote Trigg: 'By remembering an event of heightened proportions [such as the 1947 partition] we simultaneously invoke a broader range of properties, places, and objects that remain implicated in the event.'[20] Given that change and multiple interpretations are intrinsic to sites of memory, meanings emerge as complementary or disruptive or oppositional.

CHANDIGARH

Chandigarh was the city that was developed with the express purpose of obliterating the memory of the partition. Yet, ironically, until 2017 it was also the only city in South Asia with a monument to this cataclysmic event.[21] In *Oblivion*, Marc Augé insists that '[o]ne must know how to forget in order to taste the full flavour of the present, of the moment, of expectation . . . memory itself needs forgetfulness.'[22] However, as Paul Connerton points out, 'All beginnings contain an element of recollection . . . the absolutely new is inconceivable [because] in all modes of experience we always base our particular experiences on a prior context in order to ensure that they are intelligible at all. . . .'[23] How does this city of the future, the city that demanded a new beginning, carry memories of the past?

When the state of Punjab was partitioned, the capital city, Lahore, had become part of Pakistan. East Punjab, which had been apportioned to India, now needed to have a new capital. Since Punjab was at the border between the two newly formed nations running through it, the state was flooded with refugees. Indeed, all the towns of East Punjab had doubled in population with the partition, though the infrastructure such as roads, drainage, water supply, schools and hospitals were woefully inadequate to accommodate the large number of refugees. Existing cities such as Shimla and Ambala could not be upgraded into the state capital either. Shimla, which is located in the southwestern ranges of the Himalayas, had been the summer capital of the British Raj, with the Viceroy and the civil servants making their annual trek to it every summer, as the plains where Delhi is located tend to get extremely hot. But it was accessible only through a long and narrow ascent which would not have been suitable for a state capital that had to function round the year. In its turn, Ambala was a cantonment city and the main base of military operations for the Northwest, and it was perceived to be a target in case of an attack from Pakistan. Accordingly, a site was chosen which contained twenty-four villages of 21,000 residents who had to be dislocated and resettled—not unlike the partition refugees—for the development of Chandigarh.

The initial plans to build a city for 150,000 with a capacity for future expansion were drawn by two American architects, Albert Mayer and Matthew Nowicki. The project was subsequently taken over by Le Corbusier, the renowned Swiss-French architect, urban planner and painter, and the city was built between 1951 to the present.[24] The only city built on a grid pattern in India, Chandigarh is divided into sectors, with the Capitol Complex located in Sector 1. For Corbusier, the city was a metaphor for the human body, with the Capitol Complex at the head, the city centre and the work area in Sector 17 as the heart, the green spaces as the lungs, the cultural and education spaces as the intellect, and the network of roads as the circulatory system.

The first prime minister of India, Jawaharlal Nehru, decided that Chandigarh, the new capital of Indian Punjab, was to be 'a glorious stage set where the tableau of state might be enacted.'[25] He said, 'Let this be a new town, symbolic of the freedom of India, unfettered by the traditions of the past . . . an expression of the nation's faith in the future.'[26] Chandigarh is also noteworthy for the fact that it was the first venue for 'tropical architecture'[27] in India and the place where India's first generation of modernist architects learnt their craft. Chandigarh is now the capital of not one but two states—Punjab and Haryana—and is also a Union Territory (territory directly ruled by the Central government), as a result of which three distinct governments function in this city.

In April of 2016 I paid a visit to Chandigarh, a city I had never seen before. Chandigarh was unlike other Indian cities, with wide roads, systematic numbering, green traffic islands and gardens everywhere. The grid city pattern permits a constant sense of direction for the directionally challenged such as me; however, the similarity of vast numbers of buildings simultaneously seemed to disorient me if I were ever to stop walking to take a look around—did I not pass that building just now or was it another one? In which direction had I been walking? It is the Capitol Complex in Sector 1 that is the most visited by tourists in Chandigarh, now a UNESCO world heritage site, as it was designed and planned by Corbusier; magnificent, but unusual, buildings for the Secretariat, the Assembly, the High Court, the Museum of Knowledge and the Open Hand monument (see figure 6.1), among others.

Included in the complex are the Martyr's Monument, which I will discuss shortly, and the Tower of Shadows, an abstraction of a *brise soleil*. The Capitol Complex is still in the process of being completed, as the Museum

**Figure 6.1.   Le Corbusier. The Open Hand monument, Chandigarh, 1964. Copyright ©
by F.L.C./ADAGP, Paris and DACS, London 2019. Reprinted by permission of Design
and Artists Copyright Society. All rights reserved. Photo courtesy of Luisa Pèrcopo.**

of Knowledge along with the Geometric Hill and the Martyr's Monument
remain unfinished.

Since terrorists attacked the Assembly building a few years ago, any visitor to the Capitol Complex requires police permission before walking to the
Secretariat, an experience that requires you to walk from the Tourist Office
through a walkway and onto a bridge before you suddenly come upon the
magnificent, breathtaking Open Hand monument (designed and gifted to
Chandigarh by Corbusier) that faces the plaza and is profiled against the
mountains. The Capitol Complex—a mix of remarkable buildings with beautifully modulated open spaces—is meant to promenade in, to be impressed
by, to be amazed at.

How, then, can we interpret Chandigarh and, more importantly, the Capitol
Complex within the frames of affect and bodily memory? It is precisely the
modernist style of buildings, the grid pattern of streets, the wide roads in the
spread-out city made for driving rather than for walking, that establish Chandigarh as a place without memories of the wretched past of a colonized India
or the anguish of the partition. Indeed, nothing remains of the twenty-six
villages that were erased to facilitate the establishment and development of
Chandigarh. The Capitol Complex, too, with its modernist style that does not
resemble in the least the official buildings of other Indian cities, establishes

its newness, the hope for the future. The primary material with which most of Chandigarh is built, including in the Capitol Complex, is affordable concrete rather than marble to signify not only the humble monetary beginnings of independent India but also its post-colonial state, in which investments needed to be made on people and underdeveloped infrastructure and not on grandiose buildings. In these and in many other ways, Chandigarh hails the future, the modern, the hopes of India to transform from poverty and wretchedness caused by colonial rule to the pragmatic, and to take its place among other developed nations.

But yet, there is one reference to the past in this city that signifies the absence of the past and memories. As mentioned before, the only monument (until recently) commemorating the trauma of the 1947 partition lies in Chandigarh, right in the heart of the Capitol Complex. The Martyr's Monument, built with Chandigarh's favourite material, concrete, consists of a slowly inclining ramp which has, cut within it, some rectangular peepholes. The ramp descends into a sheltered space (see figure 6.2) with a nook which is meant to eventually contain sculptures of an abstracted body and other forms, but this monument is yet to be completed. On the grey concrete wall, there are two sculptural forms, one on each wall, of an Ashoka Chakra (see figure 6.3), or a wheel with twenty-four spokes, and another of an Indian swastika to signify

Figure 6.2. Le Corbusier. Chandigarh, 1951–1959, exterior (1). Copyright © by F.L.C./ ADAGP, Paris and DACS, London 2019. Reprinted by permission of Design and Artists Copyright Society. All rights reserved. Photo courtesy of Luisa Pèrcopo.

good luck or auspiciousness (see figure 6.4). The Ashoka Chakra mirrors the Indian flag, which has the twenty-four-spoked wheel at its centre, thus establishing the monument as a national one, reflecting the hopes of a nation.

How does the partition function phenomenologically in Martyr's Monument? Its location, diagonally opposite the more imposing Tower of Shadows and to the side of the Assembly building with its magnificent, colourful doors designed by Corbusier, results in your eyes being drawn not to the Martyr's Monument but to these two other buildings. As you can approach these buildings only on foot, the plaza upon which this monument is located functions as the vast forecourt to the more important and impressive Assembly building. The Martyr's Monument is discrete, sparse and completely different in its grey, concrete simplicity. Rather than being a place in its own right, you have to make an effort to notice and approach it.

Walking on the gentle slope (see figure 6.2) which is part of the monument and which does not lead you to anything particular (as the monument is still incomplete), you notice the noise, the disruption of the constant movement that envelopes the Assembly building, with Assembly members of the two governments and guards walking to and fro, vanishing into a silence that descends onto the person walking on the Martyr's Monument. In this silence enveloping you, walking on the gentle slope and gentle descent towards blank walls, memories of the violent past of the partition are allowed to surface. It is this difference of the monument—its plain appearance different from the other, more striking buildings—that elicits the silent presence refocusing and demanding our attention. This silence itself, as much as the monument, is a commemoration of the millions that lost their lives, their homes and their livelihood in the partition violence. The silence, a ceasing of movement, noise and time, allows for a new temporality—not the partition as it had been, but what it means in the present. Furthermore, this moment of commemoration also suspends the present moment—the busyness of the Assembly building—and the past unfurls and unfolds in the present. The Martyr's Monument is definitely not meant to function as a mere foil to the more eye-catching buildings; its very structure—to frame the workaday world of the Assembly building, while simultaneously bringing about a memory independent of that world—establishes the deliberate significance of the building. Thus, the structure of the monument elicits silence, memory, commemoration and history.

But does the Martyr's Monument allow for the free surfacing of memory? Pierre Nora states:

> [T]he most fundamental purpose of the *lieu de mémoire* is to stop time, to block the work of forgetting, to establish a state of things, to immortalize death, to materialize the immaterial . . . all this to capture a maximum of meaning in the fewest of signs, it is also clear that *lieux de mémoire* only exist because of

their capacity for metamorphosis, an endless recycling of their meaning and an unpredictable proliferation of their ramifications.[28]

If *lieux de mémoire* cannot be pinned down in their meanings because of their tendency to metamorphose, what else can be said about the Martyr's Memorial? I suggest that the recuperation of memory that it allows is not ideologically free or unbound, but is a mediated one through a nationalistic discourse, as is evident in the sculptural forms—the Ashoka Chakra and the Indian swastika on the walls of the monument.

The Ashoka Chakra, the twenty-four-spoked wheel (see figure 6.3) is a reference to ancient India and the edicts of Emperor Ashoka, signifying the wheel of eternal law. The adjoining sculptural form, of the Indian swastika (the right-hand swastika with arms bent clock-wise), is specifically a Hindu symbol referring to the Hindu god, Vishnu (see figure 6.4).

In short, the partition monument seems to be not just about the event, or even the victims or refugees, but the nation-state which professes itself to be constitutionally secular but ideologically dominantly Hindu. In not including either Sikh or Muslim grief in the losses of partition, the monument recuperates a very specific memory that is completely Hindu. Even the Ashoka Chakra, which does not refer to any specific religious denomination but rather

Figure 6.3.   Le Corbusier. Chandigarh, 1951–1959, exterior (2). Copyright © by F.L.C./ ADAGP, Paris and DACS, London 2019. Reprinted by permission of Design and Artists Copyright Society. All rights reserved. Photo courtesy of Luisa Pèrcopo.

Figure 6.4.   Le Corbusier. Chandigarh, 1951–1959, exterior (3). Copyright © by F.L.C./
ADAGP, Paris and DACS, London 2019. Reprinted by permission of Design and Artists
Copyright Society. All rights reserved. Photo courtesy of Luisa Pèrcopo.

the maintenance of law, does not compensate for such a Hindu reading of the
monument.

One final point needs to be made about the monument. On the day that
I took the guided tour of the Capitol Complex, the guide referred to the
Martyr's Monument as one which was dedicated to the participants of the
independence movement, 'the freedom fighters.' I was confused because I
had read references to it earlier in several sources[29] as being the only monument to partition victims in all of South Asia. I asked him to clarify whether
it was to commemorate all freedom fighters or whether it was for the partition refugees. 'Yes,' he admitted, 'it was for partition refugees.' There were
no plaques anywhere, however, that said that the Martyr's Memorial was for
partition refugees. I decided that it was a slip of the tongue that had led him
to refer to the monument as being dedicated to 'freedom fighters' until I did a
search for Martyr's Monument on the internet. The images for this monument
were not of the one I had seen but, rather, another one in the Bougainvillea
Garden which was dedicated to the soldiers who had died in the war. The
Martyr's Memorial, according to internet sources, was the War Memorial.
Confused by now, I emailed Chandigarh architect Vikramaditya Prakash,
who has done extensive work on the architecture of this city.[30] He clarified
to me that the Martyr's Memorial was, indeed, the one in the Capitol Com-

plex and was dedicated to partition victims. This has left me with questions: Was the guide on the guided tour wrong? The internet? Or was this popular memory mediated by nationalistic discourses that once again had obliterated references to the 1947 partition?

FORGETTING

In my analysis of the Martyr's Monument, my valorisation of memory with the injunction to remember everything is an inheritance from the Holocaust and Holocaust studies. For survivors of the Holocaust and for the Jewish people, remembering the atrocities of the Nazi era is a deeply political act in the face of their obliteration. Following WW2 and the Vietnam era, the rise of trauma studies saw the same conviction in the necessity to allow memories to surface, to articulate them in words, and to 'speak the unspeakable.'[31] This restoration of memory is perceived as significant because of its immensely therapeutic value, in both private and public life, as it restores both the individual to themselves as well as the social order to harmony. Yet philosophers such as William James and Friedrich Nietzsche have also pointed to the burden, the impossibility of remembering everything, and advocated the value of forgetting. Nietzsche's advocacy of active forgetting or a wilful abandonment of the past is justified, because '[i]n the case of the smallest or of the greatest happiness . . . it is always the same thing that makes happiness happiness: the ability to forget or, expressed in more scholarly fashion, the capacity to feel un-historically during its duration.'[32] Nietzsche's urging to forget, then, is so as to facilitate a normal and happy life.

If memory becomes embedded in an individual and has meaning only through a social context, as Halbwachs has argued, then the three significant mnemonic communities that affect the qualities and conditions of memories—the depth, which bits to be remembered, and how far back to remember—are the family, the ethnic group and the nation.[33] By adhering to a mnemonic community, we identify with its collective past and attain a social identity. Barbara Misztal points out that there is a 'cognitive bias' that shapes the memories of a group, which confers 'an emotional tone and style' to the group.[34] The nation as one of the primary mnemonic communities often demands a forgetting on the part of its citizens. In 'What Is a Nation,' Ernest Renan suggests how shared memories are significant for a nation to have a cohesive society. He also places a high value on forgetting within the context of a nation in that 'historical enquiry brings to light deeds of violence which took place at the origin of all political formations, even of those whose consequences have been altogether beneficial. Unity is always effected by means of brutality.'[35] In short, then, built into the subjectivity of a citizen belonging to a mnemonic community such as the nation is a demand to forget specific instances of the past.

The nationalist injunction to forget runs counter to the demand to 'always remember' in the aftermath of the Holocaust. Given the vast amounts of information that we as citizens must remember, postmodernity's compromise has been to let something or someone else remember things for us. This can be seen in the archivalization of knowledge and information in databases, archives, museums and the internet that we can access. Following Nora's train of thought, we can say that technological advances have created new ways of carrying personal memory. In 'Seven Types of Forgetting,' Paul Connerton describes prescriptive forgetting as one prescribed by the state when it aims to 'prevent a chain of retribution for earlier acts from running on endlessly.'[36] In an echo of Renan here, the state encourages an amnesia in order to bring about social cohesiveness and order. Among the various types of forgetting, Connerton also differentiates this form of amnesia from the one he describes as being constitutive in the formation of a new identity.[37] Here, Connerton explains that identities follow established narratives which directly shape behaviour. In the formation of new identities requiring new narratives, some of the older narratives have to be forgotten as they have no significance in the new era. Importantly, this form of forgetting is to prevent a 'cognitive dissonance' in the newly formed identity.[38]

In their classic work, *The Inability to Mourn*, Alexander and Margarete Mitscherlich examine post-war German denial of Nazi atrocities and suggest that the aggression displayed under National Socialism had transmuted and re-manifested itself as an energetic restoration of Germany in the wake of its destruction in WW2. Their refusal to mourn, according to the authors, was caused by a defense mechanism that demanded an *affective* rupture with the past. The Mitscherlichs point out that post-war Germany, in particular, refused to engage with its history of anti-Semitic violence in the Nazi era, preferring to perceive itself instead as the victim of the Allied forces that resulted in the partitioning of their country. This identification with the victim thus prevented the onset of guilt.[39] Forgetting, one can see, requires an enormous amount of psychic energy, but the outcome of this amnesia was social cohesion and an ability to re-establish a legitimacy to a state where the basis of civil behaviour had been destroyed by National Socialism.[40] Ironically, in the German case, this forgetting becomes the *antithesis* of the injunction to remember brought about by the Holocaust. Contemporary Germany, post-reunification, especially Berlin, remembers the Holocaust and the Nazi past everywhere—the Holocaust Memorial, the Jewish Museum, the Memorial to Homosexuals Persecuted under Nazism, to name a few of Berlin's monuments.

The Martyr's Memorial in Chandigarh negotiates between remembering and forgetting in that it seemingly marks the memory of the 1947 partition losses and victims, albeit with a nationalist and Hindu majority reading. Yet, there is a simultaneous relegation of this memorial to a shallow memory, so that details of the partition are not commemorated—the absence of Sikh and Muslim citizens whose losses were equally great, the conflation of partition victims with fallen soldiers in the war, the conflation of partition victims with freedom fighters. Indeed, one could say that the ambivalent meaning of the Martyr's Memorial lies within *the intent to remember but also the coaxing to forget.* The shallow memory of the partition functions to prevent a cognitive dissonance in the newly formed Indian identity as that of a citizen of a secular state: If we keep the memory of the slaughter of Hindus and Sikhs by Muslims during the partition, what does it mean for our Muslim citizens in the present? Indeed, the periodic communal violence in contemporary India, especially between Hindus and Muslims, seems to suggest that notwithstanding the desire to preserve a shallow version of partition memory, memory is slow to die without a trace. As Homi Bhabha describes in a different context, this ambivalence in memory is a product of that which is 'uttered *inter dicta*: a discourse at the crossroads of what is known and Permissible and that which though known must be kept concealed; a discourse uttered between the lines and as such both against the rules and within them.'[41] So what is uttered *inter dicta* over here, especially in the Hindu-Muslim relationship pre- and post-partition? That we were the same once (pre-1947) and now we are completely opposed to each other (post-1947). It is love turned to hate, familiarity to enmity, intimacy to unacceptable strangeness, and family to foe. In his description of repressive erasure, Connerton suggests that 'the explicit purpose of casting the memory of a person into oblivion has the effect of drawing attention to them, and so of causing them to be remembered. The requirement to forget ends in reinforcing memory.'[42]

For now, I want to ask if the inability to forget the partition is a form of counter-memory, a Foucauldian notion that is a critique of totalizing public narratives. Within this notion, subordinated voices surface and lay bare the close links between, and the seamless interpretations of, the dominant order and their often-ambiguous historical representations. In 'Nietzsche, Genealogy, History,' Foucault points out that the hegemonic order's domination 'is fixed, throughout its history in rituals, in meticulous procedures that impose rights and obligations. It establishes marks of its power and engraves memories on things and even within bodies.'[43] In our instance, dominant, indigenous history re-inscribes a Hindu perspective through the two exclusionary sculptural forms of the swastika and the Ashoka Chakra to shape the narrative. However, the counter-memory emerges when we destabilize the power invested in dominant meanings and include those details that fall outside 'its monotonous finality,'[44] which is revealed to be merely a fraction of the whole narrative of the Indian partition. Thus, memories can be continuously revised and promote competitive views of the past.

Finally, I want to point out the obvious—that in the Martyr's Memorial in Chandigarh, it is *not* that memory resurfaces from forgetting but rather the reverse—it is forgetting that resurfaces, notwithstanding the efforts of maintaining memory via a memorial. I conclude this chapter by suggesting an alternative reading to the memorial. The simultaneity of independence with partition has meant the relegation and subordination of partition discourse to that of decolonization, linking these two discourses metonymically in the South Asian imaginary in post-colonial Indian history. As is often the function of metonyms, the two terms establish a hierarchy with one term being re-pressed by the visibility of the other, more prominent term. The visible term is often perceived to be the positive term, the other term being rendered absent. However, notwithstanding its visibility, it is the repressed term that is gener-ally privileged in that it has 'a psychic investment in it,'[45] and remains hidden because 'it falls to the position of the signified, while the other functions as its signifier . . .'[46] What Chandigarh's monument reveals is that initially their relationship of contiguity gives the partition and independence value, sig-nificance and meaning. Yet in a desire to forget, nationalistic determinations have privileged one concept over the other, psychically investing in it, trying to designate the less visible term to the bin of forgetfulness. Nevertheless, the partition functions as a counter-memory, a defiant remembering despite the erasures of history. Indeed, the eruption of memories of partition from time to time seems to suggest that what seems forgotten in public memory is, in fact, perhaps a strong part at the core of Indian identity, far more than that of the discourse of independence struggle. Indeed, it is the suppression of memories that gives the chaos of partition the power of periodic eruption. It might not have many monuments, but the partition will not completely disappear from the Indian imaginary.

Finally, when will the partition get relegated to the past? When will the trauma of partition be overcome? The healing of trauma will not fully occur until the issue of Kashmir is finally resolved by the two countries—but that is another chapter, yet to be written.

NOTES

1. The title, of course, is an echo of James E. Young's magnificent *The Texture of Memory: Holocaust Memorials and Meanings* (New Haven, CT: Yale University Press, 1993).

2. Paul Connerton, *How Modernity Forgets* (Cambridge: Cambridge University Press, 2009), 84.

3. As cited in Connerton, *How Modernity Forgets*, 90–91.

4. Patrick Hutton as cited in Stephen Legg, 'Contesting and Surviving Memory: Space, Nation and Nostalgia in *Les Lieux de Mémoire*,' *Environment and Planning D: Society and Space* 23.4 (2005): 481.

5. See Dylan Trigg, *The Memory of Place: A Phenomenology of the Uncanny* (Athens: Ohio University Press, 2012), xviii.

6. Pierre Nora, 'Between Memory and History: *Les Lieux de Memoire*,' *Representations* 26 (Spring 1989): 7–24.

7. See, for instance, my article 'Specters of Democracy/The Gender of Spectres: Cultural Memory and the Indian Partition,' in *Revisiting India's Partition: New Essays on Memory, Culture and Politics*, eds. Amritjit Singh, Nalini Iyer and Rahul K. Gairola (Lanham, MD: Lexington Books, 2016), 3–20; also see 'Sexuality After Partition: The Great Indian Private Sphere,' in *Partitions and Their Afterlives*, eds. Radhika Mohanram and Anindya Raychaudhuri (London: Rowman & Littlefield, 2019), 49–82.

8. Trigg, *The Memory of Place*, 3.

9. Trigg, *The Memory of Place*, 3.

10. Maurice Halbwachs, 'The Social Frameworks of Memory,' in *On Collective Memory*, ed., trans. and Intro. Lewis A. Coser (Chicago: University of Chicago Press), 1992, 38.

11. Nora, 'Between Memory and History,' 7.

12. Nora, 'Between Memory and History,' 12.

13. As cited in Frances A. Yates, *The Art of Memory* (London: Routledge, 1999), 2.

14. Paul Connerton, *The Spirit of Mourning: History, Memory and the Body* (Cambridge: Cambridge University Press, 2011), 85.

15. Maurice Merleau-Ponty, *Phenomenology of Perception*, trans. Colin Smith (London: Routledge, 2006), 330.

16. Trigg, *The Memory of Place*, 5.

17. Trigg, *The Memory of Place*, 5.

18. Trigg, *The Memory of Place*, 6.

19. Trigg, *The Memory of Place*, 74.

20. Trigg, *The Memory of Place*, 75.

21. In 2017, the Partition Museum was finally opened in Amritsar, in Punjab, India. It is the only museum that exists at this time in South Asia to commemorate this event. The Kolkata (Calcutta) Partition Museum is currently being developed and will focus specifically on the experience of the Bengal partition (as the Amritsar Museum focuses on the Punjab partition). A sort of re-memorialization of the partition is also done at the Wagah border near Amritsar and consists of a daily flag-lowering ceremony and the ceremonial closing of the border for the day by both India and Pakistan. The Punjab Tourism Board is also involved in this ceremony, and both countries have invested in the spectacle of this sundown event that is attended by thousands every day on both sides of the border. The audience on both sides wave flags, dance and shout patriotic slogans led by DJs. I attended this event in March 2018 and was struck

by how Bollywoodized the ceremony was with the song and dance, especially on the Indian side. It was the disturbing effect of the nationalisms evoked by both sides and the references to the violence of 1947 now embodied in the marching Border Security Forces' rifle-carrying, goose-stepping guards in this ceremony that seemed to keep the memory of the partition alive.

22. Marc Augé, *Oblivion*, trans. Marjolijn de Jager (Minneapolis: University of Minnesota Press, 2004), 3.

23. Paul Connerton, *How Societies Remember* (Cambridge: Cambridge University Press, 1989), 6.

24. Charles-Édouard Jeanneret, better known as Le Corbusier, had a long career as an architect, urban planner, designer and painter. He was one of the pioneers of modern architecture. Seventeen projects by Corbusier in seven countries have the status of a UN World Heritage Site.

25. Sunil Khilnani as quoted in Tan Tai Yong and Gyanesh Kudaisya, *The Aftermath of Partition in South Asia* (London and New York: Routledge, 2000), 187.

26. Norma Evenson, *Chandigarh* (Berkeley: University of California Press, 1966).

27. Tropical architecture was developed by two British architects, Maxwell Fry and Jane Drew, who developed this style in Africa where they had been working prior to their involvement with Chandigarh. Drew's low-cost housing developed in Chandigarh is still popular.

28. Pierre Nora, 'Between Memory and History,' 19.

29. See, for instance, Yong and Kudaisya.

30. Personal correspondence with Vikramaditya Prakash. Also see his work *CHD Chandigarh* (New Delhi: Bloomsbury, 2014).

31. Judith Herman, *Trauma and Recovery: The Aftermath of Violence—From Domestic Abuse to Political Terror* (New York: Basic Books, 1992), 175.

32. Friedrich Nietzsche, 'On the Uses and Disadvantages of History for Life,' *Untimely Meditations*, trans. R. J. Hollingdale (Cambridge: Cambridge University Press, 1983), 62.

33. See Barbara Misztal, *Theories of Social Remembering* (Maidenhead: Open University Press, 2003), 15.

34. Misztal, *Theories of Social Remembering*, 16.

35. Ernest Renan, 'What Is a Nation,' trans. and annotated Martin Thom, in *Nation and Narration*, ed. Homi K. Bhabha (New York and London: Routledge, 1990), 11.

36. Paul Connerton, 'Seven Types of Forgetting,' in *The Spirit of Mourning: History, Memory and the Body* (Cambridge: Cambridge University Press, 2011), 34.

37. Connerton, 'Seven Types of Forgetting,' 36.

38. Connerton, 'Seven Types of Forgetting,' 36–7.

39. Alexander and Margarete Mitscherlich, *The Inability to Mourn: Principles of Collective Behaviour*, trans. Beverley R. Placzek (New York: Grove Press, 1975).

40. See Connerton, 'Seven Types of Forgetting,' 36.

41. Homi K. Bhabha, 'Of Mimicry and Man: The Ambivalence of Postcolonial Discourse,' in *The Location of Culture* (London and New York: Routledge: 1994), 89.

42. Connerton, 'Seven Types of Forgetting,' 41.

43. Michel Foucault, 'Nietzsche, Genealogy, History,' in *Language, Counter-Memory, Practice: Selected Essays and Interviews*, ed. Daniel F. Bouchard (Ithaca, NY: Cornell University Press, 1977), 150.

44. Foucault, 'Nietzsche, Genealogy, History,' 144.

45. Kaja Silverman, *The Subject of Semiotics* (Oxford: Oxford University Press, 1983), 113.

46. Silverman, *The Subject of Semiotics*, 112.

BIBLIOGRAPHY

AUGÉ, Marc. *Oblivion*. Translated by Marjolijn de Jager. Minneapolis: University of Minnesota Press, 2004.

BHABHA, Homi K. 'Of Mimicry and Man: The Ambivalence of Postcolonial Discourse.' In *The Location of Culture*. 85–92. London and New York: Routledge: 1994.

CONNERTON, Paul. *How Modernity Forgets*. Cambridge: Cambridge University Press, 2009.

CONNERTON, Paul. *How Societies Remember*. Cambridge: Cambridge University Press, 1989.

CONNERTON, Paul. 'Seven Types of Forgetting.' In *The Spirit of Mourning: History, Memory and the Body*. 33–50. Cambridge: Cambridge University Press, 2011.

EVENSON, Norma. *Chandigarh*. Berkeley: University of California Press, 1966.

FOUCAULT, Michel. 'Nietzsche, Genealogy, History.' In *Language, Counter-memory, Practice: Selected Essays and Interviews*. Edited by Daniel F. Bouchard. 138–64. Ithaca, NY: Cornell University Press, 1977.

HALBWACHS, Maurice. 'The Social Frameworks of Memory.' In *On Collective Memory*. Edited, translated and with an Introduction by Lewis A. Coser. 35–189. Chicago: University of Chicago Press, 1992.

HERMAN, Judith. *Trauma and Recovery: The Aftermath of Violence—From Domestic Abuse to Political Terror*. New York: Basic Books, 1992.

LEGG, Stephen. 'Contesting and Surviving Memory: Space, Nation and Nostalgia in *Les Lieux de Mémoire*.' *Environment and Planning D: Society and Space* 23.4 (2005): 481–504.

MERLEAU-PONTY, Maurice. *Phenomenology of Perception*. Translated by Colin Smith. London: Routledge, 2006.

MISZTAL, Barbara. *Theories of Social Remembering*. Maidenhead: Open University Press, 2003.

MITSCHERLICH, Alexander and Margarete. *The Inability to Mourn: Principles of Collective Behaviour*. Translated by Beverley R. Placzek. New York: Grove Press, 1975.

MOHANRAM, Radhika. 'Sexuality After Partition: The Great Indian Private Sphere.' In *Partitions and their Afterlives*. Edited by Radhika Mohanram and Anindya Raychaudhuri. 49–82. London: Rowman & Littlefield, 2019.

MOHANRAM, Radhika. 'Specters of Democracy/The Gender of Spectres: Cultural Memory and the Indian Partition.' In *Revisiting India's Partition: New Essays on Memory, Culture and Politics.* Edited by Amritjit Singh, Nalini Iyer and Rahul K. Gairola. 3–20. Lanham, MD: Lexington Books, 2016.

NIETZSCHE, Friedrich. 'On the Uses and Disadvantages of History for Life.' *Untimely Meditations.* Translated by R. J. Hollingdale. 57–124. Cambridge: Cambridge University Press, 1983.

NORA, Pierre. 'Between Memory and History: *Les Lieux de Memoire.*' *Representations* 26 (Spring 1989): 7–24.

PRAKASH, Vikramaditya. *CHD Chandigarh.* New Delhi: Bloomsbury, 2014.

RENAN, Ernest. 'What Is a Nation.' Translated and annotated by Martin Thom. In *Nation and Narration.* Edited by Homi K. Bhabha. 8–22. New York and London: Routledge, 1990.

SILVERMAN, Kaja. *The Subject of Semiotics.* Oxford: Oxford University Press, 1983.

TRIGG, Dylan. *The Memory of Place: A Phenomenology of the Uncanny.* Athens: Ohio University Press, 2012.

YATES, Frances A. *The Art of Memory.* London: Routledge, 1999.

YONG, Tan Tai and Gyanesh Kudaisya. *The Aftermath of Partition in South Asia.* London and New York: Routledge, 2000.

YOUNG, James E. *The Texture of Memory: Holocaust Memorials and Meanings.* New Haven, CT: Yale University Press, 1993.

Chapter Seven

How Do We Mourn?

A Look at Makeshift Memorials

Irene Scicluna

Just over fifty years ago, in October 1966, in Aberfan, South Wales, a tip of more than 150,000 cubic metres of rain-soaked mining debris collapsed and slid towards the village primary school, killing 144 people. As typically happens in events of unexpected mass trauma, a sense of community immediately emerged. Locals organized volunteer search-and-rescue operations, collected relief money and attended a joint funeral *en masse* with over 2,000 people in attendance. Moreover, for the first time in the history of British television, reporters brought the tragedy into the homes of more than 54 million people around the United Kingdom. As a result, letters of condolence poured into Aberfan and the communal mourning broadened its scope to include people who were, strictly speaking, unrelated to the tragedy, but still were compelled to offer their compassion and to share in Aberfan's grief.

Despite these unmistakable signs of group mourning, one ritual of public and communal mourning stands out by its absence. If the grim events in Aberfan had happened today, a makeshift memorial—a fragmented whole made up flowers, candles, graffiti, hastily scribbled notes and various personal items—would have emerged in the very brief moments following the violent disaster. The broadcasts would have shown footage of people participating in the makeshift memorial by laying down their tributes in distinctive, yet chaotic configurations. In 2018, there would surely have been newspaper reports featuring stretches of makeshift memorials erupting out of immediate reactions to loss. What are we to make of this conspicuous absence? Are makeshift memorials as we know them an unprecedented cultural product? And if so, what is the cultural place and effect of the makeshift memorial as a contemporary mourning ritual?

Makeshift memorials as we know them today represent the possibility to express one's individual feelings of mourning on the public stage. In itself, this is nothing new. In their study about how we currently memorialize public death, Peter Jan Margry and Cristina Sánchez-Carretero point out that crude memorials which mark an unexpectedly interrupted life is a well-documented Hispanic tradition which goes back hundreds of years.[1] The Spanish word *descansos*, meaning 'resting place,' refers to the pallbearers' resting place on the journey between the rural church and the cemetery, or *camposanto*. Wherever they put down the coffin, they would erect colourful memorials of crosses and flowers, which would remind travellers to pray for the soul in purgatory.[2]

In more recent times of war, spontaneous memorials have often marked the ground of fallen comrades with personal items. One such tribute was photographed on Normandy beach in 1944. A helmet is set atop a rifle gun, as if representing a particular soldier who perished on that spot. Despite being minimalistic, the Normandy makeshift memorial has all the qualities that our sprawling contemporary memorials do: it is immediate, likely to have been erected within a short time after the soldier's death. It is personal—constructed by mourning comrades who had a connection to the deceased and who used a symbolic object (the helmet). It is constructed as a temporary memorial, with the full awareness that it would be torn down soon after its erection. Furthermore, its function is not as a grave marker, but more as a visually striking effort in commemoration or statement about the war itself. In summary, the rifle-*cum*-memorial seems to anticipate the political and ritualistic mourning culture that we associate with our own makeshift memorials.

There are indeed historical precedents for makeshift memorialization. Perhaps, then, it is the sheer magnitude of the contemporary makeshift memorials that accounts for their distinctly current feel. It is certainly true that their size and frequency is rapidly increasing, in direct proportion to the increasing frequency of large-scale incidents of mass violent death. Perhaps the point of cultural interest lies in the fact that they are now such a consistent and automatic mourning practice that they are rituals in their own right. The widespread custom of makeshift memorials gives rise to questions about what has changed—and what has stayed the same—in our mourning practices and the way we, both as individuals and as a community, confront sudden death.

In tracing the conditions that helped establish this mourning practice, we shall first look at the memorials as a collection of individual expressions of grief and, simultaneously, as an aggregated mass. Secondly, viewing the makeshift memorial as a dynamic system raises questions about what kind of internal interactions arise within the memorial itself. Is the makeshift memorial the hegemonized whole which it appears to be at first glance? Thirdly, we shall see that if the memorials take on the emotional intensities of those who participate in them, they likewise emit that intensity back into the community. Makeshift memorials are never static accumulations of objects but, crucially, they ask pointed, politically charged questions; they contest and protest. Lastly, we shall consider how makeshift memorials are specifically characterized by their finite temporality; that is, they are eventually always cleared away. This leads to questions about the finitude of mourning itself: is there a correlation between 'moving on' and the removal of the makeshift memorial? What resonances remain after the community's expressions of grief have been disposed of? It is the import of these resonances, whether they are a result of the makeshift memorial's presence or absence, which we seek to chronicle and account for in this chapter.

CHANGING ATTITUDES TO MOURNING

What has changed in our mourning practices that would explain the contemporary recourse to public grief at makeshift memorials? As a starting point, I propose to look into general attitudes towards public mourning. In his book *The Hour of Our Death*, historian Philippe Ariès discusses the nineteenth-century shift from burials in churchyards to out-of-town cemeteries. The desire for separation between the living and the dead is attributed to hygiene, but Ariès also demonstrates that we can assume a certain level of discomfort with the spatial proximity of death. This is made even more palpable by the popularization of cremation in the twentieth century, which removes death and the body even more completely than burial. The modern banishment of death, then, is linked with the nullifying of places related to death. Ariès notes how those who are bereaved tend to avoid designated memorial sites: 'the relative of the [deceased] person rejects the physical reality of the site, its association with the body, which inspires distaste.'[3] Here already we start to see the singular nature of the contemporary makeshift memorial, where mourners actively seek out sites of death, marking them with plastic flowers and Christmas tree cuttings because '[t]his is where my daughter's spirit was last.'[4]

The death-denying phenomenon that Ariès identifies in modern western society is reflected in the decline of religion's influence in the twentieth century. Whereas in pre-modern societies it had been religious institutions that upheld a common understanding of death and mourning rituals, steady secularization meant that the burden of mourning now fell on the private individual and the closest family members. Questions about the senseless finitude of life that were once directed to a higher power now required a look inwards.[5] As inner life was cultivated, mourning was passed to the domain of the furtively personal. On this note, in 1965, the social anthropologist Geoffrey Gorer observed how 'at present death and mourning are treated with much the same prudery as sexual impulses were a century ago.'[6] Analogously, one must learn to stoically dominate the public expression of one's mourning.

The 1966 Aberfan landslide is a helpful demonstrative example in this regard. As the first televised national disaster unfolded before the nation's eyes, the grief-restraint of the families of the young victims, at least when confronted by the rolling cameras, was nothing short of extraordinary. To illustrate the point, a BBC documentary exploring the British stiff upper lip shows an Aberfan news bulletin, where a coal miner calmly talks to a reporter:

> Well, I know where my son is at the moment—he's buried in that end class-
> room up there.
> And what about your other child?
> Well, she's alright, she is. My little girl is all right.[7]

The locals' emotional response to the tragedy, if displayed at all, seemed to be redirected either towards anger at the National Coal Board or in relentless rescue work. It was only decades later that survivors and locals openly talked to newspapers about their trauma. To note that private response to death was the rule in 1966 is to highlight a jarring contrast to the public, open-view mourning which we are more familiar with today and to emphasize the cultural realignment that mourning has undergone. The twentieth century saw a hard-fought dichotomous struggle between steadfast modesty in mourning and the erosion of the 'great taboo' of mourning. It is that erosion that produces the contemporary type of public grief and, consequently, the twenty-first-century sprawling makeshift memorials.

Of course, no cultural shift is unequivocal. Emotionally detached attitudes around death remain and reverberate in our cultural consciousness. Still today, the very presence of a person who has suffered a recent loss will cause general awkwardness. Conversation can become stilted, and if we make any efforts to comfort the bereaved, the attempt will soon embarrass us and we will try desperately to change the conversation.[8] Nevertheless, we seem to be steadily shifting away from such a censored approach to mourning. The cultural reframing can be observed in the 'death positivity' coalition led by Britain's Department of Health, whose slogan reads: 'Dying Matters: Let's Talk About It.' Among other things, the initiative aims to broaden public knowledge about issues related to death and grief. Similarly, when violent death occurs nowadays, the taboo of grief seems to be giving way to more expressive attitudes. One instance is the increasing common usage of phrases like 'five stages of grief' or 'the grief process,' which recognize the normality of grief and reject the impulse to suppress it. Another example is the unprecedented ordinariness of grief counselling, support groups, blogs and communities, all of which specifically emphasize the universal aspects of mourning. In all these settings, the cultural norm encourages candid verbalization of feelings of loss in varying shades of public or private environments. It may yet be premature to say that mourning is currently free from taboo, but it certainly bears stating that in the twenty-first century, mourning percolates in collective consciousness and is no longer expected to be done entirely behind closed doors.

The cultural shift from silence to expression may go some way toward explaining not only the presence of makeshift memorials but also their sheer physical volume. Certainly, the '*sea* of balloons, cuddly toys and flowers' which materialized in St. Ann's Square in Manchester after the 2017 Manchester Arena bombing runs directly counter to the stoic grief-denial which Ariès and Gorer discuss in their anthropological studies.[9] The makeshift memorial in Manchester (figure 7.1) is typical of its kind in that it points to a general cultural disillusion with the supposed efficacy of repressing grief. Instead of 'gritting our teeth and bearing it,' we now do the exact opposite: we put on grief performances of great magnitudes, the strength of which lies in their intended purpose to be witnessed by a general audience.

The impression one gets from the strong public component in a makeshift memorial is that one is better able to freely express emotional vulnerability if it is in the context of a coalition of other individuals across the country and the world, all united in feeling some type of loss at the same time. The potential for connectedness comes with the temporal immediacy: mourning at the makeshift memorial is inherently tied to the *current* crisis situation and to the *immediate* feelings of vulnerability which reside on the surface. A memorial is volatile and unpredictable because it is ad hoc and not restricted by the structured distance with which commemorative plaques or funerary rites are imbued. Similarly, a makeshift memorial is distinct from a permanent one because the former is an outlet for mourning that is actively happening now,

Figure 7.1. St. Ann's Square makeshift memorial.

rather than mourning that has already happened. The cultural disposition in this context, then, decidedly shuns the stoicism which denies (or rather hides) the mourning self and instead encourages open, 'exorbitant, frenzied and extreme' reactions to death.[10]

Furthermore, since the informal action of writing messages and placing items is open to all potential participants, the memorial takes on an inclusive dimension. Anyone can be either an actor or a spectator. As a case in point, we may choose the memorials that began to form at the foot of French embassies around the world after the November 2015 terrorist attacks in various locations in Paris. Though the attack was localized, the felt losses—not only for the casualties but also, more broadly, for ideals of security, safety and peace—were not limited to one location, nor to one group of people of any one nation. In the collective atmosphere of grief, bereavement is no longer associated with isolation but rather with global comradeship. Instead of being an exclusive or insulated affair, then, mourning at a makeshift memorial is universal, outward bound and expansive.

INTERACTIONS: INDIVIDUAL AND COMMUNITY

The makeshift memorial is evidently a communal scene. Yet does the makeshift memorial, a ritual that depends on the public force of congregation, indicate that the social response to loss now favours the communal domain at the expense of private introspection? In the face of the ever-growing role of public self-expression in mourning, what is the place of the private facet of mourning? These questions become ever more pressing if we consider that each person lining up to place an object at the site of trauma is performing an individualized act. Each person may determine the extent of their own participation—whether they decide to place a candle, a flag, a note or some flowers, whether they remain at the site after they have placed the object of their choosing or prefer to retreat to a more private space falls under the remit of first-person experience. It is appropriate, then, to recognize that the makeshift memorial introduces a degree of exchange between highly publicized mourning and the quieter, more traditional role of solitary mourning. The most prudent way to approach the questions we posed at the start of this paragraph is to acknowledge that the private and the public aspects of mourning are not truly contrary, but that both tendencies may, in fact, be complementary to each other.

In his 1917 essay 'Mourning and Melancholia,' Sigmund Freud states that mourning is 'the reaction to the loss of a loved person, or the loss of some abstraction which has taken the place of one, such as country, liberty, an ideal, and so on.'[11] For him, mourning is a complex *internal* process whereby the mourner attempts to negotiate two conflicting dispositions within his innermost mental state: on the one hand, the expectation that the lost object should be present, and on the other hand, the encroaching consciousness that the lost object is now decidedly out of reach. It is the inexorable discrepancy between these two dispositions (one towards the object and the other towards a reality without the object) which is the source of the pain which we call grief. Accordingly, the grief is resolved and the work of mourning is completed when 'respect for reality [without the object] gains the day.'[12] Freud's account of mourning crucially illustrates the inner experience of mourning insofar as it relies on individual 'psychological energy' and 'mental struggle and labour.'[13] Consequently, even if one is standing in spatial proximity to others who are also mourning (as is the case when one places a memento at a makeshift memorial), it is entirely plausible that the mourning process must, ultimately, be undergone by oneself.

The makeshift memorial depends on the private mental state of mourning. Personal grief sentiments are the smallest common denominator of any makeshift memorial, which, in its most basic form, is rooted in the individual experiences of its participants and made up of contributions like flowers, messages or flags which are representative of those experiences. In other words, the makeshift memorial is effectively a voluminous assemblage of individual mourning processes and the singular items which represent them. Yet this is not the whole story. A makeshift memorial's sum total cannot be explained exclusively with reference to its individual parts since it crucially also refers to a culturally well-established practice of grief expression. We can surmise that this is what Margaret R. Yocom is referring to when she suggests that makeshift memorials are not makeshift at all since they 'have a rhythm, a precision, an aesthetic arrangement all their own.'[14] What she is pointing to is the fact that though they are made up of scattered components, makeshift memorials nevertheless have a particular identity, a sense of style and a clear effect on their surroundings. This is not to say that they are entirely given over to a prescribed range of permissible grief-expressive acts as, for instance, traditional funerary rites are. Rather, the salient point is that while makeshift memorials absorb the individual components they are made up of, they also necessarily exceed the scope of those components and become—in cultural and social affective terms at least—more than the sum of their parts.[15]

In effect, makeshift memorial mourning appears to take two simultaneous forms: the aggregated collection of individual contributions and the collective social force it derives from its parts. Though this chapter shall now consider these two modes of communal mourning separately based on how they work and to what ends, it is important to note that they are instrumental to each other: there can be no aggregation of individual objects without the unified social framework that supports it, and there likewise cannot be a collective force without the individual aspects which it draws its impetus from. By the same token, when one adds an item to a makeshift memorial, the act is two-fold. By expressing one's personal grief in a communal way, one is reinforcing the collective ethos which is already underway, and in turn, the cultural force facilitates the possibility for further collection of symbolic objects. It is this interdependent, circuitous process which includes both the aggregation of the parts and the collective whole that is the quintessential condition of mourning at a makeshift memorial.

AGGREGATED PARTICULARS

Does the circular loop model of a makeshift memorial imply that the individual and the collective fit together seamlessly into one harmonious ritual? It seems clear that the answer must be in the negative. If the tensions and clashes that develop at makeshift memorials are indicative of anything at all, they attest to the fact that the individual elements therein retain the idiosyncratic, sometimes conflicting, properties that were bestowed upon them by the mourners who laid them there. In her study about the makeshift memorial after the 2004 Madrid train bombings, Sánchez-Carretero likens the makeshift memorial structure to a palimpsest, a document created by erasing the original text such that the parchment could be used again, for another purpose. Most crucially, the erasure is never pristine, and centuries later it is possible to still make out layers of text, written and overwritten. In the same way, the various items at a makeshift memorial overwrite each other for lack of space, yet still leaving behind an essential trace: 'A printed sheet of paper bearing the words "Immigrants are not to be blamed" serves as support for other texts in Spanish and Arab [*sic*] written by different hands.'[16] This is an example of the makeshift as fractured whole, where the overwriting between its parts is as likely to be harmonious as it is to be jarring. Angry messages towards select groups of people lie alongside or erase others which express their grief in a more reverent tone and vice versa.

Keeping in mind such superimposed and often conflicting tensions, Sánchez-Carretero's textual metaphor of the palimpsest is a particularly useful lens through which to view the makeshift memorial. Not only does the analogy allow us to critically evaluate the mechanism of overwriting at makeshift memorials, it also brings to the fore the vibrant resonances between elements which are independent yet held together by the fact that they refer to the same violent event. In her monograph titled *The Palimpsest*, Sarah Dillon suggestively toys with the word 'palimpsestuous' to highlight the interlacing relations therein before going on to define the palimpsest as 'an involuted phenomenon where otherwise unrelated texts are involved and entangled, intricately interwoven, interrupting and inhabiting each other.'[17] In other words, the intertwining texts in a palimpsest not only erase but also *create* each other, insofar as each is a crucial intervention into understanding the other. Similarly, examining the communal mourning at a makeshift memorial is a matter of asking about the back-and-forth intersections of its various constituents. It is these kinetic interactions between overlapping items which make the makeshift memorial active and fundamentally unpredictable.

Issues surrounding the relationality of singular contributions to the makeshift memorial arose around the Columbine High School massacre memorial. Shortly after the school shooting, fifteen wooden crosses were put up on a nearby hill to represent the thirteen victims and the two shooters who died in the tragedy. People lined up to write messages of condolence on the wooden crosses. The crosses which represented the shooters, Dylan Klebold and Eric Harris, became the meeting place of various divergent mourning voices. One mourner scrawled 'Fuck you' on Dylan Klebold's cross, another mourner crossed it out. Local police removed signs that read 'Murderer, burn in hell,' while other messages inscribed on the cross directly responded to each other: 'How can anyone forgive you?'; 'Through Jesus Christ, that's how!'[18]

On the one hand, the monolith of communal mourning at Columbine can be broken down by focusing on any of these individual messages. Like the reader of the palimpsest, we may alternate between one layer and another. On the other hand, the makeshift memorial palimpsest takes us back and forth between the layers like a pendulum, never standing still nor progressing but always somehow stuck in no-man's-land. The fragmented mechanism of collective mourning is quite literally reflected in the makeshift memorial, where it is not only the case that the memorial is made up of fragments, but also that they can be altered, removed or even destroyed, revealing the fractured psyche of the community. Nowhere is this clearer than in the Columbine example: the two offending crosses were actually taken down and destroyed by the father of one of the victims. Nevertheless, the six-foot crosses were shortly replaced with smaller versions of them. Overwhelmed by all the controversy, Greg Zanis, the carpenter who had made and erected the original fifteen crosses, ultimately removed all of them for good.[19] Zanis's intervention continues to demonstrate the volatile nature of the makeshift memorial, where the expressions of individualized mourning are motile in a very literal way; that is, they can be repeatedly erased and reconstituted.

The Columbine back-and-forth is testimony to the fact that memorialization (whether makeshift or not) always 'involve[s] choices about who or which values will be honoured, and what form the remembrance will take.'[20] Nevertheless, the makeshift memorial is disposed to a heightened permissiveness with regards to disparate individual grief-expressing choices. Such fluidity is perhaps indicative of shifting tendencies in mourning practices, which lean more towards the unprescribed rather than the choreographed. The key point is that the makeshift memorial sustains a hitherto unseen unstructured mode of mourning by allowing for competing and discordant voices to come into contact and converse with one another about shared trauma in a very real and sometimes tangibly uncomfortable way. Much like a palimpsest, where there is no one author, at the makeshift memorial there is no archetypal expression of grief at the exclusion of other modes of mourning, no master builder, no architect in the essential sense of the word as one with a prescribed blueprint. There is no set of precisely organized functions, but only objects—each charged with the grief of the individual person who has laid it there—conversing with each other as if they were nodes that make up a highly volatile mourning network.

COLLECTIVE FORCE

The interactions within such a network, however, do not remain exclusively concentrated within the boundaries of the makeshift memorial, but always emanate outwards as much as they reverberate inwards. The act of lighting a candle, laying down flowers or simply visiting the memorial speaks to other individual mourning acts of that nature, but it is also outwardly public and available. It follows that we can expect the makeshift memorial's influences to go beyond the memorial itself, to encounter the world, to affect and be affected by it. In her recent account of participatory art, Erin Manning perfectly captures the bi-directionality of what she calls the 'art of participation.' Not only do we have, as our starting point, a 'melting pot of common denominators,' she argues, we must also ask how the 'techniques of encounter' are mired in 'opening up the existing fields of relation toward new forms of perception, accountability, experience and collectivity.'[21] Likewise, to get a complete picture of the cultural place of the makeshift memorial as mourning ritual, we must not only consider the interactions between its various constituents, but also the interaction of the makeshift memorial with the complex socio-political environment in which it is embedded. It is to this issue of a makeshift memorial's outward resonances that we now turn.

In his discussion of the political nature of makeshift memorials, Jack Santino characterizes them as 'silent witnesses.'[22] Crucially, however, this silence is not the silence of gravestones; that is, it is not placid in its com-

Figure 7.2. Arturo Aguilera ghost bike.

memoration. Rather, the very presence of the makeshift memorial actively exposes the trauma to public awareness. The lost object is underscored while its loss is elevated to a heightened state of relevance and urgency. Persistent testimony is precisely the impetus behind the emerging practice of ghost bikes, or makeshift memorials for bicyclists who are killed on the street (figure 7.2). A bicycle is painted white and locked to a street sign near the crash site, accompanied by a plaque with the victim's name and the usual flowers and candles. The intimate nature of using the deceased's own bike is a visually arresting expression of raw grief which interrupts the typical urban setting. The aesthetic intrusion of the makeshift memorial serves to translate personal grief in terms of social imperatives, namely, fixing traffic deaths to the memory of the passerby.

Furthermore, in their refusal to let the death be forgotten, ghost bikes serve as an indirect political call-to-action for better infrastructural policy or more acute awareness of road safety for other cyclists. The efficacy of ghost bikes as makeshift memorials is thus founded on the fact that they 'refocus critical attention on issues which are not only contentious and emotionally charged but also largely ignored and/or poorly contextualized in mass media.'[23] Even if the ghost bike is silent, then, its silent presence foregrounds political ideology by eliciting the public's attention and directing it, first towards deaths which are so frequent that they blend together, and second towards issues like infrastructure for cyclists, which are hardly attended to with urgency in legislative rooms.[24] The makeshift memorial acts as a magnifying lens with the capacity for instrumental socio-political force. As Santino so vividly puts it:

> You don't think drunk driving is a problem? My daughter was killed—here, at this spot—because of it. Teenage drinking? Responsible for the deaths of a carload of kids—right here. The county doesn't want to spend money on road improvement? Look at all the crosses along this stretch of road. . . . Now. Defend your actions, your politics, in the light of that.[25]

Makeshift memorials thus become not only a locus of mourning but also of negotiation and insistence, of action and confrontation. Those who build shrines will not allow the deceased to be written off as mere numbers. They insist that action be taken, that their children's deaths should not fall between the cracks of history. In this sense, they provoke productive movements; they are, in effect, not only mourning sites but also efficacious political call-to-actions.

Nevertheless, if the makeshift memorials are truly engaged in an active relation with their socio-political environments, this raises a number of pressing questions. To what extent can the makeshift memorial condition, alter or reinforce a specific interpretation of violent death? Should we be wary of the makeshift memorial's potential to become a political apparatus? Or should we celebrate its shaping and conditioning capacity as a welcome tool in the hands of the populace? To address these issues, we shall turn to Judith Butler's discussion of the representability of violent death. In *Frames of War*, Butler proposes that beyond war photojournalism's most self-evident function to depict scenes of war, it also serves to manipulate what will become the dominant established narrative and, in doing so, always leaves some things, or some lives, out of the frame: 'Now the state works on the field of perception,' she warns, 'and, more generally, the field of representability, in order to control affect.'[26] The frame of representation affects perception. To be clear, we are not dealing in social constructivism, a cultural theory which holds that we have no access to knowledge beyond our subjective interventions into reality. Rather, the violent events in Butler's study do have an objective existence beyond their representation. However, the problem lies with these events' susceptibility to being framed or otherwise packaged for a consumer whose understanding of the event will be filtered through the frame of representation. Needless to say, the interpretative practice of framing is fraught with moral and ethical concerns, not least since framing is typically contin-

gent on those with a vested interest in highlighting and excluding certain narrative elements. The issue becomes even more tangled when we consider that
representation animates thought processes, values, commitments and actions,
which circularly reinforce the framed representation.

Butler's insight into framing and representability can be transposed onto
the discussion of the socio-political resonances of the makeshift memorial in
the sense that they too represent and frame violent events. As visual representations of trauma, makeshift memorials have 'the power to excite and enrage
us in such a way that we might change our political views and conducts,' or
at the very least, trigger emotional reactions based on how they represent the
traumatic event.[27] The capacity to induce political action was arguably the
lasting significance of one of the earliest makeshift memorials as we know
them today. On 5 July 1934 (Bloody Thursday), between two and three thousand strikers in San Francisco took to the streets demanding fairer wages and
safer working conditions. In an effort to control the protest, police fired at the
crowd and two workers were fatally wounded. The area where the two were
injured was hastily (but neatly, far different from the sprawling memorials
of today) cordoned off with flowers and chalk markings. The construction
of the makeshift memorial had the very deliberate effect of organizing the
visual experience of the strike, especially for those who saw the extensive
newspaper coverage of the memorial. The memorial acted as a mechanism in
which the deaths (and ergo, police actions) were put in sharp focus: '2 ILA
Men Killed—*Shot in the Back*' and '*Police Murder*,' as the chalk inscriptions
at the memorial read. The stakes of the strikes were immediately raised.

In this case, we can clearly see how the memorial functions as an 'affective
frame.' The strikers' movement strategically used the emotional capital of the
flowers and chalk to highlight the deaths of the two innocent strikers. When
the police removed the flowers and scuffed out the inscriptions, they appeared
as oppressive forces whereas the 'only weapons used by the strikers were
chalk and flowers.'[28] The makeshift memorial thus presented an impression
of reality which, true or not, swayed public perceptions and intensified anger
in the community of San Francisco. The memorial reinforced the repressors/
repressed narrative, and its reconstruction came to signify resilience in the
face of authoritative rule. The memorial was, in fact, not merely a commemorative display but a spark 'of protest and resentment, instrumentalized
to articulate social or political disaffection,' spurring on the passions of those
who would later participate in an iconic funeral/protest march.[29] Journalist
Paul Eliel's assessment was that it was in no small part thanks to this grief
turned to political currency that 'the visionary dream of a small group of
the most radical workers, became for the first time a practical and realizable
objective.'[30] In their capacity for political affect, the memorials, like Butler's

imagery of war, deploy a particular interpretation of what has transpired. It is in this sense that they are politically active: they frame perception, enact narratives and incite a dramaturgy of collectivized mourning which can then serve as an instrumental catalyst to substantial political action.

At this juncture, it is worth noting a crucial difference between Butler's analysis of war photography as interpretative frame and the framing mechanism at play at the makeshift memorial. Butler highlights how the embedding of journalists in the military units during the Iraq War was an operation of power mandated by the United States, where 'state authorities were clearly interested in regulating the visual modes of participation during the war.'[31] There, the framing mechanism is employed by those who have the socio-cultural/economic/historical capital to make decisions which affect '*our* responsiveness.' The analogy between the makeshift memorial and the war photograph collapses here, since in the case of the memorial, there is no mandate, no designated action and no established parameters by an institution. Instead, the makeshift memorial *qua* frame is constructed by the individual members of the populace, and as such, produces a democratic and self-governing interpretation of events. In the case of the memorials, it is the grassroots, rather than the state, which expresses its own representation of violent events with the aim of influencing the socio-political surroundings.

An illuminating example is the assassination of Russian politician Boris Nemtsov.[32] It is fair to say that the makeshift memorials constructed along the bridge where he was assassinated (figure 7.3) stand not only for the man himself, but also for his political stances—scrutiny of the Ukraine War and the Russian economic crisis—as well as in protest of the manner in which Nemtsov died. However, the memorial has been repeatedly removed by Moscow authorities who insist that it has 'created a safety hazard' for pedestrians on the bridge.[33] Since February 2015, the bridge has become a sometimes metaphorical, sometimes literal battleground between the municipal employees who consistently remove the memorial and the activists who consistently replenish it. Fearing retaliation in the form of attack or arrest, protesters have gone so far as organizing an online delivery service to keep flowers flowing to the site.[34] Such fears, it turns out, were well-founded, since volunteer activist Ivan Skripnichenko died in August 2017 as a result of an attack he suffered while guarding the memorial. By claiming the bridge, people are exercising political agency in the absence of the ability to physically assemble. Placing a flower on this makeshift memorial is not merely commemorative but becomes a deliberate reiteration of a suppressed political narrative that interrupts the one offered by the broader operation of power. Under such harrowing conditions the memorial is a protest; every new addition to the memorial seems to bolster an affective frame where the prevailing narrative

Figure 7.3. Site of Boris Nemtsov's assassination, Moscow.

is that Boris Nemtsov was murdered and those who ordered his murder ought to be brought to justice.

Of course, we might still question the ethics of framing a violent event at all, whether that framing is done by the grassroots or by the state. As there is no monolith grassroots movement, the makeshift memorial might still not recognize a myriad of fringe interpretations of the Nemtsov assassination which are outside of the framed image the memorial presents us with. Nevertheless, the makeshift memorial is still a democratically led interruption or transition away from the Kremlin-mandated presentation of events. Responding to Butler's pointed question: 'What might be done to produce a more egalitarian set of conditions for recognizability? What might be done, in other words, to shift the very terms of recognizability in order to produce more radically democratic results?', we may answer that the makeshift memorial has the inbuilt potential to satisfy these criteria.[35] The interpretative frame of a memorial speaks to a bottom-up rather than top-down process of organizing violence, and the effect that a makeshift memorial generates can emerge as a threat to the authoritative narrative. Aspects of public trauma that would either go unnoticed (as in the cases memorialized by ghost bikes) or obliterated in official records (as in the San Francisco strikers and the Russian protesters) now have the physical and political space to exist.

FINITE DURATION

It is striking that the San Francisco memorial and the Moscow memorial were both forcibly removed by authorities and reconsolidated multiple times. As long as the memorials kept being reconstructed, the expediency of the grief had not yet run its course. While these two memorials might be particular due to the political circumstances of their removal, it is worth closing the chapter with a discussion on the fraught issue of clearing away makeshift memorials. On the one hand, there are a number of reasonable concerns: safety of the streetscapes, the unkempt aesthetics of rotting flowers, and the discomfort of having morbid reminders of trauma. On the other hand, removing them seems disloyal to the deceased. It can feel as if the act of dismantling represents the world's recovery from a loss that some have not quite recovered from yet. Debates and tensions notwithstanding, makeshift memorials are, by their nature, short-term installations.

Makeshift memorials operate in a similar manner to other death-related rites of passage: like funerals, they help traverse the grieving process by marking the end of one phase in a person's life and the beginning of an-other. However, unlike funerals, which are typically over by the afternoon, makeshift memorials prolong the transitional period to months, even years. In the case of the Charlie Hebdo shooting in January 2015, the tributes to the victims had not yet been removed by the terrorist attacks in Paris of the same year. The memorials for both attacks were only taken down in August 2016. The extended grieving process surrounding makeshift memorials is probably owing to a sense of sympathy towards those who are only gradually with-drawing from their loss. Nevertheless, the removal of the memorial is part of the overall rite of passage, whereby the clearing of the objects that made up the memorial signifies a step towards healing and moving forward.[36]

There are resonances here with Freud's 'Mourning and Melancholia.' The key concept is 'working through' mourning, which refers to a process of emotional labour before ultimate resolution. The work of mourning, as we have indicated before, consists in a rift between opposing vistas of real-ity: the libidinal position towards the lost object clashes with the reality that the lost object is not there. Subsequently, 'working through' mourning is a process that works towards the goal of accepting 'the command of reality.' Memory and detachment play a fundamental role in this acceptance: 'work-ing through' involves recollecting memories of the lost object piece by piece and painfully disassociating from the intense inclination towards each one. As Freud puts it, 'Each single one of the memories and expectations in which the libido is bound to the object is brought up and hypercathected, and de-tachment of the libido is accomplished in respect of it.'[37] In other words, for mourning to come to resolution, the trauma must first be engaged with once more and the libidinal energy that was previously invested in the lost object must be relocated to new objects, 'bit by bit, at great expanse of time and cathectic energy.'[38] The gradual shift in energy allows the mourner to inter-nalize the absence of the lost object and truly accept the loss. In summary, the measure of successful mourning resolution is the complete detachment from the lost object, so that 'the ego becomes free and uninhibited again' and the mourner is ready to invest in new objects.[39] For Freud, then, mourning is a process with an abrupt beginning and a natural end.

Freud's structural approach towards mourning could be used for an understanding of the makeshift memorial. It is entirely conceivable that the desire to accept a reality without the lost object underlies people's interest in keeping the streets clean and returning to an aesthetic of normality. For example, after the 2016 Nice truck attack, in the spirit of carrying out 'the command of reality,' hundreds of citizens formed a human chain four days after the attack, moving the commemorative items that had accumulated along the Riviera to designated places of meditation. The next day, news sources published an article with a headline expressing relief: 'On Nice's Riviera: Signs of Normal Returning after Attacks.'[40] It appears, then, that there is a pragmatic societal desire to complete the work of mourning, to rise above overwhelming sorrow, to not become so overpowered by public grief that it becomes dysfunctional or paralysing.[41] Freud's notion of 'working through' remains influential, not only because it offers a path towards much-desired closure but also, as evidenced by the Nice memorial deconstruction, because its impetus is geared towards bookending the social mourning process and thereby re-establishing the status quo.

We ought, however, to qualify the extent of the reach of the Freudian analogy. As Erika Lee Doss reminds us, 'Freud's . . . "breaking bonds" presupposition became the cornerstone of modern Western psychoanalytic understanding of bereavement,' and yet the cultural shift in mourning practices has moved towards an emphasis on 'the "continuing" bonds between the living and the deceased.'[42] The desire for continuing these bonds manifests itself in the strong public reluctance to dismantle the makeshift memorials. Consider, for instance, the town-wide polemic surrounding the removal of the scattered makeshift memorials for the victims of the Sandy Hook Elementary School shooting in Newtown, Connecticut, in 2012. On the one hand, taking the memorials down was an impending social imperative, driven by members and leaders of the community alike. On the other hand, the final decision to dismantle them caused reticence among residents, many of whom were torn over the prospect of the memorials' disappearance.[43] Once the material objects at the memorial have been affixed with the power to 'evoke memories, sustain thoughts, constitute political conditions and conjure states of being' all related to mourning, it appears difficult to dispose of them completely.[44] Even when the flowers have long since rotted, to dispose of them would be a betrayal of the conditions accrued while in mourning. Permanent clearance perhaps represents too clean a break between the mourning self and the healed self. In this respect, while still honouring the Freudian desire for resolution, contemporary mourning appears unconvinced by the prospect of a decisive break from the mourning process. Instead, there are mixed desires: the wish to alleviate the intensity of loss is coupled with a desire to preserve the grief and, by extension, the objects which represented it.

Can the conflicting gap between a desire for closure and a wish for grief preservation be bridged? What is needed is some act of transition, where the ordering process of resolution manifests itself as a transposal rather than a disposal of the memorial objects and the mourning they represent. This is precisely what one particular bystander witnessing the cleanups in Paris in August 2016 points to when she indicates that she views the removal of the makeshift memorial as a necessary resolution to the public facet of mourning, but simultaneously leaves the door open to mourning relegated to the private sphere: 'The pain has been expressed, but it's now inside us. The cleaning doesn't mean it has gone away. It's in our memories.'[45] Yet what about the objects themselves? In their case, too, a ritualized translation is necessary: from chaotic grief expressions at the trauma site to a more ordered spatial displacement. This is the domain of permanent memorialization of the trauma, which increasingly integrates elements of the makeshift in its structures in the form of museum exhibits or archival projects 'so visitors can once again experience the outpouring of human compassion they represent.'[46]

It appears that even after the work of mourning has been completed, there is still a palpable desire not to fall into complacency about past mourning. Instead the overriding wish is to be relieved from the intensity of mourning, yet retrospectively remember. Permanent memorials which integrate their makeshift predecessors do just this. From the vantage point of temporal distance, they allow us to revise our relationship not only with the traumatic event itself, but also with the immediate grief that went alongside it. Dismantling the makeshift memorial, then, is made easier with the promise that the memorial, at least, will find an emotional afterlife.

NOTES

1. Peter Jan Margry and Cristina Sánchez-Carretero, 'Rethinking Memorialization: The Concept of Grassroots Memorials,' in *Grassroots Memorials: The Politics of Memorializing Traumatic Death*, eds. Peter Jan Margry and Cristina Sánchez-Carretero (New York and Oxford: Berghahn Books, 2011), 31–32.

2. See John O. West, *Mexican-American Folklore* (Little Rock, AR: August House, 1988), 237–39.

3. Philippe Ariès, *The Hour of Our Death: The Classic History of Western Attitudes toward Death over the Last One Thousand Years*, trans. Helen Weaver (New York: Knopf, 1981), 577.

4. Ian Urbina, 'As Roadside Memorials Multiply, A Second Look,' *New York Times*, 6 February 2006, http://www.nytimes.com/2006/02/06/us/as-roadside-memorials-multiply-a-second-look.html, accessed 23 March 2019.

5. The connections between secularization and decline in mourning rituals go beyond the scope of this chapter but are developed extensively in Ariès, 'The Invisible Death,' *The Hour of Our Death,* 559–601, and Peter Homans, 'Introduction' to *Symbolic Loss* (Charlottesville: University Press of Virginia, 2000), 1–42. Everett Yuehong Zhang refers to the decline of agricultural production and the development of transportation as mitigating factors. Everett Yuehong Zhang, 'Mourning,' in *A Companion to Moral Anthropology*, ed. Didier Fassin (Malden, MA: Wiley-Blackwell, 2015), 276.

6. Geoffrey Gorer, *Death, Grief, and Mourning in Contemporary Britain* (London: Cresset Press, 1965), 111.

7. Tom McCarthy, dir., *Ian Hislop's Stiff Upper Lip—An Emotional History of Britain*, episode 3, 'Last Hurrah?,' aired 18 October 2012, on BBC Two, https://www.bbc.co.uk/programmes/b01nhccs, accessed 23 March 2019.

8. David Mellor, 'Death in High Modernity: The Contemporary Presence and Absence of Death,' in *The Sociology of Death: Theory, Culture and Practice*, ed. David Clark (Oxford: Blackwell, 1993), 11–12.

9. Tom Michael, 'We'll Never Forget: Tear-Jerking Moment Thousands Gather in Silence in Manchester to Remember the Victims of the Ariana Grande Concert Bomb Attack,' *The Sun*, 29 May 2007, https://www.thesun.co.uk/news/3674269/manchester-cop-breaks-down-tears-flowers-st-anns-square-vigil-video, my emphasis, accessed 23 March 2019.

10. Erika Lee Doss, *The Emotional Life of Contemporary Public Memorials: Towards a Theory of Temporary Memorials* (Amsterdam: Amsterdam University Press, 2008), 7.

11. Sigmund Freud, 'Mourning and Melancholia,' in *The Standard Edition of the Complete Psychological Works of Sigmund Freud*, vol. 14, *On the History of the Psycho-Analytic Movement, Papers on Metapsychology and Other Works*, trans. and ed. James Strachey (London: Hogarth Press, 1953), 243.

12. Freud, 'Mourning and Melancholia,' 244.

13. Homans, 'Introduction' to *Symbolic Loss*, 8.

14. Margaret R. Yocom, '"We'll Watch out for Liza and the Kids": Spontaneous Memorials and Personal Response at the Pentagon, 2001,' in *Spontaneous Shrines and the Public Memorialization of Death*, ed. Jack Santino (New York: Palgrave Macmillan, 2006), 61.

15. We shall say more about the collective force in the next section when we discuss how makeshift memorials tangibly exert socio-political influence.

16. Cristina Sánchez-Carretero, 'The Madrid Train Bombings: Enacting the Emotional Body at the March 11 Grassroots Memorials,' in *Grassroots Memorials*, 248.

17. Sarah Dillon, *The Palimpsest: Literature, Criticism, Theory* (London: Continuum, 2007), 3–4.

18. Michael Paterniti, 'Columbine Never Sleeps,' *GQ*, 11 April 2004, https://www.gq.com/story/columbine-shooting-littleton-colorado-200404. Pictures of Dylan's

cross can be found at A Columbine Site, 'Dylan Klebold's Cross,' http://www.acolumbinesite.com/dylan/cross.php, accessed 23 March 2019.

19. Lorraine Adams, 'Columbine Crosses Can't Bear Weight of Discord,' *Washington Post*, 3 May 1999, http://www.washingtonpost.com/wp-srv/national/longterm/juvmurders/stories/memorial03.htm, accessed 23 March 2019.

20. Grace Y. Kao, 'Of Tragedy and Its Aftermath: The Search for Religious Meaning in the Shootings at Virginia Tech,' in *From Jeremiad to Jihad: Religion, Violence, and America*, eds. John D. Carlson and Jonathan H. Ebel (Berkeley: University of California Press, 2012), 185.

21. Erin Manning, 'Artfulness,' in *The Nonhuman Turn*, ed. Richard Grusin (Minneapolis: University of Minnesota Press, 2015), 52, 61.

22. Jack Santino, 'Performative Commemoratives: Spontaneous Shrines and the Public Memorialization of Death,' in *Spontaneous Shrines and the Public Memorialization of Death*, ed. Jack Santino (New York: Palgrave Macmillan, 2006), 12.

23. Zach Furness, *One Less Car: Bicycling and the Politics of Automobility* (Philadelphia: Temple University Press, 2010), 97.

24. Aaron Rogan, 'Cyclist Is 15th Victim This Year,' *The Times*, 4 December 2017, https://www.thetimes.co.uk/article/cyclist-is-15th-victim-this-year-msfp9b7r5. The Dublin Cycling Campaign, for instance, has repeatedly called attention to government silence on traffic infrastructure after the fifteen cyclists' deaths on Irish roads in 2017 were each met with inaction.

25. Santino, 'Performative Commemoratives: Spontaneous Shrines and the Public Memorialization of Death,' 13.

26. Judith Butler, *Frames of War: When Is Life Grievable?* (London: Verso, 2009), 72.

27. Butler, *Frames of War*, 72.

28. 'Labor: On the Embarcadero,' *Time*, 16 July, 1934, quoted in Dolores Flamiano, *Women, Workers, and Race in LIFE Magazine: Hansel Mieth's Reform Photojournalism, 1934-1955* (Abingdon, Oxon: Routledge, 2016), 86.

29. Margry and Sánchez-Carretero, 'Rethinking Memorialization,' 2.

30. Paul Eliel, *The Waterfront and General Strikes, San Francisco, 1934: A Brief History* (San Francisco: Hooper Printing Co., 1934), 128.

31. Butler, *Frames of War*, 65.

32. Boris Nemtsov was a Russian opposition figure, notable for his criticism of Putin's government. On February 27, 2015, he was fatally shot on Bolshoy Moskvoretsky Bridge (Moscow) by assailants who are now imprisoned.

33. 'Shrine to Russian Opposition Leader Nemtsov Removed,' British Broadcasting Corporation, 27 February 2017, https://www.bbc.co.uk/news/av/world-europe-39102184/shrine-to-russian-opposition-leader-nemtsov-removed. Video of the removal can be found at 'Немцов мост 01 02 2017,' Video, 1:22, Removal of the Makeshift Memorial at Nemtsov Bridge, posted by 'Ирэн Аброскина' 1 February 2017. https://www.youtube.com/watch?v=Tem0DJIW-NY, accessed 23 March 2019.

34. Anna Dorozhkina, 'Flower Shop Network "Mostsvettorg" Was Asked to Refuse from Deliveries to Boris Nemtsov Memorial,' *Russia-IC*, 3 April 2015, http://russia-ic.com/news/show/20338#.WbLQebKGPcs, accessed 23 March 2019. The site

previously found at https://nemtsov.flowwow.com/ has been taken down after 'the company was urged to stop delivering flowers to the memorial to Boris Nemtsov.'

35. Butler, *Frames of War*, 6.

36. Arnold van Gennep, *The Rites of Passage* (New York: Routledge, 2010), 10–11.

37. Freud, 'Mourning and Melancholia,' 245.

38. Freud, 'Mourning and Melancholia,' 245.

39. Freud, 'Mourning and Melancholia,' 245.

40. Frank Jordans, 'On Nice's Riviera: Signs of Normal Returning after Attacks,' *Business Insider*, 19 July 2016, http://www.businessinsider.com/ap-on-nices-riviera-signs-of-normal-returning-after-attacks-2016-7?IR=T. Most articles with this headline were published on July 19, 2016.

41. Jonathan Freedland, 'Mourning Diana: A Moment of Madness?,' *The Guardian*, 12 August 2007, https://www.theguardian.com/uk/2007/aug/13/britishidentity.monarchy, accessed 23 March 2019.

42. Erika Lee Doss, *Memorial Mania: Public Feeling in America* (Chicago and London: University of Chicago Press, 2010), 71.

43. Ray Rivera, 'Newton Struggles with When to Remove Makeshift Memorials,' *Seattle Times*, 5 January 2013, https://www.seattletimes.com/nation-world/newtown-struggles-with-when-to-remove-makeshift-memorials/, accessed 23 March 2019.

44. Doss, *Memorial Mania*, 71.

45. Julia Dumont and Stéphanie Trouillard, 'Paris Clears Makeshift Memorial for Victims of French Terror Attacks,' *France 24*, 2 August 2016, http://www.france24.com/en/20160802-paris-terror-attacks-memorial-cleared-france-republique, accessed 23 March 2019.

46. Colleen M. Sullivan, '"Dear Boston" Exhibit at the Boston Public Library,' *Patch*, 26 April 2014, https://patch.com/massachusetts/medfield/dear-boston-exhibit-at-the-boston-public-library, accessed 23 March 2019.

BIBLIOGRAPHY

ADAMS, Lorraine. 'Columbine Crosses Can't Bear Weight of Discord.' *Washington Post*, 3 May 1999. http://www.washingtonpost.com/wp-srv/national/longterm/juvmurders/stories/memorial03.htm. Accessed 23 March 2019.

ARIÈS, Philippe. *The Hour of Our Death: The Classic History of Western Attitudes toward Death over the Last One Thousand Years.* Translated by Helen Weaver. New York: Knopf, 1981.

BRITISH BROADCASTING CORPORATION. 'Shrine to Russian Opposition Leader Nemtsov Removed.' 27 February 2017. https://www.bbc.co.uk/news/av/world-europe-39102184/shrine-to-russian-opposition-leader-nemtsov-removed. Accessed 23 March 2019.

BUTLER, Judith. *Frames of War: When Is Life Grievable?* London: Verso, 2009.

A Columbine Site. 'Dylan Klebold's Cross.' http://www.acolumbinesite.com/dylan/cross.php. Accessed 23 March 2019.

DILLON, Sarah. *The Palimpsest: Literature, Criticism, Theory*. London: Continuum, 2007.

DOROZHKINA, Anna. 'Flower Shop Network "Mostsvettorg" Was Asked to Refuse from Deliveries to Boris Nemtsov Memorial.' *Russia-IC*, 3 April 2015. http://russia-ic.com/news/show/20338#.WbLQebKGPcs. Accessed 23 March 2019.

DOSS, Erika Lee. *The Emotional Life of Contemporary Public Memorials: Towards a Theory of Temporary Memorials*. Amsterdam: Amsterdam University Press, 2008.

DOSS, Erika Lee. *Memorial Mania: Public Feeling in America*. Chicago and London: University of Chicago Press, 2010.

DUMONT, Julia and Stéphanie Trouillard. 'Paris Clears Makeshift Memorial for Victims of French Terror Attacks.' *France 24*, 2 August 2016. http://www.france24.com/en/20160802-paris-terror-attacks-memorial-cleared-france-republique. Accessed 23 March 2019.

ELIEL, Paul. *The Waterfront and General Strikes, San Francisco, 1934: A Brief History*. San Francisco: Hooper Printing Co., 1934.

FLAMIANO, Dolores. *Women, Workers, and Race in LIFE Magazine: Hansel Mieth's Reform Photojournalism, 1934–1955*. Abingdon and Oxon: Routledge, 2016.

FREEDLAND, Jonathan. 'Mourning Diana: A Moment of Madness?.' *The Guardian*, 12 August 2007. https://www.theguardian.com/uk/2007/aug/13/britishidentity.monarchy. Accessed 23 March 2019.

FREUD, Sigmund. 'Mourning and Melancholia.' In *The Standard Edition of the Complete Psychological Works of Sigmund Freud*. Volume 14. *On the History of the Psycho-Analytic Movement, Papers on Metapsychology and Other Works*. Translated and edited by James Strachey. 243–58. London: Hogarth Press, 1953.

FURNESS, Zach. *One Less Car: Bicycling and the Politics of Automobility*. Philadelphia: Temple University Press, 2010.

GENNEP, Arnold van. *The Rites of Passage*. New York: Routledge, 2010.

GORER, Geoffrey. *Death, Grief, and Mourning in Contemporary Britain*. London: Cresset Press, 1965.

'Немцов мост 01 02 2017.' Video, 1:22. Removal of the Makeshift Memorial at Nemtsov Bridge. Posted by 'Ирэн Аброскина.' 1 February 2017. https://www.youtube.com/watch?v=Tem0DJIW-NY. Accessed 23 March 2019.

HOMANS, Peter. 'Introduction' to *Symbolic Loss*, 1–42. Charlottesville: University Press of Virginia, 2000.

JORDANS, Frank. 'On Nice's Riviera: Signs of Normal Returning after Attacks.' *Business Insider*, 19 July 2016. http://www.businessinsider.com/ap-on-nices-riviera-signs-of-normal-returning-after-attacks-2016-7?IR=T. Accessed 23 March 2019.

KAO, Grace Y. 'Of Tragedy and Its Aftermath: The Search for Religious Meaning in the Shootings at Virginia Tech.' In *From Jeremiad to Jihad: Religion, Violence, and America*. Edited by John D. Carlson and Jonathan H. Ebel. 177–93. Berkeley: University of California Press, 2012.

MANNING, Erin. 'Artfulness.' In *The Nonhuman Turn*. Edited by Richard Grusin. 45–80. Minneapolis: University of Minnesota Press, 2015.

MARGRY, Peter Jan and Cristina Sánchez-Carretero. 'Rethinking Memorialization: The Concept of Grassroots Memorials.' In *Grassroots Memorials: The Politics of Memorializing Traumatic Death*. Edited by Peter Jan Margry and Cristina Sánchez-Carretero. 1–48. New York and Oxford: Berghahn Books, 2011.

MCCARTHY, Tom, director. *Ian Hislop's Stiff Upper Lip—An Emotional History of Britain*. Episode 3, 'Last Hurrah?.' Aired 18 October 2012. BBC Two. https://www.bbc.co.uk/programmes/b01nhccs. Accessed 23 March 2019.

MELLOR, David. 'Death in High Modernity: The Contemporary Presence and Absence of Death.' In *The Sociology of Death: Theory, Culture and Practice*. Edited by David Clark. 11–30. Oxford: Blackwell, 1993.

MICHAEL, Tom. 'We'll Never Forget: Tear-Jerking Moment Thousands Gather in Silence in Manchester to Remember the Victims of the Ariana Grande Concert Bomb Attack.' *The Sun*, 29 May 2007. https://www.thesun.co.uk/news/3674269/manchester-cop-breaks-down-tears-flowers-st-anns-square-vigil-video. Accessed 23 March 2019.

PATERNITI, Michael. 'Columbine Never Sleeps.' *GQ*, 11 April 2004. https://www.gq.com/story/columbine-shooting-littleton-colorado-200404. Accessed 23 March 2019.

RIVERA, Ray. 'Newton Struggles with When to Remove Makeshift Memorials.' *Seattle Times*, 5 January 2013. https://www.seattletimes.com/nation-world/newtown-struggles-with-when-to-remove-makeshift-memorials. Accessed 23 March 2019.

ROGAN, Aaron. 'Cyclist Is 15th Victim This Year.' *The Times*, 4 December 2017. https://www.thetimes.co.uk/article/cyclist-is-15th-victim-this-year-msfp9b7r5. Accessed 23 March 2019.

SÁNCHEZ-CARRETERO, Cristina. 'The Madrid Train Bombings: Enacting the Emotional Body at the March 11 Grassroots Memorials.' In *Grassroots Memorials: The Politics of Memorializing Traumatic Death*. Edited by Peter Jan Margry and Cristina Sánchez-Carretero. New York and Oxford: Berghahn Books, 2011.

SANTINO, Jack. 'Performative Commemoratives: Spontaneous Shrines and the Public Memorialization of Death.' In *Spontaneous Shrines and the Public Memorialization of Death.* Edited by Jack Santino. 5–17. New York: Palgrave Macmillan, 2006.

SULLIVAN, Colleen M. '"Dear Boston" Exhibit at the Boston Public Library.' *Patch*, 26 April 2014. https://patch.com/massachusetts/medfield/dear-boston-exhibit-at-the-boston-public-library. Accessed 23 March 2019.

URBINA, Ian. 'As Roadside Memorials Multiply, A Second Look.' *New York Times*, February 6, 2006. http://www.nytimes.com/2006/02/06/us/as-roadside-memorials-multiply-a-second-look.html. Accessed 23 March 2019.

WEST, John O. *Mexican-American Folklore*. Little Rock, AR: August House, 1988.

YOCOM, Margaret R. '"We'll Watch out for Liza and the Kids": Spontaneous Memorials and Personal Response at the Pentagon, 2001.' In *Spontaneous Shrines and the Public Memorialization of Death.* Edited by Jack Santino. 57–98. New York: Palgrave Macmillan, 2006.

YUEHONG Zhang, Everett. 'Mourning.' In *A Companion to Moral Anthropology.* Edited by Didier Fassin. 264–82. Malden, MA: Wiley-Blackwell, 2015.

Part III

INTIMATE HEALING

Chapter Eight

Literature between Antidote and Black Magic

The Autofiction of Chloé Delaume

Laurent Milesi

I do not write in order to heal . . .[1]

—Chloé Delaume, *Une femme avec personne dedans*

I write so that you die[2]

—Chloé Delaume, *Dans ma maison sous terre*

Reading the two epigraphs side by side does not bode well for beginning an essay whose aim should be to show the curative or restorative virtues of literature rather than exhuming its deadly aspirations. If anything, writing appears here as a murderous weapon or poison, at best an antidote (etymologically) 'given against' something or somebody, and certainly an expressive tool endowed with effective power.

Such a denial of the therapeutic function of literature is not a unique occurrence in the texts and oral interventions of the subject registered at birth as Nathalie-Anne Abdallah who, in 1999, while writing her first novel, *Les mouflettes d'Atropos*, changed her name to 'Chloé Delaume'[3] in an attempt to free herself from a family trauma—at age ten, she witnessed her often absent, violent father shooting her mother dead, then pointing his gun at her before turning it against himself and committing suicide. In a joint interview with Claire Castillon in the same month as the publication of *Une femme avec personne dedans*, her last single-authored work of autofiction,[4] to Grégoire Leménager's question whether literature was a therapy, Delaume's reply was that 'writing isn't therapeutic; I believe one doesn't heal. Just as one doesn't undergo an analysis in order to heal but to be as close as possible to one's speech [*parole*] and to oneself.'[5]

Officially diagnosed as a bipolar psychotic,[6] for whom, therefore, as the *idée reçue* goes and she often states, psychoanalysis is not a viable solution, Delaume has also dismissed the talking cure on grounds that it mostly deals with *unconscious* trauma, whereas her practice of autofiction engages with strictly real events, however fictionalized, relating to a consciously experienced drama.[7] In *Dans ma maison sous terre*, for instance, Delaume insists that she is not a neurotic and that her bipolar psychotic symptoms are not fit for a comfortable lie-down on the 'soft couch' of an analyst but rather call for no-nonsense management by a psychiatrist, whose recurrent figure in her texts is that of Dr Lagar(r)igue.[8] Autofiction for Delaume is thus, punningly in French, an '*autopsy*,' the self-analysis and postmortem (*autopsie*) of an ego damaged by parental deaths.[9]

After surveying the various negative forms of the ego's representations in her fiction, this essay will link their marked disease-related tendency to what Delaume self-diagnoses as her 'thanatopathy,' the 'bipolar' (inward/outward) orientation of the death drive in her writings (her 'death write') towards either suiciding the self or murdering the other. At the core of this ambivalent symbiosis between writing and death, I will locate her identification of literature as black magic, a performative practice which will allow me to revisit her rejection of literature as therapy, her ultimate affirmation of life-writing as she conjures death away, and ask whether its potential as a cure might not lie in its perlocutionary experience of empowerment through which a new, enfranchised 'I' can come about.

THE EGO AS (FAMILY) CANCER

Delaume has repeatedly argued for the view of writing as a performative empowerment of the self, to free an I (*je*) from the ego (*moi*) trapped in 'collective fictions' written by others:[10]

My name is Chloé Delaume. I am a fictional character. . . . I decided to become a fictional character when I realized I was one already. With this difference that I was not writing myself. Others were busy doing that for me.[11]

This alienating entrapment is also repeatedly expressed as the feeling of being cramped in a mediating abject prison-body which is 'inhabited' physiologically but not invested in mentally and psychically, a housing for her former entitled self whose eviction by the aspiring squatter 'Chloé Delaume' is staged especially in *La Vanité des Somnambules*, then *Corpus Simsi*, as two 'virtually temporary incarnations.'[12] Here is how the beginning of Delaume's autofictional essay *La règle du Je*, taking stock of the evolution some six to seven years later, depicts this sense of dispossession and disjunction from a 'real estate,' which can be compared with a similar beginning in *La Vanité des Somnambules*, that is, before the grafted parasite was eventually rejected:

> My name is Chloé Delaume. I am a fictional character. My body was born in the Yvelines on the tenth of March nineteen seventy-three; I waited a long time before curling up in it. . . . I very officially took possession of the premises when it was twenty-six summers old. In the vacant heat I unpacked my cardboard boxes; they contained books of spells [*grimoires*] and some willpower. The premises were dark and rather insalubrious, I spent a season whitewashing the cervical walls. The nerves were unkempt and the heart in tatters; it took me a long while to mend it.[13]

> My name is Chloé Delaume. I am a fictional character. I invested the body which I made my own on a muggy Friday in 1999 . . .

> My name is Chloé Delaume. I was born on 10 March 1973 a few kilometres away from the body in which I live as a parasite. During twenty-six years I lived in Somnambulia . . .

> My name is Chloé Delaume. I erred for a long time before being able to embody myself. So long that I feared I would never meet the amplectant organism.[14]

Delaume's fiction abounds in morbid, clinical depictions of the body's most unsavoury secretions, excreta and excrescences, the better to drive home the fact that the subject is estranged from the frame that usually provides anchoring in the world. As a result, the ego is afflicted[15] with all possible ailments and diseases, central to which is the ubiquitous metaphorical *cancer du nénuphar*, or water-lily cancer on the lung from which Chloé, Vian's heroine in *L'Écume des jours*, eventually succumbs.

Delaume's second novel, *Le Cri du sablier*, harbours one of the earliest and most gruesome evocations of the cancer since it is uttered by the dead mother as a curse to her daughter:

> How many times my daughter my torment my disgust have I hoped that finally you're nothing but a mirage. . . . My Chloé my mistake do you understand your forename I spat you out in March into life and my death thinking I was infecting you with water-lily cancer and . . . I ended up first buried in July. Your father killed me 30 June and you buried me on the very day . . . minus nine years of your procreation. The day of this orgasm which filthed you in me. . . . Be cursed, I say, daughter unworthy of me, the cruel tallow god always will pursue you.[16]

By unexpectedly ascribing the writer's own chosen name Chloé to the mother's premonition, this scene makes the cancer part of a morbid family romance and heritage, which Delaume's books needed to work through, or 'write through.' This is implicitly stated in the 'autofiction in four hands' *Où le sang nous appelle*, an account of her visit to her Lebanese family on her father's side with her then-partner and co-author Daniel Schneidermann, in which Delaume writes that 'family is a cancer for me. But the ablation of metastases, how many books already written, hoping that chemo propagates from household to household through reading.'[17] Similarly, her own body is felt to be a communal grave haunted by her deceased relatives in the short 'Genealogy' section of *Dans ma maison sous terre*:

> My body is the abode of the dead of my family. Dead people and ghosts, I won't heal. . . . Every night, the same dream: they inhabit my skull, a doll's house cut off with a chain saw, a dinner scene and putrefaction.[18]

Born (of) a parasite flower,[19] 'Chloé Delaume' is a malignant tumour, a 'water lilith,' or Vian's aquatic nymphaea crossed with the female night demon, witch or monster associated with sexual wantonness in Jewish mythology and occultism.[20] A similarly mythological dimension affects the author-narrator-heroine in *La Vanité des Somnambules*, who declares 'I am a viral cousin and a peeling from Atreides,'[21] whose reference, shared with Delaume's contemporaneous *Monologue pour épluchures d'Atrides*, is to Atreus's descendants, beset by murder, parricide, infanticide and incest.

Writing, then, is a 'chemotherapy' designed to resorb the family's cancerous tumours, an interminable process (comparable to Freud's interminable analysis) since it metamorphoses into a tenacious[22] tapeworm (*ténia*) which contaminates the father, the child as an 'abject presence' within the mother's womb,[23] and even spreads to Delaume-as-narrative 'réciténia'[24] in the pirated body contaminated by a 'Chloéra.'[25] More generically, 'Chloé Delaume' is a virus, a parasite, or a Trojan, that poisoned gift whereby a seemingly innocuous programme deceptively smuggles and installs a harmful piece of software on a computer, as when 'Chloé Delaume' infiltrates Sims gamers' consoles and lives as a downloadable, customizable avatar in *Corpus Simsi*:

> The character Chloé Delaume can be used by any gamer who has imported it. This fiction of one's own can infiltrate somebody else's and propagate in it. The fictional character confirms its status as a virus by circulating in this way.[26]

Predictably, many of her former selves and fictional alter egos are also plagued by such medical disorders; for instance, Adèle Trousseau, the prototype of the suicide girl in *Éden matin midi et soir*, who, 'born parasitized by a funereal virus,' suffers from an existential cancer in terminal stage: an incurable, rampant thanatopathy,[27] or what Delaume first called *la maladie de la mort*.

THANATOPATHY AND THE
'DEATH WRITE': MURDER AND/OR SUICIDE?

Death stalks throughout the writings of Chloé Delaume, from the many itera-tions and dissections of the double parental murder-suicide, and Delaume's several botched suicide attempts, to fictional, fantasized or desired deaths: the Solanas-like cutting-up of the immature, parasitic lover/tenant in *Les mouflettes d'Atropos*, whose title alludes to the oldest of the Three Fates or Moirai (in Rome: Morta), goddesses of fate and destiny, responsible for cut-ting the thread and dispensing death;[28] the young girl's prayer to God that her father may die in *Le Cri du sablier*; the metaphorical gang murder of the hospital doctor, alias the characters' Conscience, in a game of Cluedo® in the lunatic asylum of *Certainement pas*;[29] the gamebook adventure of the reader cast as Buffy the vampire slayer in *La nuit je suis Buffy Summers*, set in a murderous Los Angeles asylum; the pending suicide of Adèle Trousseau in *Éden matin midi et soir*; those of Esther Duval in *Certainement pas* and Clotilde Mélisse in *Dans ma maison sous terre*; the mourning and burial of the word *maman* in *Le deuil des deux syllabes*; the announcement of the suicide of Isabelle Bordelin aka 'Silence Majuscule,' one of Delaume's female readers and admirers, which opens *Une femme avec personne dedans*; and more. Not to mention the cemeteries and coffins that periodically adorned the various versions of her personal website.[30]

Delaume herself, as author-narrator-heroine, dates her morbid attraction to death to the fateful day of the double family tragedy:

> I caught the malady of death on 30 June 1983. Since then, I have been merely abseiling forward. I have tried love, friendship and drugs. But nothing changed. Still the same ill-being which as a dirty parasite devours heart and soul: I will not heal.[31]

A similar condition is ascribed to one of her earlier fictional characters and possible alter egos in *Certainement pas*, Aline Maupin, alias Miss Scarlet in the game of Clue®: '[Y]ou think I'm healing, but I know I've caught the malady of death.'[32]

Delaume's most macabre, death-ridden novel—the narrative is inter-spersed with fictional characters' death notices—*Dans ma maison sous terre*, is a self-proclaimed 'revenge book,' a Lovecraftian *Necronomicon* 'ordered' Nemesis-like[33] to kill Mamie Suzanne after the author learnt in 2004 from the female cousin with whom she had been raised after the tragedy, rather than directly from her grandmother, the 'good news' that her father, also diag-nosed with schizophrenic tendencies and hated by the mother's relatives on account of his Lebanese origins, was not her biological father.[34] (The repeated injunction to do away with the cowardly grandmother, in a signed letter to 'Madame la Mort,' becomes a near-incantation on the blank page titled 'Re-call,' looking as if an anonymous death threat letter was being issued: 'This is a murder attempt / I repeat / This is a murder attempt.'[35]) Set in a cemetery and featuring the narrator's necrophagous poet-companion Théophile, *Dans ma maison sous terre*, itself radically rethought as a consequence of the shat-tering revelation of the family secret, mentions how this unforeseen disclo-sure not only triggered an identity crisis and disorder which had cascading effects on Delaume's refashioning of her *je*[36] but also impacted one of her fictional constructs in the novel she was then completing.[37] In *Certainement pas* the third guilty character, Séraphine Derdega (alias Madame Leblanc/ Mrs. White), spares no medical or emotional effort to make sure that she does not beget a child so as not to transmit the genes of her violent, crazy father[38] (incidentally of Maghrebin extraction) until, aged thirty-one—the same age Delaume was when the 'good news' was sprung on her[39]—she finds out in her mother's suicide note that Azzâm Derdega was not her real father. Together with the mother's similarly bitter rejection of her progeny, this fictional ele-ment also coincides with Delaume's decision in real life, often reaffirmed in her texts, to be 'nulliparous.'[40] In 'Chloé Delaume' fiction and the real, writing and living, are intertwined in a two-way (re)shaping process—here, the adjustment of writing to life's cruel discovery as a compensation visiting upon a former school bully the plight of being a barren emotional failure in life.[41] As Clotilde Mélisse, Delaume's most consistent literary alter ego, ex-plains to her rebellious character Charlie, who reproaches her with practising a lazy form of autobiographical life-writing:

> This is not what autofiction is. It's a literary experiment. To make one's life into a novel, and to make a novel out of one's life. To mix the real and fiction, to inject the one into the other, and vice versa . . .[42]

Structured like a game of Cluedo® and adapting Agatha Christie's original formula in *Murder on the Orient Express*,[43] *Certainement pas* stages the col-lective murder of Dr. Lenoir (Dr. Black) by six characters who have found refuge in various pathologies in order not to confront their moral bankruptcy and lack of ethical conscience. In *La règle du Je*, Delaume retrospectively analysed how internment in a psychiatric hospital influences the structure of the 'I' that tries to write itself (*s'écrire*). The reader then realizes that the location of *Certainement pas* matches a similar venue where the writer partly composed her 'murder story,' settling old scores with real-life counterparts,[44] and is told that '[e]ach character embodies a real person, including myself, in some cases.'[45] Staged like a play, the one-page 'endgame' (*Fin de partie*) of

Certainement pas 'loops the loop,' as 'Chloé' asks Dr. Lagarigue, alias the reader, to whom she had given the book we have just read, whether she can be discharged, and whose reply 'is in your title.'[46]

Designed to last the length of time that separates two suicides in France—'A suicide is reported every fifty minutes; this morning that's it, it's my turn'[47]—*Éden matin midi et soir*, set between two glossy black inside pages, begins with Adèle Trousseau declaring that '[l]ast night I voted death,' then conversing with her death drive until the moment to act out her decision merges with the book's ending.[48] The 'dramatic monologue' offers the most sustained reflection on the 'virus' of thanatopathy, the word the heroine herself chooses for the malady of death, after she recounts her first suicide attempt at age six:

> To die while emptying oneself, I was ready to live this . . .
>
> Diagnostic: malady of death. . . . I cannot be cured . . . my case is not listed in your handbooks.
>
> The malady of death. . . . They the doctors say it doesn't exist. . . . But I say that the malady of death does exist. That it is an ill in itself, that it deserves being looked into and that a name be found for it. In Greek, to be credible. Thanatos is death, pathos what one suffers from.[49]

Adèle Trousseau also briefly evokes anosognosia (from *nosos*: malady; *gnosis*: knowledge), a condition in which a person during a psychotic episode is unaware of the disease, unlike her, since

> I am myself aware of all my limbs, of all the bawling parts that make up my Self. I know that I'm ill, and each piece of myself says so to me, repeats it. But it can't be cured. Yet the psychiatrist, he will want to. They all want to cure me. As if one could be healed from the malady of death.
> I'm going to tell him that, the psychiatrist. That I have the malady of death. I can't see what other name it could be given, because I'm ill, but from wanting to die from it.[50]

Adèle knows herself to the point of challenging her official diagnosis as a psychotic with suicidal tendencies, claiming rather that she has a subdivided ego and a constant, incurable urge to die,[51] and eventually becomes at one with her true self, her *je* being reunited with her *moi*, only when she resolves to end her life: 'I call on the death drive. . . . Its breath is icy, deep, you we I say: me. For the first time, whole. I say I [*Je dis Moi*], yes, whole.'[52]

Opening with an accusing mother's phone call to Delaume after her daughter, an admiring reader who mistakenly wanted to emulate her style as a therapeutic salvation, killed herself, *Une femme avec personne dedans* further dwells on the theme of thanatopathy in a more directly autofictional mood in the chapter 'Éden matin midi bonsoir'—the substituted 'good evening' here being a farewell to life:

> Young girls commit suicide, my books in their bedrooms; their mothers get in touch because they try to understand. To understand why their child, firmly, said no to life. I committed a work on the refusal to live. *Éden matin midi et soir*, every fifty minutes a person commits suicide in France, make a monologue out of it, invent Adèle. . . . Through her mouth to let a tanatopathic [*sic*] soul be heard: *tanathos* [*sic*] is death, *pathos* what one suffers from. *The Malady of death* would have been much better suited but it was already taken.[53]

To these mothers' objection that, unlike their suicide daughters, she has her books to sustain her and help her stay alive, Delaume replies, adamantly refuting the idea of writing operating as a life support:

> I do not write in order to heal from tanathopathy [*sic*], no, really not at all. To modify the real as a unique objective and sole motivation. To write in order not to die cannot have any meaning. I write in order to deconstruct: modifying the real, fiction and language are warlike tools. . . . The real is hostile to all its survivors, and I have far too much hatred, too much resentment, to allow it to crush my subjectivity. That's where the secret is, the secret as to why, why them and not me. Ladies, look at me: I am a natural child of Nemesis, *the gift of what is owed* is what I make my mission of. . . . I cannot kill myself even if the desire gnaws at me morning noon and evening . . .[54]

First featured in this very equation in Delaume's revenge book, which wishes the dead grandmother as a Christmas gift (*cadeau*),[55] the goddess who enacted due retribution in ancient Greek religion brings me back to the notion of antidote ventured at the beginning of this essay. In *La nuit je suis Buffy Summers*, the gamebook's reader-hero(ine) encounters twice a talismanic formula as s/he inherits the destiny of being the Slayer: 'death is your gift' (*la mort est ton cadeau*).[56] Taken together with the above quotation from *Une femme avec personne dedans*, this ambivalent gift of a 'license to kill,' also the father's suicide death spat out at the daughter's face,[57] warrants a dual interpretation of the gift as an antidote or a double-edged, (self-)deconstructive *pharmakon*, at once poison (German *Gift*) and cure, crime/victory or suicide/defeat. Thanatopathy, therefore, would not be reserved exclusively for the drive to kill oneself, but, as we saw repeatedly, it could also be construed as the murderous desire to kill the other in/through writing. This Janus-faced orientation of Delaume's 'death-write' is captured economically in *Où le sang nous appelle*, in the words of Daniel Schneidermann in a fictive interview with a mysterious interlocutor who, at the very end of the joint work, reveals itself to be behind the book's title as 'the voice of blood': 'writing or death. To write in order to kill.'[58] If writing cannot kill you and cannot heal you from thanatopathy, then let it turn into a lethal weapon and another's Nemesis.

Although the 'gift of death' (to use Derrida's formula) appears in a ludic environment, it can be seen as crucial to the interface between life, death and writing in Delaume's autofictional project, tensed between suicide as the gift of death to one's dissociated selves (*se donner la mort*), as with Adèle Trousseau's finally reconciled 'you are I am's' and 'you all that make me up,'[59] and the gift of death as retribution and payment of a debt owed by the other.[60] What Delaume punningly calls 'régler ses contes,' that is, to settle one's accounts (*régler ses comptes*) in a well-adjusted tale (*conte*),[61] and 'la règle du je,' the rule by which the I (*je*) plays the autofictional game (*jeu*), allows her to start—to use Cathy Caruth's phrasing—'owning the trauma' through writing while taking possession of the body once inhabited by her former legal occupant, rather than being repeatedly possessed by the overwhelming events of the past in untamed images and thoughts.[62]

WRITING AS BLACK MAGIC

To write is to practise a form of witchcraft[63]

—Chloé Delaume, *La règle du Je*

Being possessed or taking possession: this alternative between the traumatic real (being trapped in others' collective fictions) and emancipation through autofictional writing also entails a vision of the literary act as a kind of witchcraft. Poised in the 'limbic' no-woman's-land between incarnation and expulsion—'Between your fiction and my reality'[64]—*La Vanité des Somnambules* increasingly homes in on this theme as 'Chloé Delaume' fails to fully incarnate herself in the body of her former identity, Nathalie-Anne. 'Chloé Delaume' is then put on trial and to the 'Question' (also in the sense of the application of torture during a judicial examination) as a maleficent witch, and finally warded off in a 'fiction which is aborted by dint of auto-da-fé' just as the guilty sorceress was burnt at the stake[65]—to the last question in the staged inquisitorial trial, '*Has the Devil set a limit to your malevolent action?*,' the reply points to page 147, or the real final page of the fictional narrative.[66] Complete with references to Pierre de Lancre, the French judge who conducted a massive witch-hunt in Labourd in 1609, and especially to *Le Marteau des sorcières*, or *Malleus maleficarum*, a famous fifteenth-century treatise written by two German Dominicans used to persecute witches throughout Europe from which 'Third part and Question 5' is borrowed,[67] the novel draws the connection between the willpower to reformat one's *Je* and fiction's magical power to bring about such a transformation.

However, in *Dans ma maison sous terre*, Théophile casts doubts upon Delaume's abilities to master the necessary craft and performative power to exact her revenge through writing, with a covert allusion to failures in her previous fiction: 'A witch of the 12th level wouldn't even manage that. . . . A book that could kill. You can barely cast the spell of incarnation.'[68] Indeed, instead of directly killing the grandmother, the book ends up with Delaume's letter to her family relatives proposing that her former self (Nathalie Dalain) and dates (1973–1999) be engraved on the family tombstone.[69] In her role as Clotilde Mélisse, she even confesses that 'I am as typical a borderline as they come, I have no magical power,'[70] despite 'practis[ing] the witch's kiss,' according to the blurb of *Au commencement était l'adverbe*, a collection of two short plays in which she takes centre stage as a writer of autofiction meting out life and death to her creations.

But would-be witches have their own curses and, if we believe Adèle Trousseau, thanatopathy is one such spell,[71] whose unleashing, however, would testify to its enormous power even if the dosage is less accurate than psychiatric medication:

> Magic thought. Will I have to tell him, the psychiatrist, that twenty-five minutes after I woke up, while I was lying on my bed stoned out of my mind with Valium without the staff mobilizing, I made a deed of magic thought . . .
>
> Right now I'm concentrating . . . in order to curse Grégoire over ten generations. . . . It's because of the fidelity potion, I always get the bloody doses wrong when I practise witchcraft.
>
> I'm not sure it's a good idea to talk to him, the psychiatrist, about witchcraft. The members of the Medical Association have replaced the hunters of yore, I know. There's no more burning at the stake but a dosage so that one doesn't believe in anything anymore.
>
> I don't believe in anything anymore, except in the power of my own malady.[72]

Performing a Satanic inversion of divine incarnation, Delaume's attempted embodiments are, more than mere magic, a kind of black magic, a feature of autofiction which Delaume emphasized in an interview with Barbara Havercroft as well as in the third, final reader's choice of *Une femme avec personne dedans*, published soon before the exchange:

Autofiction is practised in a laboratory. Because the materials come from living matter, from the dead and the living, in test tubes, acid, iron filings, words, precipitates. Autofiction is not merely magic, alchemy, handbook and observed bacteria microscope. Autofiction often comes close to black magic. The I [*Je*] is not the Ego [*Moi*]; it demands rituals and often victims.[73]

Autofiction stems from a kind of black magic. It breeds corpses since it has been named.[74]

Recalling the project of *Dans ma maison sous terre* but also how mothers of suicide readers bitterly accused her on the phone, Delaume then warns that

what is specific to autofiction is that it manipulates living matter; the bodies and souls are real, and above the book of spells [*grimoire*] Nemesis, the goddess of revenge, smiles at us, but more precisely 'the gift of what is owed.' The project of my novel *Dans ma maison sous terre* was to kill my grandmother. It worked well, but I have no merit, she was so old. On the other hand, I paid for it. Black magic implies the concept of Return shock. Fate comes back like a boomerang multiplied by three. Total apocalypse . . . , one female reader who committed suicide, her mother accused me, my books made to kill; I lost, lost everything, even writing itself.[75]

In *Une femme avec personne dedans*, Delaume self-ironically proclaims herself a powerful witch after buying 'protection stones,' which like a boomerang or an apotropaic shield '*reflect the negative energies towards their emitter*,' those who like Silence Majuscule try to become Chloé Delaume as she herself had managed to do by reinventing herself and ousting her former ego. If the aim of autofiction is to invite the reader to write themselves, Silence Majuscule's capital mistake was precisely to have wanted to usurp somebody else's script in order to modify her own family life and exact revenge: 'The true book of spells [*grimoire*] with the right ritual is needed. Otherwise the I cannot bear the pressure . . . , implosion of the ego, quartering of the Self [*Moi*].'[76]

In order to operate, black magic needs to rely on the right linguistic formulas of one's own *grimoire*—a word which shares the same etymology as 'grammar'—which will work their performative charm, not a borrowed 'mixture of chemo water-lilies altars of magic,'[77] so that writing can modify life:

To say is to do . . . we have the russet April moon tonight let's add a few worms and many a maggot, it's boiling . . . , hop, white rabbits hats off one stick two carrots, look at me, admire, blue slugs all righty-roo raccoon slobber, vendetta vinaigrette, without the hands, yes, hop hop, a pinch of pixels, whisk it up hop hop and abracadabra. My name is Chloé Delaume, yes Ladies and Gentlemen, it's true, it's possible, yes, I'm proof of it.

To write one's life, to write oneself, to modify is possible. It's possible, Abracadabra.[78]

Still, in the third, final choice of endings to *Une femme avec personne dedans*,
Delaume will perform an interesting twist on her usual definition of autofiction as the linguistic fictionalization of strictly real events and facts:

> Real, of strictly fictional events and facts. If one wants, autofixion, from having
> injected some adventure into such a programmed life.
>
> To modify the real thus imposes itself as a mission. I pick up my book of spells
> [*grimoire*] and I turn over the page, a necessary act.[79]

A 'return to the real' which may be accompanied by most powerful rituals of
'white magic' . . .[80]

Rather than the instance of a symptomatic *Wiederholungszwang*, the
ritualized leitmotif 'My name is Chloé Delaume. I am a fictional character'
should be seen as a sort of home-grown (and unappropriatable) Coué method
countering the ceaseless tidal waves of memories, through which, by dint of
perseverance, a new I can be born since '[t]he I is the effect of a repetition.'[81]
In this respect, it is no doubt significant that the iterative trademark formula
seems to have been dropped when Delaume turned to writing other(s') fictions, from *Les sorcières de la République* onwards—at the time when she
was contemplating facing the bureaucratic hassle of having her new name
legally endorsed—since the incantatory power of the autofictional mantra had
de facto lost its *raison d'être*.

EMPOWERMENT AS ALTERNATIVE CURE?

Imperceptibly scattered throughout her twenty-plus works, Delaume's casual
hints at the possible therapeutic function of fiction should legitimately allow
one to broach again the question, seemingly settled negatively by the author
herself, whether literature is a form of healing.[82] In *Dans ma maison sous
terre*, among the reasons why she needs to write the book that will kill her
grandmother, Delaume argues that '[p]ills against the grandmother do not
exist, yet symptoms persist. Therefore, an appropriate therapy must be found
which mixes revenge and healing. Note that psychotics cannot undergo an
analysis and that it is most urgent to find a solution.'[83]

However, such concessions are vastly outnumbered by the textual fragments (some of which we have already encountered and will revisit here),

bolstered up by interviews, which not only deny the curative potential of writing—witness the witty ending of *Certainement pas*—but on the contrary emphasize its catalytic force. In her retrospective autofictional essay, Delaume returns to the fateful year 2004 and comments:

> Sometimes in my brain the ongoing fictions become entangled with the synapses; I no longer know how to write myself in the real at all, I no longer know how to write myself, barely to put up with myself. My texts prophesy the psychotic episode which will happen before long . . .[84]

And rather than mitigating the effect of pain and draining it through violent verbal outpourings—for instance, against the grandmother—Delaume feels her anger swelling, not subsiding, and gets worse rather than feels better.[85] The task of autofiction is therefore not merely to arrange retrospective material, events and feelings (her oft-reiterated formula, lifted from Alain Resnais and Marguerite Duras's film *Hiroshima mon amour*, 'tout vu, rien inventé'[86]) but also prospectively and predictively to heed to what will have happened afterwards: '*Write then what you saw, what is, and what must happen next.*'[87]

Une femme avec personne dedans is perhaps the most sustained engagement with the impossibility of literature as healing; indeed, instead of offering a prop to a bruised life (as the mothers of Delaume's suicide female readers mistakenly assume), writing is said to magnify the pain:

> As if writing were just that, a crutch, the famous something which is akin to life buoys. Writing is useless when faced with this felt experience [*ce ressenti*], I can assure you, absolutely useless. Writing does not pacify, it reduplicates the pain since one solicits it. Writing merely enables one to drown with grace, slowly . . . , the elegance of 'I'm sinking,' a dissociation which makes the movement bearable; my name is Ophelia I live in asphyxia but I'm extremely well dressed.[88]

The categorical denial of the healing power of literature in *Une femme avec personne dedans* comes as a response to the demand for recognition by Silence Majuscule at the beginning of the novel: 'I made it clear to her that literature was in no way a therapy, that it was even probably quite the contrary.'[89] For Delaume, what the young woman did not grasp is that 'a wound only barely sings,'[90] that is, that literature does not find its validation merely in the true reality of the trauma, in spite of Jacques Lacan's view that 'I consider the fact of having stated the real in question in the form of this writing to possess the value of what is generally called a trauma.'[91]

A metaphor to be understood in a similar vein as the graceful drowning afforded by writing, the literary aphorism is a recurrent motif in Delaume's texts and interviews:

> As if suffering only could be the mainspring [of autofiction]. As if it was just about self-therapy, of the Ego's restoration, not of literature. As if each practitioner merely sang their wound, nothing but the wound, not through it.
>   'I sing through my wound'; the sentence is from Pierre Guyotat's 'Légende,' in *Vivre*.[92]

Writing's enterprise of 'modifying the real' (Delaume's pet formulation) can happen successfully only on the necessary condition that the latter be transmogrified in the experimental crucible of language, in which remembering becomes re-membering otherwise, repeatedly, through one's own idiom and rhythms. In that sense, writing is, as Roland Barthes ventured, an intransitive verb,[93] unless it takes the subject as its self-reflexive object and material: *s'écrire*.

In a recent study focusing on several contemporary French writers, Michèle Bacholle enlisted Delaume among the 'post-traumatic fictional characters in mourning,' seeing in her repeated suicide attempts the mixture of a desire to kill the introjected suicide father and to punish herself for her guilt feelings about his desperate gesture.[94] Often distinct rather than conjoined phenomena—one leading to the other—trauma and mourning are indissociable in Delaume's specific case, as are suicide and murder both in the fiction's foundational *Urszene* which she survived and in the dual thematization of death in her subsequent texts. For Bacholle, who conducts her study with reference to canonical psychiatric works on the relationship between trauma and mourning, Delaume's autofictional writing, with its reprises and occasional, symptomatic occultations (such as the existence of her younger brother, who was present when the family drama unfolded), is a protracted work of mourning as much as a process of reconstruction and reinvention.[95] The only occasion when the word 'healing' appears in her meticulous analysis is in a quotation from *Seize leçons sur le trauma* by Louis Crocq, a French psychiatrist specializing in wartime neurosis and trauma, which I extract in its near-entirety:

> The subject will be . . . freed from their trauma when 1) they have ceased fixating upon it through repetition . . . ; 2) they have extricated themselves from the straitjacket of frozen time in order to get the fluid succession of their lived time going again and inscribe the memory . . . of their traumatic adventure within their life-story . . . ; 3) when they have got rid of the imposture of their traumatic

personality . . . to build for themselves a freer personality, liberated from constraints and blockages, and made up of elements from their old personality and from new elements, brought about by the wisdom of their healing; and 4) when they have found the deep meaning of their adventure and ascribed a meaning to where there was a lack thereof . . .[96]

Throughout her chapter on Delaume, Bacholle's reliance on Crocq emphasizes the cathartic method whereby the enunciation of the subject's truth about trauma holds the key to making sense of and reappropriating the foundational event.[97] This finds an echo in Delaume's oft-reiterated statement that her own autofictional practice is concerned not with right versus wrong, but rather with what sounds and feels 'just.'[98] Hence, perhaps, her exploration of all the variables and combinations to 'play all the roles,'[99] occupy in turn all the positions (child, father, mother, as victim and/or victimizer) and test *ad infinitum* the possible hypotheses and 'scenarios' that led to the double murder-suicide, let alone after the 'good news,' from the revenge book written while spending weeks on the mother's grave (*Dans ma maison sous terre*) to the 'travel book' and trip to the father's grave to lay to rest *papa*'s own 'two syllables' (*Où le sang nous appelle*).[100]

However, exhausting all real-fictional possibilities is not merely tantamount to draining the original trauma and its aftermaths of their poisonous affect, it is also in line with Delaume's proliferation of selves beyond the unicity of her mantra 'My name is Chloé Delaume' and the parthenogenesis of her double name.[101] To Leménager she insists, as does her fiction, that she is not schizophrenic but rather has 'a real problem of dissociation,'[102] a consequence of the original trauma which finds an extension in 'the implosion of the hosting body'[103] during her attempt to incarnate herself. Delaume's fascination with the cult role-playing game The Sims® can even be explained by the versatility of embodiments it affords and its analogy to her real-life trajectory, from her too-many name changes as a child (including her near-constant depersonalization by her father) to her triunity and polyvalence as autofictional subject, her several fictional alter egos and incarnations:

> Yes, at least three inside. Because I am many and weary of making us shut up. I am Chloé Delaume, author, narratrix, heroine. I am also the Queen, her majesty demands that there be . . . a community, not merely pseudonyms. . . . I am Clotilde Mélisse and maybe Melisandre, I will have to be baptized, legion, I am legion, each voice has its function, the Little One, the Stupid Bitch, the Missus, Carapace, Egeria and Sibyl. The Slayer, the Stage Manageress, Miss Puny, Princess Panic, Powdery, Collapse and Death Agony.[104]

Near the end of *Une femme avec personne dedans*, in the third and last of the future possibilities beyond the novel, Delaume explicitly refers to her dissociated self:

> Life and writing so intermingled, to write myself too much in advance risks freezing me [*me figer*], to say nothing of the danger of self-prophecy. . . . The pact becomes cumbersome, as much as its trinity. Author narratrix heroine, I've yielded to it so much that dissociation quarters my soma, by turns one of the three, autofiction: my faith, but from now on a crisis.[105]

A well-documented condition associated with the 'dialectic of trauma,' dissociation in Delaume's case never took the form of an oscillation between 'the will to deny horrible events and the will to proclaim them aloud';[106] rather, in the many re-memberings and retellings, it has affected the relation between life-death and writing down to the subject's own existential questioning. This tug-of-war is approached most consistently in *Dans ma maison sous terre*, which Delaume felt the need to write to (once again) close the autofictional cycle that had worked through her former self and the family drama. Let us follow how she stages the dilemma in several rhythmic phases:

> Because I affirm that I write myself, but I also live myself. I don't tell stories, I experiment with them always from within. Writing or life, this seems to me impossible, impossible to settle, it cancels the pact.
>
> Writing or life. I reply writing. But can writing survive a psychotic episode? Each book precedes one, inscribing its own modalities word for word. I already no longer know who I am, and the crisis will soon happen.
>
> Writing or life. Life, not writing.
>
> Writing or life, life has carried the day.
>
> I give up death, death by writing. Writing or death, I choose, here again. . . .Théophile is right, something must be done. Something which imposes life. Life and writing, to write oneself merely [*juste*] in life.
>
> I won't do a novel capable of killing her. Life or writing, I've chosen life too much.[107]

Autofiction, or the 'life-writing' of 'Chloé Delaume real fiction':[108] the project's 'borderline' and ultimate test is that choosing writing might not prove powerful enough to anchor the subject in the real and that therefore one should eventually opt for life over writing if one wishes to preserve the latter, even though Delaume's aim is '[t]o live one's writing, not to live in order to write.'[109]

Referencing both Michel Foucault in 'Le sujet et le pouvoir,' for whom one should 'promote new forms of subjectivities,'[110] as well as Judith Butler on 'the power of words: politics of the performative' (used in the French title of *Excitable Speech*), Delaume the *performeuse* insists that a new subject can come about through the repetitive practice of a new hybrid genre since

> [a]utofiction contains performative genes.
> My name is [*Je m'appelle*] and I am, nature. From the real I topple into fiction, from the bottom of fiction I address the real to inscribe myself in it at last, after transformation. Autofiction, fiction/autobiography: some kind of gender trouble.[111]

The French *je m'appelle*, literally 'I call myself,' captures more readily the performative force of Delaume's iterative act of enunciation: I call myself, therefore I am, all the more since '[t]he I reconstitutes itself with each representation of the self' and '[t]he I is an effect of repetition.'[112] Soon before stressing that 'empowerment is not a fable' in the middle of a black magician's performing act quoted previously, Delaume had remarked in *Où le sang nous appelle* that 'I am almost forty I possess nothing except this I, this interface, an enunciative agency created and imposed.'[113] Never merely a 'pen name' or pseudonym, 'Chloé Delaume' is the performative signature of a reinvented 'I' through an enunciative, literary act, and it is perhaps the liberating empowerment born of this resubjectivation through a repeated, ritualistic linguistic and literary act that can be called 'therapeutic.'

Towards the end of her autofiction in four hands, after dialoguing with the deceased on his tomb, Delaume resolves to turn over a new leaf as she departs for good: 'I'm going to get out, dad. Pass the gate of the cemetery, and for ever. . . . I no longer have any reason to make a big deal out of this story . . . , and you know what, dad? I'll move on.'[114] It is no doubt this firm resolution that Bacholle has in mind when, in the light of Delaume's next project, she writes that 'Chloé Delaume is no longer turned towards herself but towards the other, the feminine, sisterly other. She would then no longer be in LaCapra's working-through but in the moving-on which solves the "enigma of suicide".'[115]

Throughout my argument, I have resisted the facile temptation to reduce Delaume's formulaic self-naming to a mere repetition compulsion, bearing in mind, in view of the formula's performative efficacy, the following distinction by LaCapra: 'Working-through . . . should be understood as an open, self-questioning process that never attains closure and counteracts acting-out (or the repetition compulsion) without entirely transcending it, especially with respect to trauma and its aftermath.'[116] A disputed borderline genre in its own right, autofiction thwarts taxonomic boundaries even further, such as the relation between trauma and writing based on trauma studies' reliance on the traditional psychoanalytic notions of (unconscious) acting-out and repetition compulsion.

NOTES

1. Chloé Delaume, *Une femme avec personne dedans* (Paris: Seuil, 2012), 74. Unless otherwise specified, all translations from Delaume's texts are mine.

2. Chloé Delaume, *Dans ma maison sous terre* (Paris: Seuil, 2009), 7.

3. The decision to give herself a new full name with a double literary pedigree—Chloé is the heroine of Boris Vian's *L'Écume des jours* (*Froth on the Daydream*) and the patronymic is derived from Antonin Artaud's poetic rendering of Lewis Carroll's *Through the Looking-Glass* in *L'Arve et l'Aume*, both incidentally published in 1947, the year Delaume's mother was born—was soon translated into her well-known iterative mantra, almost a trademark of her autofictional work: 'My name is Chloé Delaume' (often followed by 'I am a fictional character'), which appeared no fewer than forty-five times first in *La Vanité des Somnambules* (Tours: Farrago; Paris: Léo Scheer, 2002).

4. Born 'officially' with the 1977 novel *Fils* by Serge Doubrovsky, for whom it designates the fictionalization of strictly real events (cf. Delaume, *La règle du Je. Autofiction: un essai* (Paris: PUF, 2010), 16, 18–19, and *Une femme avec personne dedans*, 138), the term 'autofiction' was prompted by a dissatisfaction with the taxonomic limitations of the literary genre of autobiography in Philippe Lejeune's influential *Le Pacte autobiographique* (1975). Based on the affirmation of a triune identity between author, narrator and character throughout Delaume's works, autofiction is described as a 'pact' between life (the real) and writing involving the fictionalization of lived experience (for example, *Dans ma maison sous terre*, 186, and *La règle du Je, passim*).

5. 'Ni prudes ni soumises,' Propos recueillis par Grégoire Leménager, *Nouvel Observateur*, 19 January 2012, at http://bibliobs.nouvelobs.com/romans/20120118. OBS9095/castillon-delaume-niprudes-ni-soumises.html, accessed 16 April 2019. A similar point was made more specifically about autofiction in *La règle du Je*, 18.

6. The technical description of her manic-depressive condition is quoted in *La règle du Je*, 89: 'Borderline state. Schizo-affective disorders. Long-term condition, dysthymic psychosis.'

7. See, for example, *La règle du Je*, 19. I have attempted to reconstruct a Lacanian trajectory of 'Chloé Delaume' through her autofictional works in '*Cyberego sum*: Autofiction versus Psychoanalysis,' to appear in *Knots: Literature & Psychoanalysis after Lacan*, ed. Jean-Michel Rabaté (London: Bloomsbury, forthcoming 2019).

8. Delaume, *Dans ma maison sous terre*, 62. Explained in *La règle du Je*, 88.

9. Chloé Delaume, *Le Cri du sablier* (Tours: Farrago, 2001), 123. The book's 'autopsy' was the outcome of a failed dual structure, one of whose egos turned into a psychoanalyst who had to be silenced since this presence did not square with De-

laume's view of the talking cure as a 'dangerous joke [*fumisterie*].' See Minh Tran Huy's 'Entretien avec Chloé Delaume,' *Zone littéraire*, 8 November 2001, at http://www.zone-litteraire.com/litterature/interviews/entretien-avec-chloe-delaume.html, accessed 16 April 2019.

10. For this aspect, see, for example, Chloé Delaume, *La règle du Je*, 6; *Les juins ont tous la même peau. Rapport sur Boris Vian* (Paris: Points, 2009), 34; and Chloé Delaume and Daniel Schneidermann, *Où le sang nous appelle* (Paris: Seuil, 2013), 113.

11. Chloé Delaume, 'S'Écrire mode d'emploi,' publie.net (2008), 1.

12. Delaume, *La Vanité des Somnambules*, 143, and the subtitle of *Corpus Simsi*.

13. Delaume, *La règle du Je*, 5. See also *La dernière fille avant la guerre* (Paris: Naïve, 2007), 9.

14. Delaume, *La Vanité des Somnambules*, 7–8, and also 129: 'I was expelled from the body which I couldn't make my own on a stormy Wednesday in 2002,' reworked as a 'spongy Friday' in *Corpus Simsi* (Paris: Léo Scheer, 2003), 4.

15. Cf. Delaume's variation 'Je suis un personnage d'affliction,' which could be rendered as 'I am an afflictional character,' in *Dans ma maison sous terre*, 205; see also 'Exercice & définitions,' in *Le roman, quelle invention! Assises du roman 2008* (Paris: Christian Bourgois, 2008), 3 (the page number refers to the downloadable file on the writer's website at http://www.chloedelaume.net/), and, for the parallel between fiction and affliction, *La nuit je suis Buffy Summers* (Montreuil-sur-Mer: è®e, 2007), 60.

16. Delaume, *Le Cri du sablier*, 65–66. An earlier scene makes the mother, who wanted to shut the nursling up ('clouer le bec'), responsible for choosing the whole name 'Chloé la fille de l'aume' (29).

17. Delaume and Schneidermann, *Où le sang nous appelle*, 287.

18. Delaume, *Dans ma maison sous terre*, 169.

19. Delaume, *La dernière fille avant la guerre*, 114. The book retraces Delaume's unbounded passion, as her adolescent self Anne, for French pop-rock new-wave band Indochine and the bitter disappointment at having the lyrics she was commissioned to write for one of their songs turned down. On her website she confessed that she wanted to hang herself afterwards (cf. 103: 'narrative thread and nooses'); the end of the book recasts the sad dénouement of Vian's *L'Écume des jours* with references to their album *Alice & June* and a Carrollian twist since 'Alice' also happens to be the name of the friend who lent her Vian's novel at school.

20. Delaume, *La Vanité des Somnambules*, 114. The figure of Lilith makes several appearances throughout Delaume's texts—for instance, the chapter 'Lilith dolorosa' in *Une femme avec personne dedans*, 119–28, a phrase used previously in *Le deuil des deux syllabes* (Paris: L'Une & l'Autre, 2011), 29, and in *Les sorcières de la République* (Paris: Seuil, 2016), 194–201—and is at the centre of the 'Club Lilith,' a forum of discussions about the figure of the witch and witchcraft, and their cultural and political reappropriation; see *Les sorcières de la République*, especially 238–46, and '15 mars: Le Club Lilith est IRL' (3 March 2017) on Delaume's website at http://www.chloedelaume.net/?p=5217, accessed 16 April 2019. In *Le Cri du sablier*, 80, Lilith is humorously fused with Lot (French *Loth*), whose wife turned into a pillar of

salt, in 'Loloth,' when Madame la Mort fulfils the young girl's wish to kill her father against a 'stiff' price—in French *salé*, literally 'salty.'

21. Delaume, *La Vanité des Somnambules*, 10.

22. Cf. 'téniacité (*ténia* + tenacity) in *La Vanité des Somnambules*, 48.

23. Delaume, *Le Cri du sablier*, 83, 64; also *La Vanité des Somnambules*, 106.

24. Delaume, *Dans ma maison sous terre*, 105. Cf. also *La Vanité des Somnambules*, 68, 106.

25. Delaume, *La Vanité des Somnambules*, 40. Relying on homophony and homography, Delaume revealed that the Oulipian constraint behind *Le Cri du sablier* was the use of *vers blanc*, in French both the blank verse contaminating the book's diction and rhythms, and the white maggots contaminating and eating away at the bodies of her dead parents (cf. also *La règle du Je*, 72). See, for example, Thierry Guichard, 'Laboratoire de génétique textuelle,' *Le Matricule des anges* 100: 'Dossier Chloé Delaume' (February 2009): 25.

26. Delaume, *Corpus Simsi*, 125. See also Marika Piva, 'Cybervariation autour de la littérature: *Corpus Simsi* de Chloé Delaume,' *Fabula / Les colloques*, Internet est un cheval de Troie, at http://www.fabula.org/colloques/document4173.php, accessed 16 April 2019.

27. Chloé Delaume, *Éden matin midi et soir* (Nantes: joca seria, 2009), 43, 32.

28. See also Delaume, *Dans ma maison sous terre*, 103–4. In *Le Cri du sablier*, the narrator stages herself as Atropos 'putting an end to her rope cutting off the thread herself' (129).

29. Chloé Delaume, *Certainement pas* (Paris: Verticales / Seuil, 2004), translated into English as *Not a Clue*, trans. and Intro. Dawn M. Cornelio (Lincoln and London: University of Nebraska Press, 2018). Page references will be to the French original followed by the English translation between parentheses. Cornelio's felicitous choice for the book's title alludes to the North American version of the detective board game.

30. http://www.chloedelaume.net/, accessed 16 April 2019 via The Internet Archive Wayback Machine. To this unending list one should also add intertextual allusions to sinister psychos or murderers on the rampage: doctor Caligari, from the film *The Cabinet of Dr. Caligari* (1920), in which a somnambulist commits murders, alongside Dr. Mabuse (*La Vanité des Somnambules*, 87), and especially Jack Torrance, of *The Shining* fame, in *Certainement pas*, 81, 307–8, which emulates his celebrated manic typing of 'All work and no play makes Jack a dull boy,' 334, as 'Tawrance' (*Not a Clue*, 46, 189–90, 207)—recalled in 'Suite 411,' in *Sillages* (Sainte-Anastasie: Cadex, 2010), 46. For the latter, see Marika Piva, *Nimphœa in fabula. Le bouquet d'histoires de Chloé Delaume* (Passignano s.T.: Aguaplano, 2012), 77, 86–87, and Delaume herself in Thierry Guichard, 'Personnage de roman,' *Le Matricule des anges* 100: 'Dossier Chloé Delaume' (February 2009): 20.

31. Delaume, *Dans ma maison sous terre*, 127. Compare with *Éden matin midi et soir*, 42.

32. Delaume, *Certainement pas*, 81 (*Not a Clue*, 46).

33. Delaume, *Dans ma maison sous terre*, 10. The motif of Nemesis or retribution, to which I will return later, will last until *Où le sang nous appelle*, 344.

34. Delaume, *Dans ma maison sous terre*, 45 ff. This cataclysmic, rather than religious, 'annunciation of the good news' is evoked also in several interviews and in Delaume and Schneidermann, *Où le sang nous appelle*, 35, which later allusively mentions that the grandmother retracted (88). Referring to work by Claude Lévi-Strauss and James Frazer, Piva reads Delaume's unusual recourse to first-naming the hated granny as a voodoo or black magic spell (*Nimphœa in fabula*, 43).

35. Delaume, *Dans ma maison sous terre*, 65.

36. Delaume, *Dans ma maison sous terre*, 17, 49, 68, 71, 90–91, 102, 135, 138.

37. Delaume, *Dans ma maison sous terre*, 45.

38. Delaume, *Certainement pas*, 248 (*Not a Clue*, 151).

39. Compare *Certainement pas*, 248 (*Not a Clue*, 151), and *Dans ma maison sous terre*, 16.

40. 'I would have reproduced myself without fearing I would transmit a failing paternal gene' (Delaume, *Dans ma maison sous terre*, 91). See also *Une femme avec personne dedans*, 13, 76, 122–24, 127; *Le deuil des deux syllabes*, 29; *Mes bien chères sœurs* (Paris: Seuil, 2019), 26, 103–4, 107; and Delaume and Schneidermann, *Où le sang nous appelle*, 78. The first chapter dedicated to Françoise Pithiviers, the mother, opens with Hugues Aufray's *Céline* 'oozing out of the radio' as her waters break, a hint at her daughter's later plight since the hit song's theme is about a spinster sacrificing her life for her siblings without conceiving children of her own. See Delaume, *Certainement pas*, 237 (*Not a Clue*, 144).

41. See Delaume and Schneidermann, *Où le sang nous appelle*, 102, where the coincidence of names is revealed.

42. Delaume, *Au commencement était l'adverbe* (Nantes: joca seria, 2010), 43. See also Delaume in Guichard, 'Laboratoire de génétique textuelle,' 23.

43. Cf. Delaume, *Certainement pas*, 9; also 279 (*Not a Clue*, 2, 170), featuring Miss Marple, one of Christie's best-known characters, as the Third Officer.

44. See '24 h dans la vie de Chloé Delaume,' interview with Colette Fellous, *France Culture*, 9 August 2009, at http://www.fabriquedesens.net/24-h-dans-la-vie-de-Chloe-Delaume, accessed 16 April 2019.

45. Delaume, *La règle du Je*, 88-89.

46. Delaume, *Certainement pas*, 363 (*Not a Clue*, 225).

47. Delaume, *Éden matin midi et soir*, 46, also 17; the book's closing words, before the initial portrait reappears, broken. In *Dans ma maison sous terre*, which also mentions this statistic in passing (154)—as does *Les sorcières de la République*, 182—Delaume had already used this real-time device to introduce the section of Clotilde Mélisse, lying inside an onyx grave fitted with a screen on which a fourteen-minute video montage plays out in a loop (23), arguably the same length of time it takes to read her following part (25–32). The chapter thus becomes equivalent to the grave, with the page as video screen, in this revenge book set in a cemetery.

48. Delaume, *Éden matin midi et soir*, 7 (also 10, 43), 16. Influenced by Sarah Kane's play *4.48 Psychosis*, this monologue features a young woman whose family name evokes a lineage of doctors and a famous maternity hospital in Paris—the book's title refers to the false security of the artificial 'Paradise' provided by psychiatric medication three times a day (20, 44).

49. Delaume, *Éden matin midi et soir*, 20–21; also 23, 25–27, 29–30, 32, 38.

50. Delaume, *Éden matin midi et soir*, 19.

51. Delaume, *Éden matin midi et soir*, 16–19. See also 9: 'I am not schizophrenic, I hear only myself in my head, only I am many.'

52. Delaume, *Éden matin midi et soir*, 45.

53. Delaume, *Une femme avec personne dedans*, 71–72, referring to Marguerite Duras's eponymous novel (see *Éden matin midi et soir*, 20). See also 9: 'Thirty-seven years old, like me, not a young woman is she, thanatopathy is an incurable disease.'

54. Delaume, *Une femme avec personne dedans*, 74–75; cf. also 77. In *Mes bien chères sœurs* she will write: 'I write in order not to die since I've already done so' (44).

55. Delaume, *Dans ma maison sous terre*, 120; 16. See also Delaume, *Les sorcières de la République*, 62, 313–15, 325.

56. Delaume, *La nuit je suis Buffy Summers*, 85, 109; reprised in *Les sorcières de la République*, 200, 349; and *Mes bien chères sœurs*, 119.

57. Delaume, *Le Cri du sablier*, 127–28. Note the parallel with, and linguistic recall of, the scene of the mother's expulsion of her daughter into life, quoted previously (*Le Cri du sablier*, 65–66).

58. Delaume and Schneidermann, *Où le sang nous appelle*, 353, 359; 59.

59. Delaume, *Éden matin midi et soir*, 8–9, 24, and *passim* for recurrent instances of pronominal fluctuations. Dissociation also characterizes those narratives in which 'Chloé Delaume' clashes against a former avatar or self, such as *La Vanité des Somnambules* and *La dernière fille avant la guerre*.

60. Jacques Derrida, *The Gift of Death*, trans. David Wills (Chicago and London: University of Chicago Press, 1995). The French idiom for 'to take away one's own life' is also central to Derrida's inquiry into 'the gift of death as being-towards-death within the horizon of the question of being' (47).

61. Delaume, *La Vanité des Somnambules*, 65.

62. In *Trauma: Explorations in Memory*, ed. and intr. Cathy Caruth (Baltimore and London: Johns Hopkins University Press, 1995), 151.

63. Delaume, *La règle du Je*, 6.

64. Delaume, *La Vanité des Somnambules*, 96. This 'limbic' (42) space, or *Somnambulie*, is related to the limbic system of memory (41–42) extracted from the website on 'Gingko: le remue-mémoire!,' dealing with memory as a basic function of the human brain, at https://pages.csrs.qc.ca/ginko/, accessed 16 April 2019.

65. Delaume, *La Vanité des Somnambules*, 119–27; 118.

66. Delaume, *La Vanité des Somnambules*, 121.

67. Delaume, *La Vanité des Somnambules*, 115, 117, 119, 123–24.

68. Delaume, *Dans ma maison sous terre*, 122.

69. Delaume, *Dans ma maison sous terre*, 205, and before: 'I won't write a novel capable of killing her' (204).

70. Delaume, *La nuit je suis Buffy Summers*, 85.

71. Delaume, *Éden matin midi et soir*, 26.

72. Delaume, *Éden matin midi et soir*, 28–29. It should be noted that Delaume's fiction is saturated with pharmaceutical products (often against psychosis, schizo-

phrenia and depression), complete with dosage and technical medical terms as well as digressions, culled from websites and textbooks, on various diseases, bodily and mental (dys)functions, etc.

73. 'Le soi est une fiction: Chloé Delaume s'entretient avec Barbara Havercroft,' *Revue critique de fixxion française contemporaine / Critical Review of Contemporary French Fixxion* 4: 'Fictions de soi / Self-fictions,' ed. Barbara Havercroft and Michael Sheringham (June 2012), 129. Delaume then alludes to two fateful cases of autofiction that could kill their intended readers: Serge Doubrovsky's *Le Livre brisé* (his wife, who drank herself to death) and Christine Angot's *L'Inceste* (her father). Compare with *Dans ma maison sous terre*, 120: 'When I write these sentences [describing the many tortures inflicted upon the grandmother], it liberates tension. I imagine her reading them, and to read them is to live them.'

74. Delaume, *Une femme avec personne dedans*, 136; also 138.

75. 'Le soi est une fiction,' 129; see also the Mediapart video clip, dated 31 January 2012 (soon after the publication of *Une femme avec personne dedans*—see 9 for the accusation that Delaume wrote '*books made to kill*'), 'Chloé Delaume. Exister si peu dans le réel,' at https://www.dailymotion.com/video/xo9x9g, accessed 16 April 2019. For the idea of a return shock accompanying revenge, see *Dans ma maison sous terre*, 115, and *Les sorcières de la République*, 62, 191, 327.

76. Delaume, *Une femme avec personne dedans*, 14.

77. Delaume, *Une femme avec personne dedans*, 14.

78. Delaume, *Où le sang nous appelle*, 136–37. The title in italics, also quoted on the preceding page, is of course an allusion to J. L. Austin's study of performative utterances *How to Do Things with Words*, for which see also *La règle du Je*, 79; *Les sorcières de la République*, 139, 181, 189–90, 248; *Mes bien chères sœurs*, 78.

79. Delaume, *Une femme avec personne dedans*, 138.

80. Delaume, *Une femme avec personne dedans*, 139.

81. Delaume, *La règle du Je*, 80.

82. See, for example, *La nuit je suis Buffy Summers*, 110 (referring to the interactive story itself); *Au commencement était l'adverbe*, 104 (Anaïs's reproach to Clotilde Mélisse, who gave her life as a character to cure herself of her jealousy); and *La dernière fille avant la guerre*, 59 (about language).

83. Delaume, *Dans ma maison sous terre*, 117.

84. Delaume, *La règle du Je*, 88. See also *Dans ma maison sous terre*, 189, quoted below.

85. Delaume, *Dans ma maison sous terre*, 124.

86. See, for instance, Chloé Delaume, *Les mouflettes d'Atropos* (Tours: Farrago, 2000), 181; *Dans ma maison sous terre*, 188–89, 191; and *La règle du Je*, 8, 55, 84. For an analysis of the matrix phrase symbolic of the survivor of a cataclysmic tragedy, see Marie-Chantal Killeen, '"Tout vu, rien inventé": *Hiroshima mon amour* dans l'œuvre de Chloé Delaume,' *French Forum* 42.2 (Fall 2017): 265–79.

87. Delaume, *Une femme avec personne dedans*, 16 and *passim*, original emphasis. See also the entry in Delaume's Facebook profile reading 'Studied Oracle Belline option Delphes at Sunnydale High School,' at https://www.facebook.com/

chloedelaumeTPE/about, accessed 16 April 2019; and *Une femme avec personne dedans*, 22–23, 29, 139.

88. Delaume, *Une femme avec personne dedans*, 74, insertion mine.

89. Delaume, *Une femme avec personne dedans*, 11.

90. Delaume, *Une femme avec personne dedans*, 11.

91. Jacques Lacan, *The Seminar of Jacques Lacan. Book XXIII: Le Sinthome*, trans. A. R. Price (Cambridge: Polity, 2016), 112.

92. Delaume, *La règle du Je*, 74, in the eponymous chapter. See also *Où le sang nous appelle*, 341, and 'Chloé Delaume. Exister si peu dans le réel,' in which Delaume also alludes to writing not as therapy but as palliative to boredom.

93. Roland Barthes, 'Writing: An Intransitive Verb?' (1966), in *The Rustle of Language*, trans. Richard Howard (Oxford: Basil Blackwell, 1986), 11–21.

94. Michèle Bacholle, *Récits contemporains d'endeuillés après suicide. Les cas Fottorino, Vigan, Grimbert, Rahmani, Charneux et Delaume* (Leiden and Boston: Brill, 2018), 211–62, selecting two out of the three interpretations given by Theodore L. Dorpat as cited by Michel Hanus in *Le Deuil après suicide*. The second hypothesis here might explain at least two passages in *Le Cri du sablier* (22, 80), to be correlated with her prayer to God that he might kill her father (37). In the same book, Delaume describes herself the day after the fateful event as a 'post-traumatic doll' (11).

95. For the occlusion of Frédéric Dalain from Delaume's autofictional writing, see Bacholle, *Récits contemporains d'endeuillés après suicide*, 234–37. Delaume herself, including via her fictional doubles, has emphasized the omnipresence of mourning in her texts, and the end of 'Exister si peu dans le réel' peters out on the admission that she has a rather 'monstrous' relation to it. Leaving out its explicit thematization in *Le deuil des deux syllabes*, see, for instance, *Le Cri du sablier*, 75: 'deuil pour deuil an pour an' (literally: mourning for mourning, year for year; a pun on the revenge formula of the *lex talionis* in French: *œil pour œil, dent pour dent*); *La dernière fille avant la guerre*, 9 (about 'the girl who was inside,' whose voice was 'granular like mourning'); *Éden matin midi et soir*, 40: 'I have made my own mourning, yes, the mourning of myself'—compare with *La règle du Je*, 13: 'I have made the mourning of an I who knew only to be She'—; *La règle du Je*, 66, 71; *Une femme avec personne dedans*, 24 (as a third person); and *Mes bien chères sœurs*, 105 (about one's dreams as opposed to the self).

96. Bacholle, *Récits contemporains d'endeuillés après suicide*, 247; quoted from Louis Crocq, *Seize leçons sur le trauma* (Paris: Odile Jacob, 2012), 186; my translation.

97. Bacholle, *Récits contemporains d'endeuillés après suicide*, 219.

98. Delaume, *Dans ma maison sous terre*, 133; *La règle du Je*, 56, 67.

99. Delaume, *Une femme avec personne dedans*, 92.

100. Delaume, *Dans ma maison sous terre*, 83–86 (chapter titled 'One woman, two men, 666 possibilities'); Delaume and Schneidermann, *Où le sang nous appelle*, 337–49 (chapter titled 'Grave for 500,000 dads').

101. Delaume, *La règle du Je*, 6: '[Boris Vian and Antonin Artaud] were flatly refusing to beget me, I know. . . . born of father and father, I knocked myself up';

and Delaume and Schneidermann, *Où le sang nous appelle*, 202: 'I have just given birth to myself.'

102. 'Ni prudes ni soumises.'

103. Delaume, *La règle du Je*, 86. The term used, *corps hébergeant*, recalls how the young orphan girl perceived her adoptive foster family as *hébergeurs*.

104. Delaume, *Une femme avec personne dedans*, 132. The list partly reworks and extends her childhood appellations in *Le Cri du sablier*, 19. See also *Éden matin midi et soir*, for example, 9: 'I am many,' and *Où le sang nous appelle*, 39. For an exhaustive list of Delaume's fictional surrogates, see Bacholle, *Récits contemporains d'endeuillés après suicide*, 245–46. Some of these, like Clotilde Mélisse and the Sibyl, will last beyond the closed autofictional cycle, in the 'Liberté, Parité, Sororité' project and its two books: *Les sorcières de la République* and *Mes bien chères sœurs*.

105. Delaume, *Une femme avec personne dedans*, 136 (insertion mine); cf. also, implicitly, 132.

106. See Judith Herman, *Trauma and Recovery: The Aftermath of Violence— From Domestic Abuse to Political Terror*, with a New Epilogue by the Author (New York: Basic Books, 2015 [1992]), 1.

107. Delaume, *Dans ma maison sous terre*, 186, 189, 190, 191, 201–2, 204 (before Delaume's proposal that 'Nathalie Dalain' be engraved with her dates on the family tombstone). Some of these excerpts dovetail with those in *La règle du Je*, 22–23.

108. Delaume, *Où le sang nous appelle*, 136.

109. Delaume, *La règle du Je*, 8.

110. Delaume, *Une femme avec personne dedans*, 139; quoted at greater length in *La règle du Je*, 77.

111. Delaume, *La règle du Je*, 79 (insertion mine), before quoting a fragment from Butler's eponymous book, alluded to alongside the French version of *Excitable Speech* also in *Les sorcières de la République*, 125 (chapter on empowerment).

112. Delaume, *La règle du Je*, 80.

113. Delaume and Schneidermann, *Où le sang nous appelle*, 136; also 202. See also *La règle du Je*, 9, which distinguishes between the 'I' of enunciative agency and the Ego (*Moi*) to be ultimately done away with. For Delaume's emphasis on empowerment, a word she leaves in English (in *La règle du Je*, 81, alongside its French equivalent: *encapacitation*), see also *Les sorcières de la République*, 124–25, 326; *Mes bien chères sœurs*, 105; and the Mediapart video clip, dated 31 January 2012, 'Chloé Delaume, c'est juste moi. Seulement nous sommes légions,' at https://www. dailymotion.com/video/xo9xad, accessed 16 April 2019.

114. Delaume and Schneidermann, *Où le sang nous appelle*, 348–49.

115. Bacholle, *Récits contemporains d'endeuillés après suicide*, 262; referring, here and throughout her study, to Dominick LaCapra's use of the Freudian notion first developed in the 1914 paper 'Remembering, Repeating and Working-Through.'

116. See Dominick LaCapra, *Writing History, Writing Trauma*, with a New Preface (Baltimore and London: Johns Hopkins University Press, 2014), xxiii.

.

BIBLIOGRAPHY

BACHOLLE, Michèle. *Récits contemporains d'endeuillés après suicide. Les cas Fottorino, Vigan, Grimbert, Rahmani, Charneux et Delaume*. Leiden and Boston: Brill, 2018.

BARTHES, Roland. 'Writing: An Intransitive Verb?.' In *The Rustle of Language*. Translated by Richard Howard. 11–21. Oxford: Basil Blackwell, 1986.

CARUTH, Cathy, editor. *Trauma: Explorations in Memory*. Introduction by Cathy Caruth. Baltimore and London: Johns Hopkins University Press, 1995.

'Chloé Delaume, c'est juste moi. Seulement nous sommes légions.' Mediapart, 31 January 2012. https://www.dailymotion.com/video/xo9xad. Accessed 16 April 2019.

'Chloé Delaume. Exister si peu dans le réel.' Mediapart, 31 January 2019. https://www.dailymotion.com/video/xo9x9g. Accessed 16 April 2019.

Chloé Delaume. Facebook profile. https://www.facebook.com/chloedelaumeTPE/about. Accessed 16 April 2019.

DELAUME, Chloé. *Au commencement était l'adverbe*. Nantes: joca seria, 2010.

DELAUME, Chloé. *Certainement pas*. Paris: Verticales / Seuil, 2004.

DELAUME, Chloé. *Corpus Simsi*. Paris: Léo Scheer, 2003.

DELAUME, Chloé. *Dans ma maison sous terre*. Paris: Seuil, 2009.

DELAUME, Chloé. *Éden matin midi et soir*. Nantes: joca seria, 2009.

DELAUME, Chloé. 'Exercice & définitions.' In *Le roman, quelle invention! Assises du roman 2008*. Paris: Christian Bourgois, 2008. Accessed 16 April 2019.

DELAUME, Chloé. *La dernière fille avant la guerre*. Paris: Naïve, 2007.

DELAUME, Chloé. *La nuit je suis Buffy Summers*. Montreuil-sur-Mer: è®e, 2007.

DELAUME, Chloé. *La règle du Je. Autofiction: un essai*. Paris: PUF, 2010.

DELAUME, Chloé. *La Vanité des Somnambules*. Tours: Farrago; Paris: Léo Scheer, 2002.

DELAUME, Chloé. *Le Cri du sablier*. Tours: Farrago, 2001.

DELAUME, Chloé. *Le deuil des deux syllabes*. Paris: L'Une & l'Autre, 2011.

DELAUME, Chloé. *Les juins ont tous la même peau. Rapport sur Boris Vian*. Paris: Points, 2009.

DELAUME, Chloé. *Les mouflettes d'Atropos*. Tours: Farrago, 2000.

DELAUME, Chloé. *Les sorcières de la République*. Paris: Seuil, 2016.

DELAUME, Chloé. *Mes bien chères sœurs*. Paris: Seuil, 2019.

DELAUME, Chloé. *Not a Clue*. Translated and Introduction by Dawn M. Cornelio. Lincoln and London: University of Nebraska Press, 2018.

DELAUME, Chloé. 'S'Écrire mode d'emploi.' publie.net, 2008.

DELAUME, Chloé. 'Suite 411.' In *Sillages*. Sainte-Anastasie: Cadex, 2010. 39–50.

DELAUME, Chloé. *Une femme avec personne dedans*. Paris: Seuil, 2012.

DELAUME, Chloé and Daniel Schneidermann. *Où le sang nous appelle*. Paris: Seuil, 2013.

DERRIDA, Jacques. *The Gift of Death*. Translated by David Wills. Chicago and London: University of Chicago Press, 1995.

'Gingko: le remue-mémoire!.' https://pages.csrs.qc.ca/ginko/. Accessed 16 April 2019.

GUICHARD, Thierry. 'Laboratoire de génétique textuelle.' *Le Matricule des anges* 100: 'Dossier Chloé Delaume' (February 2009): 22–27.

GUICHARD, Thierry. 'Personnage de roman.' *Le Matricule des anges* 100: 'Dossier Chloé Delaume' (February 2009): 18–21.

HERMAN, Judith. *Trauma and Recovery: The Aftermath of Violence—From Domestic Abuse to Political Terror.* With a New Epilogue by the Author. New York: Basic Books, 2015 [1992].

KILLEEN, Marie-Chantal. '"Tout vu, rien inventé": *Hiroshima mon amour* dans l'œuvre de Chloé Delaume.' *French Forum* 42.2 (Fall 2017): 265–79.

LACAN, Jacques. *The Seminar of Jacques Lacan. Book XXIII: Le Sinthome.* Edited by Jacques-Alain Miller. Translated by A. R. Price. Cambridge: Polity, 2016.

LACAPRA, Dominick. *Writing History, Writing Trauma.* With a New Preface. Baltimore and London: Johns Hopkins University Press, 2014.

'Le soi est une fiction: Chloé Delaume s'entretient avec Barbara Havercroft.' *Revue critique de fixxion française contemporaine / Critical Review of Contemporary French Fixxion* 4: 'Fictions de soi / Self-fictions.' Edited by Barbara Havercroft and Michael Sheringham (June 2012): 126–36.

'Ni prudes ni soumises,' Propos recueillis par Grégoire Leménager.' *Nouvel Observateur*, 19 January 2012. http://bibliobs.nouvelobs.com/romans/20120118.OBS9095/castillon-delaume-niprudes-ni-soumises.html. Accessed 16 April 2019.

PIVA, Marika. 'Cybervariation autour de la littérature: *Corpus Simsi* de Chloé Delaume.' *Fabula / Les colloques*, Internet est un cheval de Troie. http://www.fabula.org/colloques/document4173.php. Accessed 16 April 2019.

PIVA, Marika. *Nimphæa in fabula. Le bouquet d'histoires de Chloé Delaume.* Passignano s.T.: Aguaplano, 2012.

TRAN, Minh Huy. 'Entretien avec Chloé Delaume.' *Zone littéraire*, 8 November 2001. http://www.zone-litteraire.com/litterature/interviews/entretien-avec-chloe-delaume.html. Accessed 16 April 2019.

'15 mars: Le Club Lilith est IRL' (3 March 2017). http://www.chloedelaume.net/?p=5217. Accessed 16 April 2019.

'24 h dans la vie de Chloé Delaume.' Interview with Colette Fellous. *France Culture*, 9 August 2009. http://www.fabriquedesens.net/24-h-dans-la-vie-de-Chloe-Delaume. Accessed 16 April 2019.

Chapter Nine

Queer Trauma, Paternal Loss and Graphic Healing in Alison Bechdel's *Fun Home: A Family Tragicomic*

Olga Michael

In this essay, I investigate the representation of inter-generationally transmitted queer trauma and paternal loss in Alison Bechdel's graphic memoir, *Fun Home: A Family Tragicomic*, arguing for the potential offered by the comics medium for the display of what I perceive as Bechdel's attempt of healing.[1] Identifying a form of trauma that is subtle, embedded in structures of the everyday, and transmitted by Bruce Bechdel to his daughter, Alison, I investigate the ways in which *Fun Home* also depicts the process of working through it via Bechdel's intertextual references to Oscar Wilde's aestheticism. I propose that these references produce 'queer temporalities' that allow the reconfiguration of space from the domain of the Gothic and the monstrous into a positive, artistic articulation of Bruce's closeted homosexuality. In revisiting her childhood and adolescent years, Bechdel reinterprets her family home as well as her distant, closeted father in an effort to come to terms with his loss. This reinterpretation is facilitated through her references to Wilde's life and art, traces from which she projects onto Bruce by portraying him as a fin-de-siècle Wildean aesthete. Through this portrayal, Bechdel offers her father the life of the artist he had declined in favour of passing as a heterosexual father, reconciling with him via her adult wise take on him, and on his love for beauty, art(ifice) and literature.[2]

TRAUMA AND LIFE WRITING IN COMICS: TOWARDS GRAPHIC HEALING

The depiction of trauma has been a stable theme in life narratives told via comics since the emergence of the genre in the US underground comix scene in the 1960s and 1970s.[3] Art Spiegelman's landmark *Maus*, which signalled the legitimization of the genre and won the Pulitzer prize in 1992, attests to the suitability of comics for the expression of inter-generationally transmitted trauma. Narrating Holocaust survival as experienced by Vladek, an Auschwitz survivor, and Art, his son, Spiegelman chose to depict the Jews as mice, showing the nuanced potential of the (until recently) marginalized medium of comics for the telling of traumatic life stories.[4] Indeed, Hillary Chute observes a 'peculiar relation' between 'the form of comics' and 'the expression of life stories,' noting the medium's suitability particularly for traumatic narratives, since it can make 'literal the presence of the past by disrupting spatial and temporal conventions to overlay or palimpsest past and present.'[5] In *Graphic Women*, Chute also explains that because of their fragmented nature and their visual/verbal hybridity, comics can mediate the difficulties emerging from the unrepresentability and unspeakability of trauma.[6]

Meaning in comics is formed through combinations of visual and textual parts as well as through readers' active participation in filling in the gaps between panels, otherwise known as gutters, in order to move from one narrative fragment to the next.[7] Panels include visual images, speech balloons, narrators' captions and the visual embodiments of characters, like the autobiographical avatar in autobiographical comics.[8] All these structural elements allow complex and nuanced representations of trauma because in comics, 'pictures are part of the writing and the drawing moves rather than merely illustrates the narrative. . . . Words and images create unsynthesized narrative tracks' in which one part 'is not redundant of the other.'[9] In this chapter, I am interested in the ways in which the form of comics allows readers to identify traces of healing in addition to the representation of queer trauma in Bechdel's graphic memoir. My aim is to point to the potential of the medium for the performance of what I would describe as an attempt of *graphic healing*, which is achieved, in *Fun Home*, through Bechdel's intertextual references to Wilde's life and art.

Scholarly criticism has acknowledged the healing effect of testimonial (life) writing, with Shoshana Felman and Dori Laub suggesting that in addition to recording historic events, testimonial literature can function as 'the unsuspected medium of healing.'[10] Similarly, Marilyn Chandler McEntyre introduces post–World War I literary autobiographies as 'narratives of crisis' and 'healing acts' because they 'address the central problems of finding words for the inexpressible, form for the chaotic, and a way out of isolation and despair back into human community through writing.'[11] Autobiography, she further adds, can be a means of 'restructuring, redescribing, reevaluating, and remythologizing the world.'[12] Suzette A. Henke has introduced the term 'scriptotherapy' to refer to healing through writing in women's life narratives.[13] Such healing effects emerge from 'the dual possibilities of performance and revision' existing in life writing.[14] When telling traumatic life stories, authors are involved, according to Chandler McEntyre, 'in a wrestle "with words and meanings" that can be deeply regenerative' since narration 'is a way of purging guilt and pain, re-centering the self, and reconnecting with community.'[15] Helen M. Buss explains that, because of this impact of trauma life narratives, readers 'must work with [writers] as . . . psychoanalytic detective[s] with good grasp of historical and cultural contexts [as well as] the linguistic consequences of trauma,' to identify one's move from the condition of being 'possessed by the past, to a condition' of possessing it.[16] For this end to be achieved, readers must be aware of their engagement with 'a form of literature that claims to be testimony' and, thus, 'more than a fictive contract.'[17]

Cartoonists rely on verbal as well as visual means to depict trauma and the journey through it. To identify the healing function of such texts, readers are therefore required to pay close attention to the meanings produced through a visual/verbal interplay, as the visual realm of a narrative often forms stories that complicate and enrich the verbal account of trauma, and vice versa. For instance, Phoebe Gloeckner and Lynda Barry incorporate, visually or verbally, elements from the genre of the fairy tale in their graphic memoirs, to invest their autobiographical subjects with agency over their pasts and in relation to their abusers, which they lacked during the occurrence of traumatic events.[18] However, it is up to readers to trace, through their interpretative stance, the healing function of such references in relation to the trauma that is narrated. In *Fun Home*, trauma is caused by the emotional and physical alienation existing between Alison and her father and by his eventual loss when he was hit by a truck four months after she came out to her family as a lesbian at the age of twenty. Alison suggests that Bruce's death was not accidental, but a carefully planned suicidal act, connected to her own coming out and to the exposure of his closeted homosexuality by her mother upon her own sexual revelation (*FH*, 57–89).

Hence, the work of healing I trace in the book concerns the wounds that emerged from Bruce's death and from the autobiographical subject's childhood inability to approach her father and to connect with him physically as well as emotionally since his unspeakable secret triggered unpredictable behaviours that harmed their relationship. By choosing to lead a double life and to pass as a heterosexual family man, Bruce shows the injurious impact of 'queer trauma' on himself and on his family, and particularly his daughter.[19] This type of trauma stems from the violence of compulsory heterosexuality, which according to Judith Butler renders some lives livable and grievable and others unlivable and ungrievable.[20] Gust A. Yep writes that compulsory heterosexuality operates as 'the invisible center and the presumed bedrock of society, . . . the quintessential force creating, sustaining, and perpetuating the erasure, marginalization, disempowerment, and oppression of sexual others.'[21] For this reason, individuals may internalize homophobia, injuring either themselves, via closeting processes and by passing as heterosexuals, or others, through hate crimes or by forcing them to conform to heteronormative standards.[22]

Laura S. Brown explains that many queer people suffer oppression within their families because of their gender identification and/or sexuality. They may suffer betrayal by family members and society in general when they decide to come out, and in more extreme cases, they may be vulnerable to the threat of hate crimes. Because of their daily exposure 'to small doses of trauma,' queer individuals are thus more prone to psychological distress and behavioural dysfunctions.[23] In *Fun Home*, Bruce's life choices embody both internalized and externalized symptoms of queer trauma. He chooses to repress his drives and to lead a double life as a heterosexual paterfamilias. He is largely unable to connect with his children and his wife, being constantly preoccupied with the restoration of the Gothic Revival family home, through which he channels his sexual frustration.[24] He is obsessed with maintaining the anachronistic beauty and perfection of the family's dwelling place at the expense of his children, and he becomes inexplicably enraged and occasionally abusive when he suspects that they might have slightly displaced his art objects (*FH*, 11, 18). The narrator explains that she and her brothers felt inferior to Bruce's artificial items because, unlike those, they were imperfect. As she puts it, her father 'treated his furniture like children, and his children like furniture' (*FH*, 14).

Alison's lack of communication with her father as a child caused her feelings of embarrassment. In fact, the distance between and isolation of the Bechdel family members seem to have been the causes of the obsessive-compulsive disorder she developed at the age of ten, which she managed to overcome with her mother's help (*FH*, 134–143). In addition to the 'Arctic climate' existing within the Bechdel family, Alison's failure to perform a heteronormatively feminine bodily stylization put further strain on her relationship with Bruce, who is depicted in an ongoing effort to force onto her a conventional feminine gender representation during her childhood, adolescence and early adulthood—occasionally through threats of physical abuse (*FH*, 67). Bruce, then, projects (his) queer trauma onto Alison, who shares with him the inability to fit in the norms of compulsory heterosexuality. Unlike Bruce, who is closeted and ineffectively passes as a heterosexual father, Alison is open about her sexuality as well as her gender identification. Bechdel draws her autobiographical avatar as a tomboy during childhood and adolescence and as a masculine woman during adulthood.[25] In her refusal to pursue the gendered stylization her father desires for her, she drifts further away from him, thus causing additional tension in their already troubled relationship.

Bruce's preoccupation with the family house, and with art(ifice) and literature, in addition to his closeted secret, also function as barriers that disrupt the father/daughter relationship. Below, I look at the initial presentation of these barriers via Bechdel's depiction of the Gothic Revival family home, focusing particularly on the representation of family roles and male homosexuality through Gothic literary and spatial elements. Then, I proceed to identify an attempt to reorient readers' perspectives in ways that allow the reinterpretation of space as Bruce's Wildean artwork, which articulates his closeted secret. Noting the 'queer temporalities' created via the comics medium and Bechdel's intertextual references to Wilde's life and art, I suggest that present and past conflate to allow the display of her wiser, reconciling adult perspective on her father. Ultimately, Bechdel seems to have made sense of her distant father and to have been able to tell his (unspeakable) life story by inscribing it on space. In the end, by presenting him 'with compassion and complexity,' she offers him, in Ann Cvetkovitch's words, 'a different form of visibility,' which poses a challenge on 'celebratory queer histories that threaten to erase more disturbing and unassimilable inheritances.'[26] *Fun Home* therefore shows the suitability of the comics medium for the representation of queer inter-generational relations.

FAMILY RELATIONS, MALE HOMOSEXUALITY AND THE GOTHIC

When interviewed by Chute, Bechdel explained that, because of Bruce's elusiveness, she had to read and research a lot to make sense of his character and his death when she was writing *Fun Home*.[27] The richness of her 'archival turn' is evident in the amount of materials in the form of police reports, photographs, diary entries, personal letters and books she reproduces in the narrative.[28] In addition, and most importantly, it can be traced in how literary and artistic genres, styles and devices become essential for the development of the story, the expression of trauma and the identification of the narrative's healing impact. The first chapter of *Fun Home*, 'Old Father, Old Artificer,' presents the child protagonist's perspective on an incomprehensible, aggressive, 'monstrous' father through the use of the Gothic, which can be traced in how the family home and family relations as well as Bruce and his closeted secret are depicted. In her analysis of this chapter, Valerie Rohy notes that 'as *Fun Home* develops the child's difference from her father, the narrative voice resonates with that of a much younger Alison.'[29] Occasionally, she continues, it seems that 'the child's consciousness [enters] the narrator's voice,' and then, 'Bechdel goes on to revise earlier assertions, including the notion of her father's falsehood on which Alison's identity and her view of the archive seem to depend.'[30] It is precisely the child's perspective on Bruce and his closeted secret, as embedded in the narrator's voice, that becomes foregrounded through Bechdel's use of the Gothic for the expression of his closeted homosexuality within the domestic domain. This double perspective presents to readers an autobiographical subject that is possessed by the past.

In describing her father's obsessive preoccupation with the restoration of the Gothic Revival family home, the narrator explains that she and her brothers were perceived by Bruce as 'free labor' and 'extensions of his own body, like precision robot arms' that facilitated his work around the house (*FH*, 13). In addition to feeling that Bruce's objects were more valuable for him than his children, Alison notes that as a child, she believed that all his 'useless' ornaments were lies, which 'obscured function' becoming 'embellishments in the worst sense' (*FH*, 16). In chapter one, then, the child autobiographical avatar seems unable to feel at home in her family home and this has to do with Bruce's tastes, which become expressed through his excessive, anachronistic home decoration. In parallel to her descriptions of the house, Alison mentions her father's unpredictable mood swings, his inability to handle criticism well and her family's incapability of showing affection for each other because they were not 'physically expressive' (*FH*, 18–19). In her account of the embarrassment she felt upon her unsuccessful attempt to kiss her father goodnight once, the narrator explains that her feelings constituted 'a tiny scale model of [Bruce's] more fully developed self-loathing. His shame,' she adds, 'inhabited our house as pervasively as the aromatic musk of aging mahogany. In fact, the meticulous, period interiors were expressly designed to conceal it. Mirrors, distracting bronzes, multiple doorways. Visitors often got lost upstairs' (*FH*, 20). The visual register offers readers access to the empty spaces of the house, with a panel presenting a confused old woman almost running into a mirror. In this way, Alison introduces domestic space as a labyrinth in which Bruce attempts to conceal both his secret and his feelings.[31]

This depiction of the family home becomes underscored through her description of her father as the mythical Daedalus, the 'skilful artificer [and] mad scientist who . . . designed the famous labyrinth . . . and who answered not to the laws of society, but to those of his craft' (*FH*, 6, 7). In the visual register of the text, Bruce is preoccupied with home decoration, while Alison declares her distaste for the pink flower-patterned wallpaper he chose for her room. The combination of the narrator's reference to Daedalus and his labyrinth with the visual depiction of Bruce's work in the Bechdel family home guides readers to form a correlation between the two. Later, as Bruce is drawn beating one of Alison's brothers because he was not able to hold the Christmas tree straight long enough so that he could identify its perfect positioning, the narrator notes that like her father, 'Daedalus, too, was indifferent to the human cost of his projects' (*FH*, 11). Daedalus, she continues, also betrayed the king by creating, upon the queen's request, a 'cow disguise' that would help her 'seduce the white bull' (*FH*, 11). The outcome of this 'unnatural' seduction was 'a half-bull, half-man monster [that] inspired Daedalus' greatest creation yet[;] the labyrinth—a maze of passages and rooms opening endlessly into one another,' in which he 'hid the Minotaur' (*FH*, 12). When Alison refers to the monstrous outcome of Pasiphae's unnatural mating with the bull, the visual register shows the autobiographical avatar fearfully looking towards her enraged father, whose presence is visually captured through a black shadow threateningly directed towards her.

This graphic metaphor depicts Bruce's rage and dark secret as a hybrid monster. Like the Minotaur, Bruce's 'unnatural' closeted passion seems to have triggered the obsessive restoration of the Bechdel family home in which it is trapped as well as the rage he projects onto his children. As the narrator describes the youth who hopelessly attempted to escape Daedalus's labyrinth, the autobiographical avatar is drawn running, leaving the house and escaping Bruce's rage. As she walks away, Alison thinks about Daedalus's relationship with his son, Icarus, wondering whether he was 'really stricken with

Figure 9.1. From *Fun Home: A Family Tragicomic* by Alison Bechdel. Copyright © 2006 by Alison Bechdel. Reprinted by permission of Houghton Mifflin Company. All rights reserved.

grief when Icarus fell into the sea or just disappointed by the design failure'
of the wings he had created for him (*FH*, 12). In implicitly identifying with
Icarus, the narrator once again mediates her inability to understand whether
her father cared about his art(ificial) works more than he did for her and
her brothers. The maze-like design of the family home, its Gothic Revival
architectural style, the presentation of Bruce as a tyrannical father similar to
Daedalus, and of his repressed, 'monstrous' closeted secret in parallel to the
Minotaur, render the domestic domain a space of the Gothic, in which Alison
is called to survive.[32] In the first chapter of *Fun Home*, then, Bechdel's artistic
choices and intertextual references seem to be driven by the need to depict
her child autobiographical subject's discomfort with the family home and her
father, which is mediated through the use of the Gothic.

Anne Williams explains that the conventions of the Gothic include 'a vulnerable and curious heroine; a wealthy, arbitrary, and enigmatic hero/villain;
and a grand mysterious dwelling concealing the violent, implicitly sexual
secrets of this *homme fatal*.'[33] The Gothic, she proceeds, 'is overdetermined
by structures of the [patriarchal] family,' which re-appear in various components of the genre like 'the architecture of the haunted castle or house, [and]
the experience of horror and terror' (*FH*, 22, 87). In the case of *Fun Home*,
the *homme fatal* is also the tyrannical paterfamilias of the Gothic and the
man distinguished by his double life, which is structured around the secret
of his closeted homosexuality. Nevertheless, it is not homosexuality itself
that haunts the Bechdel family home, but the shame, frustration and rage that
emerge from its repression. As Eve Kosofksy Sedgwick points out, the literary Gothic explores 'perverse secrets of sexuality,' and it operates as a 'locus
for the working-out of some of the terms by which nineteenth- and twentieth-
century European culture has used homophobia to divide and manipulate
the male-homosocial spectrum.'[34] It is also a genre that displays workings
of the Oedipal family, like 'the absolutes of licence and prohibition, . . . , a
fascinated proscription of sexual activity [and] an atmosphere dominated by
the threat of violence between generations.'[35] In this sense, the child autobiographical avatar is trapped not only within her labyrinth-like Gothic Revival
home that hides her father's sexual secrets, but also in a particular type of
femininity which Bruce imposes on her, manifesting the father-to-daughter
inter-generational transmission of queer trauma.

Judith Halberstam writes of the centrality of the monster in the Gothic,
which 'announces itself . . . as the place of corruption' and sexual deviance.[36]
Referring to the duality and the conflict staged within a single person in the
Gothic, Halberstam analyses Oscar Wilde's *The Picture of Dorian Gray*. In
Wilde's book, Dorian's portrait is monstrous because it reveals too much
by becoming 'a record of his life, his desires [and] his corruption, while he

maintains his youth.'[37] *Fun Home* graphically employs these Gothic elements to re-create Bruce's passing, his double life, and its harmful impact on his family. In addition, it re-creates Alison's troubled relationship with her father, and the inter-generational transmission of queer trauma. Bruce becomes Daedalus, his repressed secret is presented as the Minotaur, and the house, like Dorian's painting, tells too much by becoming a screen on which Bruce's 'lies' and feelings are inscribed. Interestingly, Halberstam describes the literary Gothic in relation to the 'ornamental excess' of Gothic architecture, noting that both produce too much through their 'rhetorical extravagance.'[38] In *Fun Home*, the Gothic Revival style of the family home, which Bruce obsessively restores, is meticulously reproduced by Bechdel herself, who also introduces a child protagonist that is trapped in it, being simultaneously terrified of her father's monstrous, inexplicable behaviour. Nevertheless, as the narrative unfolds, Bechdel alters her perspective, distancing herself from her child self's view of Bruce and reconfiguring the meaning of the house.

Halberstam explains that Dorian's hidden self in *The Picture* is, similarly to Bruce's, 'a sexual' and 'decadent self . . . too much preoccupied with art, representation, and beauty, rather than life, experience, the common lot.'[39] During the fin-de-siècle, traits like 'effeminacy, sensuality, love of art, uselessness [and] idle leisured existence,' which previously characterized the 'corruption of aristocracy,' came to 'stereotype homosexual behavior' according to Halberstam.[40] In Wilde's novel, Dorian's corruption is embodied in an artwork. His identity becomes written on the painting, which becomes 'equivalent to narrative.'[41] By the end of the story, Dorian decides to destroy it with a knife. 'As it killed the painter,' the narrator relates, the knife 'would [also] kill the painter's work, and all that it meant. It would kill the past, and when that was dead [Dorian] would be free. It would kill this monstrous soul-life, and, without its hideous warnings, he would be at peace.'[42] Art came to dominate Dorian's life, and by 'murdering' the painting, he hoped to find peace. Eventually, however, the portrait was found intact, capturing his exquisite, youthful beauty, while 'lying on the floor was a dead man, in evening dress, with a knife in his heart. He was withered, wrinkled, and loathsome of visage,' and so the darkness and ugliness of Dorian's life returned to his body.[43]

The Picture illustrates Wilde's views on the superiority of art over nature as these are described in 'The Decay of Lying,' where taking up the persona of Vivian, Wilde explains that art unveils nature's lack of design and ugliness. Art, he explains, 'takes life as part of its rough material, recreates it, and refashions it in fresh forms, [art] is absolutely indifferent to fact, [it] invents, imagines, dreams, and keeps between herself and reality the impenetrable barrier of beautiful style, of decorative or ideal treatment,' making and unmaking worlds, and abiding to no laws.[44] In *The Picture*, the painting is what preserves eternal beauty as Dorian becomes, at the end, a grotesque, old, ugly spectacle. In 'The Decay,' Vivian declares that the 'proper aim of art' is 'the telling of beautiful untrue things.'[45] For Wilde and his contemporaries, the untrue, the artificial, the unnatural and the perverse found a locus for their expression not in nature, but in art and literature.[46] Fin-de-siècle aesthetes invented codes to express 'the love that dared not speak its name' through artistic and literary styles and devices, like, for instance, their use of flowers.[47] Art therefore allowed the articulation of unspeakable desires and identities against medical, scientific and legal discourses that pathologized and criminalized them.[48] It is through this subversive dimension of Wildean art that *Fun Home* shows Bechdel's attempt of *graphic healing*, allowing the reorientation of readers' perspectives on Bruce and the family home. This reorientation helps readers trace how Bechdel revises and ultimately undoes the Gothic dimension of her intimate space, and of her father and his closeted secret.

UNDOING THE GOTHIC: GRAPHIC HEALING THROUGH WILDE'S AESTHETICISM

Readers are guided to form correlations between Bruce and Wilde early in the narrative, when Alison describes him as an 'aesthete,' and mentions that he 'appeared to be an ideal husband and father' who nevertheless secretly 'had sex with teenage boys' (*FH*, 15, 17). In addition, she explains that her father 'liked to imagine himself as a nineteenth century aristocrat,' as Bruce is drawn sitting in his almost excessively decorated library, where he used to secretly seduce some of his young students (*FH*, 60). By referring to her father's appearance as an ideal husband and explaining that underneath this disguise lay his secret, the narrator evokes Wilde's eponymous play. Indeed, the penultimate chapter of *Fun Home* is titled 'The Ideal Husband.' The chapter contains a number of references to Wilde's plays and life in the depiction of the family home, which functions as a spatial life-narrative and an artwork mirroring Bruce's life story. The blurring of the boundary between the fine and the applied arts that allows the interpretation of the domestic space as a work of art was common in the context of the Aesthetic Movement, which developed from the work of architects and designers in the nineteenth century and had Oscar Wilde and William Morris as its most significant representatives.[49] In *Fun Home*, Bruce's beautification of the domestic place and the preservation of its late nineteenth-century Gothic Revival style function as an anachronism that keeps alive, a century later, the core values of the move-ment, which expanded from architectural design to the visual arts and lit-erature, through which Wilde and his contemporaries expressed homosexual desire.

While the inscription of male homosexuality on interior design and home decoration has remained largely unnoticed by critics, Michael Hatt describes 'the Aesthetic interior, the self-conscious creation of a beautiful home' as a means through which 'private (homosexual) desire and public self were integrated.'[50] He further suggests that the aesthete is reflected on the surfaces of his house and this is how the 'dialectic of self and space collapses into intrasubjectivity or narcissism.'[51] The house emerges, therefore, as performa-tive of the aesthete's homosexuality and can be understood as an 'autotopog-raphy,' a spatial autobiographical performance, a metaphorical writing of the self on space. Deirdre Heddon explains that 'the relationship between identity and place is one of mutual construction,' noting that 'autotopography is writ-ing place through self (and simultaneously writing self through place).'[52] For Simon Trezise, 'autotopography' concerns both 'the territory we can touch and see and . . . the mind with which we respond to this territory.'[53] Thus, perceiving space as Bruce's autotopography has to do with a reader's under-standing of Bruce as a Wildean artist and his/her approach to the (domestic) space beyond its utility which can recast it as an aesthetic artwork, and a spatial life narrative. In *Fun Home*, Bechdel's references to Wilde's life and art can guide readers to change their perspective both on Bruce, who was previously depicted as a monstrous paterfamilias, and on the family home that was presented as the domain of the Gothic.

'The Ideal Husband' in *Fun Home* narrates the participation of Alison's mother in a local production of Wilde's *The Importance of Being Earnest*. Its title, however, refers to Bruce, who has to attend a hearing at court after hav-ing been accused of buying beer for a minor, the seventeen-year-old Mark, with whom he was also sexually involved (*FH*, 161). Although the narrator only speculates about Bruce's relationship with Mark and his brother, Dave, she notes that in the end, like 'Oscar Wilde who was condemned by the testimony of his rough trade,' her father too was exposed by the two broth-ers he knew (*FH*, 175). Similar references to Wilde's life and plays appear in the diegetic realm of the Bechdel family story to enrich it. For instance, the narrator explains that as a child during her mother's rehearsals, she took *The Importance* 'at face value' and her enjoyment remained 'unencumbered by Wilde's martyrology' (*FH*, 165). Going back to it as an adult, she knows that 'right after *The Importance* opened . . . Wilde's trials begun' (*FH*, 166). She is aware of Wilde's relationship with Alfred Douglas and their trip to Algiers, where they 'had been disporting themselves with the local boys.'[54]

She also knows of the accusation of sodomy that Douglas's father directed against Wilde, of the trials and of Wilde's imprisonment for 'indecent acts' (*FH*, 166). After relating this information, Alison explains that in *The Importance*, 'illicit desire is encoded as a character's uncontrollable gluttony.' Immediately after this, Bechdel offers readers visual access to her family home, where Bruce is drawn devouring cucumber sandwiches (*FH*, 166). In this way, she guides readers to interpret Bruce's behaviour, as depicted in the particular panel of *Fun Home*, similarly to how they would interpret gluttony in *The Importance*—that is, as a metaphorical mediation of his 'illicit desire.'

It is precisely through these traces of the past in the diegetic present that 'queer temporalities' are formulated, allowing readers to reinterpret Bruce and the family home beyond the monstrous and the Gothic. According to Carolyn Dinshaw, 'queer temporalities' refer to 'the possibility of touching across time, [and] collapsing time through affective contact between marginalized people now and then.'[55] Dinshaw suggests that 'with such queer historical touches we could form communities across time.'[56] This 'refusal of linear historicism,' she suggests, has the potential to free us 'to think further about multiple temporalities in the present.'[57] Sam McBean explains that the moments in which the past 'touches' the present in ways that expand it carry both an erotic and an affective element.[58] *Fun Home* performs this touch of the past on the present through Bechdel's references to Wilde's life and art in Bruce's life story, which guide readers to decipher further layers of meaning within the mise-en-scène trauma narrative. Through this conflation, Bechdel also situates her work in the male homosexual literary and artistic canonical tradition to foreground the healing possibilities emerging from her engagement with Wilde—her literary (fore)father. It is through this engagement that she can reinterpret her biological father, Bruce, who shares with Wilde a common love for art(ifice) that poses itself against nature. The queer touch of the past on the diegetic present of *Fun Home* is located in Bruce's love for art(ificial) beauty, in the anachronistic Gothic Revival style of the family home (which is among the most representative styles of the Aesthetic Movement), and in traces from Wilde's plays and life in Bruce's story. These elements help readers identify the artistic, rhetorical function of the family home in relation to Bruce's secret.

Commenting upon the outcome of the hearing, during which 'the real accusation dared not speak its name,' Alison mentions a significant difference between Wilde and her father, despite the similarities of their stories. Bruce 'did not provoke a burst of applause in the courtroom, as [the former] had, with an impassioned plea for the understanding of "such a great affection of an elder man for a younger man as there was between David and Jonathan",' she explains.[59] In this sense, Bruce becomes an anti-hero. His artistic work remained unknown during his lifetime. His own martyrology and trauma of passing as a heterosexual husband and father were never acknowledged. His life was marked by shame, which was transmitted to the rest of his family. Indeed, Bechdel herself explains that when she found the police report with Mark's testimony she 'felt triumphant as a writer [and a] researcher' but 'embarrassed as [a] daughter.'[60] In addition, she describes *Fun Home* as 'a huge violation of [her] family,' when called to comment on her mother's response to it.[61] It seems then, that like Bruce and Daedalus, Bechdel too had to become disinterested in the human cost of her project, which functions as a homage to her father by acknowledging his martyrology and art. As she reinterprets *The Importance* in adulthood, she also reinterprets the Gothic Revival family home and her father, moving from being possessed by the past as a child, to possessing it as a wiser adult cartoonist. In order to foreground her reconfiguration of the family home into Bruce's Wildean 'autotopography,' Bechdel incorporates in her graphic memoir the narration of a storm and the damage it left behind.

Among other things that interrupt and delay the story of Bruce's legal entanglements, the narrator refers to a storm that damaged their garden. While this may be perceived as an interval that merely prolongs narrative development, I interpret it as purposefully positioned in the text since it foregrounds the function of domestic space as a Wildean artwork that reflects Bruce's life story. In parallel to the surfacing of his secret through the court hearing, and her references to Wilde's trials and plays, Alison mentions that the storm caused the trees that had sheltered the house for two centuries to fall down (*FH*, 178). In this context, Bechdel seems to have turned to the language of horticulture and to flower imagery that were also used by Wilde and his contemporaries for the expression of male homosexual desire, to reconfigure the house beyond its utility as the family's dwelling place. Wilde himself famously had a green carnation attached to his buttonhole as a symbol for his homosexuality, and in *Fun Home*, Bechdel's meticulous reproduction of Bruce's obsession with real and artificial flowers, inside and outside the house, is quite noticeable. Moreover, Bechdel chooses to structure the harm inflicted on Bruce and his family through the revelation of his secret during his hearing in parallel to the damage the storm caused to their garden, thus mirroring Bruce's ordeals in the domestic space.

The narrator explains that the storm only harmed their garden, leaving the rest of the neighbourhood and their house untouched, indicating 'a narrow escape' from destruction, which she connects to another 'narrow escape [that] was yet to happen' (*FH*, 180). With the latter, Alison refers to the magistrate's

Figure 9.2. From *Fun Home: A Family Tragicomic* by Alison Bechdel. Copyright ©
2006 by Alison Bechdel. Reprinted by permission of Houghton Mifflin Company. All
rights reserved.

decision to drop charges against Bruce on the condition that he would 'complete six months of counselling,' a decision that led to Bruce and his family's
escape from the harmful impact the exposure of his desire for adolescent boys
would have on them (*FH*, 180). The function of the house as a spatial embodiment of Bruce's identity changes after Alison's coming out, when she found
out, through her mother, about his past. Upon her return home after she had
learned about her father, Alison finds her home uncanny with 'some crucial
part of the structure . . . missing, like in dreams [she] would have later when
termites had eaten through all the floor joists' (*FH*, 216). While the domestic
space was previously dominant in the visual register (see figure 9.2), after the
revelation of Bruce's secret, the narrative perspective shifts and focuses on
the actual people residing in the house (see figure 9.3).[62]

Figure 9.3. From *Fun Home: A Family Tragicomic* by Alison Bechdel. Copyright © 2006 by Alison Bechdel. Reprinted by permission of Houghton Mifflin Company. All rights reserved.

The autobiographical avatar returns home again after her father's death with her girlfriend Joan. During her stay there, she is depicted with her mother, Helen, and Joan in the library, where Bruce used to secretly seduce his male students. In her reading of the scene, Janine Utell observes that, unlike Bruce's secret desires, 'Joan and Alison's erotic intimacy is . . . made visible in the family home.'[63] In addition to her same-sex desire, Alison's female masculinity is also visible and inscribed on her body. As the three women are sitting in the library, Helen gives Joan a book of poetry by Wallace Stevens. The narrator explains that 'over the years, [her] mother [had] given away or sold most of [Bruce's] library [beginning] immediately after the funeral, [by] bestowing a book on Joan' (*FH*, 82).[64] Consequently, Helen initiates the ending of the family home's rhetoric in revealing Bruce's secret to Alison. She is also the one who puts an end to the function of the house as a performance of his homosexuality. By giving away Bruce's books, by selling the library, and ultimately the house itself, Helen also eliminates its significance as an anachronistic Wildean artwork. As such, she begins what can be read as a healing process that would aid her recovery from the past by unburdening herself from the strain that Bruce's homosexuality had inflicted on her. In this respect, Helen acts similarly to Dorian in *The Picture*, when he decides to destroy his painting in order to find peace.

Bechdel, however, preserves the queer rhetoric of space in *Fun Home*, and after Bruce's death, she shifts her attention away from the family home to his grave—his post-mortem dwelling place. The narrator notes that 'his headstone was an obelisk, a striking anachronism among the ungainly granite slabs in the new end of the cemetery' (*FH*, 29). Like the family home, the

Figure 9.4. From *Fun Home: A Family Tragicomic* by Alison Bechdel. Copyright © 2006 by Alison Bechdel. Reprinted by permission of Houghton Mifflin Company. All rights reserved.

tombstone is also distinguished through its anachronistic Gothic Revival style, and the narrator implies that her father's homosexuality was demarcated through it, as the obelisk also has 'a shape that in life [Bruce] was unabashedly fixated on' (*FH*, 29).[65] If we are to consider the space occupied in the graveyard as a post-mortem embodiment of Bruce's aestheticism and same-sex desire, then the arrangement of objects there, like in the Bechdel family home, is of utmost importance. Interestingly, when Alison visits her father's grave years after his death, she finds it 'desecrated with a cheesy flag, placed there by some well-meaning armed services organization' (*FH*, 53). As she throws the flag away, the narrator's caption informs readers that 'there was some fleeting consolation in the sheer violence of [her] gesture,' similar to the one she had felt years before at her father's funeral, when she violently shook the funeral director's hand off her arm, on which he had placed it in an act of consolation (*FH*, 53).

In the second chapter, titled 'A Happy Death,' the final panel shows a distanced perspective of the graveyard with Alison lying on her father's grave after having thrown the flag away, restoring it to its ideal state. Similarly to the previous graveyard panels, this one also underscores the uniqueness of Bruce's tomb. The narrator's captions offer readers access to Alison's attempt to come to terms with her father's loss: 'My father really was down there, I told myself. Stuck in the mud for good this time' (*FH*, 54). That her autobiographical avatar is drawn lying on Bruce's tomb functions as a means through which she can metaphorically 'touch' her father through space. In contrast to his life, which he led as a Wildean aesthete and a distant father obsessed with art(ificial) beauty, with his death, Bruce is forced to return to mud and, like Dorian, he becomes trapped in nature's lack of design. Never-

Figure 9.5.   From *Fun Home: A Family Tragicomic* by Alison Bechdel. Copyright © 2006 by Alison Bechdel. Reprinted by permission of Houghton Mifflin Company. All rights reserved.

theless, his grave, his post-mortem anachronistic, Wildean artwork, preserves in *Fun Home*, like Dorian's picture, the (un)truth of Bruce's life for those who can decipher it.

Dana Luciano discusses the lipstick marks left by admirers on Wilde's grave in France, a 'monument that speaks at once, of the affirmation and the repression of queer energies.'[66] While Wilde's biological descendants are annoyed by these marks, Luciano reads them as 'meant not to deface the memorial but to activate memory' manifesting what Dinshaw describes as 'the touch of time' and presenting an alternative form of contact with the past.[67] Space, then, becomes an intermediary entity between admirers and the lost object that is Wilde. In *Fun Home*, Bechdel's attentive reproduction of the spaces that Bruce inhabited, before and after his death, indicates that they have the same function for the father/daughter pair. The Gothic Revival family home, in which Alison spent her childhood years, feeling trapped by its 'artificiality' and exaggerated ornamentation, transforms into Bruce's 'autotopography,' as does his anachronistic grave. The centrality of the family home in the graphic memoir is also noted by Chute, who mentions that the book's first edition 'is configured like a home, with the exterior drawn' on its covers and the William Morris chrysanthemum wallpaper pattern that decorated the walls of the Bechdel family home 'on the inside as endpapers.'[68]

CODA

In her analysis of *Fun Home*, Chute writes that 'the act of drawing' bodies 'as Bechdel does proposes both drawing and vision itself as a kind of touching the past. Comics,' she notes, 'is above all a haptic form [that demands] tactility.'[69] For Bechdel, comics function as the means through which 'to touch the subjects on which her work focuses and insert herself in their past.'[70] It is precisely through this ability to 'touch' Bruce, not only via the tactility of the comics medium, but also by preserving the details of his spatial, Wildean artworks, that *Fun Home* performs Bechdel's attempt of healing and her act of homage to her father. Through her use of comics and by infusing the medium with intertextual references to Wilde's art and life, Bechdel demonstrates the potential the genre offers in relation to the representation of queer lives, spaces and temporalities, and of the working through of inter-generationally transmitted queer trauma. The violence of compulsory heterosexuality, which injured the father/daughter pair and was initially mediated via the use of the Gothic and the monstrous, becomes undone through Bechdel's wiser adult perspective on her father and what she presents as his spatial Wildean artworks. Her performance of 'the queer touch of time' allows her to work through trauma and loss, and to positively reconfigure those same spaces and attitudes that alienated the young autobiographical avatar from her father, performing her attempt of *graphic healing*.

NOTES

1. For some of the scholarly investigations of the representation of queer trauma in *Fun Home*, see Jennifer Lemberg, 'Closing the Gap in Alison Bechdel's Fun Home,' *WSQ: Women's Studies Quarterly* 36.1–2 (2008): 129–40; Hillary L. Chute, *Graphic Women: Life Narrative and Contemporary Comics* (New York: Columbia University Press, 2010), 175–217; Hélène Tison, 'Loss, Revision, Translation: Re-Membering the Father's Fragmented Self in Alison Bechdel's Graphic Memoir *Fun Home: A Family Tragicomic*,' *Studies in the Novel* 47.3 (2015): 346–64.

2. The narrator in *Fun Home* explains that during her family's trip to Europe when she was a child, she 'cemented the unspoken compact with [her parents] that [she]

would never get married [and] that [she] would carry on to live the artist's life they had each abdicated' in order to get married and have a family. Alison Bechdel, *Fun Home: A Family Tragicomic* (London: Jonathan Cape, 2006), 73. Hereafter abbreviated as *FH*, with page number in the text. In the graphic memoir there are references to her mother's artistic interests, for instance, in acting. In this essay I am focusing on Bechdel's negotiation of Bruce's artistic tendencies, which are not as explicitly mentioned, apart from the description of his obsessive preoccupation with house restoration and his reading of literature and books about art.

3. See Chute, *Graphic Women*, 13–27.

4. For an analysis of inter-generationally transmitted trauma in *Maus*, see Marianne Hirsch, 'Mourning and Postmemory,' in *Graphic Subjects: Critical Essays on Autobiography and Graphic Novels*, ed. Michael Chaney (Madison: University of Wisconsin Press, 2011), 17–44.

5. Hillary L. Chute, 'Comics Form and Narrating Lives,' *Profession* 11 (2011): 108.

6. Chute, *Graphic Women*, 3.

7. Scott McCloud describes the reader's move from panel to panel by filling in the gaps as a process whereby closure is provided. Elisabeth El Refaie also notes that the 'gappiness' of comics requires reader participation in meaning formation. See Scott McCloud, *Understanding Comics* (New York: HarperCollins, 1994), 67; and Elisabeth El Refaie, *Autobiographical Comics: Life Writing in Pictures* (Jackson: University Press of Mississippi, 2012), 183.

8. The term 'autobiographical avatar' refers to the visually structured self in graphic memoirs. See Sidonie Smith and Julia Watson, *Reading Autobiography: A Guide for Interpreting Life Narratives* (Minneapolis: University of Minnesota Press, 2010), 169.

9. Chute, 'Comics Form and Narrating Lives,' 108.

10. Shoshana Felman and Dori Laub, *Testimony: Crises of Witnessing in Literature, Psychoanalysis, and History* (New York: Routledge, 1992), 9.

11. Marilyn Chandler McEntyre, *A Healing Art: Regeneration through Autobiography* (Abingdon: Routledge, 2016), x.

12. McEntyre, *A Healing Art*, 5.

13. See Suzette A. Henke, *Shattered Subjects: Trauma and Testimony in Women's Life Writing* (New York: St. Martin's Press, 2000), xviii–xix.

14. Charles M. Anderson and Marian M. MacCurdy, eds., 'Introduction,' in *Writing and Healing: Towards an Informed Practice* (Urbana, IL: National Council of Teachers, 2000), 7.

15. McEntyre, *A Healing Art*, ix.

16. Helen M. Buss, *Repossessing the World: Reading Memoirs by Contemporary Women* (Toronto: Wilfrid Laurier University Press, 2002), 140.

17. Buss, *Repossessing the World*, 139.

18. My previous work concerns the reparative uses of intertextuality in relation to childhood (sexual) trauma in Phoebe Gloeckner's and Lynda Barry's graphic memoirs. For some examples, see Olga Michael, 'Excavating Childhood: Fairy Tales, Monsters and Abuse Survival in Lynda Barry's *What It Is*,' *a/b: Auto/biography Stud-

ies 32.3 (2017): 541–66; Olga Michael, 'Graphic Autofiction and the Visualization of Trauma in Lynda Barry and Phoebe Gloeckner's Graphic Memoirs,' in *Autofiction in English*, ed. Hywel Dix (Basingstoke: Palgrave Macmillan, 2018), 105–25; and Olga Michael, 'The Other Narratives of Sexual Abuse in Phoebe Gloeckner's *A Child's Life and Other Stories*,' *Journal of Graphic Novels and Comics* 9.3 (2018): 229–50.

19. Laura S. Brown, 'Sexuality, Lies, and Loss,' *Journal of Trauma Practice* 2.2 (2003): 66.

20. For Butler's elaboration on this, see Judith Butler, *Undoing Gender* (London: Routledge, 2004), 17–19.

21. Gust A. Yep, 'The Violence of Heteronormativity in Communication Studies,' *Journal of Homosexuality* 45.2–4 (2003): 18.

22. Yep, 'The Violence of Heteronormativity in Communication Studies,' 18–26.

23. Brown, 'Sexuality, Lies, and Loss,' 63.

24. This is suggested by Alison in *Fun Home*, particularly when she describes her father's passion for the restoration of the house as 'libidinal [,] manic [and] martyred.' See *FH*, 7.

25. For an analysis of female masculinity, see Judith Halberstam, *Female Masculinity* (London: Duke University Press, 1998), 1–44.

26. Ann Cvetkovich, 'Drawing the Archive in Alison Bechdel's *Fun Home*,' *WSQ: Women's Studies Quarterly* 36.1–2 (2008): 125, 126.

27. See Hillary L. Chute, 'An Interview with Alison Bechdel,' *Modern Fiction Studies* 54.4 (2006): 1005.

28. Jared Gardner notes that this 'archival turn' has been a prevailing tendency in contemporary graphic memoirs. See Jared Gardner, 'Archives, Collectors, and the New Media Work of Comics,' *Modern Fiction Studies* 52 (2006): 788.

29. Valerie Rohy, 'In the Queer Archive: *Fun Home*,' *GLQ: Journal of Lesbian and Gay Studies* 16.3 (2010): 347.

30. Rohy, 'In the Queer Archive,' 348.

31. Critics have discussed the role of the family home as a screen that veils Bruce's homosexuality through its association with heteronormative family life. See Hélène Tison, 'Drag as Metaphor and the Quest for Meaning in Alison Bechdel's *Fun Home: A Family Tragicomic*,' *GRAAT* 1 (2007): 26–39; Ariela Freedman, 'Drawing on Modernism in Alison Bechdel's *Fun Home*,' *Journal of Modern Literature* 32.4 (2009): 131; and Robin Lydenberg, 'Under Construction Alison Bechdel's *Fun Home: A Family Tragicomic*,' *European Journal of English Studies* 16.1 (2012): 61.

32. Bechdel's descriptions of playing in the funeral home run by her father that was next to their home, her references to bats entering her home, and the parallelism of her family with the Addams Family accentuate the Gothic attribute of her domestic life and space. In fact, the narrator explains that in a photograph depicting her in 'a black velvet dress [her] father had wrestled [her] into, [she] appear[s] to be in mourning,' but also, identical to Wednesday Addams. See *FH*, 34–5.

33. Anne Williams, *Art of Darkness: The Poetics of Gothic* (Chicago: University of Chicago Press, 1995), 38.

34. Eve Kosofsky Sedgwick, *Between Men: English Literature and Male Homosocial Desire* (New York: Columbia University Press, 1985), 90.

35. Sedgwick, *Between Men*, 91.

36. Judith Halberstam, *Skin Shows: Gothic Horror and the Technology of Monsters* (Durham, NC: Duke University Press, 1995), 54, 56.

37. Halberstam, *Skin Shows*, 57.

38. Halberstam, *Skin Shows*, 54.

39. Halberstam, *Skin Shows*, 66.

40. Halberstam, *Skin Shows*, 66.

41. Halberstam, *Skin Shows*, 74.

42. Oscar Wilde, *The Picture of Dorian Gray* (Oxford: Oxford University Press, 2006), 187.

43. Wilde, *The Picture of Dorian Gray*, 188.

44. Oscar Wilde, *Intentions* (New York: Brentano's, 1905), 3.

45. Wilde, *Intentions*, 22.

46. For discussions on the expression of homosexuality through art and literature during the fin-de-siècle, see Ed Cohen, 'Writing Gone Wilde: Homoerotic Desire in the Closet of Representation,' in *Critical Essays on Oscar Wilde*, ed. Reginia Gagnier (New York: Macmillan, 1991): 68–87; and Reginia Gagnier, 'Sexuality, the Public, and the Art World,' in *Critical Essays on Oscar Wilde*, 23–67.

47. For elaborations on this, see Eve Kosofsky Sedgwick, *Epistemology of the Closet* (London: Harvester Wheatsheaf, 1990), 4; and Alison Syme, *A Touch of Blossom: John Sargent and the Queen Flora of Fin-de-Siècle Art* (University Park: Pennsylvania State University Press, 2010), 4–12.

48. For an analysis of the medicalization and criminalization of the homosexual, see Michel Foucault, *The Will to Knowledge*, Vol. 1, *The History of Sexuality*, trans. Robert Hurley (London: Penguin, 1998), 17–43.

49. Elisabeth Aslin, *The Aesthetic Movement: A Prelude to Art Nouveau* (London: Elek, 1969), 13.

50. Michael Hatt, 'Space, Surface, Self: Homosexuality and the Aesthetic Interior,' *Visual Culture in Britain* 8.1 (2007): 105.

51. Hatt, 'Space, Surface, Self,' 117.

52. Deirdre Heddon, *Autobiography and Performance* (Basingstoke: Palgrave MacMillan, 2008), 90.

53. Simon Trezise, *The West Country as a Literary Invention: Putting Fiction in Its Place* (Exeter: University of Exeter Press, 2000), 13.

54. Trezise, *The West Country as a Literary Invention*, 13.

55. Carolyn Dinshaw et al., 'Theorizing Queer Temporalities: A Roundtable Discussion,' *GLQ: Journal of Gay and Lesbian Studies* 13.2–3 (2007): 178.

56. Dinshaw et al., 'Theorizing Queer Temporalities,' 178.

57. Dinshaw et al., 'Theorizing Queer Temporalities,' 178.

58. Sam McBean, *Feminism's Queer Temporalities* (London: Routledge, 2016), 12. Elizabeth Freeman also discusses 'the bonds of love, not only attachments in the here and now but also those forged across both spatial and temporal barriers' through 'queer temporalities.' See Elizabeth Freeman, 'Time Binds, Or, Erotohistoriography,' *Social Text* 23.3–4 (2005): 61.

59. McBean, *Feminism's Queer Temporalities*, 180.

60. Chute, 'An Interview with Alison Bechdel,' 1006.
61. Chute, 'An Interview with Alison Bechdel,' 1009.
62. For the alterations in narrative perspective, see *FH*, 177–79, 216.
63. Janine Utell, 'Intimacies in Alison Bechdel's *Fun Home*: The Case of Joan,' *The Comics Grid* (2011): np.
64. In Alison Bechdel's second graphic memoir, *Are You My Mother? A Comic Drama*, which focuses on her problematic relationship with her mother during her adulthood, Bruce and the family home are not mentioned, apart from a passing reference to the fact that her mother sold the house seven years after Bruce's death. See Alison Bechdel, *Are You My Mother? A Comic Drama* (London: Jonathan Cape, 2012), 236.
65. For discussions on the popularity of the obelisk during the fin-de-siècle as part of the Gothic Revival Trend of the Aesthetic Movement in commemorative arts, see Richard V. Francaviglia, 'The Cemetery as an Evolving Cultural Landscape,' *Annals of the Association of American Geographers* 61.3 (2005): 501; and Peggy McDowell and Richard Meyer, *The Revival Styles in American Memorial Art* (Bowling Green, OH: Bowling Green State University Popular Press, 1994), 134–44.
66. Dana Luciano, 'Nostalgia for an Age Yet to Come: Velvet Goldmine's Queer Archive,' in *Queer Times, Queer Becomings*, eds. Ellen L. McCallum and Mikko Tuhkanen (Albany: State University of New York Press, 2011), 121.
67. Luciano, 'Nostalgia for an Age Yet to Come,' 122–23.
68. Chute, 'An Interview with Alison Bechdel,' 1008.
69. Chute, 'Comics Form and Narrating Lives,' 112.
70. Chute, 'Comics Form and Narrating Lives,' 113.

BIBLIOGRAPHY

ANDERSON, Charles M. and Marian M. MacCurdy, editors. 'Introduction.' In *Writing and Healing: Towards an Informed Practice*, 1–22. Urbana, IL: National Council of Teachers, 2000.
ASLIN, Elizabeth. *The Aesthetic Movement: A Prelude to Art Nouveau*. London: Elek, 1969.
BECHDEL, Alison. *Are You My Mother? A Comic Drama*. London: Jonathan Cape, 2012.
BECHDEL, Alison. *Fun Home: A Family Tragicomic*. London: Jonathan Cape, 2006.
BROWN, Laura S. 'Sexuality, Lies, and Loss.' *Journal of Trauma Practice* 2.2 (2003): 55–68.
BUSS, Helen M. *Repossessing the World: Reading Memoirs by Contemporary Women*. Toronto: Wilfrid Laurier University Press, 2002.
BUTLER, Judith. *Undoing Gender*. London: Routledge, 2004.
CHUTE, Hillary L. 'An Interview with Alison Bechdel.' *Modern Fiction Studies* 54.4 (2006): 1004–13.
CHUTE, Hillary L. 'Comics Form and Narrating Lives.' *Profession* 11 (2011): 107–17.

CHUTE, Hillary L. *Graphic Women: Life Narrative and Contemporary Comics.* New York: Columbia University Press, 2010.

COHEN, Ed. 'Writing Gone Wilde: Homoerotic Desire in the Closet of Representation.' In *Critical Essays on Oscar Wilde.* Edited by Regenia Gagnier. 68–87. New York: Macmillan, 1991.

CVETKOVICH, Ann. 'Drawing the Archive in Alison Bechdel's *Fun Home.*' *WSQ: Women's Studies Quarterly* 36.1–2 (2008): 111–28.

DINSHAW, Carolyn, Roderick A. Ferguson, Carla Freccero, Elizabeth Freeman, Judith Halberstam, Annamarie Jagose, Christopher Nealon and Nguyen Tan Hoang. 'Theorizing Queer Temporalities: A Roundtable Discussion.' *GLQ: Journal of Gay and Lesbian Studies* 13.2–3 (2007): 177–95.

EL REFAIE, Elisabeth. *Autobiographical Comics: Life Writing in Pictures.* Jackson: University Press of Mississippi, 2012.

FELMAN, Shoshana and Dori Laub. *Testimony: Crises of Witnessing in Literature, Psychoanalysis, and History.* New York: Routledge, 1992.

FOUCAULT, Michel. *The Will to Knowledge.* Volume 1. *The History of Sexuality.* Translated by Robert Hurley. London: Penguin, 1998.

FRANCAVIGLIA, V. Richard. 'The Cemetery as an Evolving Cultural Landscape.' *Annals of the Association of American Geographers* 61.3 (2005): 50–59.

FREEDMAN, Ariela. 'Drawing on Modernism in Alison Bechdel's *Fun Home.*' *Journal of Modern Literature* 32.4 (2009): 125–40.

FREEMAN, Elizabeth. 'Time Binds, Or, Erotohistoriography.' *Social Text* 23.3–4 (2005): 57–68.

GAGNIER, Regenia. 'Sexuality, the Public, and the Art World.' In *Critical Essays on Oscar Wilde.* Edited by Regenia Gagnier. 23–67. New York: Macmillan, 1991.

GARDNER, Jared. 'Archives, Collectors, and the New Media Work of Comics.' *Modern Fiction Studies* 52 (2006): 787–806.

HALBERSTAM, Judith. *Female Masculinity.* London: Duke University Press, 1998.

HALBERSTAM, Judith. *Skin Shows: Gothic Horror and the Technology of Monsters.* Durham, NC: Duke University Press, 1995.

HATT, Michael. 'Space, Surface, Self: Homosexuality and the Aesthetic Interior.' *Visual Culture in Britain* 8.1 (2007): 105–30.

HEDDON, Deirdre. *Autobiography and Performance.* Basingstoke: Palgrave MacMillan, 2008.

HENKE, Suzette A. *Shattered Subjects: Trauma and Testimony in Women's Life Writing.* New York: St. Martin's Press, 2000.

HIRSCH, Marianne. 'Mourning and Postmemory.' In *Graphic Subjects: Critical Essays on Autobiography and Graphic Novels.* Edited by Michael Chaney. 17–44. Madison: University of Wisconsin Press, 2011.

LEMBERG, Jennifer. 'Closing the Gap in Alison Bechdel's *Fun Home.*' *WSQ: Women's Studies Quarterly* 36.1–2 (2008): 129–40.

LUCIANO, Dana. 'Nostalgia for an Age Yet to Come: Velvet Goldmine's Queer Archive.' In *Queer Times, Queer Becomings.* Edited by Ellen L. McCallum and Mikko Tuhkanen. 121–55. Albany: State University of New York Press, 2011.

LYDENBERG, Robin. 'Under Construction Alison Bechdel's *Fun Home: A Family Tragicomic.' European Journal of English Studies* 16.1 (2012): 57–68.

MCBEAN, Sam. *Feminism's Queer Temporalities*. London: Routledge, 2016.

MCCLOUD, Scott. *Understanding Comics*. New York: HarperCollins, 1994.

MCDOWELL, Peggy and Richard Meyer. *The Revival Styles in American Memorial Art*. Bowling Green, OH: Bowling Green State University Popular Press, 1994.

MCENTYRE, Marilyn Chandler. *A Healing Art: Regeneration through Autobiography*. Abingdon: Routledge, 2016.

MICHAEL, Olga. 'Excavating Childhood: Fairy Tales, Monsters and Abuse Survival in Lynda Barry's *What It Is.' a/b: Auto/biography Studies* 32.3 (2017): 541–66.

MICHAEL, Olga. 'Graphic Autofiction and the Visualization of Trauma in Lynda Barry and Phoebe Gloeckner's Graphic Memoirs.' In *Autofiction in English*. Edited by Hywel Dix. 105–25. Basingstoke: Palgrave Macmillan, 2018.

MICHAEL, Olga. 'The Other Narratives of Sexual Abuse in Phoebe Gloeckner's *A Child's Life and Other Stories.' Journal of Graphic Novels and Comics* 9.3 (2018): 229–50.

ROHY, Valerie. 'In the Queer Archive: *Fun Home.' GLQ: Journal of Lesbian and Gay Studies* 16.3 (2010): 340–61.

SEDGWICK, Eve Kosofsky. *Between Men: English Literature and Male Homosocial Desire*. New York: Columbia University Press, 1985.

SEDGWICK, Eve Kosofsky. *Epistemology of the Closet*. London: Harvester Wheatsheaf, 1990.

SMITH, Sidonie and Julia Watson. *Reading Autobiography: A Guide for Interpreting Life Narratives*. Minneapolis: University of Minnesota Press, 2010.

SYME, Alison. *A Touch of Blossom: John Sargent and the Queen Flora of Fin-de-Siècle Art*. University Park: Pennsylvania State University Press, 2010.

TISON, Hélène. 'Drag as Metaphor and the Quest for Meaning in Alison Bechdel's *Fun Home: A Family Tragicomic.' GRAAT* 1 (2007): 26–39.

TISON, Hélène. 'Loss, Revision, Translation: Re-Membering the Father's Fragmented Self in Alison Bechdel's Graphic Memoir *Fun Home: A Family Tragicomic.' Studies in the Novel* 47. 3 (2015): 346–64.

TREZISE, Simon. *The West Country as a Literary Invention: Putting Fiction in Its Place*. Exeter: University of Exeter Press, 2000.

UTELL, Janine. 'Intimacies in Alison Bechdel's *Fun Home*: The Case of Joan.' *The Comics Grid* (2011): np.

WILDE, Oscar. *Intentions*. New York: Brentano's, 1905.

WILDE, Oscar. *The Picture of Dorian Gray*. Oxford: Oxford University Press, 2006.

WILLIAMS, Anne. *Art of Darkness: The Poetics of Gothic*. Chicago: University of Chicago Press, 1995.

YEP, Gust A. 'The Violence of Heteronormativity in Communication Studies.' *Journal of Homosexuality* 45.2–4 (2003): 11–59.

Chapter Ten

Concrete Loss

Attesting to Trauma in Teresa Margolles's Karla, Hilario Reyes Gallegos

Nicholas Chare

CONCRETE ART

Teresa Margolles's 2016 installation artwork *Karla, Hilario Reyes Gallegos*, on display at the Hirschhorn Gallery in Washington, DC, at the time of writing, relates to the life and death of a sixty-four-year-old trans* woman, Karla.[1] Karla, a sex worker in Ciudad Juárez, was murdered in December 2015. The installation includes an audio-track in Spanish and English (in which another trans* sex worker, Ivon, describes the circumstances of the murder), an eight-foot-high black and white inkjet print of a photograph of Karla, a copy of the death certificate for Hilario Reyes Gallegos (Karla's given name), and a piece of reinforced concrete from the scene of the crime. The photograph shows Karla, who is wearing a white strapless dress, posing for the camera. Behind her in the middle-distance is a mound of rubble and some piping, a construction site.[2] In the background there are numerous buildings; this is a residential area. Karla lifts the hem of the dress slightly so as to better reveal her open-toe shoes. The photograph was taken by Margolles in July 2015. It was conceived as one of the *Pistas de baile* series, a succession of photographs of trans* sex workers standing in the remains of demolished nightclubs. Karla's shoes are those she would have worn when dancing. The buildings that are visible behind Karla also appear in several other images from the series including *Pista de baile del club 'Irma's'* and *Pista de baile del club 'Mona Lisa.'* Karla had also been slated to appear in a work Margolles was planning for Manifesta 11 in 2016. She was, however, murdered on 22 December 2015, beaten to death by a client in an abandoned building. The lump of concrete in the installation was found there. Painted white in parts with a metal bar embedded in it to act as reinforcement, it functions as a visual synecdoche for the crime scene. The chunk is reported to bear traces of blood.[3]

211

Crime scenes and the victims of crime often form the focus of Margolles's art. She also explored the theme of crime as part of the artist's collective SE-MEFO, named after the Servicio Médico Forense (Forensic Medical Service) of Mexico City. One of SEMEFO's works, a 1998 installation titled *Memoria Fosilizada* (Fossilized Memory), was a shallow concrete block within which were encased the possessions of murder victims.[4] In *The Historian's Craft*, Marc Bloch notes that the geologist [*sic*] who discovers a fossilized ammonite does not capture the living creature.[5] The fossil is not the thing itself. In *Memoria Fosilizada*, comparably, the possessions should not be mistaken for the lives they commemorate. Their relation to the victims is indirect. In addition to indexing the victims, the work also invites reflection on the socio-economic conditions within which the crimes were committed. Michael Bax-andall describes paintings as 'fossils of economic life,' referring to how style in Quattrocento paintings is influenced by financial considerations.[6] It is simi-larly possible to read *Memoria Fosilizada* and *Karla* as preserving a kind of record of a given economic situation, here a broader one, in which economic disparities shape the kinds of lives and deaths that people in Mexico's cities experience. Pascal Beausse has interpreted Margolles's art practice in general as one that 'summons the viewer to a political and metaphysical meditation on death and on the social and economic inequalities surrounding it.'[7] In the context of *Karla*, sex workers of all genders in Mexico suggest their choice of profession is linked to a need for money, influenced by a 'lagging economy and the lack of opportunities for other employment.'[8]

Memoria Fosilizada has been read as removing 'valuable citations of iden-tity' from usage for any judicial purpose.[9] *Karla* also raises questions of iden-tity and its appropriation. Ivon's affect-laden account of Karla's murder con-trasts with the impersonal death certificate, the official record of the death, a legal document that forcibly imposes Karla's given name upon her. In death, she must return to the name and sex assigned her at birth. Karla's lived real-ity here collides with the violent inflexibility of bureaucratic formalities. The document, in its seeming neutrality, its tick-box indifference, travesties the complexity of the life it brings to an administrative close. The inclusion of the facsimile of the death certificate draws attention to the inadequacies of state-sanctioned conceptualizations of gender as they are embedded in such documents. The reference to the state also indirectly signals broader failings at the level of regional and national government institutions, particularly law enforcement, towards trans* sex workers.

In their study of violence against trans* sex workers in Tijuana, Debra Cas-tillo, María Gudelia Rangel Goméz and Armando Rosas Solís describe how violence is more commonplace for trans* workers compared to women work-ers, and that it is perpetrated by both law enforcement and clients.[10] A history of violence and abuse 'has made transgender/transsexual sex workers highly distrustful' about coming forward and seeking help from law enforcement when subject to violence. A study conducted in Ciudad Juárez and Tijuana shows that female sex workers also endure physical and sexual abuse leading to psychological traumas.[11] Their negative experiences echo those of Mexican women subject to violence who have sought help from public institutions including the police.[12] Kathleen Staudt has examined how the police frequently manifest 'disrespect, disregard, complicity, and incompetence' in relation to violent crimes against women.[13]

The way the elements of *Karla* are installed together—with the block of concrete positioned on the gallery floor in front of the nearly life-size photograph of Karla—gives it somewhat the appearance of a shrine.[14] When read in this way, the concrete block comes to resemble a votive offering. In Mexico, votive images, or *ex voto*, are sometimes created to offer gratitude for a miracle. In *Karla*, however, no thanks is being given. The concrete is instead presented as a form of condemnation. This visually uninteresting, bland, cold material is what killed, rather than saved, Karla. This is not to say the concrete was the murder weapon, as some critics have maintained, but rather that for Margolles it is not a neutral material, it embodies contemporary beliefs and values. Concrete has an ancient history, but its usage became broader and more widespread in the industrial era thanks to the invention of modern cement and reinforced concrete. It is a relatively cheap yet durable building material. Many buildings in modern cities feature concrete in their construction. Artworks that employ concrete, either found or expressly fashioned, therefore embrace a material associated with modernity.

As Adrian Forty notes in *Concrete and Culture*, concrete 'is one of the agents through which our experience of modernity is mediated.'[15] It can sometimes be viewed as emancipatory, linked with architectural progress and expanding access to housing, yet is also associated with urban ugliness, the so-called 'concrete nightmares,' Brutalist tower-blocks made in the 1950s and 1960s. It is likely in response to architecture of this kind that Marcel Joray felt the need to mount a defence of concrete and its potential beauty as a building material.[16] Concrete also possesses a dark history. It was used, for example, to construct the crematoria at Birkenau and also the *Führerbunker*. Forty suggests that WW2 acted to reconfigure 'concrete's base associations, aligning it with violence, destruction and death.'[17] Through events such as the Holocaust, concrete became linked with genocide and trauma. The concrete that appears in *Karla*, sourced from an abandoned building in Juarez, is connected with traumas caused by a specifically Mexican experience of modernity, one that is allied to rapid industrialization and the globalization of the economy, particularly at the US-Mexico border.[18]

In the context of *Karla*, the spectator is also encouraged to see concrete as figuring other themes. In crime, for instance, the method of encasing a victim in 'concrete boots' or 'cement shoes' has become mythologized as a form of gangland execution in the United States. The former teamster boss Jimmy Hoffa is reputed to have been murdered by members of the Mafia and buried in concrete at a Detroit construction site. In Mexico, murder victims associated with the country's so called 'drug wars' have been found hidden in concrete-filled barrels. In 2005 in Ciudad Juárez, a murdered child was found inside a plastic container filled with cement (a part constituent of concrete).[19] Concrete is therefore a material associated with violent crimes and with efforts to conceal them. It is also a material celebrated for its hardness and durability.[20] The production of concrete involves a complex process of mixing, moulding and curing, in which malleability gradually gives way to an enduring rigidity, the material assuming 'the status of stone-like consistency.'[21] Concrete is therefore often linked with solidity, conceptualized in its ostensible end-state. In this context, placing the concrete block in combination with the callous death certificate may also be read as figuring something of the inflexibility of contemporary conceptions of gender, an inflexibility which feeds transphobia. The traumas experienced by victims of transphobia can be traced back, at least in part, to a too rigid conceptualization of gender itself. This inflexible conceptualization is also signalled in *Karla* by the death certificate.

Concrete is a signature material for Margolles, one she has employed repeatedly in her individual art practice and as part of the SEMEFO collective. The block in *Karla* therefore links this work with earlier works in the artist's corpus. In addition to *Memoria Fosilizada*, concrete was employed, for example, to make *Banca* (Chair) (2002) and *Mesa y dos bancos* (Table and Two Chairs) (2003). The water which was mixed with the cement used in the manufacture of these items of furniture had previously been utilized in a morgue. It was suffused with residues of the deceased. Furniture is used in living spaces. It frequently carries traces of lives lived, such as scratches and stains. Here furniture is manufactured with the aid of dregs from the dead. The two works have been read as reifying corpses, as making that which is usually thought of in the abstract become concrete.[22] The morgue water was likely used to clean the space. It was a means of removing traces—blood, hair, flakes of skin and other perceived detritus—of the dead from a workspace, a workplace. By saving and using this water, Margolles simultaneously preserves corporeal remainders and indexes a particular place and the attitudes towards the dead that are associated with it. Margolles understands the morgue to be a 'thermometer of society,' indicative of the social climate in a given location and moment.[23] Morgues are transit stations for corpses rather than resting places. Bodies are stored there as they await identification, or in preparation for autopsies or for burial. The space is one designed for temporary preservation. Through incorporating the water in the concrete furniture, Margolles makes this preservation more permanent, yet what she conserves are not corpses but traces of them preserved by way of efforts to remove all vestiges of them. The concrete furniture is therefore a complex meditation on remembering and forgetting.

The furniture sculptures connote earlier minimalist artworks such as Robert Morris's *Hearing* (1972) with its metal furniture, a zinc table, copper chair and lead bed. Art historians and critics such as Edward Bacal, Sydney Hart and Jean-Philippe Uzel recognize that Margolles is in dialogue with minimalism and some of the values the movement is perceived to embody.[24] It is, however, rare for minimalist artists to employ concrete as a medium.[25] Minimalist artworks are sometimes read as providing critiques of capitalism. Drawing on the art writings of Dan Graham, Alistair Rider, for instance, examines how Carl Andre's works can be seen to subvert art market criteria of value linked to notions of quality and to '[turn] the terms of a bourgeois economy against itself.'[26] He also explores how Andre's artworks proffer materials that operate 'outside the realm of commodified exchange values.'[27] According to Rider, 'Andre's sculptures could be said to waver relentlessly between having things in circulation and withdrawing them from circulation, between establishing equivalences and refusing all such substitutions and exchanges.'[28]

For Douglas Crimp, Richard Serra's massive work *Tilted Arc* (1981)— which was installed in Foley Federal Plaza, New York, until its controversial destruction—presented spectators with the truth of their social condition, one governed by egotism.[29] Egotism, self-centred feelings of superiority, is similar to egoism which also involves preoccupation with oneself. As Robert Reiner explains, ethical harms caused by 'cultures of egoism, short-termism [and] *irresponsibility* towards others' arise within materialistic market societies.[30] The culture of egoism leads to a 'me' society.[31] In this context, *Tilted Arc* can be read as providing a critique of Keynesian economic policies and the social outlooks they generate. The work had a strongly political dimension. Both Crimp and Rider tease out ways in which minimalist works register and invite reflection upon the economic conditions of the society in which they were made. This aspect of minimalism may appeal to Margolles, whose works register the miseries caused by the North American Free Trade Agreement (NAFTA) and the economic climate it has created in Mexico, particularly along the border with the United States in cities such as Juarez, a climate of massively unequal distribution of wealth and of cyclical commercial crises.

In his discussion of Serra, as well as exploring the political critique embodied in his sculptures, Crimp feels it necessary to defend the artist's corpus from accusations of being 'macho, overbearing, aggressive [and] oppressive.'[32] Minimalism has been strongly linked with practices of domination and brutality, most notably by Anna Chave, whom Crimp appears to be indirectly responding to. For Chave, minimalism is a violent art movement both in terms of its attacks upon artistic conventions and its forcefulness towards its audiences.[33] Minimalist artists do not critique violence, they perpetrate it. Chave also focuses on the critical reception of the works which involves vocabulary linked to strength and rigour, to hardness. It seems that Margolles is sensitive to this masculinist facet of minimalist idioms and sometimes seeks to subvert it. A case in point is *La promesa* (2012), a work comprised of crushed materials from a demolished house in Ciudad Juárez which was fashioned into a block. The block was then displayed at the Musée d'art contemporain de Montréal for the exhibition *Teresa Margolles: Mundos* (16 February–14 May 2017), where it was scraped at for one hour a day for eleven days during the exhibition, repetitive actions that gradually caused it to disintegrate. On one level, the work can be read as providing commentary on the false economic promise of Juárez, where 100,000 houses created for migrant workers have been abandoned in recent years.[34] Additionally, *La promesa* can be interpreted as demolishing minimalist pretensions, the hard, neat rectangular block gradually losing its shape, its structural integrity, being reduced to a pile of loose rubble spread out across the gallery floor. If, as Chave posits, minimalism does embody a rhetoric of power, a work such as *La promesa* contests that rhetoric. The reduction of *La promesa* to rubble, to waste, also links the work with a major theme for Margolles, that of social abjection.

The debris gestures towards the marginalized, the migrant underclass in Juárez who are forced to give up on their expectations of a better life and confront the harsh realities of precarious employment and inadequate infrastructure. The house used to make *La promesa* was located in an area at the edge of the neighbourhoods of Praderas de Oriente and Tierra Nueva which is surrounded by *maquiladoras*, transnational factories which often involve assembly lines. The *maquiladora* forms an example of what Sergio González Rodrígues describes as 'abject architecture.'[35] He sees it as on a continuum with 'extermination camps, collapsible garrison houses or blockhouses, bunkers, and criminal/political torture chambers,' a structure that, at its extreme, represents 'the femicide machine's antechamber.'[36] The femicide machine, for Rodríguez, 'is composed of hatred and misogynistic violence, *machismo*, power and patriarchal reaffirmations that take place at the margins of the law or within a law of complicity between criminals, police, military, government officials, and citizens who constitute an a-legal old-boy network.'[37] Gendered violence was also noted by Margolles during the making of *Cimbra Frame-*

work (2006). This work involved coating the clothes of victims of femicide and of their families in cement and depositing them in a trough.[38] Two male contractors employed to help realize the work were angered at Margolles's perceived lack of creative input and 'threw the clothes into the cement and then into the trough haphazardly.'[39] This lack of respect towards the artist and also the possessions of the deceased and the bereaved revealed the entrenched patriarchal attitudes towards women, including artists, in Mexico. An absence of respect also extends to the economically disenfranchised, who are often treated like trash.

LOOKING BEYOND THE ABJECT

In the bourgeois imaginary, the poor are frequently perceived as abject, as social detritus.[40] Alicia Schmidt Camacho refers to subaltern Mexican women as dispensable non-citizens, treated as throwaway lives by civil society.[41] As Gregg Horowitz observes, 'garbage is what society ejects in order to keep itself orderly; it is social superfluity incarnate.'[42] The impoverished, when viewed as refuse, come to function as society's constitutive outside. In a depressed economy, the poor and the dead poor become perceived as social flotsam. Sometimes the metaphor of the economically disenfranchised as garbage becomes literalized. The cost of burial means that many bodies in morgues in Mexico are abandoned, left unclaimed by family members. This leads to situations where 'these victims of violent deaths are frequently thrown out with the trash.'[43] Margolles has been seen to be seeking to draw attention to this shocking reality through works such as *Fosa Común* (Communal Grave) (2005). This work involved smashing and then remaking the floor of an exhibition space. The new floor was manufactured using a concrete mix that again incorporated water from a morgue. Visitors therefore walked upon residues of the dead. Beausse reads this work as offering 'a burial ground to those who have been deprived of it.'[44] In the light of this interpretation, it bears remembering that no bodies are interred in *Fosa Común*. It is composed, in part, of a liquid intended to wash away the abject traces of corpses, a liquid that was itself a waste product. The artwork therefore thinks death beyond the corpse.[45]

   Although material sourced from a morgue is used in the production of the work, it is re-appropriated as a means to withhold death as it is condensed in the figure of the corpse. The corpse, Julia Kristeva explains, is the 'utmost of abjection' in modern society:

> In that compelling, raw, insolent thing in the morgue's full sunlight, in that thing that no longer matches and therefore no longer signifies anything, I behold the

breaking down of a world that has erased its borders: fainting away. The corpse, seen without God and outside of science, is the utmost of abjection. It is death infecting life. Abject.[46]

Julia Banwell uses this quotation from Kristeva as part of her discussion of Margolles's art practice, a practice she reads as confronting 'the spectator with the abject.'[47] In *Fosa Común*, however, we are not presented with a body of the kind described by Kristeva, a body which might best be defined as concrete in its brutal directness of being. For Kristeva, 'as in true theater, without makeup or masks, refuse and corpses *show me* what I permanently thrust aside in order to live.'[48] The corpse provides an unmediated encounter with thingness. Margolles's *Fosa Común* is, by contrast, studiously oblique, providing a non-presentation of the dead. The gallery floor—walked upon, talked above—is akin to an unmarked grave, an unremarked grave. It is an artwork which, like so many by Margolles, conceals as much as it reveals.

In 2005 Margolles travelled to Ciudad Juárez and visited several locations where murdered women had been found. She collected earth from these crime scenes which she then used to fashion numerous adobes, or sun-dried bricks. Like concrete, adobes are often used as a building material. Rebecca Scott Bray sees these bricks as forming 'headstones without a grave.'[49] Her reading foregrounds the absence of the bodies of the murdered women from the works. Their presence is figured through association, by way of a place which has been carried into each brick. Bray reads them as seeming 'to stand in for the dead, but lacking names, epitaphs, they are sadder, both more silent and articulate than any other grave space.'[50] Jean-Philippe Uzel sees the bricks as reminiscent of Carl Andre's *Flanders Field* (1978).[51] The latter work, despite some visual similarity, was manufactured from wood. Andre's most famous brick work is *Equivalent VIII* (1966/1969), which is now installed at Tate. The bricks, multiple units combined into a large rectangle, seem self-contained, encouraging reflections that are limited to their use and exchange values. Rosalind Krauss reads the firebricks used by Andre as remaining 'obdurately external, as objects of use rather than vehicles of expression.'[52] Rider identifies the concretist aesthetic as being one that 'celebrated the plain facticity of the object' and rejected the notion of art objects as 'expressions of subjective emotions.'[53] This passionless art—compassionless in its conception of what art should and can be—appears the antithesis of Margolles's art practice. Her adobes, for example, seem meditations on memory and loss rather than calculated musings on the exchange values of material artefacts. If Margolles uses a minimalist vocabulary, clearly she also extends it. Abstract ruminations regarding capitalism of the kind embarked upon by artists such as Andre and Serra are here literally coupled with traces of flesh and blood, with concrete evidence of the detrimental effects of a particular economic system and the violent conditions it generates.

The adobes were exhibited alongside a video on a loop that retraced the journeys—along roads and dirt tracks—which the murdered women would have had to take between work and home, and also a card including information about Juárez and the crimes. Bray explains that 'the juxtaposition of these pieces, of sight and visual motion, of silence, text and wordlessness, provides a minimalist posthumous biography, a writing which is never enough because it is made in the gap of loss.'[54] This sense of an unsaid is crucial for understanding the artwork and, indeed, Margolles's broader project. When viewed cumulatively, Margolles's artworks progressively gesture towards the unsaid and the unseen. Through their opacity, their withholding of ready sense, the artworks reject what Griselda Pollock has referred to as 'the relief of signification,' the balm of symbolization that allays traumatic experiences.[55] Pollock's conception of trauma is indebted to the thinking of Bracha Ettinger. Ettinger's meditations on the nature of trauma occur both in her theoretical writings and through her art practice. Her art and her writings can be understood as operating in a symbiotic relationship.

Ettinger builds on the ideas of Jacques Lacan, particularly those of his later seminars. For Lacan, trauma is associated with the Real, with the register of psychic reality linked with maternal plenitude, the absence of difference and the lack of lack of the infant. In the Real, the infant's wants are all fulfilled by the psychic figure of the Mother (or the Thing [*das Ding*, *la chose*]) such that there are no lasting unfulfilled wishes. Once the infant has entered the two other registers of psychic reality, the Imaginary and the Symbolic, the emergence of desire and the embrace of signification (the cut of difference) lead to a schism with the Real. The Real continues to resonate for the subject but as a traumatic kernel, as some Thing resistant to symbolization. Lacan describes the Thing, *das Ding*, as 'the beyond-of-the-signified.'[56] The Real is not absent in any simple sense from the Imaginary and the Symbolic—it is keenly felt—but it resists imagining and does not signify. In this sense, its traumatic dimensions are clear. Georges Didi-Huberman, for example, refers to the extermination camp of Auschwitz-Birkenau as a Real, as somewhere that seems to exceed our capacities for imagining or describing.[57] For Julia Kristeva, the Real as it is conceived in a text such as *Powers of Horror* is abject, a source of extreme anxiety and of revulsion. Ettinger offers a radically different conception of the Real, one that some of Kristeva's more recent writings are proximate to, in which it is not a source of fear but of possibility, an ethical resource. Both Ettinger and Kristeva can be seen to explore the relationship between aesthetic practices as loci of socio-political transformation.[58]

For Ettinger, the matrixial which relates to 'the prenatal, the intrauterine, gestation and pregnancy,' can potentially 'deconstruct and dissolve the concept of the unitary separate phallic subject split by the castration mechanism, rejecting its abject, and mourning its m/Other.'[59] In a culture in which the Real is simply viewed as repulsive, it risks being co-opted, employed to justify acts of violence against those identified as abject. Karen E. Tatum, for instance, has argued that domestic violence emerges from out of the logic of castration, one in which the fear of the abject mother is an unconscious motivating factor. In *Explaining the Depiction of Violence against Women in Victorian Literature*, Tatum draws on Kristeva's concept of abjection to explain men's violence towards women. She suggests that this is because men associate women in the Symbolic order with the 'abjected maternal/female body.'[60] Tatum emphasizes that this association is the product of cultural construction.[61] It is through cultural coding that women or other groups within society become labelled as Other and abject. In contemporary culture (which continues to manifest misogyny), transphobia might also be understood as, in part, symptomatic of this psychic logic. Trans* identities are currently viewed by some as incarnating a frightening Otherness, one they respond to with enmity and aggression. Karla can be seen as a tragic victim of this phenomenon.

Susan Stryker explores how transgender (her term) has been mobilized 'to contain all gender trouble, thereby helping to secure both homosexuality and heterosexuality as stable and normative categories of personhood.'[62] In this reading, transgender becomes the abject, the excluded: a constitutive outside that renders the 'normal' possible by way of its perceived abnormality. Stryker's response to this violent exclusionary process is to celebrate this exclusion, drawing on social abjection and the rage it generates in those who must endure its consequences as an inspiration for practices of resistance. In 'My Words to Victor Frankenstein above the Village of Chamounix: Performing Transgender Rage,' an essay based upon a performance piece, Stryker offers a manifesto for appropriating the abject, repurposing an abject-status and transforming it (as much as is possible) into something positive.[63] Here there are echoes of Judith Butler's exploration of the idea of critically adopting queerness, of laying claim to the power to name oneself, yet, as Butler foregrounds, with an awareness that any such claim must be tentative and partial.[64] Butler and Stryker offer invaluable reflections on how to craft strategies of resistance from out of existing conditions of oppression. Gloria Anzaldúa, however, writes of our modern perceptions of the *mita' y mita'* (half and half)—a person she identifies as 'both male and female,' someone we might nowadays describe as refusing to conform to binary norms of gender—that 'we are suffering from . . . an absolute despot duality that says we are able to be only one or the other.'[65] For Anzaldúa then, what is needed is a way to escape the trapping poles of binary conceptions of gender. Ettinger may gesture towards a possible means of effecting such an escape through her willingness to address the generative conditions for the processes of exclusion that underpin abjection.

Ettinger uses the term m/Other to distinguish the maternal of the matrixial from the Mother or Other of the Symbolic, the psychic figure that features in the oedipalizing scenario. The small 'm' signals that this is a becoming mother rather than an accomplished entity. The 'm/' also accentuates that the matrixial stratum of subjectivity is 'feminine.' Ettinger writes that the matrixial 'is shaped by feminine difference that is linked to the female body and relates to *her* "hole" in the Real and to the originary matrixial times and spaces that differentiate themselves before repression.'[66] Feminine difference is therefore not to be confused with sexual difference; the latter emerges and is regulated during the Oedipus complex.[67] It is through sexual difference (and the rise of 'norms' of desire across this difference) that sexes and sexualities become labelled as accepted or are abjected.

As Griselda Pollock stresses, sexuality as it is conceived by Ettinger is more complex and accommodating than sexuality as it manifests purely within the Symbolic. Drawing on Ettinger's thinking, she suggests that:

> [i]f the subject is constituted both in relation to identifications that are incorporated, plural, and diverse from the beginning, and are themselves . . . emitting the enigmatic signals of their own desiring sexualities, and if the subject is also shaped in relation to the ever-enigmatic signifier the phallus, we need to read across the surface of aesthetic forms for impressions, if not inscriptions, of co-existing forms of desire and desirability that may, under the traumatic conditions of the Oedipus complex, coalesce into a predominant 'orientation' of desire and affection, or remain diffused and uncertain, or layer each other in relation to fantasy, imagination, and actualization.[68]

In this conception of sexuality, predominant orientations (heteronormativity, for example) potentially become concretized in the Symbolic, yet they do so against a more dispersed and open backdrop. There are alternative desires operating in the matrixial 'that must be differentiated not only from phallic desire, but also from *maternal* or *female* desire as defined in the phallic universe.'[69]

The psychoanalytic framework Ettinger contends with is one in which physical violence against those labelled as abject and socially marginalized is triggered by the projection of cultural constructions of the maternal onto them. Others are thus socially constructed as the source of a 'natural, pre-discursive power of horror.'[70] In this structure, the psychic category of the Mother (a role that can be fulfilled by an other who biologically identifies as female, male or trans*), the Other, is imposed upon all of those who are registered as abject. Rather than offering modes of embracing the abject and building resistance to violent oppression from within the negative, Ettinger thinks about ways of fostering reconciliation within culture with the maternal, the Mother as an anxiety-inducing, potentially border-troubling psychic figure. It is this dimension of her thinking which Butler foregrounds in her essay of the artist-analyst's work, 'Disturbance and Dispersal in the Visual Field.' Butler suggests that Ettinger 'concerns herself with the ethical and political question of what it means to make a link across a border when the dominant ethos maintains that no link can be made.'[71]

THE MATRIXIAL BORDERSPACES

Ettinger seeks to look beyond the phallus (without disavowing its Symbolic necessity) and draw attention to an aesthetic dimension to subjectivity that is the matrixial. This dimension is subjacent to the castration paradigm associated with the Symbolic. Griselda Pollock observes of the matrixial:

> As Ettinger underlines, the matrixial plays in/on a *borderspace*. This implies a borderlinking that is also the spatial co-difference of the several. If the feminine is to gain non-phallic meaning, it must *not* be thought in relation to organs (penis versus womb) or anatomies (inside versus outside). Instead it must invoke a psychic *event-encounter* understood through such concepts as borderspace, borderlinking. Borderspaces are subject to a perpetual returning and rehoning, and are thus never stabilized as a cut, split, or division. The borderlinking borderspace is not a confusion; it implies a bordertime and offers the possibility of moments when borderlines may become thresholds and the passage from one to the other may produce possible transformations, circulations, sharings. Since these co-affectings are contingent on specificities of singular subjectivities, histories, conditions, and semiotic offerings, virtuality, potentiality, and provisionality are a part of the system.[72]

The art practice of Margolles often actively resists logics of division, privileging instead acts of diffusion. Her works strive to produce conditions conducive to what Ettinger calls wit(h)ness-Thing, a perceptual process that fosters encounters with the Thing of the Real that are registered affectively in aesthetic experience. Lacan regarded the Thing, the lost object desired by the subject, as unattainable from within the Symbolic. Ettinger's work contrasts with the Lacanian psychoanalytic narrative which, as Pollock explains, 'depends upon initiating subjectivity only with birth, thus imagining a process of formation that involves an accumulating series of separations, cleavages and finally "castration" which has the effect of rendering the maternal both abject and the site of endless desire while "it" is nothing but that lostness.'[73] For Ettinger, by contrast, something of the maternal, the Thing can be conveyed through aesthetic encounter by way of the registration of intensities, affects, rather than the recognition of signs. Pollock describes affect as it is conceived within psychoanalysis as a diffuse phenomenon that colours the psychic disposition.[74] Emotions such as happiness or sadness are not affects in that they are already too shaped, too specific. Ettinger calls the felt communication of affect co-poiesis. Works such as Margolles's *Banca* and *Mesa y dos bancos*, which embody the dead in their very structure yet withhold all signs of them, generate intense reactions which signal that an aesthetic encounter of the kind described by Ettinger is potentially taking place.

Similarly, a work such as *Entierro* (Burial) (1999), which is made of a human foetus encased in concrete, figures the traumatic kernel that is the Real yet also gestures to a beyond to figuration. The mother of the unborn child could not afford to pay burial expenses and asked Margolles for help. The impact of the work is highly affective. *Entierro* has the appearance of a brick, although in reality it is more like a coffin or tomb. It could be mistaken for one of the units in Carl Andre's fire-brick work *Equivalent VIII*, yet that would be a false equivalence. *Entierro* may outwardly embody the 'inert thingness' which Alex Potts describes as forming minimalism's dynamo in the 1960s, yet there is more than meets the eye to Margolles's work.[75] The stilled life that inhabits the block of concrete, potently registered despite its invisibility, expresses the violence of economic disenfranchisement in ways that the calculated commentary on modern industry of the minimalists could not. Like the minimalists, there is a resistance to what Potts calls 'image-based consumerism,' yet it is of a different order.[76] Margolles draws attention to the traumatic by-products of rapid industrialization and global economics by way of 'quiet' indications of tragedy. Tragedies are alluded to throughout Margolles's corpus yet not sensationalized.[77]

In Margolles's rendering invisible of the bodies of the dead, her touching upon them indirectly, one can trace a resonance with the art of Alejandro Luperca Morales, who produced a series *Post Meridiem/Post Mortem* that involved gently erasing images of the dead bodies of victims of violence from pages of the Juárez-based evening newspaper *PM*.[78] Here the bodies as signifiers of violence cease to be; instead, only scuffed space remains. Both Luperca and Margolles embrace what John Paul Ricco has referred to as a disappeared aesthetics. Writing in the context of what he calls 'the time of AIDS,' Ricco has noted of loss that it becomes lost when subject to symbolization and narrativization, to recuperative logics of representation.[79] Like Pollock, Ricco recognizes the consolation that accompanies signification. In a sense, once a traumatic death is represented, lent substance, something of the trauma becomes dissipated. The affective dimension to Margolles's works means that trauma still registers, yet not as sign but as intensity. Signs function by way of detachment, discrete spacings, and require mastering through acts of interpretation. Encounters with artworks such as *Entierro* involve opening towards unbound affects, embracing intimacy, engaging with the matrixial, the aesthetic dimension to subjectivity.

In *Borderland/La Frontera*, Gloria Anzaldúa suggests that 'the work of a *mestiza* consciousness is to break down the subject-object duality that keeps her prisoner and to show in her flesh and through the images in her work how duality is transcended.'[80] For her, the 'uprooting of dualistic thinking in the individual and collective consciousness is the beginning of a long struggle, but one that could, in our best hopes, bring us to the end of rape, of violence, of war.'[81] Artworks that foster the matrixial, that generate borderspaces, provide a way to look beyond the constraints of binary-logic. Ettinger writes that the matrixial comprises '[r]elations-without-relating and distance-in-proximity [that] preserve the co-emerging Other as both subject *and* object without turning the Other into an object only; and they preserve the matrixial woman as both subject *and* object, not as Object or other only.'[82] Artworks that provide potential encounters with the matrixial therefore enable insights into how to think across binaries, beyond borders.

Karla is also a work that proffers such a potential encounter. It is a work that encourages oscillation between its varied aspects: the death certificate, the concrete block, the photograph, and the voices (of Ivon and of the English translator). These multiple sights and sounds, sites, that signify Karla, ultimately work to undo the idea of any secure symbolization of the life and death that was hers. The concrete, in its brute materiality, might seem to offer a cruel monument. As a broken, fragmentary form, however, it possesses a compromised monumentality. The block remembers but indirectly. It indexes the abandoned architectural space in which Karla met her violent end, holding something of her history yet certainly not all. The four elements in the work combine to refuse any chance of possessing her, standing in for her. There is no relief of signification here. The spectator engages in a series of unsettled, unsettling aesthetic encounters with discrete yet related aspects of the piece. Karla is rendered multiple, not reduced, not condensed into a seeming unified subjectivity. The chilling logic of the death certificate is refused.

Ivon's voice, which can be listened to while contemplating the other aspects of the work, weaves them together—connecting the living and dead Karla. Ivon's words are the words of a specific individual and possess a distinctive grain. They are laden with affect. Beneath the signs, the words that describe Karla's fate, there is something else present, an intensity, a moment of encounter. When this affect is felt, there is a shared borderspace, a connection. *Karla* therefore both records the traumatic effects of an exploitative and unfair economic system and an overly *machista*, or macho culture, and offers a way to look beyond the logics that contributed to Karla's violent death.

Margolles nourishes an art practice that resists particular strands of avant-gardism with their unreflective embrace of phallic subjectivity and their hard-edged certitude in the symbolic power of artworks. In a way, the broken block at Karla's feet can be seen to offer a critique of the abstract pretentions of minimalist art, its dry claims to matter. Critiques of capitalism and of phallocentrism require more human elements, traces of individual traumas linked with these value systems, if they are to register effectively, affectively. Margolles offers no relief in relation to the traumas she confronts but she does enable affective encounters, encounters that are potentially transformational. The urgency of the need to generate artworks such as *Karla* is evidenced by the tragic reality that another trans* sex worker involved in the series *Pistas de baile* has now been murdered. La Gata, who appears in the work *Pista de baile del club 'Las Vegas,'* was killed in Ciudad Juárez in 2016. Through the space of encounter a work such as *Karla* generates, one that invites sharing in traces of trauma by way of aesthetic processes, the beholder is potentially subject to change. Pollock writes that such encounters as acts of wit(h)nessing are transformative.[83] In this they possess a healing dimension, not in the sense of offering a cure for trauma but rather through providing enhanced understanding of it.[84] By way of such understanding, one not premised on mastering affective experiences but on sharing in them, legacies of trauma become open to life-enhancing reflection.

NOTES

1. This work will henceforth be referred to as *Karla*. A reproduction of this artwork can be found at the following website: https://www.peterkilchmann.com/artists/teresa-margolles/overview/karla-hilario-reyes-gallegos-2016. The use of trans* with an asterisk as my preferred term aims for inclusivity. I have used transgender and transsexual when authors that I am referring to have adopted those terms.
2. Following Ivon, I refer to Karla by the pronoun 'her.'
3. Thérèse St-Gelais, 'The Violence of Order,' in *Teresa Margolles: Mundos*, ed. Chantal Charbonneau, 88–93. (Montréal: Musée d'art contemporain de Montréal, 2017), 90.
4. Margolles was a member of SEMEFO from 1990 to 1998.
5. Marc Bloch, *The Historian's Craft*, trans. Peter Putnam (New York: Alfred A. Knopf, 1953), 52.
6. Michael Baxandall, *Painting and Experience in Fifteenth-Century Italy* (Oxford: Oxford University Press, 1988), 2.

7. Pascal Beausse, 'Teresa Margolles: Primordial Substances,' in *Materiality*, ed. Petra Lange-Berndt (Cambridge, MA: MIT Press, 2015), 136.

8. Debra A. Castillo et al., 'Violence and Transvestite/Transgender Sex Workers in Tijuana,' in *Gender Violence at the US-Mexico Border: Media Representation and Public Response*, eds. Héctor Domínguez-Ruvalcaba and Ignacio Corona (Tucson: University of Arizona Press, 2010), 19. Employment opportunities for trans* people in Mexico are also limited by discrimination.

9. Rebecca Scott Bray, 'En piel ajena: The Work of Teresa Margolles,' *Law Text Culture* 11 (2007): 24.

10. Castillo et al., 'Violence and Transvestite/Transgender Sex Workers in Tijuana,' 31.

11. Monica Ulibarri et al., 'History of Abuse and Psychological Distress Symptoms among Female Sex Workers in Two Mexico-US Border Cities,' *Violence Vict.* 24.3 (2009): 399–413.

12. Rebecca Scott Bray describes the city of Juárez as a place that has 'come to symbolize the gendered failure of criminal justice in the region.' Bray, 'Margolles's Crime Scene Aesthetics,' *South Atlantic Quarterly* 110.4 (2011): 939.

13. Kathleen Staudt, *Violence and Activism at the Border: Gender, Fear, and Everyday Life in Ciudad Juárez* (Austin: University of Texas Press, 2008), 121

14. Roadside shrines featuring the Virgin Mary are not uncommon in Mexico.

15. Adrian Forty, *Concrete and Culture: A Material History* (London: Reaktion, 2012), 14.

16. Marcel Joray, *Le Béton dans l'art contemporain* (Neuchâtel: Éditions du Griffon, 1977), 13–15.

17. Forty, *Concrete and Culture*, 178.

18. See Elvia R. Arriola, 'Accountability for Murders in the *Maquiladoras*,' in *Making a Killing: Femicide, Free Trade, and La Frontera*, eds. Alicia Gaspar de Alba and Georgina Guzmán (Austin: University of Texas Press, 2010), 25–61. Nuala Finnegan also provides a sophisticated overview of how neoliberalism and geopolitics have shaped Juárez in *Cultural Representations of Feminicidio at the US-Mexico Border* (New York: Routledge, 2018).

19. Sergio González Rodríguez, *The Femicide Machine*, trans. Michael Parker-Stainback (Los Angeles: Semiotext(e), 2012), 74.

20. In reality, concrete can be fragile depending on factors such as the ingredients used to make it and the conditions it experiences post-manufacture.

21. Rowan Bailey, 'Concrete Thinking for Sculpture,' *parallax* 21.3 (2015): 242.

22. Beausse, 'Teresa Margolles,' 138.

23. Julia Banwell, *Teresa Margolles and the Aesthetics of Death* (Cardiff: University of Wales Press, 2015), 88.

24. See Edward Bacal, 'The Concrete and the Abstract: On Doris Salcedo, Teresa Margolles and Santiago Serra's Tenuous Bodies,' *parallax* 21.3 (2015): 259–70; Sydney Hart, 'Crisis and Representation: The Representations of Flows in Teresa Margolles' Recent Work,' *Espace: art actuel* 118 (2018): 42–7; and Jean-Philippe Uzel, 'Her Blood is Going to Help Us All: Teresa Margolles, Indigenous Feminicide,'

in *Teresa Margolles: Mundos*, ed. Chantal Charbonneau (Montréal: Musée d'art contemporain de Montréal, 2017).

25. Forty, *Concrete and Culture*, 197-98.

26. Alistair Rider, *Carl Andre: Things in their Elements* (New York: Phaidon, 2011), 185.

27. Rider, *Carl Andre*, 185.

28. Rider, *Carl Andre*, 188.

29. Douglas Crimp, *On the Museum's Ruins* (Cambridge, MA: MIT Press, 1993), 179.

30. Robert Reiner, *Law and Order: An Honest Citizen's Guide to Crime and Control* (Cambridge: Polity, 2007), 6.

31. Reiner, *Law and Order*, 96.

32. Crimp, *On the Museum's Ruins*, 159.

33. Anna Chave, 'Minimalism and the Rhetoric of Power,' in *Art in Modern Cultures: An Anthology of Critical Texts*, eds. Francis Frascina and Jonathan Harris (London: HarperCollins, 1992), 269.

34. Anonymous, 'La promesa,' in *Teresa Margolles: Mundos*, ed. Chantal Charbonneau (Montréal: Le Musée d'art contemporain de Montréal, 2017), 34.

35. Rodríguez, *The Femicide Machine*, 31.

36. Rodríguez, *The Femicide Machine*, 31.

37. Rodríguez, *The Femicide Machine*, 11.

38. Alice Driver, *More or Less Dead: Feminicide, Haunting, and the Ethics of Representation in Mexico* (Tucson: University of Arizona Press, 2015), 145.

39. Driver, *More or Less Dead*, 145.

40. See Griselda Pollock, 'Proximity and the Color of Desire: The Laboring Body and Its Sex,' in *Looking Back on the Future: Essays on Art, Life and Death*, ed. Penny Florence (Amsterdam: G+B Arts, 2001), 177–226.

41. Alicia Schmidt Camacho, 'Ciudadana X: Gender Violence and the Denationalization of Women's Rights in Ciudad Juárez, Mexico,' in *Terrorizing Women: Feminicide in the Américas*, eds. Rosa-Linda Fregoso and Cynthia Bejarano (Durham, NC: Duke University Press, 2010), 276.

42. Gregg M. Horowitz, *Sustaining Loss: Art and Mournful Life* (Stanford: Stanford University Press, 2001), 189.

43. Beausse, 'Teresa Margolles,' 139.

44. Beausse, 'Teresa Margolles,' 139.

45. Bacal reads Margolles's art practice as one that calls to mind abstract bodies which are 'absent, invisible or otherwise virtual bodies which have disappeared from the scene of the work but nevertheless leave their impression upon it.' Bacal, "The Concrete and the Abstract," 259. Amy Sara Carroll similarly claims that Margolles 'has driven the body to abstraction.' Carroll, '*Muerte sin fin*: Teresa Margolles's Gendered States of Exception,' *TDR: The Drama Review* 54.2 (2010): 107.

46. Julia Kristeva, *Powers of Horror: An Essay on Abjection*, trans. Leon S. Roudiez (New York: Columbia University Press, 1982), 4.

47. Banwell, *Teresa Margolles and the Aesthetics of Death*, 74.

48. Kristeva, *Powers of Horror*, 3.

49. Bray, 'En piel ajena,' 37.

50. Bray, 'En piel ajena,' 37.

51. Uzel, 'Her Blood is Going to Help Us All,' 96.

52. Rosalind E. Krauss, *Passages in Modern Sculpture* (Cambridge, MA, MIT Press, 1981), 250.

53. Alistair Rider, 'The Concreteness of Concrete Art,' *parallax* 21.3 (2015): 343-4.

54. Bray, 'En piel ajena,' 38-39.

55. Griselda Pollock, *Encounters in the Virtual Feminist Museum: Time, Space and the Archive* (London: Routledge, 2007), 180.

56. Jacques Lacan, *The Ethics of Psychoanalysis 1959–1960: The Seminar of Jacques Lacan Book VII*, trans. Dennis Porter (London: Routledge, 1992), 54.

57. Georges Didi-Huberman, *Images in Spite of All: Four Photographs from Auschwitz*, trans. Shane B. Lillis (Chicago: University of Chicago Press, 2008), 3

58. For a discussion of Kristeva in this context, see Maria Margaroni's essay 'Recent Work on and by Julia Kristeva: Toward a Psychoanalytic Social Theory,' *Signs* 32.3 (2007): 793–808.

59. Bracha L. Ettinger, *The Matrixial Borderspace* (Minneapolis: University of Minnesota Press, 2006), 183.

60. Karen E. Tatum, *Explaining the Depiction of Violence against Women in Victorian Literature* (Lewiston, NY: Edwin Mellen Press, 2005), 14.

61. Tatum, *Explaining the Depiction of Violence Against Women in Victorian Literature*, 33.

62. Susan Stryker, 'My Words to Victor Frankenstein above the Village of Chamounix: Performing Transgender Rage,' in *The Transgender Studies Reader*, eds. Susan Stryker and Stephen Whittle (New York: Routledge, 2006), 274.

63. For a powerful reading of this essay as a manifesto for originary queerness and for the trans* animacy of matter, see Karen Barad, 'Transmaterialities: Trans*/Matter/Realities and Queer Political Imaginings,' *GLQ* 21.2-3 (2015): 387–422.

64. Judith Butler, *Bodies that Matter: On the Discursive Limits of 'Sex'* (New York: Routledge, 1993), 223–42.

65. Gloria Anzaldúa, *Borderland/La Frontera: The New Mestiza*, 3rd ed. (San Francisco: Aunt Lute Books, 2007), 41.

66. Ettinger, *The Matrixial Borderspace*, 66.

67. See Sheila Cavanagh's article 'Transsexuality as Sinthome' for further discussion of sexual difference in relation to the matrixial. Cavanagh, 'Transsexuality as Sinthome: Bracha L. Ettinger and the Other (Feminine) Sexual Difference,' *Studies in Gender and Sexuality* 17. 1 (2016): 27–44.

68. Griselda Pollock, 'To Play Many Parts: Reading Between the Lines of Charlotte Salomon/**CS**'s *Leben? oder Theater?' RACAR* 43.1 (2018): 75–76.

69. Emphases in the original. Ettinger, *The Matrixial Borderspace*, 67.

70. Tatum, *Explaining the Depiction of Violence Against Women in Victorian Literature*, 34

71. Judith Butler, 'Disturbance and Dispersal in the Visual Field,' in *Art as Compassion: Bracha L. Ettinger*, eds. Catherine de Zegher and Griselda Pollock (Brussels: ASA Publishers, 2011), 151.

72. Emphases in the original. Griselda Pollock, 'Femininity: Aporia or Sexual Difference,' in *The Matrixial Borderspace*, ed. Brian Massumi (Minneapolis: University of Minnesota Press, 2006), 19.

73. Griselda Pollock, 'A Matrixial Installation: Artworking in the Freudian Space of Memory and Migration,' in *Art as Compassion: Bracha L. Ettinger*, eds. Catherine de Zegher and Griselda Pollock (Brussels: ASA Publishers, 2011), 220.

74. Griselda Pollock, *Art in the Time-Space of Memory and Migration, Sigmund Freud, Anna Freud and Bracha L. Ettinger in the Freud Museum: Artwriting after the Event* (Leeds: Wild Pansy Press, 2013), 54.

75. Alex Potts, *The Sculptural Imagination: Figurative, Modernist, Minimalist* (New Haven, CT: Yale University Press, 2000), 4.

76. Potts, *The Sculptural Imagination*, 4.

77. For another discussion of images of Juárez that resist spectalurarization, see my article 'The Skin of the Photograph: Representing the Murdered Women of Juárez,' *West Coast Line 53* 41.1 (2007), 26–31.

78. Alejandro Luperca Morales, a resident of Cuidad Juárez, began this series in 2010 and has so far subjected roughly 500 images to the very time-consuming procedure of gently erasing the bodies of the dead, a procedure he equates with the process of mourning. A selection of these images have been published as *PM* (Madrid: Chaco/Gato Negro, 2018).

79. John Paul Ricco, *The Logic of the Lure* (Chicago: University of Chicago Press, 2002), 40-41.

80. Anzaldúa, *Borderland/La Frontera*, 102.

81. Anzaldúa, *Borderland/La Frontera*, 102.

82. Emphases in the original. Ettinger, *The Matrixial Borderspace*, 72.

83. Griselda Pollock, *After-affects/After-images: Trauma and Aesthetic Transformation in the Virtual Feminist Museum* (Manchester: Manchester University Press, 2013), 15.

84. I am indebted here to Hans Loewald's conception of 'understanding' as it manifests in analysis as therapeutic act. See Loewald, 'Reflections on the Psychoanalytic Process,' in Hans W. Loewald, *Papers on Psychoanalysis* (New Haven, CT: Yale University Press, 1980), 381–83.

BIBLIOGRAPHY

ANZALDÚA, Gloria. *Borderland/La Frontera: The New Mestiza*. Third Edition. San Francisco: Aunt Lute Books, 2007.

ARRIOLA, Elvia R. 'Accountability for Murders in the *Maquiladoras*.' In *Making a Killing: Femicide, Free Trade, and La Frontera*. Edited by Alicia Gaspar de Alba and Georgina Guzmán, 25–61. Austin: University of Texas Press, 2010.

BACAL, Edward. 'The Concrete and the Abstract: On Doris Salcedo, Teresa Margolles and Santiago Serra's Tenuous Bodies.' *parallax* 21.3 (2015): 259–70.

BAILEY, Rowan. 'Concrete Thinking for Sculpture.' *parallax* 21.3 (2015): 241–58.

BANWELL, Julia. *Teresa Margolles and the Aesthetics of Death*. Cardiff: University of Wales Press, 2015.

BARAD, Karen. 'Transmaterialities: Trans*/Matter/Realities and Queer Political Imaginings.' *GLQ* 21.2-3 (2015): 387–422.

BAXANDALL, Michael. *Painting and Experience in Fifteenth-Century Italy*. Oxford: Oxford University Press, 1988.

BEAUSSE, Pascale. 'Teresa Margolles: Primordial Substances.' In *Materiality*. Edited by Petra Lange-Berndt. 136–39. Cambridge, MA: MIT Press, 2015.

BLOCH, Marc. *The Historian's Craft*. Translated by Peter Putnam. New York: Alfred A. Knopf, 1953.

BRAY, Rebecca Scott. 'En piel ajena: The Work of Teresa Margolles.' *Law Text Culture* 11 (2007): 13–50.

BRAY, Rebecca Scott. 'Teresa Margolles's Crime Scene Aesthetics.' *South Atlantic Quarterly* 110.4 (2011): 933–48.

BUTLER, Judith. *Bodies that Matter: On the Discursive Limits of 'Sex.'* New York: Routledge, 1993.

BUTLER, Judith. 'Disturbance and Dispersal in the Visual Field.' In *Art as Compassion: Bracha L. Ettinger*. Edited by Catherine de Zegher and Griselda Pollock. 149-65. Brussels: ASA Publishers, 2011.

CAMACHO, Alicia Schmidt. 'Ciudadana X: Gender Violence and the Denationalization of Women's Rights in Ciudad Juárez, Mexico.' In *Terrorizing Women: Feminicide in the Américas*. Edited by Rosa-Linda Fregoso and Cynthia Bejarano. 275-89. Durham, NC: Duke University Press, 2010.

CARROLL, Amy Sara. '*Muerte Sin Fin*: Teresa Margolles's Gendered States of Exception.' *TDR: The Drama Review* 54.2 (2010): 103–25.

CASTILLO, Debra A., María Gudelia Rangel Gómez and Armando Rosas Solís. 'Violence and Transvestite/Transgender Sex Workers in Tijuana.' In *Gender Violence at the US-Mexico Border: Media Representation and Public Response*. Edited by Héctor Domínguez-Ruvalcaba and Ignacio Corona. 15–34. Tucson: University of Arizona Press, 2010.

CAVANAGH, Sheila L. 'Transsexuality as Sinthome: Bracha L. Ettinger and the Other (Feminine) Sexual Difference.' *Studies in Gender and Sexuality* 17.1 (2016): 27–44.

CHARE, Nicholas. 'The Skin of the Photograph: Representing the Murdered Women of Juárez.' *West Coast Line* 53 42.1 (2007): 26–31.

CHAVE, Anna. 'Minimalism and the Rhetoric of Power.' In *Art in Modern Cultures: An Anthology of Critical Texts*. Edited by Francis Frascina and Jonathan Harris. 264–81. London: HarperCollins, 1992.

CRIMP, Douglas. *On the Museum's Ruins*. Cambridge, MA: MIT Press, 1993.

DIDI-HUBERMAN, Georges. *Images in Spite of All: Four Photographs from Auschwitz*. Translated by Shane B. Lillis. Chicago: University of Chicago Press, 2008.

DRIVER, Alice. *More or Less Dead: Feminicide, Haunting, and the Ethics of Representation in Mexico*. Tucson: University of Arizona Press, 2015.

ETTINGER, Bracha L. *The Matrixial Borderspace*. Minneapolis: University of Minnesota Press, 2006.

FINNEGAN, Nuala. *Cultural Representations of Feminicidio at the US-Mexico Border*. New York: Routledge, 2018.

FORTY, Adrian. *Concrete and Culture: A Material History*. London: Reaktion, 2012.

HART, Sydney. 'Crisis and Representation: The Representations of Flows in Teresa Margolles' Recent Work.' *Espace: art actuel* 118 (2018): 42–47.

HOROWITZ, Gregg M. *Sustaining Loss: Art and Mournful Life*. Stanford, CA: Stanford University Press, 2001.

JORAY, Marcel. *Le Béton dans l'art contemporain*. Neuchâtel: Éditions du Griffon, 1977.

KRAUSS, Rosalind E. *Passages in Modern Sculpture*. Cambridge, MA: MIT Press, 1981.

KRISTEVA, Julia. *Powers of Horror: An Essay on Abjection*. Translated by Leon S. Roudiez. New York: University of Columbia Press, 1982.

LACAN, Jacques. *The Ethics of Psychoanalysis, 1959-1960: The Seminar of Jacques Lacan Book VII*. Translated by Dennis Porter. London: Routledge, 1992.

LOEWALD, Hans W. 'Reflections on the Psychoanalytic Process.' In Hans W. Loewald, *Papers on Psychoanalysis*. 372–83. New Haven, CT: Yale University Press, 1980.

MARGARONI, Maria. 'Recent Work on and by Julia Kristeva: Toward a Psychoanalytic Social Theory.' *Signs* 32.3 (2007): 793–808.

MARTÍNEZ, Oscar J. *Ciudad Juárez: Saga of a Legendary Border City*. Tucson: University of Arizona Press, 2018.

MORALES, Alejandro Luperca. *PM*. Madrid: Chaco/Gato Negro, 2018.

POLLOCK, Griselda. 'A Matrixial Installation: Artworking in the Freudian Space of Memory and Migration.' In *Art as Compassion*. Edited by Catherine de Zegher and Griselda Pollock. 191–241. Brussels: ASA Publishers, 2011.

POLLOCK, Griselda. *After-affects/After-images: Trauma and Aesthetic Transformation in the Virtual Feminist Museum*. Manchester: Manchester University Press, 2013.

POLLOCK, Griselda. *Art in the Time-Space of Memory and Migration, Sigmund Freud, Anna Freud and Bracha L. Ettinger in the Freud Museum: Artwriting after the Event*. Leeds: Wild Pansy Press, 2013.

POLLOCK, Griselda. *Encounters in the Virtual Feminist Museum: Time, Space and the Archive*. Abingdon: Routledge, 2007.

POLLOCK, Griselda. 'Femininity: Aporia or Sexual Difference?.' In *The Matrixial Borderspace*. Edited by Brian Massumi, 1–38. Minneapolis: University of Minnesota Press, 2006.

POLLOCK, Griselda. 'Proximity and the Color of Desire: The Laboring Body and Its Sex.' In *Looking Back on the Future: Essays on Art, Life and Death*. Edited by Penny Florence. 177–226. Amsterdam: G+B Arts, 2001.

POLLOCK, Griselda. 'To Play Many Parts: Reading Between the Lines of Charlotte Salomon/**CS**'s *Leben? oder Theater?*' *RACAR* 43.1 (2018): 63–80.

POTTS, Alex. *The Sculptural Imagination: Figurative, Modernist, Minimalist.* New Haven, CT: Yale University Press, 2000.

REINER, Robert. *Law and Order: An Honest Citizen's Guide to Crime and Control.* Cambridge: Polity, 2007.

RICCO, John Paul. *The Logic of the Lure.* Chicago: University of Chicago Press, 2002.

RIDER, Alistair. *Carl Andre: Things in their Elements.* New York: Phaidon, 2011.

RIDER, Alistair. 'The Concreteness of Concrete Art.' *parallax* 21.3 (2015): 340–52.

RODRÍGUEZ, Sergio González. *The Femicide Machine.* Translated by Michael Parker-Stainback. Los Angeles: Semiotext(e), 2012.

ST-GELAIS, Thérèse. 'The Violence of Order.' In *Teresa Margolles: Mundos.* Edited by Chantal Charbonneau. 88-93. Montréal: Musée d'art contemporain de Montréal, 2017.

STAUDT, Kathleen. *Violence and Activism at the Border: Gender. Fear, and Everyday Life in Ciudad Juárez.* Austin: University of Texas Press, 2008.

STRYKER, Susan. 'My Words to Victor Frankenstein above the Village of Chamounix: Performing Transgender Rage.' In *The Transgender Studies Reader.* Edited by Susan Stryker and Stephen Whittle. 244–56. New York: Routledge, 2006.

TATUM, Karen E. *Explaining the Depiction of Violence against Women in Victorian Literature.* Lewiston, NY: Edwin Mellen Press, 2005.

ULIBARRI, Monica et al. 'History of Abuse and Psychological Distress Symptoms among Female Sex Workers in Two Mexico-US Border Cities.' *Violence Vict.* 24.3 (2009): 399–413.

UZEL, Jean-Philippe. 'Her Blood is Going to Help Us All: Teresa Margolles, Indigenous Feminicide.' In *Teresa Margolles: Mundos.* Edited by Chantal Charbonneau. 94–101. Montréal: Musée d'art contemporain de Montréal, 2017.

Chapter Eleven

The Monstrosity of the New Wounded

Thinking Trauma, Survival and Resistance with Catherine Malabou and Julia Kristeva

Maria Margaroni

THE NEW WOUNDED: CATHERINE MALABOU'S CHALLENGE TO PSYCHOANALYSIS

Catherine Malabou's *The New Wounded: From Neurosis to Brain Damage* was originally published in 2007, following a number of philosophical treatises where she set out to explore the concept of plasticity, most notably in the work of G. W. F. Hegel and Martin Heidegger but also in connection with Derridean deconstruction, Levinasian ethics and current feminist debates on sexual difference. In all of these works, Malabou aims to announce the inauguration of a new philosophical era, one no longer based on the structuralist and poststructuralist privileging of an enlarged concept of *writing* but on the neurologically informed motor scheme of plasticity.[1] Since her emergence as a philosopher, Malabou has sought to pursue the implications of employing this motor scheme in approaching a key philosophical theme, namely, the dialectic between freedom and determinism as this is reconfigured in the contemporary landscape of advanced global capitalism (characterized by a concern with productivity and flexibility), terror (foregrounding the precarity of human life, its exposure to fatal accident) and in light of increasing advances in the neurosciences. What distinguishes Malabou from other thinkers of her generation is her willingness to take on board neurological findings on the human brain, thus situating her research at the crossroads between the sciences and the humanities. As an advocate of New Materialism, Malabou insists on the need to ground philosophical thought in the material economy of the human brain. From her perspective, taking current neurobiological concerns into consideration can help us approach the old question of the relationship between brain and mind or nature and nurture in novel ways. In this context,

her turn to Sigmund Freud and her attempt to rethink the legacy of psychoanalysis from the vantage point offered by the field of the neurosciences was
far from a surprise.

The New Wounded constitutes an attempt on her part to articulate a materialist theory of trauma outside the traditional Freudian framework. In this
book Malabou takes as her starting point the premise that all trauma, be it
psychic or lesion-based, has a serious impact on the affective part of the brain
and leads to the production of a new type of patient, one characterized by
cool indifference not only to the world outside but to his or her own suffering. It is this kind of patient, whose auto-affection is radically damaged, that
enables the philosopher to introduce and theorize the concept of 'destructive
plasticity,' referring to a form of plasticity which, as she explains, transforms
the psychic economy of the subject through the annihilation of his or her past
identity. In her view, recognizing and reflecting on the emerging category of
the new wounded constitutes an important philosophical task today, given
that, as she characteristically puts it, 'emotional indifference' announces itself
'as the monstrosity of our time.'[2]

To fully appreciate Malabou's project in *The New Wounded*, it is important, I believe, that we take the time to unpack the diverse contexts, concerns
and stakes behind her invocation of a *new* type of patient. If, as she herself
points out in her Preamble to the book, the 'determination of psychic dis-
turbances—their definition, their clinical picture, and their therapy' is not
context-free but 'is always contemporaneous with a certain state or a certain age of war,' (*NW*, xvi), then it is imperative to understand the distinct
socio-political coordinates that have led the philosopher to introduce new
pathological paradigms. Clearly, as the subtitle to the book suggests, Malabou's 'new wounded' is posited beyond and against the *old* type of neurotic
patient theorized by Freud in response to the devastating impact of WW1 on
the human psyche. The main problem Malabou has with Freud's analysis of
traumatic neurosis is that it disregards the lesional aspect of the trauma, be it
the actual lesion suffered by the subject or the cerebral damage produced by
the traumatic shock. As she explains, what matters for Freud is neither the
organic lesion as such nor the impact of the event on the structure of the brain
but the internal conflict that gets revived and remobilized through the action
of the external event. This is why Malabou insists that Freud is reluctant to
think the brute accident, which is subsumed under the function of the psychic
event Freud privileges, namely, sexuality as the 'site of an encounter between
the exogenous and the endogenous' or, in other words, 'the connection between an *incident* and a *signification*.' (*NW*, 5, original emphasis)

In Malabou's view, it is precisely this connection that is missing in the new
cases of trauma we are witnessing. Cerebral trauma, she argues, renders any

kind of interpretation impossible. The new wounded are patients who have survived the hermeneutic void of their own accidents. They are radically cut off from their history and hence unable to draw from past resources to 'fiction' some kind of narrative thread that would keep their psychic economy intact. The new forms of trauma, according to Malabou, teach us that the '*enemy, today, is hermeneutics*.' (*NW*, 155, original emphasis)

In *The New Wounded*, Malabou refers explicitly to two contexts that constitute what she calls the distinct states of war in relation to which contemporary psychic pathologies need to be studied. Terrorism and the overwhelming threat of a terrorist attack have clearly shaped Malabou's conceptualization of the traumatic event as brute, unmotivated accident, a violent rupture of both historical and subjective continuity, an ambiguous occurrence at the borders between natural catastrophe and premeditated crime. In its impersonality and chance impact, the terrorist attack exemplifies for Malabou the senselessness of contemporary forms of trauma, their defiance of all existing hermeneutic frameworks. 'The sinister lesson of terrorism,' she writes, 'lies in its refusal to formulate a lesson' (*NW*, 155). Hence, its employment in Malabou's analysis as paradigmatic of what she calls 'cerebrality,' a concept referring to a causality *other than* sexuality, a regime of events that seriously damage cerebral functions (*NW*, 2).

Yet, this is not the only state of war Malabou invokes. According to her, the category of the new wounded cannot be understood outside the context of an aggressive global capitalism which drains its accomplices of all affect and grounds its success in the production of a host of disaffiliated rejects: the unemployed, the underemployed, the homeless, the victims of trafficking or modern slavery. Malabou's key paradigm in this context is Alzheimer's, a neurodegenerative disease which is alarmingly on the rise, especially in the affluent West. Using the Alzheimer's patient as an exemplary case of the contemporary forms of trauma, Malabou argues that the 'odd unconcern' that characterizes this patient is, significantly, one of the values promoted by an advanced, techno-mediated capitalism.[3] The cool indifference of the subject suffering from Alzheimer's, therefore, mirrors both the alienation of flexible, performance-oriented workers within the capitalist system *as well as* the drained, drifting existence of the new economic misfits and social outcasts.

Bringing together the two states of war presented above is an important strategic move that enables Malabou to demonstrate that *coolness*, far from the attitude of isolated subjects in the margins of contemporary experience, is in reality the visible symptom of the pathology of our times. Affective barrenness is becoming more and more the norm, she suggests. It is the 'gaping wound that appears on all the battlefields of contemporary society' (*NW*, 161). This is why Malabou sets out to articulate a general theory of trauma, one aiming to account not merely for patients of neurodegenerative diseases, victims of terrorist attacks or the disaffiliated within the capitalist system but, as she insists, for all types of illness that constitute part of the disabilities movement, victims of both natural catastrophes and socio-political violence, as well as for those older forms of trauma which Freudian theory has failed to understand and, as a result, to cure: schizophrenia, autism, epilepsy, or Tourette's syndrome (*NW*, 10).

Malabou is, needless to say, very much aware of the risks she is taking in treating all these diverse maladies as an 'amalgam' (*NW*, 156). Yet, she seems to think that the risks are worth taking since the stakes are high. Indeed, one of the philosopher's key concerns in *The New Wounded* is the increasing blurring of the borders between psychic, organic and socio-political trauma. It is not simply that socio-political violence has a material impact on the functions of the brain. More importantly, political violence today, she argues, takes on the guise of nature: its eruption and impact are unanticipated; it appears cut off from any causality or motivation; it obliterates all sense or affect. This is why, in her view, both philosophy and psychoanalysis need to return to 'the great question of the relation between biology and the social' (*NW*, 158). The concept of 'destructive plasticity' that she introduces aims at reopening this question in positing the operation of an annihilating power, the equivalent of the death drive, within the brain of every human being. If this biologically determined power is unleashed by non-biological forms of trauma, constituting the organism's response to extreme situations where no escape is possible, then doesn't finitude post-Heidegger manifest itself *not* in our being-towards-death but in the form of a paradoxical *survival*, that is, as a surplus of life in the very void of life? Survival, Malabou writes, 'sometimes manifests itself' as 'the indifference of life to life,' as a 'farewell that is not death, a farewell that occurs within life.'[4]

I find Malabou's foregrounding of *survival* as an existential possibility in between *Eros* (the life-binding principle) and *Thanatos* (the drive to absolute unboundedness) most important, for I agree with what the impetus of her analysis seems to be suggesting: the aim today is not to ensure survival at all costs but to resist (mere) survival as the ambiguity of this flat existence that is neither life nor death but an indifference to *both* life and death. According to Malabou, understanding this ambiguous existential mode is the first step towards recognizing the contemporary configurations not only of human suffering but also of human cruelty. As she argues, these configurations can no longer be approached from within the Freudian psychoanalytic tradition. The forms of cruelty we are currently witnessing are not the product of aggression or the expression of hatred, both of which involve an acknowledgement of the other. They need to be perceived, instead, in connection with this uncanny link between biology and the social, a link which, she reminds us, translates *'brain lesions'* into *'lesions in otherness'* (*NW*,161, original emphasis). As a result, both suffering and making suffer today share the same death-like face of emotional apathy or cool indifference. Though Malabou insists on its contemporaneity, this death-like face is, however, not deprived of a name or a history.

WITNESSING THE *MUSELMANN*—AGAIN

In her Preamble to *The New Wounded*, Malabou acknowledges the impact of twentieth-century and twenty-first-century military conflicts on the emergence as well as the evolution of our concepts of trauma. She does not explicitly refer to Walter Benjamin, one of the most penetrating analysts of the intimate and collective effects of WW1, yet his post-war testimony to the loss of communicable experience and the bankruptcy of collective narrative seems to inform Malabou's understanding of the nature of trauma in terms of a hermeneutic void.[5] Interestingly, in 'Goethe's Elective Affinities,'[6] Benjamin develops the notion of 'the expressionless,' which, Shoshana Felman argues, lies at the heart of his conceptualization of 'history as trauma.'[7] Pursuing the implications of this notion in connection with questions relating to genocide, oppression and crimes against humanity, Felman comes to define 'the expressionless' in terms that introduce an illuminating subtext to Malabou's analysis of the 'new wounded,' giving it a historical depth Malabou does not openly acknowledge and an added political significance: 'expressionless are those whom violence has deprived of expression; those who . . . have been historically made faceless. . . . Those whom violence has paralyzed, effaced, or deadened, those whom violence has treated in their lives as though they were *already dead*, those who have been made (in life) without expression, without a voice, and without a face.'[8] In other words, what in Benjamin was primarily a literary concept becomes in the hands of Felman a powerful cipher for the psychically exhausted subject, especially for that ghostly, lifeless remnant that emerges in the figure of the Holocaust survivor, one trapped in the ambiguous zone between the no-longer living and the not-yet dead, unable to give expression to anything other than history and its petrifying 'death's head.'[9]

In this light, it is no wonder that in the Preamble to *The New Wounded* Malabou refers to Bruno Bettelheim's analytic work as one of her sources of inspiration. Bruno Bettelheim, survivor of a concentration camp himself, has acquired fame (or, indeed, notoriety)[10] due to his distinct approach to autism. Rather than go along with the consensus regarding the organic origins of autism, Bettelheim insists, instead, on approaching autism as the product of extreme existential circumstances. Noting that autistic children present symptoms similar to those exemplified by a certain type of camp inmate known as a *Muselmann*, Bettelheim sets out to demonstrate that autistic children withdraw into their own universe in their attempt to defend themselves against what they experience (though it may not necessarily be true) as an extreme form of violence. According to Bettelheim, these children's unresponsiveness and their reluctance to use language and acknowledge an other need to be perceived in relation to the *Muselmann*'s 'total emotional depletion' and absolute dehumanization.[11] In *The Empty Fortress* he argues: 'The view is therefore proposed that infantile autism is a state of mind that develops in reaction to feeling oneself in an extreme situation, entirely without hope.'[12] In his view, understanding the connection between what, on the one hand, is a form of dehumanization 'inflicted for political reasons on victims of a social system' and, on the other hand, 'a self-chosen state of dehumanization' is a necessary step to the treatment of autism.[13] This is precisely the project he undertakes in his establishment of the Orthogenic School in Chicago, which has been perceived as his unique response to his devastating experience in the camp. As Giorgio Agamben puts it, the 'Orthogenic School, . . . had the form of a kind of counter-camp,' in which Bettelheim 'undertook to teach *Muselmänner* to become men again.'[14]

In her own return to Bettelheim, Malabou acknowledges her indebtedness to his 'methods,' that is, as she explains, to 'the type of gaze that he brought to the study of autistic children' (*NW*, xvii). It is this type of gaze that she seeks to adopt in her decision to think together brain lesion and socio-political trauma, a neurodegenerative disease like Alzheimer's and the spectrum of pathologies included in the category of post-traumatic stress disorder. This is, perhaps, why the figure of the *Muselmann*, employed by Bettelheim as the 'dark precursor and interpretative paradigm' of childhood autism,[15] falls like a shadow upon Malabou's conceptualization of the new wounded. Indeed, from Primo Levi to Bettelheim and Agamben, the *Muselmann* is described as a liminal figure situated at the threshold between life and death.[16] As we have seen, Malabou's traumatized subjects share precisely this liminal, in-between existence. Similarly, the *Muselmann*'s apathetic attitude to his or her surroundings, his or her emotional withdrawal, and the mask-like indifference of his or her face are all traits that reappear in Malabou's phenomenology of new forms of trauma. More importantly, what gets reiterated in all accounts of the *Muselmann* is that he or she is the paradigmatic figure of survival, a survival devoid of life. In *Remnants of Auschwitz*, Agamben seems to be especially interested in the connection between the *Muselmann* and a certain mode of survival that marks the dehumanization of the human. Discussing

If This Is a Man, he traces this connection back to Levi: '*The human being*, Levi's title implies, *is the one who can survive the human being*.'[17] Pursuing Levi's insight further, Agamben traces in the figure of the *Muselmann* the workings of a force which is very close to Malabou's destructive plasticity. As he puts it, '[L]ife bears with it a caesura that can transform all life into survival and all survival into life.'[18] Like in Malabou, in Agamben survival is the 'nightmare of a vegetative life' that is the remainder of a 'life of relation.'[19] Interestingly, 'survival' comes to function in Agamben as the 'secret cipher' for biopower. It is, he argues, its 'supreme ambition,'[20] given its interest in producing pliable, functional, dispensable bodies, bared of all emotion and communal ties.

In my analysis of Malabou's *The New Wounded*, my aim so far has been to throw light on the distinct contexts that have shaped her approach to contemporary forms of trauma. In particular, I have suggested that the global phenomena of terrorism and an advanced techno-capitalism have had a determining influence on Malabou's conceptualization of the nature of the traumatic event and her concern with the production of a new flat mode of existence, a form of *survival* as the empty husk of life. I have then moved on to bring into focus the layered history of this understanding of survival, from Benjamin and Felman to Bettelheim and Agamben. Survival, then, in Malabou is not simply the existential mode that characterizes the new wounded, but a bio-political strategy, one that appears to be central in the capitalist management of bodies, in the biomedical separation of vegetative life that is 'less than nothing'[21] from life worth saving as much as in an ever-expanding culture of death where, as Malabou argues, Hannah Arendt's conviction in the banality of evil takes on a novel significance. Malabou writes: '"Making suffer" today manifestly assumes the guise of the neutrality and senselessness of a blow without author and without history, of mechanical violence, and of the absence of interiority. . . . Evil is the becoming insensate of evil' (*NW*, 200).

The perspective offered above explains, I believe, the philosopher's insistence on articulating a comprehensive theory for both organic and socio-political forms of trauma. It also explains her persistent refusal to propose any forms of cure to the new pathologies she is analysing. Instead, she suggests that what is urgent is to take the time to reflect on 'the clinical and philosophical problem posed by destructive plasticity' (*NW*, 167), a problem which, according to her, needs to be thought in connection with the Freudian concept of the death drive, a material understanding of accident and a neurologically framed approach to the cerebral event. These are precisely the terms in which Malabou envisions the emergence of a neuro-psychoanalysis that will undertake to reclaim *life* as a form of resistance against mere survival or, as she puts it quoting Alain Ehrenberg, against the 'multiple maintenance programs' which condemn us to be 'chronically healthy' and which serve to make us 'work better, feel better,' indeed, 'obey better.'[22]

In what follows, I would like to take up Malabou's challenge to rethink life as *counter*-survival. As I will argue, her commitment to analysing the biopolitical contexts and stakes of contemporary forms of psychic violence needs to be appreciated, although her actual analysis seems limited by two theoretical choices that are significant divergences from Bettelheim's own psychoanalytic method. More specifically, it needs to be noted that, whereas Bettelheim sets out to debunk any myths that obscure the socially generated causes of autism (thus privileging socio-political over organic factors),[23] Malabou appears to move in the opposite direction, foregrounding, as we have seen, the lesional aspects of organic and sociogenic forms of trauma. In addition, Malabou does not pay any attention to a suggestion Bettelheim puts forward in *The Empty Fortress*, namely, the suggestion that what the observer interprets as cool indifference in the attitude of autistic children may, in fact, hide an affective depth that is 'kept from ever coming to awareness by a to-tal avoidance of all relatedness.'[24] In a chapter titled 'A Note on *Passionate Indifference*' Bettelheim emphasizes his conviction that the avoidance of all relatedness may be 'a strange way of relating' but it 'is certainly not a stance of indifference.'[25]

This conviction has recently been reiterated by contemporary psychoana-lyst Julia Kristeva in her brief commentary on the new forms of suffering and making suffer. Taking as a starting point the increase in cases of adolescents involved in gang rape, she notes the banalization of violence, as experienced by both perpetrators and victims. Drawing on existing commentary on such cases, Kristeva refers to the male perpetrators' social marginality and their use of violence as a form of 'compensation,' that is, as a means of claiming the virile power denied to them. As for the female victims, they seem to 're-main indifferent under the weight of a shame and a sense of guilt which they cannot share.' What is more, some of these young girls do not even appear to experience the rape as a violation, 'a victimizing situation.' She concludes the description of what constitutes a major social problem by quoting the words of 'a psychologist': 'What is striking, is the absence of affect, the great poverty of sentiments.'[26]

Clearly, however, Kristeva reproduces the position of social commenta-tors and psychologists in order to take a distance from this position. Like Bettelheim, she suggests that what is interpreted as 'indifference' points, instead, to 'the secret held in bodies-crypts,' which can find release only in the criminal act.[27] Kristeva seems to concur with Malabou on the belief that indifference *is* the monstrosity of our times. Yet this manifest insensibility, this 'anesthesia' is, according to Kristeva, the visible 'scar of an excitation or sorrow' which is inassimilable because the suffering subjects today lack the means to represent them.[28] Whereas Malabou foregrounds the impact of the traumatic event on the emotion inductors in the brain, Kristeva (faithful to the Freudian psychoanalytic tradition) seems more concerned with the capacity of the traumatized subject to negotiate this impact and assimilate it within his or her psychic economy. As we have seen, for Malabou the senselessness of the traumatic experience is due to the violence of the event, its unmotivated, brutal nature. By contrast, Kristeva shifts our attention away from the event as such to the sources of resistance within the wounded subject, those psychic spaces that in the past were cultivated through prayer, reading, writing or the 'art of conversation'[29] and that are currently atrophied in societies controlled by a culture of images, a logic of profit and the rehashed banalities of the social media.

'Survival,' suggests Kristeva, is synonymous with censuring what is insupportable, because it can neither be represented nor shared.[30] In an essay dedicated to Felman, she chooses to focus on Felman's reading of Claude Lanzmann's *Shoah* as an attempt on his part to urge the Holocaust survivor 'to break out of the very deadness that enabled the survival.' As Felman puts it, the 'narrator calls the witness to come back from the mere mode of surviving into that of living—of living pain.' It is this necessary 'return from rough "survival" to a "vital suffering"' that Kristeva defines as Lanzmann's (and our) task of *incarnation*.[31] *If* survival goes hand in hand with a sensory and affective numbing to extreme pain; *if* it results from an inability to touch the open wound and offer (tender) it to the touch of others,[32] then reincarnating life as *counter*-survival may, I will argue, take the form of *tendering* (offering a wound to an other's touch) and *tenderness* (touching the wound to diagnose, bring back and alleviate the pain).[33] Indeed, in the Preamble to *The New Wounded*, Malabou acknowledges that tenderness may be 'the only way to respond' to patients who have 'simply become vegetables' and have lost all sensation of physical or psychic pain.[34] As I propose to demonstrate, this is precisely where Kristeva and Malabou meet: namely, in their conviction that tenderness may be a means of reincarnating the empty husk of survival. To this end, I will turn to a writer (survivor and witness of some of the worst atrocities of WW2) whose works testify to this uncanny experience of death as a remnant of life and have, as a result, attracted the analytic interest of both the philosopher and the psychoanalyst.

THE BLACK SUN OF INDIFFERENCE:
KRISTEVA, MALABOU AND MARGUERITE DURAS'S FACE

Born in French Indochina in 1914, novelist, playwright and screenwriter Marguerite Duras became acquainted with the intimate violence of colonial

politics, the effects of which she saw reflected both in the dead ends experienced by her impoverished family and in her own personal relationships as a
French girl growing up in an unfamiliar, deeply hostile context. She returned
to France in 1931 where, during WW2, she lived through Nazi occupation,
joined the French Resistance and, after liberation, witnessed closely the impact of the concentration camp on the human psyche as she nursed her first
husband, the writer Robert Antelme, back to life. These experiences were
turned into the cauldron within which her writings were conceived. Although
her emphasis remained on the intimate rather than the political sphere, her
work cannot be approached in isolation from the history that has shaped and
continues to inform it. As Kristeva writes in a brief essay dedicated to Duras,
the 'history of our century passed through her pages, leaving only a ravaged
intimacy. Is the source of suffering familial or historical? . . . It's a way of
living, surviving, perhaps . . .'[35]

Indeed, and irrespective of whether the historical context is foregrounded
or not, her characters are all survivors of psychic, familial or communal
disasters. As such, they exemplify the flatness of post-traumatic existence
that Malabou analyses, an existence which Duras in a 1986 novel names
'the malady of death.'[36] In the novel an unnamed man pays an unnamed
young woman to spend a few days with him. Clearly, what he wants is not
sex but a chance to awaken his deadened feelings, an opportunity to share
an unacknowledged sorrow, which (like his sex) seeks 'somewhere to put
itself, somewhere to shed its load of tears.'[37] Although murder is only con-
templated, not actually committed, the relation between the two characters is
strikingly cruel, a cruelty which takes no other form than the monstrosity of
cool indifference Malabou posits at the heart of contemporary traumatisms.
Despite his conscious decision to try 'loving,' the man remains disaffected,
unable to connect with his partner or his own memories and emotions.[38]
The woman tells him: 'I saw you were suffering from the malady of death.'
When he asks why this malady is fatal, she answers: 'Because whoever has
it doesn't know he's a carrier, of death. And also because he's like to die
without any life to die to, and without even knowing that's what he's doing.'[39] The woman herself stays impassive throughout the period they spend
together. She allows him to enter her, but she refuses to hold and tend to
him. She is a 'stranger' who has fallen asleep in someone else's bed, both
cruelly aloof and extremely vulnerable in her naked indifference.[40] When
their contract expires, she simply disappears leaving only the 'mark of her
body . . . still there on the sheets. Cold.'[41] This is why the reader feels that,
despite her efforts not to catch the deadly virus of his malady, the man is
right to suspect that the malady of death is also in her. She too is condemned
to live *in* death and die *of* it.[42]

The same kind of cruelty characterizes the relationship depicted in her semi-autobiographical novel, *The Lover*. Emotionally depleted by a rejecting, psychically exhausted mother, an abusive older brother and an overwhelming sense of helplessness, the young girl in this novel gives herself to her adult Chinese lover with the cold indifference of a prostitute. 'She says: I'd rather you didn't love me. But if you do, I'd like you to do as you usually do with women.'[43] Although when she meets her lover, she is still an adolescent, the girl feels too old, overcome with the weight of a family which has suddenly been turned to stone. It is 'petrified so deeply it's impenetrable,' she tells the reader. 'Everyday we try to kill one another, to kill. Not only do we not talk to one another, we don't even look at one another. . . . The word conversation is banished. . . . Every sort of community, whether of the family or otherwise, is hateful to us, degrading. We're united in a fundamental shame at having to live.'[44] Like the two lovers in *The Malady of Death*, she too is a living-dead and cannot but infect others with her death, which takes the form of an intimate, infinite sadness.[45] Battered by her frigidity, unable to touch a sorrow that festers within, her Chinese lover gradually loses any semblance of life, his tender and tendering body turns rigid like a corpse. When she leaves him, she tells us he continues, he lives on—though for a long time the 'memory of the little white girl' remains his only 'link with emotion' and 'with the immensity of tenderness.'[46]

Malabou analyses *The Lover* in *Ontology of the Accident* where she focuses on the workings of destructive plasticity, tracing its explosive force which results in the transformation of the affected being, its reduction into an empty form, the form of its absence. This is why in her reading of *The Lover* Malabou chooses to discuss neither the colonial context that is formative of the relations and fate of all the characters nor the layered history of indifference and abuse that has shaped the narrator's sense of having been radically cut off from the child she used to be and the child's openness to life. Instead, she structures her analysis around the metamorphic event Duras describes in the early pages of the novel, that is, the event of 'ageing before ageing,' the narrator's conviction that her youth was stolen away, suddenly, 'too soon.'[47] Drawing connections between the narrator in the novel and Duras herself, Malabou insists: 'The transformation did not in fact occur over the years, as one might have imagined; it was well and truly *instantaneous*. *Suddenly*, right in the midst of her youth, the first woman *brutally* became the second. Duras was young for only a very short time, just eighteen years.'[48]

Similarly, Malabou shows that the end of childhood which Duras confesses to goes hand in hand with the end of love and the emergence of a new cold persona to match the new more aged face. Again, this change is presented as the product of 'the pure event, without cause or explanation': '. . . one fine day a person no longer loves their parents and family. . . . the end of love is always brutal . . . it happens all of a sudden, like a death.'[49] Turning to another novel by Duras, *The Sea Wall*, Malabou notes that the alcoholism of the female protagonist (like the addiction to alcohol Duras almost died of) emerges abruptly, 'out of nowhere.'[50] Rather than the source and explanation of this addiction, the subject and its history appear to be its inevitable, anticipated outcome. There is no subject, Malabou argues, that pre-exists its own destruction. In her view, this is precisely what 'is terrifying' in Duras, namely, the 'incredible coincidence of the beginning and becoming'[51] or, indeed, the annihilation of all becoming in a beginning that is also an end.

Malabou interprets Duras's style as the visual index of this explosion of biological, historical, psychic becoming. As she explains, Duras has the tendency to suppress 'links and causal connections.'[52] To produce the effects of disjunction, disorder, fortuitous rather than necessary happening, the writer privileges 'repetition and enumeration' as well as the figure called 'asyndeton.' The asyndeton, according to Malabou, 'is linguistic alcoholism.'[53] As such, it destroys all relations between subject and verb, it empties out any chronological references,[54] it sabotages syntax as the guarantee of both subject and meaning.

In her more comprehensive study of Duras in *Black Sun* and *Hatred and Forgiveness*, Kristeva also foregrounds the writer's distinct style which, according to her, serves *not* as a mirror to the traumatic, metamorphic event but as a surgical scalpel that dissects the cadaver we carry within us post-WW2. At the opening of her chapter on Duras, in *Black Sun* Kristeva writes: 'Auschwitz and Hiroshima have revealed that the "malady of death," as Marguerite Duras might say, informs our most concealed inner recesses.'[55] In a gesture that anticipates Malabou's in *The New Wounded*, Kristeva suggests that a 'mutilation of feelings,' a '*basic disconnection*,' a suffering that 'merges with indifference' constitute the visible symptoms of 'the horror of the Second World War,' one which remains unrepresentable and, hence, continues to exist within us as a 'monstrous nothing.'[56] On Kristeva's reading, Duras develops a 'blank rhetoric,' a 'discourse of dulled pain,' in her attempt to force us to confront this 'nothing' which takes on the face of cool indifference and condemns us to a 'devitalized existence' on 'the frontiers of life and death.'[57] Echoing Duras, Kristeva reminds us: 'We are survivors, living dead, corpses on furlough, sheltering personal Hiroshimas in the bosom of our private worlds.'[58]

As we have seen, in Malabou the face of survival resembles Duras's ravaged face, formed in the ruins of her youth and in the aftermath of a traumatic event that is as brutal as it is incomprehensible. For Malabou, Duras's face is the cartography of destructive plasticity, a force that drains it of all human feeling and reduces it to a mask. If this mask is terrifying, Malabou suggests, this is because it hides *not* the essence but the absence of a face. By contrast, while acknowledging the coldness of the mask, Kristeva (like Bettelheim) insists on the need to feel the passion-infused nothing beneath it. Borrowing a 'dazzling metaphor' from Gérard de Nerval, she associates this nothing with an 'imagined sun, bright and black at the same time.'[59] In her view, Duras's genius lies in her courage to write in the blazing shadow of this black sun, a figuration for Bettelheim's *passionate* indifference. Turning our face in the direction of this death-bearing sun is important for Kristeva since it is there, in the unlivable abyss of this nothing, that 'an alchemy of binding and un-binding' operates;[60] that death is touched and held; and that the brutal event itself, our private or communal Hiroshimas, becomes reinfused with eros, reincarnated as *life*. As I intend to demonstrate in my concluding section, this is precisely the shattering, tender alchemy of Duras's *Hiroshima mon amour.*

HOLDING AGAINST DEATH:
TENDERNESS AND MATERNAL RELIANCE

In her approach to Duras, Malabou succeeds in throwing into relief the devastating effects of destructive plasticity on a subject that seems unable to put up any resistance to it, given that what once was the subject's *ground* (its past, its bonds with others, its life-drive and auto-affective economy) has been erased and can, therefore, not serve as a material or psychic support for the subject. In her analysis of Duras but also in her theorization of destructive plasticity in general, Malabou seems to be walking on a tightrope between two biological concepts which are related though not synonymous: namely, the concepts of 'apoptosis' and 'necrosis.' Apoptosis refers to the natural process of programmed cell death, which maintains a balance in cell numbers, protects the organism by getting rid of damaged or cancerous cells and contributes to the development of a being through the formation of 'apoptotic bodies' which can be reused by other cells or can lead to the production of new structures. According to Alfons Lawen, the word 'apoptosis' comes from the ancient Greek ἀπόπτωσις meaning the '"falling off of petals from a flower" or "of leaves from a tree in autumn."'[61] As the etymology of the word suggests, apoptosis is a form of creative destruction in the course of which death turns into the opening of a chance for new life.

Malabou refers to apoptosis on several occasions in *Ontology of the Accident*, *Plasticity at the Dusk of Writing* and *What Should We Do with Our Brain?*. The process of apoptosis, she argues, shows that 'all creation can only occur at the price of a destructive counterpart.'[62] Apoptosis, then, for

Malabou is equivalent to *positive plasticity* and is inextricable from the force of life. She compares apoptosis to 'the sculptor's chisel,' which produces new life forms through slicing off unwanted scraps of clay or marble.[63] In *What Should We Do with Our Brain?* she clearly associates the suicide mechanism of cellular renewal with 'the power of *healing*' that exists as a possibility within every organism. As she puts it, the 'plastic art of the brain gives birth to a statue capable of self-repair.'[64] By contrast, destructive plasticity seems to correspond to the phenomenon of necrosis. Compared to apoptosis, necrosis is described as a messier process which involves the explosion of a cell due to severe infection, injury or any form of psychic trauma. Necrosis can cause inflammation and may damage neighbouring healthy cells. It is, therefore, a form of biological terrorism which marks the exhaustion of the organism's renewing capacities.[65]

In a true Hegelian fashion, Malabou refuses to discuss apoptosis and necrosis as oppositional pathways. She insists that necrosis, though pathological, is also a form of plasticity and, hence, as much of a creative process as apoptosis is. Life, according to Malabou, is the tension-generating dialectic between apoptosis and necrosis, 'between the birth and the destruction of possibilities, between the emergence and destruction of forms of being.'[66] In this light, life needs to be conceptualized as a permanent state of emergency, sustaining and renewing itself 'against and with the threat of destruction.'[67] The thought of destructive plasticity as precisely this threat of destruction, as the acknowledgement of finitude in the guise of the necrotic force of the event, is most important for Malabou. From her perspective, it is our commitment to the negative that can empower us to reclaim life as resilience and resistance rather than flexibility and indifference. Commitment to the negative involves primarily recognition of the plasticity of existence and the creative force of its explosive urge (i.e., apoptosis). In *What Should We Do with Our Brain?* she clarifies: 'To insist on explosive surges is to say that we are not flexible in the sense that all change of identity is a critical test, which leaves some traces, effaces others, resists its own test, and tolerates no polymorphism.' In conclusion, she emphasizes that '. . . if we didn't explode at each transition, if we didn't destroy ourselves a bit, we could not live.'[68] As we have seen, Malabou associates flexibility with the type of apathetic survival promoted by global capitalism, an existential mode that reduces the subject to an acquiescent tool in the hands of profit-oriented, normative structures. This is why commitment to the negative also involves for Malabou a refusal to positivize the explosive potentiality of existence. In other words, it necessitates a holding onto the danger and irrevocability of necrosis.

If, contra survival, *life* is inextricable from freedom and responsibility, this is because its plasticity is not a smooth transition from form to form, a compliant ability to don 'all masks,' adopt 'all postures, all attitudes,'[69] but is a turbulent, risky experience. Malabou insists on situating contemporary subjectivity at the heart of such experience which she defines as 'the plastic challenge' of preserving a 'middle course' between welcoming the crisis that transformation brings and remaining resilient in the face of it, able to with-stand the suffering and re-create itself out of it.[70] Hence the philosopher's double (and perhaps conflicting) allegiance to both the reparative *work* of the negative (apoptosis) and the uncompromising *event* of the negative (necro-sis). It is the thought of the latter that needs to be cultivated if life is to remain a risk, a form of struggle against cool, apathetic survival. It is the former, however, that enables us to reincarnate life when life has been taken over by death. In *The New Wounded*, Malabou attempts to keep a rather precarious balance between the necessary thought of the negative (the always open pos-sibility of launching oneself 'into the void of all identity'[71]) and the equally necessary working through of the negative. In the end, the philosopher's therapeutic concerns are pushed to the background.[72] Malabou limits herself to the diagnosis of evil: namely, the recognition of destructive plasticity and the type of unremitted survival it condemns us to. As a result, her analysis fails to explain how the traumatized subject's resilience may be developed and what 'the art of tendering help,' as Bettelheim puts it,[73] might entail.

This is precisely Kristeva's focus in a recent essay titled 'Reliance, Or Ma-ternal Eroticism.' Significantly, the essay constitutes an exploration of two key Kristevan ideas which show the close connection between Malabou and Kristeva, namely, the idea that life is a state of emergency and the conviction in the originary presence of the negative.[74] Like Malabou, Kristeva shows that the development of human subjectivity is inextricable from an embodied experience of crisis, the biological manifestations of which are the processes of apoptosis and necrosis. What she calls 'maternal reliance' is a bio-psychic economy within each speaking being, which serves to regulate these pro-cesses of death in the interests of life. The biological and affective sources of this economy are traced back to the period of gestation when the maternal body functions like a scaffolding for the newly conceived life, a 'place of passion, caring, vocation and responsibility.'[75] Although it is 'fragile,' this protecting structure is 'indelible,' according to Kristeva, and can continue to support the developing subject throughout his or her life.[76] As she explains, maternal reliance, infused with the life-binding force of *eros*, has a 'veiled but natural resemblance to *apoptosis*' and takes on a balancing, modulating, renewing function, translating 'the time of death into a temporality of new beginnings.'[77] This is why she insists that it is 'clearly the *work* of the nega-tive,' a binding/re-binding psychic mechanism that opens up negativity to 'a fabulous investment in the state of emergency in life' and 'the care of the living.'[78] In this light, it is important to note that, for Kristeva, the 'basic affect of reliance' is tenderness,[79] that is, a love that touches but does not seek to possess; a passionate attunement to an other's suffering; a caring that tends to and holds the vulnerable other through and against death.

Kristeva is employing an extended metaphorics of holding to describe the bio-psychic supporting structure that needs to become one of the healing resources of the analyst: from *Khora*, the Platonic receptacle to the maternal Thing as the nourishing container of the not-yet-I, Maurice Merleau-Ponty's image of two touching hands, the Virgin's holding of Jesus' dead body in a number of Pietà paintings or sculptures and Giovanni Battista Pergolesi's hymn to the mother as the tenacious principle of *amort* (i.e., love as undeath). What Kristeva calls *reliance* is, then, a refiguration of the maternal *herethics* she theorized in her earlier essay on Pergolesi's *Stabat Mater*.[80] As she acknowledges, this principle of the hold is nothing but a 'phantasm,' a long-lost memory of a 'psychic and somatic reality,' yet it can re-impassion life through and 'up to the limits of life.'[81] Interestingly, in a short film she has written, focusing on maternal reliance, Kristeva argues that the necrotic destruction of this heretical principle was one of the consequences of the rise of National Socialism in Germany in the 1930s and WW2. With close reference to the paintings of German Expressionist Max Beckmann, she suggests that it was not just the Judeo-Christian God who was killed in the Nazi camps but, along with Him, the maternally connoted principle of the hold.[82]

Duras's *Hiroshima mon amour*, the script she wrote for Alain Resnais's 1959 film, unfolds precisely around the tacit desire to recover this principle against the deadened existence of an ambivalent survival. The protagonists are both reluctant survivors of the massive trauma inflicted on victors and the defeated alike by the constellation of events that make up the cruelty of WW2. The man, a Japanese architect, has survived the loss of his family and the obliteration of his native city after the US atomic bombing of Hiroshima and Nagasaki that marked the end of the war. Duras is careful to describe him against the background of a Hiroshima that has recovered only a semblance of life. Despite the return to normality, the movement of people in the streets, the persistence of life that 'goes on,' the city is petrified, trapped in the throes of a death that refuses to draw its last breath. The faces of this death are endless and hover over the protagonists as they meet, embrace and part: the condemned patients at Hiroshima hospital, the '[h]uman skin floating, surviving still in the bloom of its agony' at the museum, the malformed children, the stillborn babies, the anonymous 'heads of hair the women of Hiroshima . . . discovered had fallen out.'[83] Though, in her portrait of the man, Duras tells us he 'hasn't "cheated" with life,' the necrotic force of the event that has transformed him and the history of his country survives in his voice, a 'flat,' 'negative voice,' compulsively reiterating the monstrous 'nothing' of the experience.[84]

The woman is a French actress who has come to Hiroshima to participate in a film about peace. She carries with her the memories of Nazi occupation, the loss of her lover (a German soldier), the disgrace imposed on her and her family with liberation, the madness that came with it and her confinement in a cellar for almost a year. Yet, in her portrait of the woman, Duras insists that it is 'not the fact of having been shaved and disgraced that marks her life,' but the fact that she has survived what ought to have killed her: namely, the death of her lover in Nevers and the deadening of her own (once young) body.[85] Like Duras's, the woman's youth ended brutally when she was eighteen. Since then, she tells the man in an equally 'flat, muffled, monotonous' voice, she (like other victims of the war, like other witnesses of Auschwitz or Hiroshima) has had to live on in the unbearable vicinity of 'indifference. And also the fear of indifference.'[86]

The two protagonists' encounter seems to take place in the hard-to-sustain spacing between indifference and the fear of indifference. This is why it is so unexpected—and so desperate. What is more, Duras points out, it 'takes place in the one city of the world where it is hardest to imagine it: Hiroshima.'[87] How can love have a chance at the heart of a future-abortive now and in the face of a life that has taken the form of absence? Duras, however, appears to be convinced that *if* love has a chance, this can only erupt in Hiroshima: the devastated place, the brutal event, the unnameable name for the monstrosity that inhabits the human. As she emphasizes, her aim in the film is not 'the description of horror by horror' but what she calls the 'miracle' of a 'resurrection.'[88] In other words, Duras mobilizes the banality of love in an attempt to break the confining mold of a banalized survival. The goal, she explains, is to make the horror 'rise again from its ashes by incorporating it' in the raw flesh of a love that spares neither death nor the pain.[89]

Significantly, this love is strangely desexualized. It takes on the disimpassioned quality of care and tenderness. Duras structures her narrative around images of bodies holding onto each other, limbs touching, hands gripping, clasping and caressing. The opening of the film introduces the ambiguous zone the characters inhabit, a zone on the borders between life and death, *eros* and *Thanatos*. As she describes the opening scene, 'we see mutilated bodies—the heads, the hips—moving—in the throes of love or death—and covered successively with the ashes, the dew, of atomic death—and the sweat of love fulfilled.'[90] After Hiroshima, Duras seems to be saying, all we are left with is a life that is too much like death, and love is only the rattle of a dying body. In the few hours they spend together the protagonists shed the hard skin of indifference, exposing their respective wounds to the touch of the other.

Emerging out of the hell of war, they become Orpheus figures,[91] each for the other, leading their lover back to the world of the living. On this journey back to life, love is neither desire nor possession. It becomes the heretical economy of reliance Kristeva theorizes, finding expression and sustenance in the reiterative rhythm of multiple embraces: the woman's memory of holding her dying lover's body all through the night to make death more bearable; her mother's 'infinite,' 'rough tenderness' and her consoling embrace when she returns home with her hair shaven;[92] the lovers' cradling arms, which erase the temporal gap between past and present,[93] comforting the suffering brought about by loss.

Duras contrasts the kind of film she wishes to make with the run-of-the mill peace film, full of empty-sounding promises that cannot heal because they keep their gaze averted from the black sun of unacknowledged suffering. *Hiroshima mon amour* moves from the unnameability of the event at the beginning (the man's insistence that the *nothing* of Hiroshima can neither be known nor seen)[94] to its naming at the end. This is why the names of the protagonists are not given in the film. As Duras explains, '[I]n fact, in each other's eyes, they *are* no one. They are names of places, names that are not names.'[95] *She* is Nevers, a small occupied town in France where the woman suddenly, abruptly grew old. *He* is Hiroshima, a place that death has preserved.[96] The farewell scene at the end of the film is, then, a scene of healing and recognition. Looking at each other's face, the lovers learn to pronounce the foreign name of the traumatic event: 'Hi-ro-shi-ma. That's your name. . . . That's my name. Yes. Your name is Nevers. Ne-vers in France.'[97] Thus, the unnameable retrieves its name and face. As a name, it gets re-signified: '. . . an overlapping of Nevers and love, of Hiroshima and love' takes place.[98] As a face, it is touched and turned in love towards another face. Face to face, the protagonists part but they offer each other all they have: namely, their survival, their 'most precious possession,' Duras notes.[99] And it is here that the miracle Duras aims at occurs: 'It is as though,' she tells us, 'through them, *all of Hiroshima was in love with all of Nevers.*'[100]

NOTES

1. See Catherine Malabou's *Plasticity at the Dusk of Writing: Dialectic, Destruction, Deconstruction*, trans. Carolyn Shread (New York: Columbia University Press, 2010), 57–60.

2. See Catherine Malabou, *The New Wounded: From Neurosis to Brain Damage*, trans. Steven Miller (New York: Fordham University Press, 2012), 168. The title of the original edition in French was *Les nouveaux blessés: De Freud à la neurologie*,

penser les traumatismes contemporaines (Paris: Bayard, 2007). All references in this essay will be to the English edition.

3. Malabou, *New Wounded*, 15.

4. Catherine Malabou, *Ontology of the Accident: An Essay on Destructive Plasticity*, trans. Carolyn Shread (Cambridge: Polity Press, 2012), 37–8.

5. See Walter Benjamin, 'Experience and Poverty,' in *Selected Writings*, vol. II, trans. Rodney Livingstone, ed. Michael W. Jennings (Cambridge, MA and London: Belknap Press of Harvard University Press, 2005).

6. See Walter Benjamin, 'Goethe's Elective Affinities,' in *Selected Writings*, vol. I, trans. Stanley Corngold, eds. Marcus Bullock and Michael W. Jennings (Cambridge, MA and London: Belknap Press of Harvard University Press, 1996), 340–41.

7. See Shoshana Felman, 'From "The Storyteller's Silence: Walter Benjamin's Dilemma of Justice",' in *The Claims of Literature: A Shoshana Felman Reader*, eds. Emily Sun, Eyal Peretz and Ulrich Baer (New York: Fordham University Press, 2007), 346.

8. Felman, 'The Storyteller's Silence,' 325–26.

9. See Felman's discussion of K-Zetnik's act of witnessing in the context of the Eichmann trial in 'A Ghost in the House of Justice: Death and the Language of the Law,' in *The Claims of Literature*, 351–86. At the end of her discussion Felman associates K-Zetnik's 'courtroom silence' with Benjamin's suggestion that everything that 'has been untimely, sorrowful, unsuccessful' about history is expressed 'in a death's head,' 386.

10. There is much controversy about Bettelheim's person and credentials, his therapeutic method and his theory of autism. In this chapter I will not enter the debate around this controversy, which Malabou does not acknowledge either. Due to lack of space, I will limit myself to a discussion of what in his work seems to attract Malabou, namely, his courage to think together autism, a neurodevelopmental disorder, and experience in a concentration camp. To understand the controversy about Bettelheim and the Orthogenic School for autistic children he established, one may want to begin with the following biographies: Nina Sutton, *Bruno Bettelheim: A Life and a Legacy* (New York: Basic Books, 1997); and Richard Pollack, *The Creation of Dr. B: A Biography of Bruno Bettelheim* (New York: Simon & Schuster, 1997).

11. Bruno Bettelheim, *The Empty Fortress: Infantile Autism and the Birth of the Self* (New York: Free Press, 1967), 65.

12. Bettelheim, *Empty Fortress*, 68.

13. Bettelheim, *Empty Fortress*, 7.

14. Giorgio Agamben, *Remnants of Auschwitz: The Witness and the Archive*, trans. Daniel Heller-Roazen (New York: Zone Books, 2002), 46, emphasis in the original.

15. Agamben, *Remnants*, 46.

16. In *Remnants of Auschwitz*, Agamben demonstrates that the image of the *Muselmann* as a 'walking corpse' recurs systematically in different accounts of camp experience. See 41, 44, 54–55.

17. Agamben, *Remnants*, 82, emphasis in the original.

18. Agamben, *Remnants*, 133.

19. Agamben, *Remnants*, 154. See also Malabou, *New Wounded*, xiv, 66.

20. Agamben, *Remnants*, 156.

21. Malabou, *Ontology*, 71. See also *The New Wounded* where, in her Preamble, Malabou describes the dominant medical attitude to Alzheimer's patients: 'I should mention that during my grandmother's illness her geriatric care facility did not offer any psychotherapeutic services. The patients were certainly not mistreated, but it was clear that they were not considered to be subjects endowed with psychic life and that no one was prepared to respond to their despair other than by numbing it with medication,' xiii.

22. Catherine Malabou, *What Should We Do with Our Brain?*, trans. Sebastian Rand (New York: Fordham University Press, 2008), 68. Malabou writes: 'What we are lacking is *life*, which is to say: *resistance*.'

23. See in particular Part III (titled 'Wolf Children') and Part IV ('A Discussion of the Literature on Infantile Autism') of *The Empty Fortress*.

24. Bettelheim, *Empty Fortress*, 90.

25. Bettelheim, *Empty Fortress*, 89–90, my emphasis.

26. All quotations in this paragraph are from Julia Kristeva, 'Les nouvelles maladies de l'âme,' in *Micropolitique* (La Tour d'Aigues: Editions de l'aube, 2001), 158–59. Translations from the original French are mine.

27. Kristeva, 'Les nouvelles maladies,' 159.

28. Kristeva, 'Les nouvelles maladies,' 159.

29. Kristeva, 'Les nouvelles maladies,' 160.

30. Julia Kristeva, 'La torture en pleine lumière,' in *Micropolitique*, 49.

31. Kristeva responds to Shoshana Felman's 'From "The Return of the Voice: Claude Lanzmann's *Shoah*",' in *The Claims of Literature*, 295–314. Here I'm quoting a passage on page 310. Kristeva's response is titled 'For Shoshana Felman: Truth and Art,' in *The Claims of Literature*, 315–21. The passage quoted can be found on pages 318–19.

32. Malabou understands the new forms of trauma in terms of an inability to touch and be touched. In *The New Wounded* she writes: 'Difficulty letting oneself be touched is the evil of our times, the paradoxical result of being wounded. To be wounded, indeed, is to be touched, struck by a blow. . . . To touch thus means precisely to wound. . . . But the "touching" of the wound, today, has generated an inability to feel touching, *an inability to be touched affectively, which is the sign that one has been "touched"—that is, wounded.*' See 160–61, emphasis in the original.

33. 'Tenderness' in medicine has a distinct meaning. It refers to the pain or discomfort felt when an ailing part of the body is palpated (i.e., examined by touch). As I will move on to suggest, 'tenderness' is, then, a most appropriate term to use in the context of pathologies where the patient has become insensible to his or her own pain. s.v. 'tenderness,' Marie O'Toole, *Miller-Keane Encyclopedia and Dictionary of Medicine, Nursing, and Allied Health*, 7th ed. (Amsterdam: Elsevier: 2003) and other definitions of the medical term at https://medical-dictionary.thefreedictionary.com/tenderness, accessed 29 March 2019.

34. Malabou, *New Wounded*, xiv.

35. Julia Kristeva, 'A Stranger,' in *Hatred and Forgiveness*, trans. Jeanine Herman (New York: Columbia University Press, 2010), 246.

36. See Marguerite Duras, *The Malady of Death*, trans. Barbara Bray (New York: Grove Press, 1986).

37. Duras, *Malady*, 1.

38. Thinking about the possibility of staging the novel as a play, Duras emphasizes that the man in the story should not appear. His thoughts and words need to be reported by a male actor/narrator who would be seen reading a script. The man and the woman in the play, she explains, 'should speak as if they were reading the text in separate rooms, isolated from one another.' Duras, *Malady*, 56–57.

39. Duras, *Malady*, 3, 18–19.

40. Duras, *Malady*, 23.

41. Duras, *Malady*, 51.

42. Duras, *Malady*, 34, 46.

43. Marguerite Duras, *The Lover*, trans. Barbara Bray (London: Harper Perennial, 2006), 41.

44. Duras, *Lover*, 50, 58–59.

45. Duras, *Lover*, 48–49.

46. Duras, *Lover*, 121–22.

47. Malabou, *Ontology*, 55.

48. Malabou, *Ontology*, 56, my emphasis.

49. Malabou, *Ontology*, 57, 59.

50. Malabou, *Ontology*, 63.

51. Malabou, *Ontology*, 60, 63.

52. Malabou, *Ontology*, 61.

53. Malabou, *Ontology*, 61-62.

54. Malabou, *Ontology*, 62.

55. Julia Kristeva, *Black Sun: Depression and Melancholia*, trans. Leon S. Roudiez (New York: Columbia University Press, 1989), 221.

56. Kristeva, *Black Sun*, 223, 225, 231, 243, 244, emphasis in the original.

57. Kristeva, *Black Sun*, 4, 221, 223.

58. Kristeva, *Black Sun*, 236.

59. Kristeva, *Black Sun*, 13.

60. Kristeva, 'A Stranger,' 247.

61. Alfons Lawen, 'Apoptosis—An Introduction,' *BioEssays* 25.9 (2003): 888.

62. Malabou, *Ontology*, 4.

63. Malabou, *Ontology*, 5; Malabou, *Brain*, 19.

64. Malabou, *Brain*, 27-28.

65. For a clear analysis of necrosis, see Pierre Golstein and Guido Kroemer, 'Cell Death by Necrosis: Towards a Molecular Definition,' *Trends in Biochemical Sciences* 32.1 (2006), 37-43. See also Malabou, *Ontology*, 5.

66. Malabou, *Plasticity*, 70.

67. Malabou, *Brain*, 76.

68. Malabou, *Brain*, 74.

69. Malabou, *Brain*, 72.

70. Malabou, *Brain*, 82; Malabou, *Plasticity*, 70.

71. Malabou, *Brain*, 80.

72. See Malabou's Conclusion in *The New Wounded*, 211–15.

73. Bettelheim, *Empty Fortress*, 12.

74. See Julia Kristeva, 'Reliance, Or Maternal Eroticism,' *Journal of the American Psychoanalytic Association* 62.1 (2014): 73, 77.

75. Mitchell Wilson, 'Maternal Reliance: Commentary on Kristeva,' *Journal of the American Psychoanalytic Association* 62.1 (2014): 108.

76. Kristeva, 'Reliance,' 78.

77. Kristeva, 'Reliance,' 73, 77, emphasis in the original.

78. Kristeva, 'Reliance,' 77, my emphasis. As the translator of the essay notes, 'reliance' means binding or linking. See note 5 on page 71.

79. Kristeva, 'Reliance,' 75.

80. See Julia Kristeva, 'Stabat Mater,' *The Kristeva Reader*, ed. Toril Moi (Oxford: Blackwell, 1986), 160-86. In this essay Kristeva defines the mother's love (*amour*) as a heretical ethics (or a her-ethics), which serves as a source of resistance against death (*amort*).

81. Kristeva, 'Reliance,' 78, 79.

82. See 'Reliance: De l'érotisme maternel,' film written by Julia Kristeva, dir. G. K. Galabov (2011). https://vimeo.com/62742478, accessed 25 March 2019.

83. Marguerite Duras, *Hiroshima mon amour*, trans. Richard Seaver (New York: Grove Press, 1959), 17, 22.

84. Duras, *Hiroshima*, 110, 15, 8.

85. Duras, *Hiroshima*, 112.

86. Duras, *Hiroshima*, 15, 33.

87. Duras, *Hiroshima*, 9.

88. Duras, *Hiroshima*, 9, 53.

89. Duras, *Hiroshima*, 9.

90. Duras, *Hiroshima*, 8.

91. Referring to Claude Barrois's distinction between the Orpheus myth and the Oedipus myth in his analysis of war trauma, Malabou writes: 'Traumato-neurotic personalities have returned from hell not from childhood.' *New Wounded*, 154.

92. Duras, *Hiroshima*, 96.

93. Through the woman's eyes, the two male lovers merge, their hands and touch come to resemble. The Japanese man himself identifies with the woman's dead lover, in an attempt to restore the sense of continuity that death has brutally disrupted. See Duras, *Hiroshima*, 29, 54–66.

94. Duras, *Hiroshima*, 15, 18–23.

95. Duras, *Hiroshima*, 13, emphasis in the original.

96. Duras, *Hiroshima*, 9.

97. Duras, *Hiroshima*, 83.

98. Duras, *Hiroshima*, 12.

99. Duras, *Hiroshima*, 112.

100. Duras, *Hiroshima*, 13, emphasis in the original.

BIBLIOGRAPHY

AGAMBEN, Giorgio. *Remnants of Auschwitz: The Witness and the Archive.* Translated by Daniel Heller-Roazen. New York: Zone Books, 2002.

BENJAMIN, Walter. 'Experience and Poverty.' In *Selected Writings.* Volume II. Translated by Rodney Livingstone. Edited by Michael W. Jennings. 731–36. Cambridge, MA and London: Belknap Press of Harvard University Press, 2005.

BENJAMIN, Walter. 'Goethe's Elective Affinities.' In *Selected Writings.* Volume I. Translated by Stanley Corngold. Edited by Marcus Bullock and Michael W. Jennings. 297–360. Cambridge, MA and London: Belknap Press of Harvard University Press, 1996.

BETTELHEIM, Bruno. *The Empty Fortress: Infantile Autism and the Birth of the Self.* New York: Free Press, 1967.

DURAS, Marguerite. *Hiroshima mon amour.* Translated by Richard Seaver. New York: Grove Press, 1961.

DURAS, Marguerite. *The Lover.* Translated by Barbara Bray. London: Harper Perennial, 2006.

DURAS, Marguerite. *The Malady of Death.* Translated by Barbara Bray. New York: Grove Press, 1986.

FELMAN, Shoshana. *The Claims of Literature: A Shoshana Felman Reader.* Edited by Emily Sun, Eyal Peretz and Ulrich Baer. New York: Fordham University Press, 2007.

GOLSTEIN, Pierre and Guido Kroemer. 'Cell Death by Necrosis: Towards a Molecular Definition.' *Trends in Biochemical Sciences* 32.1 (2006): 37–43.

KRISTEVA, Julia. 'A Stranger.' In *Hatred and Forgiveness.* Translated by Jeanine Herman. 245–50. New York: Columbia University Press, 2010.

KRISTEVA, Julia. *Black Sun: Depression and Melancholia.* Translated by Leon S. Roudiez. New York: Columbia University Press, 1989.

KRISTEVA, Julia. 'For Shoshana Felman: Truth and Art.' In *The Claims of Literature: A Shoshana Felman Reader.* Edited by Emily Sun, Eyal Peretz and Ulrich Baer. 315–21. New York: Fordham University Press, 2007.

KRISTEVA, Julia. 'La torture en pleine lumière.' In *Micropolitique.* La Tour d'Aigues: Editions de l'Aube, 2001. 49–52.

KRISTEVA, Julia. 'Les nouvelles maladies de l'âme.' In *Micropolitique.* La Tour d'Aigues: Editions de l'Aube, 2001. 158–61.

KRISTEVA, Julia. 'Reliance, Or Maternal Eroticism.' *Journal of the American Psychoanalytic Association* 62.1 (2014): 69–85.

KRISTEVA, Julia. 'Reliance: De l' érotisme maternel.' Directed by G. K. Galabov (2011). https://vimeo.com/62742478. Accessed 25 March 2019.

KRISTEVA, Julia. 'Stabat Mater.' *The Kristeva Reader.* Edited by Toril Moi. 160–86. Oxford: Blackwell, 1986.

LAWEN, Alfons. 'Apoptosis – An Introduction.' *BioEssays* 25.9 (2003): 888–96.

MALABOU, Catherine. *The New Wounded: From Neurosis to Brain Damage.* Translated by Steven Miller. New York: Fordham University Press, 2012.

MALABOU, Catherine. *Ontology of the Accident: An Essay on Destructive Plasticity.* Translated by Carolyn Shread. Cambridge: Polity Press, 2012.

MALABOU, Catherine. *Plasticity at the Dusk of Writing: Dialectic, Destruction, Deconstruction.* Translated by Carolyn Shread. New York: Columbia University Press, 2010.

MALABOU, Catherine. *What Should We Do with Our Brain?* Translated by Sebastian Rand. New York: Fordham University Press, 2008.

O'TOOLE, Marie. *Miller-Keane Encyclopedia and Dictionary of Medicine, Nursing, and Allied Health.* Seventh Edition. Amsterdam: Elsevier, 2003.

POLLACK, Richard. *The Creation of Dr. B: A Biography of Bruno Bettelheim.* New York: Simon & Schuster, 1997.

SUTTON, Nina. *Bruno Bettelheim: A Life and a Legacy.* New York: Basic Books, 1997.

WILSON, Mitchell. 'Maternal Reliance: Commentary on Kristeva.' *Journal of the American Psychoanalytic Association* 62.1 (2014): 101–11.

Index

About the Editors and Contributors

Mieke Bal, born 1946, in Heemstede, Netherlands, is a founder of ASCA (the Amsterdam School of Cultural Analysis), a cultural theorist, critic, video artist and curator. Mieke Bal's primary commitment is to develop interdisciplinary approaches to cultural artifacts. She focuses on gender, migratory culture, psychoanalysis and the critique of capitalism. Her thirty-nine books include a trilogy on political art: *Endless Andness* (on abstraction, 2013), *Thinking in Film* (on video installation, 2013), *Of What One Cannot Speak* (on sculpture, 2010). Her early work comes together in *A Mieke Bal Reader* (2006). Her video projects of documentaries on migratory culture have been exhibited internationally, including in the Museum of the History of Saint Petersburg in 2011. After this she embarked on making 'theoretical fictions.' *A Long History of Madness*, with Michelle Williams Gamaker, argues for a more humane treatment of psychosis, and was exhibited internationally, including in a site-specific version, *Saying It*, in the Freud Museum in London. In fall 2017 it was combined with *Reasonable Doubt* in Warsaw. *Madame B*, also with Michelle Williams Gamaker, is widely exhibited, including in the Centro Galego de Arte Contemporáneo, Santiago de Compostela (2017–2018), and combined with paintings by Edvard Munch in the Munch Museum in Oslo in a museum-wide exhibition she curated. Her film and installation, *Reasonable Doubt*, on René Descartes and Queen Kristina, explores the social and audio-visual aspects of the process of thinking (2016). The installation of that project has premiered in Kraków, and was shown in many countries, including in 2018 in two exhibition-specific installations in the Frans Hals Museum in Haarlem. Her most recent video work is a sixteen-channel video work, *Don Quixote: tristes figuras*. For more information, see www.miekebal.org.

Ivan Callus is Professor of English at the University of Malta, where he teaches courses in contemporary literature and in literary criticism. He has published widely on contemporary fiction, comparative literature, literary theory and posthumanism. His most recent volume is *European Posthumanism* (Routledge, 2016), co-edited with Stefan Herbrechter and Manuela Rossini. He is the founding co-general editor of *CounterText: A Journal for the Study of the Post-Literary*, launched with Edinburgh University Press in 2015, and is co-director of the Critical Posthumanism Network (criticalposthumanism.net).

Nicholas Chare is Associate Professor of Modern Art in the Department of History of Art and Film Studies at the Université de Montréal. In 2018, he was the Diane and Howard Wohl Fellow at the Jack, Joseph and Morton Mandel Center for Advanced Holocaust Studies at the United States Holocaust Memorial Museum in Washington, DC. He is the author of *Auschwitz and Afterimages: Abjection, Witnessing and Representation* (2011) and the co-author, with Dominic Williams, of *Matters of Testimony: Interpreting the Scrolls of Auschwitz* (2016) and *The Auschwitz Sonderkommando: Testimonies, Histories, Representations* (2019).

Arleen Ionescu is Tenured Professor of English Literature and Critical Theory at Shanghai Jiao Tong University. Her major research and teaching interests are in the fields of Modernist prose and, increasingly, in Critical Theory, Memory Studies, Holocaust Studies and Trauma Studies. She has published widely on James Joyce and other related aspects of modernism, Maurice Blanchot, Jacques Derrida, and Samuel Beckett as well as on trauma in reputed academic journals such as *James Joyce Quarterly*, *Parallax*, *Partial Answers*, *Papers on Joyce*, *Joyce Studies Annual*, and *Slovo*. She co-edited five issues of *Word and Text - A Journal of Literary Studies and Linguistics*. Her books include *Concordanţe româno-britanice* (Editura Universităţii din Ploieşti, 2004), *Romanian Joyce: From Hostility to Hospitality* (Peter Lang, 2014), and *The Memorial Ethics of Libeskind's Berlin Jewish Museum* (Palgrave Macmillan, 2017). The research on this book is supported by the Program for Professor of Special Appointment (Eastern Scholar) at Shanghai Institutions of Higher Learning.

Lucia Ispas is Lecturer in Romanian Literature at Universitatea Petrol-Gaze din Ploieşti. Her major research and teaching interests are in the fields of literary criticism, Romanian postmodernist prose and literary Avant-garde. She has published *Radu Petrescu. Monografie* (2011) and *Istoria literaturii* *române. Perioada interbelică. Poezia* (2015), as well as numerous articles on Radu Petrescu, a Joycean Romanian writer, one of the fathers of Romanian postmodernism, and the Romanian writer of Jewish origin, Mihail Sebastian.

Maria Margaroni is Associate Professor in Literary Theory and Feminist Thought at the University of Cyprus. She has held Visiting Fellowships at the Institute for Advanced Studies in the Humanities (University of Edinburgh) and the Centre for Cultural Analysis, Theory and History (University of Leeds). She has published extensively on the work of Julia Kristeva in peer-reviewed journals and collected volumes. Her publications include *Julia Kristeva: Live Theory* (with John Lechte, Continuum, 2004), *Metaphoricity and the Politics of Mobility* (with Effie Yiannopoulou, Rodopi, 2006), *Intimate Transfers* (with Effie Yiannopoulou, special issue of the *European Journal of English Studies*, 2005), *Violence and the Sacred* (special issue of *Philosophy Today*, 2012) and *Textual Layering: Contact, Historicity, Critique* (with Apostolos Lampropoulos and Christos Hadjichristou, Lexington Books, 2017). She is currently finishing her monograph focusing on the thought of Catherine Malabou and Julia Kristeva.

Olga Michael is Lecturer in English Language and Literature at the University of Central Lancashire, Cyprus. Her research interests include women's life writing, trauma and gendered violence in testimonial literature, and contemporary graphic life narratives of human rights violations. She has published on feminism, female beauty and sexual violence in Phoebe Gloeckner's graphic memoirs, on the intersections between Lynda Barry's *What It Is* and revisionist fairy tales, and on graphic autofiction in Barry and Gloeckner's graphic memoirs. Her forthcoming work includes inter alia, 'Logging in, Speaking Out: Gendered Testimony in the Age of Social Media' (co-authored with Sofia Mason, *Cultures of Testimony: A Handbook*, Palgrave Macmillan) and 'PTSD and Female Sexuality in the Aftermath of Childhood and Adolescent Sexual Abuse in Una's *Becoming, Unbecoming*' (*Journal of Graphic Novels and Comics*). Her most recent publications include 'Reading Phoebe Gloeckner's A Child's Life and Other Stories at the Time of #MeToo,' (*Life Writing*) and 'Graphic Autofiction and the Visualization of Trauma in Lynda Barry and Phoebe Gloeckner's Graphic Memoirs' (*Autofiction in English*, Palgrave Macmillan).

Laurent Milesi is Tenured Professor of English Literature and Critical Theory at Shanghai Jiao Tong University and Honorary Senior Research Fellow at Cardiff University. He has written extensively on Joyce and related aspects of modernism, twentieth-century (American) poetry, postmodernism and poststructuralism, with a particular emphasis on Jacques Derrida and Hélène Cixous. His edited collection, *James Joyce and the Difference of Language*, was published by Cambridge University Press in 2003. He has translated several works by Jacques Derrida: (with Stefan Herbrechter) *H. C. pour la vie, c'est à dire ...* (Stanford University Press, 2006) and by Hélène Cixous: *Le Voisin de zéro. Sam Beckett* (Polity, 2010), *Philippines* (Polity, 2011) and *Tomb(e)* (Seagull Books, 2014). He is one of the general editors of the 'Critical Perspectives on Theory, Culture and Politics' book series at Rowman & Littlefield International, where *Credo Credit Crisis: Speculations on Faith and Money*, co-edited with Christopher John Müller and Aidan Tynan, appeared in 2017. He serves as joint editor in chief for the international journal *Word and Text - A Journal of Literary Studies and Linguistics*. He is currently completing a monograph titled *Jacques Derrida and the Ethics of Writing*.

Radhika Mohanram teaches Critical Theory and Postcolonial Studies in Cardiff University, Wales. Her publications include *Postcolonial Discourse and Changing Cultural Contexts* (Greenwood, 1995), *English Postcoloniality* (Greenwood, 1996), *Black Body: Women, Colonialism and Space* (Minnesota, 1999), *Shifting Continents/Colliding Cultures* (Rodopi, 2000), *Imperial White* (Minnesota, 2007), and *Imperialism as Diaspora* (Liverpool, 2013). She most recently co-edited a collection of essays titled *Partitions and their Afterlives: Violence, Memories, Living* (Rowman & Littlefield, 2019). She is currently working on her next monograph on the 1947 Indian partition and is also the PI of the AHRC-funded project *Refugee Wales* (2019–2022).

Irene Scicluna, who holds an MA in Philosophy from King's College London and an MA in Modern and Contemporary Literature and Criticism from the University of Malta, is a Philosophy PhD candidate and postgraduate tutor at the School of English, Communication and Philosophy (ENCAP) at Cardiff University. Her doctoral research, generously funded by the School of English, Communication and Philosophy (ENCAP), Cardiff University and the ENDEAVOUR Scholarships Scheme, Ministry for Education and Employment, Malta, investigates the interactive development of one organism with another. Her project develops a speculative phenomenological account of feeling as an inter-relational continuum of receptivity and affect and examines how the primordial element of existence depends on non-cognitive operative intentionality. She is also interested in philosophy of ecology informed by process ontology.

Ernst van Alphen is Professor of Literary Studies at Universiteit Leiden. His publications include *Francis Bacon and The Loss of Self* (Harvard University Press, 1995), *Caught By History: Holocaust Effects in Contemporary Art, Literature, and Theory* (Stanford University Press, 1997), *Armando: Shaping Memory* (NAi Publishers, 2000), *Art in Mind: How Contemporary Images Shape Thought* (University of Chicago Press, 2005), *Staging the Archive: Art and Photography in the Age of New Media* (Reaktion Books, 2014), and *Failed Images: Photography and Its Counter-Practices* (Valiz, 2018).

www.ingramcontent.com/pod-product-compliance
Lightning Source LLC
Chambersburg PA
CBHW021809270326
41932CB00007B/114